Death, Grief and Loss in the Context of COVID-19

This book provides detailed analysis of the manifold ways in which COVID-19 has influenced death, dying and bereavement.

Through three parts: Reconsidering Death and Grief in Covid-19; Institutional Care and Covid-19; and the Impact of COVID-19 in Context, the book explores COVID-19 as a reminder of our own and our communities' fragile existence, but also the driving force for discovering new ways of meaning-making, performing rites and rituals, and conceptualising death, grief and life. Contributors include scholars, researchers, policymakers and practitioners, accumulating in a multi-disciplinary, diverse and international set of ideas and perspectives that will help the reader examine closely how Covid-19 has invaded social life and (re)shaped trauma and loss.

It will be of interest to all scholars and students of death studies, biomedicine, and end of life care as well as those working in sociology, social work, medicine, social policy, cultural studies, anthropology, psychology, counselling and nursing more broadly.

Panagiotis Pentaris is an Associate Professor of Social Work and Thanatology in the School of Human Sciences at the University of Greenwich, London, England, UK, where he is also a member of the Institute for Lifecourse Development, an internationally recognised Institute focusing on interdisciplinary research across the lifespan. Pentaris is a council member for the Association for the Study of Death and Society, and over the last ten years he has researched and published on death, dying, bereavement, culture and religion, social work, social policy and LGBTQIA+ issues.

Routledge Advances in Health and Social Policy

Effective Interventions for Unemployed Young People in Europe
Social Innovation or Paradigm Shift?
Edited by Tomas Sirovatka and Henk Spies

Social Research in Health and Illness
Case-Based Approaches
Constantinos N. Phellas and Costas S. Constantinou

Ethnic Identity and US Immigration Policy Reform
American Citizenship and Belonging amongst Hispanic Immigrants
Maria del Mar Farina

Research and Evaluation in Community, Health and Social Care Settings
Experiences from Practice
Edited by Suzanne Guerin, Nóirín Hayes and Sinead McNally

Critical Discourses of Old Age and Telecare Technologies
Gizdem Akdur

Aging Veterans with Disabilities
A Cross-National Study of Policies and Challenges
Arie Rimmerman

Creative Arts-Based Research in Aged Care
Photovoice, Photography, and Poetry in Action
Evonne Miller

Inciting Justice and Progressive Power
The Partnership for Working Families Cities
Edited by David Reynolds and Louise Simmons

Death, Grief and Loss in the Context of COVID-19
Edited by Panagiotis Pentaris

For more information about this series, please visit: https://www.routledge.com/Routledge-Advances-in-Health-and-Social-Policy/book-series/RAHSP

Death, Grief and Loss in the Context of COVID-19

Edited by Panagiotis Pentaris

Routledge
Taylor & Francis Group
LONDON AND NEW YORK

First published 2022
by Routledge
2 Park Square, Milton Park, Abingdon, Oxon OX14 4RN

and by Routledge
605 Third Avenue, New York, NY 10158

Routledge is an imprint of the Taylor & Francis Group, an informa business

© 2022 selection and editorial matter, Panagiotis Pentaris; individual chapters, the contributors

The right of Panagiotis Pentaris to be identified as the author of the editorial material, and of the authors for their individual chapters, has been asserted in accordance with sections 77 and 78 of the Copyright, Designs and Patents Act 1988.

All rights reserved. No part of this book may be reprinted or reproduced or utilised in any form or by any electronic, mechanical, or other means, now known or hereafter invented, including photocopying and recording, or in any information storage or retrieval system, without permission in writing from the publishers.

Trademark notice: Product or corporate names may be trademarks or registered trademarks, and are used only for identification and explanation without intent to infringe.

British Library Cataloguing-in-Publication Data
A catalogue record for this book is available from the British Library

Library of Congress Cataloging-in-Publication Data
Names: Pentaris, Panagiotis, editor.
Title: Death, grief and loss in the context of COVID-19 / edited by Panagiotis Pentaris.
Description: Abingdon, Oxon ; New York, NY : Routledge, 2021. | Series: Routledge advances in health and social policy | Includes bibliographical references and index.
Identifiers: LCCN 2021005383 (print) | LCCN 2021005384 (ebook)
Subjects: LCSH: Death. | Loss (Psychology) | Grief. | COVID-19 (Disease)--Psychological aspects.
Classification: LCC HQ1073 .D425 2021 (print) | LCC HQ1073 (ebook) | DDC 155.9/37--dc23
LC record available at https://lccn.loc.gov/2021005383
LC ebook record available at https://lccn.loc.gov/2021005384

ISBN: 978-0-367-64732-2 (hbk)
ISBN: 978-0-367-64739-1 (pbk)
ISBN: 978-1-003-12599-0 (ebk)

Typeset in Times New Roman
by MPS Limited, Dehradun

In memory of **Maria Yerosimou**

Your smile, grace, love and kindness are kept in my heart.
You shan't be forgotten.

Contents

List of Figures	xiii
List of Tables	xiv
List of Contributors	xv
Acknowledgements	xxii
List of Abbreviations	xxiii

Introduction: capturing the beginning of a long journey of loss, trauma and grief   1
PANAGIOTIS PENTARIS

Referring to SARS-CoV-2 and Covid-19 5
Part I: Reconsidering death and grief in Covid-19 6
Part II: Institutional care and Covid-19 8
Part III: Impact of Covid-19 in context 10
References 12

PART I
Reconsidering death and grief in Covid-19   15

1 Familiarity with death   17
PANAGIOTIS PENTARIS AND KATE WOODTHORPE

Introduction 17
The pre-Covid-19 visibility of death 18
The visibility of death in the face of the pandemic 20
Inequalities 22
A politicisation of death 23
Conclusion 24
Notes 24
References 24

2 Grief in the COVID-19 pandemic 29
KENNETH J. DOKA

Introduction 29
COVID-19 in context 30
Populations at risk for grief in the pandemic 31
Coping with grief 34
Interventive approaches 36
Conclusion 38
References 38

3 Apocalypse now: COVID-19 and the crisis of meaning 40
ROBERT A. NEIMEYER, EVGENIA MILMAN, AND
SHERMAN A. LEE

Anxiety in the context of COVID-19 41
Coronavirus Anxiety Scale (CAS) 42
Grief in the time of corona 44
Pandemic Grief Scale (PGS) 46
From screening to meaning: prescriptions for practice 51
Coda 54
References 54

4 Physically distant but socially connected: streaming funerals, memorials and ritual design during COVID-19 60
STACEY PITSILLIDES AND JAYNE WALLACE

Make do and mending: the technologies and memorials of COVID-19 60
Funeral directors' creative uses of communication technologies and presence 64
What could technology do? 67
Conclusion: design directions for COVID-19 70
Notes 71
References 71

5 Social death in 2020: Covid-19, which lives matter and which deaths count? 77
JANA KRÁLOVÁ

Introduction 78
'Archaeology' of social death: three schools of thought 80
The exceptions 84

Covid-19: which lives matter and which deaths count? 88
Concluding remarks 92
References 93

PART II
Institutional care and Covid-19 99

6 End-of-life decision-making in the context of a pandemic 101
NATALIE PATTISON AND LUCY RYAN

End-of-life decisions – a global rationing context 101
Rationing resources: a necessary evil during COVID-19? 102
Factors that influence health care decisions at the end of life:
    application to COVID-19 105
Decision-making principles in COVID-19 107
Decision aides and shared decision-making 110
Advanced Care Planning in a pandemic 111
Achieving best practice principles 113
References 114

7 NHS values, ritual, religion, and Covid19 death 121
DOUGLAS DAVIES

Worldview, ideas-identity-destiny 121
Conclusion 132
References 132

8 Non-COVID-19 related dying and death during the pandemic 134
WAI YEE CHEE, SAMUEL S.Y. WANG, WINNIE Z.Y. TEO,
MELISSA FONG, ANDY LEE, AND WOON CHAI YONG

Case 1 The effects of COVID-19 on a non-COVID-19 related,
    hospitalised palliative patient during the pandemic:
    dying, death and grieving in a foreign land 135
Discussion 136
Case 2 The effects of COVID-19 on the care plans of a
    non-COVID home palliative patient during the pandemic:
    overtreatment, ethical concerns and funerary
    constraints 139
Discussion 140
Grieving other non-COVID-19 related deaths during the
    pandemic 142

Conclusion 144
References 144

9 Covid-19 and care home deaths and harms: a case study from the UK 146
ALISOUN J. MILNE

Care homes and care home populations in the UK 146
Covid-19 and deaths in care homes 147
Covid-19 and harm 150
Discussion 153
Conclusion 155
Notes 155
References 156

10 Impact of Covid-19 on mental health and associated losses 160
MANJU SHAHUL-HAMEED, JOHN FOSTER, GINA FINNERTY, AND PANAGIOTIS PENTARIS

Introduction 160
Mental health pre Covid-19 161
Impact of Covid-19 on mental health 163
Covid-19 and the digital divide 167
Change, loss and bereavement 168
Suicidal ideation 170
Conclusion 172
Note 173
References 173

11 Assisted dying and Covid-19 178
THEO BOER AND KEVIN YUILL

Introduction 178
Legal developments 179
Practical developments 181
A necessary act of compassion? 182
Patients who want help to die: loneliness, fear, and fear of being a burden 185
A rise in telemedicine 187
A differential value on human lives 188
Conclusion 190
Notes 190
References 191

PART III
Impact of COVID-19 in context 195

12 **Losing touch? Older people and COVID-19** 197
RENSKE CLAASJE VISSER

*Introduction 197
The importance of touch 200
Loss of touch 201
New ways of keeping in touch 203
Conclusion 205
Notes 206
References 206*

13 **Between cultural necrophilia and African American activism: life and loss in the age of COVID** 209
KAMI FLETCHER AND TAMARA WARASCHINSKI

*Introduction: COVID-19 + White supremacy = thousands of African American deaths 209
Cultural necrophilia: revisiting death and grief illiteracy during a global pandemic 211
The link between death denial and White supremacy 214
African American deathways amidst COVID-19, the 2020 pandemic and White supremacy 218
African American deathways as a response to dehumanized Black Life and dishonored Black Death 220
Conclusion: Black feminist and womanist frameworks as ways through the crisis 223
References 225*

14 **The biopolitics and stigma of the HIV and Covid-19 pandemics** 229
JASON SCHAUB

*Biopolitics 231
Stigma 233
Lessons from HIV for the Covid-19 pandemic 236
Conclusion 237
References 237*

15 Suicide in the context of the COVID-19 pandemic 241
MOHAMMED A. MAMUN AND JANNATUL MAWA MISTI

The COVID-19 pandemic and mental health 241
What is suicide? 243
Prior pandemics and suicide 243
Suicide in the context of the COVID-19 pandemic 244
Theories of suicide in the COVID-19 context 247
Concluding remarks 248
Acknowledgements 249
References 249

16 Death and dying during the COVID-19 pandemic: the Indian context 254
APURVA KUMAR PANDYA AND KHYATI TRIPATHI

Introduction 254
Changing the nature of death, dying and mourning in COVID-19 255
Death rituals, stigma and coping in the era of COVID-19 256
Dying with dignity in the times of COVID-19 261
Implications for practice and research 262
References 264

Index 267

Figures

4.1 Unfinished farewell 63
9.1 The cumulative number of care home residence deaths in care homes involving Covid-19 in England between April and July 2020 148
10.1 Suicidal behaviour in vulnerable populations in the COVID-19 era 170

Tables

3.1	Coronavirus Anxiety Scale 2.0	45
3.2	Pandemic Grief Scale	47
14.1	Experiential and policy differences	234

Contributors

Theo Boer is a professor of Health Care ethics at the Protestant Theological University in Groningen, the Netherlands and a member of the Dutch Health Council. He studied theology and ethics in Utrecht, Uppsala, and Karl-Marx-Stadt (Chemnitz). From 2005–2014 he was a member of the Governmental Review Committees for the hindsight assessment of assisted dying cases. From being a supporter of the Dutch euthanasia law, he has become increasingly critical about the possibilities to safely legalise assisted dying.

Dr Yong Woon Chai is a senior consultant in the Division of Palliative Care at the NUH. She is also Head of the Supportive and Palliative Care Programme at Alexandra Hospital, aimed at championing compassionate care and quality of life for patients receiving palliative care. Dr Yong is also a senior consultant in the Division of Palliative Care at the National University Cancer Institute, Singapore (NCIS). She has also served as a Senior Clinical Lecturer at the Yong Loo Lin School of Medicine at the National University of Singapore (NUS), as well as a visiting Consultant at St. Luke's Hospital. Dr Yong has received advanced training in Geriatric Medicine, followed by Palliative Care Medicine and is dually accredited as a specialist in Geriatric Medicine and Palliative Medicine. She believes in building stronger bonds with various community partners.

Ms Wai Yee Chee founded Grief Matters, the first Centre for Bereavement Care in Singapore in her role as senior Director to Montfort Care, a charity organisation. She holds a parallel position as a Programme Director with the Singapore Hospice Council, to promote the standard of psychosocial care among palliative care providers in Singapore. Ms Chee received the Outstanding Social Worker Award in 2016.

Dr Douglas J. Davies is a Professor in the Study of Religion and Director of The Centre for Death and Life Studies at Durham University, trained in Anthropology and Theology and researches their interplay, especially in the ritual, symbolism and belief of funerary rites and also of Mormonism. A Doctor of Letters (Oxford) and Honorary Doctor of Sweden's Uppsala

University, he holds elected fellowships in The Learned Society of Wales, The Academy of Social Sciences, and The British Academy.

Dr Kenneth J. Doka is a Professor Emeritus at the Graduate School of The College of New Rochelle and senior consultant to the Hospice Foundation of America. A prolific author, Dr Doka has published books and over 100 articles and book chapters. Dr Doka is editor of both *Omega: The Journal of Death and Dying* and *Journeys: A Newsletter to Help in Bereavement*. Dr Doka was elected President of the Association for Death Education and Counseling in 1993. In 1995, he was elected to the Board of Directors of the International Work Group on Dying, Death and Bereavement and served as chair from 1997–1999. He has received a number of awards including the Lifetime Achievement Award from ADEC and the Herman Feifel Award from IWG. Dr Doka is an ordained Lutheran minister and a licensed mental health counsellor.

Gina Finnerty is a senior lecturer in midwifery at the University of Greenwich. She was awarded her PhD in midwifery education at the University of Surrey in 2008. Gina's areas of academic interest are craft knowledge in midwifery, mentorship and healthcare simulation. Gina is a member of the simulation steering group in the School of Health Sciences. She has published in a range of peer-reviewed journals and books and has presented at international conferences. Gina is currently involved in a simulation project which has a focus on communication of staff involved in end of life care.

Dr Kami Fletcher is an Associate Professor of American and African American History and co-coordinator of Women's and Gender Studies at Albright College in Reading, PA (USA). Her research centres on African American burial grounds, late 19th/early 20th century Black female and male undertakers, and contemporary Black grief and mourning.

Ms Melissa Fong is an assistant nurse clinician from Methodist Welfare Services (MWS) Homecare and Home Hospice, which is a home service that provides clinical care and support to both palliative and non-palliative patients at home. She is also part of the MWS palliative team that provides regular palliative consultation to MWS Nursing home (Yew Tee) and MWS Bethany Nursing Home (Choa Chu Kang). She graduated from Alice Lee Centre for Nursing Studies in 2011 as a staff nurse. She attained a Specialist Diploma in Palliative care Nursing from Ngee Ann Polytechnic in 2017 and has further advanced her training in palliative care in 2020 with a Masters Degree in Palliative care with King's College London School of Medicine Department of Palliative Care, Policy and Rehabilitation.

Dr John Foster is a Reader in Alcohol Policy and Mental Health Studies, he was awarded his PhD through the University of London in 2001. He is a qualified mental health nurse and has taught students at all levels from pre-registration nurses to PhD post-graduates. His main research interest is the link between drug and alcohol use and mental health, and he has written a portfolio work concerning home drinking. He is particularly interested in helping students understand the barriers to change and the importance of prioritising engagement skills through motivational interviewing.

Dr Jana Králová is a researcher, theorist, lecturer, academic writer, registered social worker and publicly engaged social death preventer, appreciative of humour and satire. Jana authored peer-reviewed publications which, alongside her PhD are in the field of social death. Jana's scholarly interest in Social Death and its prevention includes all communities that are dehumanised, marginalised, discriminated against, oppressed, excluded, stigmatised, disregarded and otherwise considered worthless by others. Jana thinks, writes, and practices with these populations in ways that promote unconditional positive regard and humane treatment for *all* human beings.

Dr Andy Lee is a Principal Resident Physician at Singapore's Methodist Welfare Services (MWS) Home Care and Home Hospice team. It cares for a continuum of patients ranging from helping homebound patients to age in place to meeting their palliative care needs when they arise. Dr Lee is an accredited family physician and has focused his work on caring for patients in the community and helping to roll out the palliative care approach in MWS's nursing homes. He has also been serving as a clinical tutor at the Yong Loo Lin School of Medicine, National University of Singapore.

Sherman A. Lee, PhD, is an associate professor of psychology at Christopher Newport University. Lee studies negative feeling states, such as anxiety and grief, and the role personality and religion play in those emotional experiences. He also teaches courses in the psychology of personality, psychology of the human-animal bond (Anthrozoology), and the psychology of death, dying, and bereavement (Thanatology). The creator of the *Trait Sympathy Scales*, *Islamophobia Scale*, *Persistent Complex Bereavement Inventory*, and the *Coronavirus Anxiety Scale*, he is currently researching the impact of the COVID-19 pandemic on the psychological well-being of people around the world.

Mohammed A. Mamun is the founder and Director at the CHINTA Research Bangladesh and belongs to the Department of Public Health and Informatics, Jahangirnagar University, Bangladesh. The CHINTA Research Bangladesh is his brainchild, aims for engaging undergraduate students in research first ever in Bangladesh. His main research interests are psychiatric epidemiology, public health, as well as clinical research. Based on the Scientific Bangladesh report, Mamun has placed as the fourth most prolific Bangladeshi author in the year 2020.

Evgenia Milman, PhD, teaches at St Edward's University, where she publishes research examining how making meaning of stressful experiences influences mental health. Having authored dozens of research publications and book chapters on grief and grief therapy, she is currently developing the Handbook of Grief Therapies for Sage. Dr Milman also practices psychology, is faculty at the *Portland Institute for Loss and Transition,* and adjunct assistant professor at the Medical University of South Carolina. She is a content expert for the Canadian Virtual Hospice, on the advisory board for TAPS, and chairs online education for the Association of Death Education and Counseling.

Dr Alisoun Milne is a Professor of Social Work and Social Gerontology at the University of Kent. Her research expertise is in four intersecting areas: mental health in later life; social work with older people and their families; family carers; and care homes. Alisoun is a qualified and registered social worker and is involved in the UK and European networks promoting, and researching, the role of social work with older people and their carers. She is a fellow of the Academy of the Social Sciences and a member of the Research Excellence Framework 2021 sub-panel for social work and social policy.

Jannatul Mawa Misti is the clinical researcher at the CHINTA Research Bangladesh, and a medical student at the Pabna Medical College, Bangladesh. From the very beginning of the CHINTA Research Bangladesh, she is being associated with its journey and worked with numerous projects published in The Lancet. Her main research interests are on clinical researches, although she works on epidemiology and public health as well. Misti is one of the youngest undergraduate researchers from Bangladesh.

Robert A. Neimeyer, PhD, directs the *Portland Institute for Loss and Transition*, and maintains an active consulting and coaching practice. Neimeyer has published over 500 journal articles and book chapters as well as 30 books, including *Techniques of Grief Therapy* (Routledge, 2015), and serves as editor of *Death Studies*. He is currently working to advance a more adequate theory of grieving as a meaning-making process.

Apurva Kumar Pandya, PhD, is a Health Psychologist and currently working as an Economic Health Specialist at Regional Resource Centre for Health Technology Assessment, Indian Institute of Public Health Gandhinagar (IIPH-G), Gujarat, India. Prior to joining the IIPH-G, he has worked with International Non-Government Organization, United Nation agency, Department of Human Development and Family Studies, Maharaja Sayajirao University of Baroda and worked as a consulting psychologist. He has more than 12 years of experience working in the field of HIV prevention, research, program management and preventive counselling services. Primarily his work focuses on helping (marginalized) population to lead healthy lives, conduct policy-relevant studies, and improve public (mental) health service delivery to reduce health disparities and inequities.

Professor Natalie Pattison is a clinical academic who has worked clinically in cancer, critical care and critical care outreach. She is the Florence Nightingale Foundation Clinical Professor of Nursing with a joint appointment across the University of Hertfordshire and East and North Herts NHS Trust. She is the clinical lead for critical care follow-up services, combining this with a research role. Her research interests focus on her clinical area of critical care and critically ill ward patients, and cancer critical care. She is widely published in critical care supportive care.

Dr Panagiotis Pentaris is an Associate Professor of Social Work and Thanatology in the School of Human Sciences at the University of Greenwich, London, England, UK, where he is also a member of the Institute for Lifecourse Development, an internationally recognised Institute focusing on interdisciplinary research across the lifespan. Pentaris is a council member for the Association for the Study of Death and Society, and over the last ten years he has researched and published on death, dying, bereavement, culture and religion, social work, social policy and LGBTQIA+ issues.

Dr Stacey Pitsillides is a Senior Research Fellow in the School of Design at Northumbria University. Her research actively inquiries into the relationship between design, technology, death and dying. Collaborating with hospices, festivals, libraries, and galleries this research curates a range of interactive events aimed at specific communities e.g. tech innovators, educators and bereaved family members. Her work has been featured in festivals including Death: The Southbank Centre's Festival for the Living, FutureFest and the Edinburgh International Science Festival. Dr Pitsillides is on the standing committee for the International Death Online Research Symposium and was part of the collective developing a Global COVID-19 Relief Coalition white paper on death, grief and virtual funerals.

Lucy Ryan is a clinical academic leading a small but highly enthusiastic research team specialising in critical care research at Nottingham. She has clinical expertise in critical care and is a Florence Nightingale Foundation Research Scholar. Lucy's research interests are focused on communication and palliative care within critical care.

Dr Jason Schaub is a Lecturer in Social Work at the University of Birmingham. He is a qualified social worker and senior fellow of the Higher Education Academy, and a founding member of European Social Work Research Association. His work focuses on gender and sexuality, particularly improving the wellbeing of LGBTQ+ young people, predominantly using evidence-based methodologies and mixed methods. His research also examines leadership in social work and social workmen. Before entering academia, he practised in the USA, Ireland and the UK in mental health and children's services for over ten years.

Manju Shahul-Hameed is undertaking PhD in Integration of Health and Social Care, on mental health provisions, at University of Greenwich. She is also the founder of a registered charity called Manju Shahul-Hameed Foundation for Mental Health (Charity Number: 1176447) and was the Chair of Health and Wellbeing Board (Croydon) during 2017–2018. In addition, Manju is the Cabinet Member for Economic Recovery and Skills at London Borough of Croydon and Chair of Croydon Plus Credit Union, which provides low-interest loans and savings to the residents of Croydon, Merton and Sutton Boroughs. She was the mayor of Croydon during 2014/15.

Dr Winnie Teo is a Consultant at the National University Cancer Institute, Singapore (NCIS) and Alexandra Hospital. She is an accredited haematologist with a strong interest in end of life care. She also serves as a clinical lecturer at the Yong Loo Lin School of Medicine at the National University of Singapore (NUS). She hopes to share her experience with dealing with Non-COVID-19 related deaths during this pandemic, which has brought unprecedented challenges for the society.

Dr Khyati Tripathi is a death researcher and has been working in the area for 12 years now. She completed her B.A.(H) and M.A in Psychology, M.Phil. in Social Anthropology and PhD in Psychology from the University of Delhi, India. Her PhD thesis focused on the cultural construction of the dead in Hinduism and Judaism through culture-specific death rituals. She was awarded the prestigious Commonwealth Split-site scholarship (2016–2017) to spend a year of her PhD in the Department of Psychosocial Studies at Birkbeck, University of London. She was also awarded the research fellowship by the University Grants Commission, India for a period of five years (2014–2019).

Dr Renske Claasje Visser is a medical anthropologist interested in ageing, dying and death. She is particularly interested in health inequalities and how place shapes end of life experiences. Currently, she is a Research Fellow at the University of Surrey conducting research on Cancer Care in English prisons. Her previous research has looked at parental bereavement in young adulthood, the meaning of home in later life, and the experience of ageing in a secure psychiatric hospital. Presently, she is the postdoctoral representative for the Association for the Study of Death and Society.

Dr Jayne Wallace is a Professor of Craft, Digital Creativity and Wellbeing in the School of Design at Northumbria University, Newcastle and based in the CoCreate research group. Her research explores the potential of design, digital technologies, and the act of making to support sense of self across a range of human contexts. Central here are creative, participatory methods particularly within the contexts of bereavement, end of life and dementia.

Dr Samuel Sherng Young Wang is a Singaporean Chinese doctor who graduated from the University of New South Wales, Sydney, Australia. He is currently working in Alexandra Hospital, Singapore and has a strong interest in end of life care and palliative medicine. He hopes to eventually specialise in Haematology and incorporate aspects of palliative medicine into his speciality interest of Haematology. This chapter on 'Non-COVID-19 related Dying and Death during the Pandemic' was written based on his clinical experience caring for patients at the peak of the COVID-19 pandemic in Singapore. He hopes that his clinical encounters with patients during the pandemic would translate into important lessons when caring for the psychosocial needs of palliative patients during a pandemic.

Tamara Waraschinski grew up in Germany and then moved to Australia, where she worked as editor and researcher, and received her PhD in Sociology from the University of Adelaide. As a social theorist and death scholar with work and volunteer experience in aged and palliative care, she is particularly interested in how capitalism shapes attitudes around end-of-life. She co-founded the non-profit 'The Collective for Radical Death Studies', a collective of Scholars, Funeral Directors, Death Work Practitioners, Activists, and Students of Death Studies who view death work as synonymous with anti-racism work, and as a way to validate cultural and social life among marginalized groups. Tamara now lives with her family in New England, USA, where she combines her expertise in sociology and her passion for death and grief literacy with her position as company manager for a mission-driven Black Theatre company to help foster awareness for Black lives and joy.

Dr Kate Woodthorpe is a Senior Lecturer in Sociology in the Department of Social and Policy Sciences at the University of Bath, where she is also a member of the Centre of Death and Society (CDAS), an internationally recognised research centre focusing on the interdisciplinary social aspects of death, dying and bereavement. Over the last two decades, Dr Woodthorpe has researched and published on funeral practice and costs, bereavement, mourning, memorialisation, cemetery use and cremation funerals.

Kevin Yuill is an Associate Professor of History at the University of Sunderland. A Fulbright Scholar, he studied History and American Studies at Cambridge, Nottingham, and Maryland, USA. Most recently, he has researched the history of euthanasia and liberal attitudes to suicide.

Acknowledgements

This book would not have been possible without the support and guidance that I received from many people, starting from those who supported me during the Covid-19 pandemic and associated measures all through 2020 and into 2021.

First and foremost, I want to thank my son, Jack G. Pentaris Baker, with whom I have had the chance to share a lot more time together following school periodic closures during the last two terms of 2019–2020 and since September 2021. I am so thankful to his wise comments about my work and aspirations, as those continuously provoke my thinking and have me better evaluate what is meaningful in life and death. Jack, thank you for being a superhero to me; having you by my side, healthy and happy, makes me appreciate life more, especially during these difficult and challenging times we have been going through. Kudos for enduring so wonderfully with both your daddies during these difficult times.

I am thankful to all my friends and family, who remained close and supportive during a year of social isolation and aloneness. They have all supported me in ways that they may not have realised. I am grateful particularly to my sister Rena Gatzounis for her continuous acknowledgement and support with everything I do (or do not do), and my dear friends Theo Serafeim, Kostia Vasilopoulou, Nelita Groppa, Panagiotis Kyvetos and Katia Liosatou for their invaluable presence during the pandemic, and immense emotional support at times when things felt somewhat difficult! We thought that the period of physical isolation would create social distance between us, but on the contrary, this period has cemented our relationships even further, helping us realise the significance of our friendship.

Lastly, this book would not have come to fruition if it were not for the kind contribution of all authors listed in this volume. Thank you to all of them who kindly agreed to be part of this project and worked with me efficiently, albeit the varied challenges we each have been facing during the pandemic. Similarly, thank you to the editors at Routledge for their kind support while working on this manuscript.

List of Abbreviations

ACP	Advanced Care Planning
AIDS	Acquired Immunodeficiency Syndrome
ASDS	Association for the Study of Death and Society
BAME	Black and Asian Minority Ethnic
CA	Coronavirus Anxiety
CAS	Coronavirus Anxiety Scale
Covid-19	Coronavirus Disease 2019
CFR	Case Fatality Rate
CFS	Clinical Frailty Score
CQC	Care Quality Commission
DAH	Development Assistance for Health
DAMH	Development Assistance for Mental Health
DHSC	Department of Health and Social Care
DNACPR	Do Not Attempt Cardio-Pulmonary Resuscitation
DNAR	Do Not Attempt Resuscitation
DNR	Do Not Resuscitate
DoLS	Deprivation of Liberty Safeguards
EOL	End of Life
FDA	Food and Drug Administration
GP	General Practitioner/Practice
HIV	Human Immunodeficiency Virus
ICD	International Classification of Disease
ICU	Intensive Care Unit
IMF	International Monetary Fund
ISARIC	International Severe Acute Respiratory and Emerging Infection
ITU	Intensive Therapy Unit
LMICs	Low and Middle-Income Countries
MAID	Medical Aid in Dying
MERS	Middle East Respiratory Syndrome
MERS-CoV	Middle East Respiratory Syndrome - coronavirus
NCPC	National Council for Palliative Care
NHA	National Housing Act

NHS	National Health Service
NICE	National Institute for Health and Clinical Excellence
OECD	Organisation for Economic Co-operation and Development
ONH	Office for National Statistics
PHE	Public Health England
PGS	Pandemic Grief Scale
PPE	Personal Protective Equipment
PPE	Proper Protective Equipment
PTSD	Post-traumatic Stress Disorder
QALYS	Quality of Life Years
SAGE	Scientific Advisory Group for Emergencies
SARS	Severe Acute Respiratory Syndrome
SARS-CoV-2	Severe Acute Respiratory Syndrome Coronavirus 2
TMT	Terror Management Theory
UK	United Kingdom
UN	United Nations
USA	United States of America
WBG	World Bank Group
WHO	World Health Organization

Introduction: capturing the beginning of a long journey of loss, trauma and grief

Panagiotis Pentaris

In December 2019, a new virus by the name Covid-19 emerged in Wuhan, China, which quickly spread across the world and by March 2020 was recognised as a global pandemic. When writing this introduction (December 2020) the coronavirus updates tell us that worldwide there have been, to date, approximately 8.5 million cases. Majority of those who have contracted the virus recover from it, and many cases remain active. However, a large number of the population does not survive the virus; more than 1.7 million people have died of Covid-19, by December 2020.

This is merely scraping the surface of the complex social phenomenon coronavirus that the world has been facing in 2020, a year that for many 'stood still', instilled fear and caused trauma and losses unexpectedly. These experiences have been further complicated, particularly when looking at the possibility that the virus does discriminate across varied groups in society. Scholars and researchers, as well as journalists, to date, have claimed that Covid-19 does not discriminate. In many ways, this may be true, given that the virus might kill someone regardless of their ethnic or religious background, or their gender and/or sexuality. Yet, statistics have by now shown us that albeit the chances that all may die of Covid, there are some subgroups that are mostly affected by it. The chance of dying if contracting the virus changes by age. For those aged between 10 and 39, the probability is 0.2%, while for younger children it is even lower. As the age increases, so does the probability, with those aged 70–79 to have an 8% chance and those aged 80 and above a 14.8% chance of death. This is reflective of the latest Case Fatality Rate (CFR) (Our World in Data, 2020; also see Munster et al., 2020) that emphasises that it is older people who are most at risk of contracting and dying of coronavirus, and more specifically those aged 70 and above, particularly with comorbidities.

Race and ethnicity are two other areas by which Covid appears to discriminate; of course, studies have not yet been conclusive or extensive enough to provide a robust argument. This is merely an observation by CFR across the world, which shows that Black and Asian communities run higher risks of contracting the virus and dying of it, too. The APM Research Lab (2020) in the US shows that not only Black but Indigenous Americans as well experience highest rates of death from Covid-19. Similarly, the Centers for Disease Control and Prevention (2020) present data that want Black or African Americans, American Indian or Alaska Native, as well as Hispanic persons to be four times more likely to contract the virus and be hospitalised, and two to three times in all probability to die of Covid-19, as opposed to their White counterparts. Similar statistics have emerged in other countries. In the UK, and especially in the first peak of the pandemic, the virus was mostly highest among Black men and women (Office for National Statistics, 2020). Further, and drawing on the same and other sources, males of Asian backgrounds like Bangladeshi, Pakistani and Indian, turn a much higher risk of contracting the virus and dying of it (Public Health England, 2020).

Other areas are continuously being examined as those that cause the divide in the world's experience of the coronavirus pandemic, and this introduction is not citing them all. Yet, this first part of the book highlights that age, race, ethnicity, perhaps gender, are not 'conditions' which impact one's health. These are simply markers of other conditions and life experiences that associate with poorer health outcomes. Pointedly, these are markers of socio-economic status (Bowleg, 2020; Ali, Asaria and Stranges, 2020), accessibility and acceptability of health services (Cénat et al., 2020; Gauthier et al., 2020), as well as risk of being exposed to the virus due to lifestyle and/or employment (Hawkins, 2020) (e.g. infrastructure workers). In other words, Covid-19 and its impact on public health and social life are primarily surfacing social and health inequalities that are neither new nor surprising to policy makers.

Death tolls and public health offer information paramount to tackle the health issues associated with the current pandemic. However, many of the Covid-19 responses (by governments and otherwise) need to tackle (and some already do) other areas of trauma and loss experienced by those affected by the virus, which in this case would include the wider population of this Earth. The virus is challenging society by placing death in the front row. People around the world are asked to periodically isolate themselves and avoid any physical contact with family members and loved ones that do not reside in the same household. The implications of this request are multidimensional and often edgy, impacting people in varied ways, many of which remain unknown to us yet.

Studies to date focused specifically on the economic impact of Covid (e.g. McKibbin and Fernando, 2020), older people and the mental and physical effects of social isolation due to Covid-19 associated measures (e.g. Sepúlveda-Loyola et al., 2020), the impact of loneliness (e.g. Banerjee and Rai, 2020), the effects on residents in care homes (e.g. Hsu et al., 2020) and disabled people (e.g. Lund et al., 2020), the influence of Covid on children and youth (e.g. Courtney et al., 2020), LGBTQ populations (e.g. Salerno, Williams and Gattamorta, 2020), the disproportionate impact of Covid on ethnic minorities (e.g. Tai et al., 2020) and the psychological effects of the

Covid-19 associated quarantine measures in 2020 (e.g. Pietrabissa and Simpson, 2020), while others have endeavoured to devise ways to tackle 'coronavirus anxiety' (Milman, Lee and Neimeyer, 2020). This is, of course, not an exhausting list, but an indication that work has been undertaken, is underway, and is focusing on certain areas more than others. In fact, a simple search on databases (in December 2020), across academic journals, policy documents, and non-peer-reviewed contributions, shows that in the space of one year, since the emergence of the virus, and before it was claimed a global pandemic by the World Health Organization in March 2020, more than 1.2 million sources/papers/policies have been published. Those may not always be drawing on critical evidence, but the number shows how the academic, research (medical and non), social and policy communities worldwide have been preoccupied.

The current pandemic did not only take us by surprise and left individuals, communities and societies in shock, but necessitated attention to the varied and complex losses that we have all been experiencing (of course, for the reader this may be in the past tense, but when this book is put together, the world is facing second and third waves of high rates in Covid cases and deaths, which has led to further quarantine measures), and which primarily seem to stem from social inequalities that pre-existed. The varied losses the world is faced with are too many to list in a simple text; some, however, that may be more universal than others include loss of freedom, loss of employment, the loss of contact with family and friends, loss of choice and access to certain services. These are but a few non-death related losses, but loss by death has been impactful, too. The death of loved ones has been traumatic differently than otherwise during the pandemic, and this is primarily due to the restrictions related to the measures tackling the spread of the virus. The inability to be near a loved one who is dying, or travel to attend a funeral, pay respects, and say goodbyes, has left many grievers in a helpless state, facing the risk of ongoing, chronic and traumatic grief. Consequently, at the risk of exacerbated or new mental health challenges, which call for immediate and careful attention, as has been the case in the recent months.

That said, the coronavirus pandemic ignited not only a worldwide experience of trauma, but a critical debate in the media about death and dying, revisiting the subject since its subtle references in the last few decades. The reality of death and the fragility of life made the headlines daily in 2020 and invaded private spaces even more than they did before. Choice of exposure to the daily death rates news has gradually declined, unless one stays away from electronic devices. Social media, mass media and everyday conversations have been preoccupied with Covid-19, quarantine measures and the risks of mortality. It is important to notice here, nonetheless, that as the pandemic evolved, and after the summer 2020, scientific and medical communities gained more knowledge and understanding of the virus in order to develop solutions that have put people's minds to rest at large, albeit the continuous worries. On 9 November 2020, the biopharmaceutical company Pfizer announced a 90% efficacy of the working vaccine to reduce the risks of Covid-19 infections (Pfizer, 2020). This led to further trials which helped release the first vaccine and, currently, thousands of people have been vaccinated and positive results are slowly emerging. Not long after the release of the first vaccine, the University of Oxford research community released the AstraZeneca vaccine, the second to protect the public from Covid-19.

It is equally important to make mention here of state-level responses during the pandemic and since March 2020 in particular. Governments have been offering messages of support to the public in their respective nations; while highlighting the need for a collaborative, large-scale and science-based response to Covid-19. The G20 Leader's Summit's input reflects the current efforts for such large-scale response to this global pandemic. Working closely with the World Health Organization (WHO), International Monetary Fund (IMF), World Bank Group (WBG), United Nations (UN), and other global organisations, the G20 Leaders attempt to develop solutions and put support in place for all health, economic and social impacts that communities and individuals are facing and will continue to face during the aftermath of the pandemic.

The current pandemic is a reminder of the fragility of life, not only the life of an individual but of communities and societies on the whole. It reminds us how people and communities are interconnected and, hence, depend on one another to persevere, but also highlights vulnerabilities, fears and resilience. Coronaviruses, or any other viruses, do not discriminate (in principle, as I mention earlier), neither are contained in one geography. As the virus Covid-19 has been spreading across the world, communities and individuals are increasingly facing the tragic loss of human life and the emotional reaction to those losses. Covid-19 has caused the sudden death of many people and intensified not only the experiences of grief and bereavement but invaded into the ways of grieving and mourning as those have been traditionally passed on from one generation to the next.

This book does not have a single starting point but draws on the many and arduous losses that the world has been facing – both universal and population-specific – and reflects on how the current pandemic has been influencing and transforming social life. This is not a task that can or should be undertaken by one person only, though, and this is if we want to gain as much of an understanding of the situation as possible. Thus, a number of scholars, researchers, policymakers and practitioners are contributing to this volume, accumulating a multi-disciplinary, diverse and international set of ideas and perspectives that will help the reader examine closely how Covid-19 has invaded social life, resulted in often irreversible outcomes of trauma and loss, and caused grief that is both intense and unexplored, particularly due to its anticipated long-term and complicated nature. In other words, the aim of this collection of essays, which is further introduced later in the introduction, is to offer the reader an initial reflection of how death, loss and grief are experienced in the context of Covid-19; how is social life impacted in varied geographical contexts, how has policy responded to currently recognised coronavirus related needs, and how has technology been used under the circumstances of death and loss.

Referring to SARS-CoV-2 and Covid-19

There are hundreds of coronaviruses; mostly spread among animals and often passed on people with what is called the 'spillover event'. Coronaviruses predominantly cause respiratory illnesses and have been mostly deadly. In the 21st century, three main such coronaviruses have emerged. The first (i.e. SARS-CoV) (Severe Acute Respiratory Syndrome – coronavirus) in 2002 and phased out in 2004. The next was MERS-CoV (Middle East Respiratory Syndrome – coronavirus), emerged in 2012 and continues to resurface periodically. The third coronavirus of the 21st century is the SARS-Cov-2 (Severe Acute Respiratory Syndrome – coronavirus – 2). This novel coronavirus that emerged in December 2019 is known as Covid-19; otherwise, Coronavirus Disease 2019 (for more information, see National Institute of Allergy and Infectious Diseases, 2020).

This book neither has a medical character, nor do I, the editor, have any such medical knowledge. But this brief section is important to emphasise the context in which the book explores what death, grief and loss is. Further, it shows briefly the varied ways in which the virus has been referred to in the media, in scholarly work and ongoing research and practice. The terms and formats Covid-19, Covid19, COVID-19, COVID19, coronavirus, coronavirus pandemic, covid pandemic, SARS-CoV-2, and other indicatives have been used interchangeably, while they all refer to the same thing, but some to the virus and others to the disease it causes. In this book, contributors have been given the space to consistently use the term and format that best facilitate their discussions. Hence, there is consistency in each chapter, but varied ways of referring to the coronavirus SARS-CoV-2 have been used across chapters.

About this book

This book is divided into three parts and 16 chapters. The first section focuses on revisiting death, dying, grief and bereavement (as well as mourning) and how the current pandemic not only transforms our experiences but surfaces new realities of death and grief, and mourning practices – particularly with the use of technology. The first section also focuses on identifying the convoluted and diversified losses associated with the coronavirus pandemic. The second part of the book examines the challenges and controversies faced by healthcare systems, addressing key queries such as end-of-life decision making during Covid-19, assisted suicide, and mental health challenges and care systems. This part of the book takes into account practical examples about how Covid has impacted on the care of patients in various institutional settings, inclusive of care homes. Last, the third part looks at the meaning of Covid-19 on few specific communities, such as LGBTQ and older individuals. These three parts, in other words, tell a story about how death, dying, grief and bereavement are transformed experiences in the context of Covid-19; how these are found in healthcare systems; and how Covid-19 and associated measures have impressed in specific contexts and populations.

Each section is comprised of a different number of chapters, and each chapter revolves around a central argument: Covid-19 and associated measures in 2020 and beyond have impacted irreversibly and undeniably on social life, leading to a labyrinthine experience of death, grief and loss. Similarly, most chapters consider the purpose and benefits of the use of technology in such times, while recognising not only current challenges but future threats as well, which call for action.

Part I: Reconsidering death and grief in Covid-19

The first part of the book comprises five chapters. In the first chapter, Panagiotis Pentaris and Kate Woodthorpe explore how Covid-19 has led to a re-familiarisation with death and grief and policy action on the basis of re-surfaced social inequalities. The authors consider the pre-Covid-19 visibility of death in the public sphere and how the mass media coverage of the coronavirus pandemic has stirred social and political debates and responses. The chapter begins with a discussion about the pre-Covid-19 concealment of death from public view and argues that the coronavirus triggered a (new) public visibility of death. Further, the chapter recognises that news media has provided extensive coverage of Covid-19 deaths, which includes exhaustive debates about social inequalities that often appear to be the underpinning cause for the disproportionate death rates among different parts of the population. The authors conclude the chapter with the argument that the abovementioned factors have demanded a political response to the matter, and a long overdue politicisation of death.

The second chapter focuses on the unique issues that the pandemic creates for individuals grieving in this period. In this chapter, Kenneth Doka explores grief in three populations: grievers of those who have died from Covid-19; grievers of those who have died from causes not related to Covid-19; grief and trauma experienced by healthcare professionals in this period. These explorations do not neglect to discuss grief stemming from losses not related to death, but linked with experiences very common to us all, such as loss of employment and human relations. Similar to other chapters, this segment impresses on us the need for future action given the risk for complicated grief reactions, which are yet to be examined. To enable future trends and forward thinking in practice, Kenneth Doka makes suggestions for therapists in mental health, which will assist when working with those coping with such losses.

Following on from the arguments in the second chapter, the third recognises coronavirus anxiety as a psychological consequence of the fear and anxiety in the face of Covid-19 and foresees 'a shadow pandemic of dysfunctional grief' that follows the coronavirus pandemic. The authors, Robert Neimeyer, Evgenia (Jane) Milman and Sherman Lee, present two scales that help develop practice that can benefit the recognised pandemic of dysfunctional grief. The first scale is the *Coronavirus Anxiety Scale* (CAS) that serves as a screener for functional impairments, and the second is the *Pandemic Grief Scale* (PGS), which helps identify bereaved survivors at a heightened risk of substance abuse and suicide. When exploring these scales and their effectiveness, the authors argue that meaning making is the medium to regulating either direct or indirect Covid stressors, and the scales can be useful tools for professionals working with people affected by Covid-19 on such levels.

Stacey Pitsillides and Jayne Wallace, in the fourth chapter, argue that in the face of Covid-19 the use of technology to express grief and perform rituals has become the norm. Whilst online environments were previously a choice and provided an alternative platform for grief, they have now become a necessity and only option. The authors emphasise this with a discussion about streaming funerals online. The chapter creates a balance between the loss of physical presence at times when most wanted (e.g. funeral attendance) and the gain of telepresence, which allows people, regardless of geography and restrictions, to be present. With a focus on the benefits of technology, the chapter recognises, but does not examine, that digital poverty and digital illiteracy are a challenge; not every person is privileged with technology or the knowledge of how to use it. Hence, often rely, where possible, on others to help them have access and enjoy such benefits.

The next and final chapter of the first section looks at social death and Covid-19. The chapter draws on the three disciplinary areas that help theorise social death – slavery, death studies and genocide – and argues that structural violence, during Covid-19, becomes the cause of social death. Government (in)actions continue to be influential and transform people's lives, especially in a period when they are much more dependent socially and financially on the input from the State. The chapter recognises that structural inequalities when responding to Covid lead to the exacerbation of social divisions in society and separate those who have the means to access and enjoy services from those who cannot. Social inequalities are thus on the surface, and with quarantine measures that keep people isolated and physically distant, the risks of social death, social disengagement, or generally the break-up of the relationship between State and an individual are high. The author of this chapter, Jana Králová, concludes that social death as a framework helps conceptualise the experiences of individuals in society, who otherwise remain invisible. This is highly pertinent to the challenges posed by the coronavirus pandemic, as circumstances lead to different results based on every person's resources, capacities and socio-financial stability.

Part II: Institutional care and Covid-19

The second part of the book includes six chapters, all of which offer arguments relevant to the challenges institutional care faces during the pandemic, especially when considering end-of-life decision making, assisted dying, mental health and suicide, and the praise of healthcare systems as a new religion and the saviour.

In Chapter 6, Natalie Pattison and Lucy Ryan endeavour to unpack the burden of ethical decision making for dying patients (both due to Covid-19 and to non-related reasons), by clinical personnel. The chapter recognises that the scope and impact of the pandemic, as well as the pace by which new cases emerge have shocked the healthcare system, leaving organisations and professionals precarious to the limitations at hand (e.g. resources). It is within this argument that the authors claim that rapid decision-making in end-of-life care in this period, can often and without choice lead to poorer practices, as the pace by which practitioners need to act does not allow for full consideration of the best evidence in order to make best decisions. Additionally, and regarding Covid-19 related deaths, evidence, especially in the first few months of the pandemic, was not available, which left clinicians helpless when making decisions. The authors draw on their clinical experiences during the pandemic to emphasise their arguments and exemplify the difficulties faced by clinicians and other healthcare staff.

In the next chapter, Chapter 7, Douglas Davies focuses on the National Health Service (NHS) in the UK and its role in the British response to the Covid-19 global pandemic. For the UK, the NHS has become, according to the author, an integral part of social and cultural life; it holds values that are elemental to the way Britons specifically run their lives. This chapter argues that during the pandemic, and while religious buildings were shuttered, and practices minimised due to restrictions, the NHS played a more holy role. The public started, quickly, to create rituals that would celebrate the NHS and its workers, while the State embraced the recognition of the risks that healthcare workers faced during the pandemic. Such rituals included weekly applauses and messages on windows and pavements, echoing the Government's messages that 'the NHS saves lives'. The transferability of this argument is apparent when one looks at how other institutions and healthcare workers altogether around the world have been treated during the pandemic (e.g. Medicare in the US and Canada).

Next, in Chapter 8, Wai Yee Chee, Samuel Wang, Winnie Teo, Melissa Fong, Andy Lee and Woon Chai Yong explore non-Covid-19 related deaths and discuss the challenges in caring for dying patients, not from Covid, during the pandemic. Quarantine and other measures have been disruptive for all, inclusive of most vulnerable patients not affected by Covid, most importantly due to the constraints placed on caregivers, families and friends, turning them unable to support patients in their daily routines, as they would otherwise. It is without doubt that during the current pandemic, Covid-19 patients became the priority – we can also see this from essential work like cancer trials being paused in the early months – and this chapter, with case studies, shows the grief and ethical dilemmas faced by non-Covid-19 patients.

Chapter 9, by Alisoun Milne, is an account about care homes in Covid-19. The chapter is a case study from the UK, which scrutinises not only how the coronavirus pandemic has impacted on care homes, their residents, staff members, caregivers, family and friends, but also how effective government responses to the situation have been. The author argues that care homes have not been a priority, albeit the abundant health demands of the residents, during the pandemic. The number of deaths in care homes was not accounted for until much later into the pandemic, and protective equipment was not sent to care homes as a priority. This led to further shortage of staff being unable to provide support without running high risks of infections themselves. This chapter's argument brings together thoughts shared in chapters two (different types of grief in the pandemic), three (coronavirus anxiety experienced by staff and residents), four (family and friends could only connect with the residents via social media and other communication technologies, but only when and where residents had the resources and skills to do so), and five (running high risks of social disengagement and isolation to the extent of social death), in a single case study. Alisoun Milne argues that the current deficits in the process revealed the gaps in the infrastructure of the care system, which need attention with long-term solutions and an attempt for effective integrated care.

Further, Chapter 10 puts focus on the prevalence of death, grief and loss during the pandemic with mental health outcomes. In this chapter, Manju Shahul-Hameed, John Foster, Gina Finnerty and Panagiotis Pentaris reflect on the diverse ways in which the many and unique to each situation losses experienced in this period, have led (and continue to lead) to highly challenging circumstances for individuals, families and communities. Some of those include the risk of suicide, heightened levels of anxiety and depression, as well as PTSD following Covid. The authors emphasise that accessibility to mental health services has been more difficult in this period, while quarantine and other measures to help reduce the spread of the virus are inevitably connected with an increased burden in mental health. The chapter concludes with a call for action in light of the anticipated need for long-term solutions to the deep-rooted mental health challenges that Covid-19 introduced or aggravated.

Theo Boer and Kevin Yuill, in Chapter 11, examine how Covid-19 and associated measures have impacted on assisted dying and assisted suicide services in countries where they are offered. The authors highlight that despite the statistics showing that assisted dying and assisted suicide are important services to some, while quarantine measures and social isolation increased the number of requests for assisted dying, the services were, for the first few months of the pandemic, shut down, leaving people precarious of social isolation that further impacted on their wellbeing. This chapter adds value to this book as it emphasises an area that is not only of controversy to many (policymakers included), but of importance when considering the long-term effects of the experiences of death, destruction, loss and trauma related to Covid-19, some of which is discussed in previous chapters, both in parts I and II, but in some of the chapters to follow, as well.

Part III: Impact of Covid-19 in context

The next five chapters comprise the third and final part of this book. These chapters specifically look at death, grief and loss related to Covid-19 and in the context of specific populations. Particularly, in Chapter 12, Renske Visser contests the age-restricted and often nullifying government responses (e.g. policies introduced to tackle Covid-19 related needs), which treat older individuals as a homogenous group, ignoring the immense diversity within this group, both physically and mentally, to focus on two main categories. The author of this chapter is arguing that quarantine measures specific to older people and general isolation has led older individuals to 'touch hunger'. The deprivation of proximity and touch and human relations in-person has resulted in the breakdown of connectedness with others. Simultaneously, in this chapter, Renske Visser acknowledges that Covid-19 and associated measures not only restricted older individuals but provided new opportunities to them; new ways of keeping in touch with families and friends.

Chapter 13 is a thorough account of *Necrophile Self* (i.e. 'a cultural trait of death phobia and consumerism within the individual') and the death of African Americans in the pandemic. Kami Fletcher and Tamara Waraschinski draw on recent events like the murder of the late Mr George Floyd, as well as activism that followed to underscore the politicisation of mourning and grief, by tackling white supremacy. The authors conclude with the argument that Black Feminist Theories are an essential vehicle to overcome death denial cultures concerning the deaths of African Americans in a political context of consumerism and white supremacy, which is aggravated with Covid-19.

In Chapter 14, Jason Schaub is examining the biopolitics of a pandemic. To do so, the author draws on learning from the HIV pandemic and reflects on how we can apply this to the current Covid-19 pandemic. Jason Schaub is, specifically, drawing on the experiences of gay men in the HIV pandemic, recognising the notion of disenfranchised grief, and explores the similarities and differences between the two pandemics (i.e. HIV and Covid-19), while arguing the biopolitics of both. Precisely, the chapter discusses biopower and the manipulation of the human body at times like Covid-19; policy, legislation and guidance during any pandemic dictates the way one lives their life, but only in relation to their human body (e.g. policies about proximity with others in public or wearing masks). Last, the chapter recognises the concept of stigma as a pertinent outcome from a pandemic as the latter associates with one part of the population more than another. This reference to previous works about stigmatised and marginalised parts of the population is complementary to previous chapters in this book, which highlight the social inequalities and discrepancies surfacing or being exacerbated during Covid-19.

Mohammed A. Mamun and Jannatul Mawa Misti, in Chapter 15, elaborate on all current data and knowledge about how Covid-19 has influenced suicidal behaviour and suicide rates altogether. The authors delve into a thorough account of varied studies that have explored these associations, and highlight the prevalence of suicidal ideation, suicidal behaviour, suicide attempts, mental health generally, Covid-19 and associated measures. The chapter argues that in light of this knowledge, policymakers, mental health practitioners and governments on the whole should further emphasise on developing prevention in such situations. This complements the thesis of the tenth chapter (mental health and high risks of suicide as a result), as well.

In the final chapter, Chapter 16, Apurva Kumar Pandya and Khyati Tripathi are providing an in-depth account of how Covid-19 and associated measures have influenced social, economic and political life in India. This chapter is unique in that it highlights the Indian context, bringing to our attention realities distant from the Western world, which are important, if we are to develop a rounded understanding of Covid-19 and the complexity of its impact. This chapter draws on two case studies to explore the transformation of religious rituals in light of death, as well as the barriers and difficulties that individuals are facing at current times.

Coda

Before we venture to the subsequent chapters of this book, I would like to reemphasise three main points made across this introduction. First, this book is neither conclusive nor exhaustive of knowledge and data about Covid-19 and the varied ways the disease has influenced human life. The book is primarily stemming from a place of reflection, where all contributors have taken a brave step forward to report on their appreciation of the situation, in their respective fields, and when available report on data and robust evidence that recognises further importance on the subject each time. Next, this book is the collection of essays authored by a range of contributors from varied disciplinary backgrounds, including healthcare, theology, medicine, palliative and hospice care, sociology, social care, social work, gerontology, thanatology, anthropology and medical anthropology, midwifery, psychology and psychotherapy, grief and bereavement expertise, nursing, mental health, health economics, design and digital design and history. Similarly, the contributors of this collection come from varied geographical backgrounds, including Singapore, the UK, USA, Canada, the Netherlands, China, India and Ireland.

The third and last point I wished to emphasise here is this. This collection of essays can be read as a whole or per chapter. The experience of the reader, however, will certainly be influenced based on how they approach it. Each chapter will, independently, provide thorough and important information about the argument it seeks to make. Yet, chapters are complementary to one another and when read as a collection, the reader can appreciate a more rounded and robust reflection of Covid-19 and its unavoidable effects on death, grief and loss.

References

Ali, S., Asaria, M. and Stranges, S., 2020. COVID-19 and inequality: are we all in this together? *Canadian Journal of Public Health*, 111(3), pp. 415–416.

APM Research LAB, 2020. The color of coronavirus: Covid-19 deaths by race and ethnicity in the U.S. Available at: https://www.apmresearchlab.org/covid/deaths-by-race (Accessed: 27 December 2020).

Banerjee, D. and Rai, M., 2020. Social isolation in Covid-19: the impact of loneliness. *International Journal of Social Psychiatry*, 66(6), pp. 525–527.

Bowleg, L., 2020. We're not all in this together: on COVID-19, intersectionality, and structural inequality. *American Journal of Public Health*, 110(7), p. 917.

Cénat, J.M., Dalexis, R.D., Kokou-Kpolou, C.K., Mukunzi, J.N. and Rousseau, C., 2020. Social inequalities and collateral damages of the COVID-19 pandemic: when basic needs challenge mental health care. *International Journal of Public Health*, 65(6), pp. 717–718.

Centers for Disease Control Prevention, 2020. COVID-19 hospitalization and death by race/ethnicity. Available at: https://www.cdc.gov/coronavirus/2019-ncov/covid-data/investigations-discovery/hospitalization-death-by-race-ethnicity.html (Accessed: 16 January 2021).

Courtney, D., Watson, P., Battaglia, M., Mulsant, B.H. and Szatmari, P., 2020. COVID-19 impacts on child and youth anxiety and depression: challenges and opportunities. *The Canadian Journal of Psychiatry*, 65(10), pp. 688–691.

Gauthier, G.R., Smith, J.A., García, C., Garcia, M.A. and Thomas, P.A., 2020. Exacerbating inequalities: social networks, racial/ethnic disparities, and the COVID-19 pandemic. *The Journals of Gerontology: Series B*, 76(3), pp. e88–e92. Doi: 10.1093/geronb/gbaa117

Hawkins, D., 2020. Differential occupational risk for COVID-19 and other infection exposure according to race and ethnicity. *American Journal of Industrial Medicine*, 63(9), pp. 817–820.

Hsu, A.T., Lane, N., Sinha, S.K., Dunning, J., Dhuper, M. and Kahiel, Z., 2020. Impact of COVID-19 on residents of Canada's long-term care homes–ongoing challenges and policy response. *International Long-Term Care Policy Network*, 17, pp. 1–18.

Lund, E.M., Forber-Pratt, A.J., Wilson, C. and Mona, L.R., 2020. The COVID-19 pandemic, stress, and trauma in the disability community: A call to action. *Rehabilitation Psychology*, 65(4), pp. 313–322.

McKibbin, W. and Fernando, R., 2020. The economic impact of COVID-19. In R. Baldwin and B.W. di Mauro (eds.), *Economics in the time of COVID-19*. London, UK: CEPR Press, pp. 45–52.

Milman, E., Lee, S.A. and Neimeyer, R.A., 2020. Social isolation and the mitigation of coronavirus anxiety: The mediating role of meaning. *Death Studies*, pp. 1–13. Doi: 10.1080/07481187.2020.1775362

Munster, V.J., Koopmans, M., van Doremalen, N., van Riel, D. and de Wit, E., 2020. A novel coronavirus emerging in China – key questions for impact assessment. *New England Journal of Medicine*, 382(8), pp. 692–694.

National Institute of Allergy and Infectious Diseases, 2020. Coronaviruses. Available at: https://www.niaid.nih.gov/diseases-conditions/coronaviruses (Accessed: 27 December 2020).

Office for National Statistics, 2020. Coronavirus Covid-19 related deaths by ethnic group: England and Wales. Available at: https://www.ons.gov.uk/peoplepopulationand community/birthsdeathsandmarriages/deaths/articles/coronaviruscovid19relateddeaths-byethnicgroupenglandandwales/2march2020to15may2020 (Accessed: 17 January 2021).

Our world in Data, 2020. Mortality risk of Covid-19. Available at: https://ourworldindata.org/mortality-risk-covid (Accessed: 27 December 2020).

Pfizer, 2020. Pfizer and biontech announce vaccine candidate against Covid-19 achieved success in first interim analysis from phase 3 study. Available at: https://www.pfizer.com/news/press-release/press-release-detail/pfizer-and-biontech-announce-vaccine-candidate-against (Accessed: 27 December 2020).

Pietrabissa, G. and Simpson, S.G., 2020. Psychological consequences of social isolation during COVID-19 outbreak. *Frontiers in Psychology*, 11, p. 2201. Doi: 10.3389/fpsyg.2020.02201

Public Health England, 2020. Disparities in the risk and outcomes of COVID-19. Available at: https://assets.publishing.service.gov.uk/government/uploads/system/uploads/attachment_data/file/908434/Disparities_in_the_risk_and_outcomes_of_COVID_August_2020_update.pdf (Accessed: 13 January 2021).

Salerno, J.P., Williams, N.D. and Gattamorta, K.A., 2020. LGBTQ populations: psychologically vulnerable communities in the COVID-19 pandemic. *Psychological Trauma: Theory, Research, Practice, and Policy*, 12(S1), pp. S239–S242.

Sepúlveda-Loyola, W., Rodríguez-Sánchez, I., Pérez-Rodríguez, P., Ganz, F., Torralba, R., Oliveira, D.V. and Rodríguez-Mañas, L., 2020. Impact of social isolation due to COVID-19 on health in older people: mental and physical effects and recommendations. *The Journal of Nutrition, Health & Aging*, 24(9), pp. 938–947. Doi: 10.1007/s12603-020-1469-2

Tai, D.B.G., Shah, A., Doubeni, C.A., Sia, I.G. and Wieland, M.L., 2020. The disproportionate impact of COVID-19 on racial and ethnic minorities in the United States. *Clinical Infectious Diseases*, 72(4), pp. 703–706. Doi: 10.1093/cid/ciaa815

Part I
Reconsidering death and grief in Covid-19

1 Familiarity with death

Panagiotis Pentaris and Kate Woodthorpe

Key points

- Pre-Covid-19, death has been concealed from public view, with recent efforts to (re)integrate death into everyday life.
- Covid-19 has triggered a (new) public visibility of death.
- News media has provided wide-ranging coverage of Covid-19 deaths, including inequalities, to the extent that death has entered people's homes as an everyday subject for discussion.
- These factors have necessitated a political response, and a long-overdue politicisation of death.

Introduction

As this book will attest to, Covid-19 and its associated lockdown measures have changed people's lives in unprecedented ways. Across the world, governments, societies, families and individuals have been affected by the virus and control measures that have led to huge disruption(s) to everyday life. Seemingly, everyday there have been reports of increased mental health challenges, growth in domestic abuse, concerns over the rationing of health and social care, and the long-term risks attached to prolonged social isolation – especially among the elderly and those at high risk. Within these reports, death, dying and bereavement have received significant coverage. It is almost as if Covid-19 has been a huge and shocking aide-mémoire about the fragility and finality of the mortal human condition. Abruptly reminded that an airborne virus such as Covid-19 'can kill',[1] tales of death and the risk of death have dominated the news for much of 2020, with much talk of 'premature' death, and vulnerabilities associated with age, morbidity and physical condition. Access to dying people in hospitals to say goodbye has become headline news, along with whether families are permitted to attend a funeral service, and the legality of their hugging a fellow mourner.

Such public recognition of death and its impact is long overdue. In this chapter, we consider the pre-Covid-19 visibility of death in the public sphere and what the virus has done to raise the social and political profile of death in the public domain. We explore what Covid-19 has thrown up, challenged, or changed in terms of how people in the UK and beyond know and understand death, dying and bereavement, and how these vary between different groups of people. We argue that such a stark reminder about mortality and inequality within the population is much welcome and needed, for socio-economic improvements to be made.

The chapter first introduces the reader to well-established ideas and theories about the presence and concealment of death in modern/late modern society, examining the evolution of ways in which societies and individuals have engaged in conversations about death in public. In the second part of the chapter, we focus on how Covid-19 and associated measures have influenced death, dying and bereavement. Specifically, we start with the argument that Covid-19 has led to a publicly visible (re)institutionalisation of death and concurrent emphasis on death inequalities. This public and ample visibility of death and associated inequalities, we argue, has led to a long-overdue politicisation of death.

The pre-Covid-19 visibility of death

The visibility and concealment of death has been discussed and debated for millennia, first seen in the Socratic period in dialectic inquiries about human nature and the moral concepts of life and death (Derrida, 1995). In probably the most well-known and oft-cited account of death(s) over time, historian Ariès (1975) argued that pre-modernity death had a much greater presence in everyday life, with individuals, families and even whole communities succumbing relatively frequently to infectious disease. Such uncontrollable 'wild death' and a corresponding lack of medical care meant that dying usually occurred at home, and the dead remained there, cared for by their family and community, until their (timely) disposal.

With the advent of modern medicine, by the arrival of the 20th century the modern world had sought to – and been able to – control, or 'tame', death (Ariès, 1975). Humans became the rulers of life and death (Riley, 1970), mastering and controlling the limits of the human body (Pentaris, 2021) in order to sustain life as long as possible. This greater understanding of causes of death resulted in greater control of illness and with advanced healthcare and medical intervention came the imperative to organise those services as efficiently as possible.

It is quite staggering what has been achieved in such a short space of time, with high levels of control and the ability to sustain life leading to massive improvements in longevity. Infant mortality rates are low, with aims to get them lower (Office for National Statistics, 2020a); people are living longer with cancer (50% live for 10 years or more), doubling in the last 40 years

(Cancer Research UK, n.d.) and around the world people are living longer and in better health (World Health Organization, 2020a). These long lives have created a whole host of challenges for healthcare systems and economies that need to support their ageing population. They have also, we argue, resulted in a collapse in familiarity with death, dying and bereavement. Death no longer occurs as a matter of course *throughout* individual's lives. Now, people – in western post-industrial countries at least – can easily reach middle adulthood before they experience and encounter a 'close' death. Correspondingly, death any time before adulthood is regarded as 'out of time', with Public Health England (PHE) (2018a) identifying death before 75 years as 'premature'.

Such unfamiliarity with death has been further exacerbated by the institutions that have been established to efficiently manage the end of life, removing dying and the dead from 'everyday' domestic settings. In the UK, three in every four people will die in an institutional setting, be it a hospital, care home or hospice (Public Health England, 2018b). After death, unless there is coroners involvement, typically deceased people are immediately handed over to funeral directors, who sanitise and store their body until the day of their disposal. Dying and the aftermath of death thus takes place behind closed doors.

Thus, everyday encounters with people who are dying or bereaved have declined, and so too has a corresponding recognition in the public sphere that *death happens*. Death is something that has become mastered and hidden from public view; it has become domesticated, taking place behind closed doors (see Stanley and Wise, 2011). This privatisation of death and its impact, pre-Covid-19, has long been of concern for sociologists (see Howarth, 2006 for a good overview): 70 years ago, in his famous essay on *The Pornography of Death*, sociologist Gorer (1955) opined that the growing concealment of everyday death in the 20th century had left people with a sensationalised version of death in the public domain – versions there were embellished and characterised principally to appeal to media consumers and voyeurs. Fast forward three decades and the 1990s saw a resurgence of sociological interest in the status and visibility of death in modern societies (see for example Mellor and Shilling, 1993). UK sociologist Walter was one of the most prolific contributors to literature during this period and argued – in contrast to anthropologists who were arguing that death as 'taboo', and psychologists who were arguing that death was 'denied' in modern societies – death was being *hidden* from public view (Walter, 1991). Such concealment was underpinned by, and contributed to, its routinisation and institutionalisation (James and Field, 1992).

As a result of growing concerns about this process of institutionalisation and a lack of public scrutiny (see Lawton, 1998), by the mid 1990s there were signs of a burgeoning 'revival' of death in the public domain, with dying people being asked to discuss death (more) openly, on the prerequisite that professionals, family and friends would do so similarly (Walter, 1994). Since then, in recent years there has been a growing interest in news coverage of death (see Hanusch, 2010) and moves towards 'de-institutionalising' death through a death positive movement (Lofland, 2019; Leland and Yalkin, 2018), which has seen the establishment of death cafes and death doulas to promote dying at home and 'naturalise' the end of life (Rawlings et al., 2019). Efforts such as these have attempted to (re)integrate death into everyday life. A (re)conceptualisation of death through a lens of spiritual transcendence has, Lee (2008) has argued, further enabled greater 'death talk' in the public domain. Such efforts to assimilate death and life have not been without critique, however, with shortcomings identified in how this increase in 'death talk' overlooks temporal and cultural contexts. For example, Cheng et al. (2019) have argued that death remains taboo (that is, unspoken) among people of Chinese origin living in the UK, to the extent that it can interfere with end-of-life decisions.[2] Elsewhere, Paul (2019) has critiqued contemporary theorisation of death for neglecting children. Indeed, it could be argued that for children death has remained embedded in their everyday worlds throughout the 20th and 21st centuries, with research showing that in children's literature death is a relatively common topic and has been since the 1600s (Gibson and Zaidman, 1991). Similarly, the 'ordinariness' of death has been reflected in children's animated films since the early 1900s (Pentaris, 2019).

So, what has happened to the visibility of death in 2020 with the Covid-19 pandemic? In the second half of this chapter, and focusing on the UK specifically, we propose that Covid-19 has resulted in a *publicly visible* (re)institutionalisation of death, and a 21st-century revival of death talk in the public domain. This revival has included a radical shift towards public recognition of inequalities associated with death and a (much needed) political reply. In other words, death has become politicised.

The visibility of death in the face of the pandemic

The arrival of Covid-19 in 2020 marks a turning point for the public visibility of death in the 21st century. Pre Covid-19, efforts to de-institutionalise and to (re)locate dying away from institutions (see above) were predicated on a small but crucial number of factors: free choice, freedom of movement and known disease trajectories that could be managed flexibly in both acute care settings and communities. Come 2020, what no one was expecting was the potential impact of a novel virus on how end of life would be managed and resulting 'death talk'. The early Spring of 2020 saw the introduction of hyper-vigilance/surveillance of individuals at the end of their life amid concerns of infection control, virus transmission and a potential overloading of the healthcare system. What resulted from this was, we argue, a (re)institutionalisation of the end of life – but a (re)institutionalisation that was, somewhat contradictorily, taking place *in public*.

This occurred for two reasons. First, individuals who were critically ill with Covid-19 were whisked away from their place of residence, close relationships and communities, and relocated within tightly controlled hospital settings, often designated as Covid wards (Mahase, 2020; Chavez et al., 2020). In the most fraught periods of lockdown in the end of March and early April 2020, with travel and proximity regarded as too 'risky' for virus transmission, visitors to these patients were not permitted (Sterpetti, 2020). As a result, many deaths happened in isolation, with no family member present or having visited to 'say goodbye'. Far from being hidden however, it was not long before stories emerged in the media of families saying goodbye over computer tablets and attending funerals online (see BBC, 2020a; Siddique and Marsh, 2020; see Chapter 16). And it was during this period that the Covid-19 Bereaved Families for Justice UK group was formed, campaigning for a public inquiry into how dying and access to patients was managed during this time. These challenges resulted in wide reporting in the news media, with specific deaths generating a lot of attention, such as the case of Ismail Mohamed Abdulwahab, a 13-year-old from London who died in hospital, and whose family were unable to visit to say goodbye or attend his funeral (BBC, 2020d). His and similar stories led to the Health Secretary, Matt Hancock MP, announcing that under new Covid-19 related guidelines, family members – with restrictions in numbers – would be able to visit hospitals to say goodbye to their dying relatives. In other words, the coverage of this (re)institutionalisation of death demanded, and received, political reply.

A second case for a (re)institutionalisation of death was for those individuals who were very ill and/or terminally ill, but who were not permitted to leave their current place of residence and/or attend hospital settings to receive care (Kunz and Minder, 2020). Although not as dramatic as those who were rushed to hospital never to return, those who would have normally expected to receive hospital-based treatment and/or to die in hospital, were now dying in the community and their place of residence, very privately with little contact with others, behind closed doors (New Scientist, 2020). Such a tightly controlled approach to managing the virus and people at the end of their lives in the community (whether they were dying from Covid-19 or another cause) was most vividly seen in care homes (Comas-Herrera et al., 2020; Pentaris et al., 2020). In these settings visits from outside parties were ceased, including even GPs – who are normally relied upon to visit residents, to support care home staff with end of life, and to certify death (Alton and White, 2020).

Such a high level of control over the end of life served, for a short period of time, to (re)segregate those who were dying from the living in a way that was unprecedented for the 21st century. Now, the risks to the population as a whole and concerns of overwhelm in the healthcare system meant that 'in the interests of public health' those who were dying had their options removed: about their treatment, their location, being with others, being attended to by medical professionals and so on. In hospitals, this high level of control challenged the deeply entrenched narrative of patient choice and autonomy, which is at the heart of UK healthcare policy (Alcock, 2014). It further undermined transparency in end-of-life care, with scrutiny of and input into care and practices at the bedside by patients' families prevented, and communication and contact between the patient and their families, and clinicians and the family, moved online.

At the same time however, and somewhat paradoxically/incredibly, the (re)institutionalisation of death was receiving *more* visibility in the public domain than ever before and was being widely debated by journalists and politicians. Thus, while dying was becoming more institutionalised in the first few months of 2020 there had never been more 'death talk'. This boom in media coverage of death and dying brought about by Covid-19 was quite staggering. Suddenly, everyone (it appeared) was interested in all issues related to mortality, and the media – intoxicated by the drama of the pandemic – were more than happy to oblige with wall to wall coverage; be they detailing how dying and to-be-bereaved people were being supported (BBC, 2020b); the restrictions on care home visiting (Borland, 2020); commentary on the creation and provision of Public Protective Equipment (PPE) to prevent virus transmission and death (Sanderson, 2020); concerns about the impact of funeral restrictions on the ability to grieve (Booth, 2020); and an upcoming 'grief pandemic' (Matsumoto, 2020) or rise in 'complicated grief' (Wegner, 2020; Marcus, 2020).

Inequalities

As part of this coverage the disparity and inequity between different groups of people was increasingly brought to light, further exacerbated by the release of information about the most vulnerable/affected groups for the virus. At the forefront of these debates was the increasing recognition of inequalities on the basis of age (Armitage and Nellums, 2020). Different age groups experienced the virus differently and, as the situation progressed, the UK Government started publicly identifying and labelling 'the elderly' as one of the most vulnerable groups and susceptible to contracting and dying of the virus (Liu et al., 2020; see Chapter 12). Widely reported in the media, associated health challenges and being older than 70 suddenly became a 'deathly combination' (Barek, Aziz and Islam, 2020), with those in this category were asked to isolate for longer periods.

Minority ethnic groups were too disproportionately affected (PHE, 2020a; see Chapter 13) and inequity between different ethnic groups and their susceptibility to the virus publicly debated (Centers for Disease Control and Prevention, 2020; PHE, 2020b). Specifically, it became apparent that people of Bangladeshi ethnicity were twice as likely to die of the virus, when compared to their White counterparts (PHE, 2020b). Similarly, those of Chinese, Indian, Pakistani or Black Caribbean and Other Black origins were at 15%

higher risk of death from Covid-19, and there was considered media debate as to why this was the case (PHE, 2020b). Such ethnic inequalities in the face of Covid-19 were not isolated to the UK (BBC, 2020c), with similar ethnic disparities and risk of death seen in the USA (World Economic Forum, 2020a). Indeed, data from the USA was clear in showing that existing inequalities in residence and geographical areas between Black Americans and other ethnic groups, influences access to resources and healthcare, and meant that for Black Americans the risk of death from Covid-19 was heightened (Centers for Disease Control and Prevention, 2020).

Another group of people who has faced tremendous inequality during the pandemic was those with a disability (mental or physical or both). The World Economic Forum (2020b) reported that two thirds of all those with a visual impairment felt that their dependency levels have risen significantly since the start of the quarantine measures, while the World Health Organization (2020b) highlighted the higher risks of death by Covid among those with a disability. Once again, such inequalities in death featured heavily in the news media (see Webster, 2020).

A politicisation of death

With greater coverage, 'death talk' and a growing realisation that there are significant inequalities around death, politicians have – finally – had to address the end of life as an issue of political importance. Through Covid-19 and its impact, politicians and policymakers, and those that report their work in the media, have suddenly become attuned to death in a way that has arguably not been seen in the 21st century. Media coverage of death has been extensive throughout 2020, with continual law and guidance being issued to manage death and ongoing concerns raised as to the variation in the susceptibility of different social groups and how this *has* to be addressed. It was as if the world was 'waking up' to the reality of the human mortal condition, suddenly aware that medicine was not the great saviour for all and that death would, and could, happen to anyone – with some groups of people more vulnerable than others.

Such a realisation and politicisation of death has been long overdue. With the enormous improvements in healthcare and public health, and a death rate that has been steadily declining since 2001 (Office for National Statistics, 2020b), there has since been a growing political complacency around death. Such complacency has, we argue, resulted in a perpetual neglect of death and its aftermath as a policy issue. Similarly, inequalities in death have been largely overlooked.

The necessity of Covid-19 for a political response has drastically altered the course of this neglect. Throughout the pandemic such responses have been relayed to and publicly debated in varied ways, via the news media. The political response and coverage of death from Covid-19 gives us considerable hope for the future of end-of-life policy and death studies more broadly; as when inequalities in death are socially acknowledged and solidified through political action, the chances are that further public awareness is raised more widely (for the politics of decision-making in health policy, see Weissert and Weissert, 2008).

Where this politicisation of death goes post-Covid-19 is up for debate. Right now, in the winter of 2020/21 as we write this chapter, there has never been greater coverage of UK deaths, the impact of (re)institutionalisation, and the inequities faced by different groups of the population. As the fallout of Covid-19 begins, we can only hope that this memory of mortality will be retained.

Conclusion

Covid-19 and the implications of its management has changed the visibility of death and dying in the UK throughout 2020. This novel virus and efforts to control its spread have brought death into the public domain as never before, reawakening the general public and political elite to the fallibility of medicine and the fragility of the human condition. Human mortality and our vulnerabilities have never been more hotly debated and contested; concerns about susceptibility and death vulnerabilities have never been more vividly apparent.

This chapter has shown how, after many years of concealment and institutionalisation, in the early 20th century there were signs of a growing integration of death back into everyday life. Covid-19 has both challenged and contributed to this process of integration, through the segregation of the dying/dead from the living as part of pandemic control measures and the simultaneous wall-to-wall media coverage and exponential growth in public 'death talk'. This coverage has raised awareness of inequities and inequalities between groups of people, based on age, ethnicity and disability; and together have necessitated a long over-due political response.

Notes

1 Despite the prevalence of flu, which kills around 7,500 people a year in the UK (PHE, 2020a).
2 This is not a view shared by all; Zhang (2020) has argued that this is not the case amongst older Chinese migrants living in the UK.

References

Alcock, P., 2014. *Social policy in Britain*. London, UK: Macmillan International Higher Education.

Alton, E. and White, C., 2020. GPs' experience of safeguarding in care homes: what do they see and what do they do? *British Journal of General Practice*, 70(suppl 1). Doi: 10.3399/bjgp20X711269

Ariès, P., 1975. *Western attitudes toward death: from the Middle Ages to the present* (Vol. 3). Baltimore, MD: Johns Hopkins University Press.

Armitage, R. and Nellums, L.B., 2020. COVID-19 and the consequences of isolating the elderly. *The Lancet Public Health*, 5(5), p. e256.

Barek, M.A., Aziz, M.A. and Islam, M.S., 2020. Impact of age, sex, comorbities and clinical symptoms on the severity of COVID-19 cases: a meta-analysis with 55 studies and 10014 cases. *Heliyon*, 6(12), p. e05684.

BBC, 2020a. Coronavirus: hospital ipads could be used 'to say goodbye'. Available at: https://www.bbc.co.uk/news/uk-england-birmingham-52185204 (Accessed: 17 December 2020).

BBC, 2020b. Coronavirus: 'Many said goodbye to loved ones in an ambulance'. Available at: https://www.bbc.co.uk/news/health-52441692 (Accessed: 17 December 2020).

BBC, 2020c. Why are more people from BAME backgrounds dying from coronavirus? Available at: https://www.bbc.co.uk/news/uk-52219070 (Accessed: 4 December 2020).

BBC, 2020d. Coronavirus: family of dead boy, 13, 'happy' with policy change. Available at: https://www.bbc.com/news/uk-england-london-52312653 (Accessed: 21 December 2020).

Booth, R. 2020. UK's Covid bereaved suffer heightened grief, finds study. Available at: https://www.theguardian.com/lifeandstyle/2020/nov/26/uks-26m-covid-bereaved-suffer-heightened-grief-finds-study (Accessed: 22 December 2020).

Borland, S., 2020. Three in four care homes say GPs won't visit residents with Coronavirus and only a third of nursing centres are accepting patients from hospital as the full horrifying scandal blighting the nation's elderly is revealed, Daily Mail. Available at: https://www.dailymail.co.uk/news/article-8313245/Three-four-care-homes-say-GPs-wont-visit-residents-coronavirus.html (Accessed: 17 December 2020).

Cancer Research UK, n.d. Cancer survival. Available at: https://www.cancerresearchuk.org/health-professional/cancer-statistics-for-the-uk#heading-Two (Accessed: 17 December 2020).

Centers for Disease Control and Prevention, 2020. COVID-19 racial and ethnic health disparities. Available at: https://www.cdc.gov/coronavirus/2019-ncov/community/health-equity/racial-ethnic-disparities/index.html (Accessed: 22 December 2020).

Chavez, S., Long, B., Koyfman, A. and Liang, S.Y., 2020. Coronavirus Disease (COVID-19): A primer for emergency physicians. *The American Journal of Emergency Medicine*, online first. Doi: 10.1016/j.ajem.2020.03.036

Cheng, H.W.B., Shek, P.S.K., Man, C.W., Chan, O.M., Chan, C.H., Lai, K.M., Cheng, S.C., Fung, K.S., Lui, W.K., Lam, C. and Ng, Y.K., 2019. Dealing with death taboo: discussion of do-not-resuscitate directives with Chinese patients with noncancer life-limiting illnesses. *American Journal of Hospice and Palliative Medicine®*, 36(9), pp. 760–766.

Comas-Herrera, A., Zalakaín, J., Lemmon, E., Henderson, D., Litwin, C., Hsu, A.T., Schmidt, A.E., Arling, G. and Fernández, J-L., 2020. Mortality associated with COVID-19 outbreaks in care homes: early international evidence. Available at: https://ltccovid.org/2020/04/12/mortality-associated-with-covid-19-outbreaks-in-care-homes-early-international-evidence/ (Accessed: 22 December 2020).

Derrida, J., 1995. *The gift of death*. Chicago, IL: University of Chicago Press.

Gibson, L.R. and Zaidman, L.M., 1991. Death in children's literature: taboo or not taboo? *Children's Literature Association Quarterly*, 16(4), pp. 232–234.

Gorer, G., 1955. The pornography of death. *Encounter*, 5(4), pp. 49–52.

Hanusch, F., 2010. *Representing death in the news: journalism, media and mortality*. Basingstoke: Palgrave Macmillan.

Howarth, G., 2006. *Death and dying: a sociological introduction*. Bristol: Polity Press.

James, N. and Field, D., 1992. The routinization of hospice: charisma and bureaucratization. *Social Science and Medicine*, 34(12), pp. 1363–1375.

Kunz, R. and Minder, M., 2020. COVID-19 pandemic: palliative care for elderly and frail patients at home and in residential and nursing homes. *Swiss Medical Weekly*, 150(1314). Doi: 10.4414/smw.2020.20235

Lawton, J., 1998. Contemporary hospice care: the sequestration of the unbounded body and 'dirty dying'. *Sociology of Health & Illness*, 20(2), pp. 121–143.

Lee, R.L., 2008. Modernity, mortality and re-enchantment: the death taboo revisited. *Sociology*, 42(4), pp. 745–759.

Leland, J. and Yalkin, D., 2018. The positive death movement comes to life. *The New York Times*, 22. Available at: https://www.nytimes.com/2018/06/22/nyregion/the-positive-death-movement-comes-to-life.html (Accessed: 22 December 2020).

Liu, K., Chen, Y., Lin, R. and Han, K., 2020. Clinical features of COVID-19 in elderly patients: a comparison with young and middle-aged patients. *Journal of Infection*, 80(6), pp. e14–e18.

Lofland, L.H., 2019. *The craft of dying: the modern face of death*. Cambridge, MA: MIT Press.

Mahase, E., 2020. Coronavirus: NHS staff get power to keep patients in isolation as UK declares "serious threat". *BMJ*, 368. Doi: 10.1136/bmj.m550

Marcus, E.N., 2020. Covid-19 has shed light on another pandemic of depression, anxiety and grief. Available at: https://www.washingtonpost.com/opinions/2020/11/24/covid-19-has-shed-light-another-pandemic-depression-anxiety-grief/ (Accessed: 22 December 2020).

Matsumoto, S., 2020. With a pandemic and isolation during the holidays, grieving can be even more complicated this year. Available at: https://www.opb.org/article/2020/12/22/with-pandemic-and-isolation-during-the-holidays-grieving-can-be-even-more-complicated-this-year/ (Accessed: 22 December 2020).

Mellor, P.A. and Shilling, C., 1993. Modernity, self-identity and the sequestration of death. *Sociology*, 27(3), pp. 411–431.

New Scientist, 2020. Coronavirus rules for care homes are too strict and not science-based. Available at: https://www.newscientist.com/article/2259044-coronavirus-rules-for-care-homes-are-too-strict-and-not-science-based/ (Accessed: 5 December 2020).

Office for National Statistics, 2020a. Child and infant mortality in England and Wales: 2018. Available at: https://www.ons.gov.uk/peoplepopulationandcommunity/birthsdeathsandmarriages/deaths/bulletins/childhoodinfantandperinatalmortalityinenglandandwales/2018 (Accessed: 17 December 2020).

Office for National Statistics, 2020b. Monthly mortality statistics, England and Wales: July 2020. Available at: https://www.ons.gov.uk/peoplepopulationandcommunity/birthsdeathsandmarriages/deaths/bulletins/monthlymortalityanalysisenglandandwales/july2020 (Accessed: 17 December 2020).

Paul, S., 2019. Is death taboo for children? Developing death ambivalence as a theoretical framework to understand children's relationship with death, dying and bereavement. *Children & Society*, 33(6), pp. 556–571.

Pentaris, P., 2021. The governance of dying in transhumanist and posthuman societies. London, UK & New York, NY: Routledge.
Pentaris, P., 2019. Locating death in children's animated films. In Teodorescu, A. and Jacobsen, M.H. (eds.), *Death in contemporary popular culture*. London, UK & New York, NY: Routledge, pp. 175–191.
Pentaris, P., Willis, P., Ray, M., Deusdad, B., Lonbay, S., Niemi, M. and Donnelly, S., 2020. Older people in the context of COVID-19: a European perspective. *Journal of Gerontological Social Work*, 63(8), pp. 736–742.
Public Health England (PHE), 2018a. Health profile for England 2018, Chapter 2: Trends in mortality. Available at: https://www.gov.uk/government/publications/health-profile-for-england-2018/chapter-2-trends-in-mortality (Accessed: 17 December 2020).
Public Health England (PHE), 2018b. End of life care profiles: February 2018 update. Available at: https://www.gov.uk/government/publications/end-of-life-care-profiles-february-2018-update/statistical-commentary-end-of-life-care-profiles-february-2018-update (Accessed: 4 December 2020).
Public Health England (PHE), 2020a. Surveillance of influenza and other respiratory viruses in the UK: Winter 2019 to 2020. Available at: https://assets.publishing.service.gov.uk/government/uploads/system/uploads/attachment_data/file/895233/Surveillance_Influenza_and_other_respiratory_viruses_in_the_UK_2019_to_2020_FINAL.pdf (Accessed: 4 December 2020).
Public Health England (PHE), 2020b. Disparities in the risk and outcomes of COVID-19. Available at: https://assets.publishing.service.gov.uk/government/uploads/system/uploads/attachment_data/file/908434/Disparities_in_the_risk_and_outcomes_of_COVID_August_2020_update.pdf (Accessed: 4 December 2020).
Rawlings, D., Tieman, J., Miller-Lewis, L. and Swetenham, K., 2019. What role do Death Doulas play in end-of-life care? A systematic review. *Health and Social Care in the Community*, 27(3), pp. 82–94.
Riley Jr, J.W., 1970. What people think about death. In Brim, O.G. Jr., Freeman, H.E., Levine, S. and Scotch, N.A. (eds.), *The dying patient*. New York, NY: Russell Sage Foundation, pp. 30–41.
Sanderson, A., 2020. Number 10 wasted millions of YOUR cash on Tory pals in sheer panic, Daily Express. Available at: https://www.express.co.uk/comment/expresscomment/1362076/Boris-Johnson-PPE-cost-NHS-Covid-19-coronavirus-lockdown-Matt-Hancock (Accessed: 17 December 2020).
Siddique, H. and Marsh, S., 2020. Coronavirus: Britons saying final goodbyes to dying relatives by videolink, The Guardian. Available at: https://www.theguardian.com/world/2020/mar/24/britons-saying-final-goodbyes-to-dying-relatives-by-videolink-covid-19 (Accessed: 17 December 2020).
Stanley, L. and Wise, S., 2011. The domestication of death: the sequestration thesis and domestic figuration. *Sociology*, 45(6), pp. 947–962.
Sterpetti, A.V., 2020. COVID-19 diffusion capability is its worst, unpredictable characteristic. How to visit a patient from a distance. *The British Journal of Surgery*, 107(7), p. e181.
United Nations, 2019. World population prospects 2019: Highlights. United Nations Publications. Available at: https://www.un.org/development/desa/publications/world-population-prospects-2019-highlights.html (Accessed: 22 December 2020).
Walter, T., 1991. Modern death: taboo or not taboo? *Sociology*, 25(2), pp. 293–310.
Walter, T., 1994. *The revival of death*. London, UK: Routledge.

Webster, L., 2020. Coronavirus: why disabled people are calling for a Covid-19 inquiry. *BBC News*. Available at: https://www.bbc.co.uk/news/uk-53221435 (Accessed: 4 December 2020).

Wegner, H., 2020. There's no tissue box on Zoom: grief support groups adapt to consoling from afar. Available at: https://eu.azcentral.com/story/news/local/arizona/2020/12/09/grief-facilitators-go-online-help-grieving-during-covid-19-pandemic/6486760002/ (Accessed: 22 December 2020).

Weissert, C.S. and Weissert, W.G., 2008. *Governing health: the politics of health policy*. Baltimore, MD: Johns Hopkins University Press.

World Economic Forum, 2020a. COVID-19 has hit Black Americans hardest. Healing this divide would lift the nation. Available at: https://www.weforum.org/agenda/2020/08/covid19-racial-wealth-gap-black-americans/ (Accessed: 4 December 2020).

World Economic Forum, 2020b. These are the countries where the internet access is lowest. Available at: https://www.weforum.org/agenda/2020/08/internet-users-usage-countries-change-demographics/ (Accessed: 4 December 2020).

World Health Organization (WHO), 2020a. World Health Statistics 2020: monitoring health for the Sustainable Development Goals. Available at: https://apps.who.int/iris/bitstream/handle/10665/332070/9789240005105-eng.pdf (Accessed: 17 December 2020).

World Health Organization (WHO), 2020b. Disability considerations during the COVID-19 outbreak. Available at: https://www.who.int/publications/i/item/WHO-2019-nCoV-Disability-2020-1 (Accessed: 4 December 2020).

Zhang, W., 2020. Is Death Taboo for Older Chinese Immigrants? *OMEGA-Journal of Death and Dying*, online first. Doi: 10.1177/0030222820927883

2 Grief in the COVID-19 pandemic

Kenneth J. Doka

Key points

- The current COVID pandemic is likely to create a future pandemic of complicated grief.
- Current travel and visiting restrictions limit opportunities for persons to be with relatives prior to death and limit the effectiveness of funeral rituals.
- Risk groups consist of not only persons who died of COVID but also people who have of other causes, medical and other professionals who have experienced a massive death toll and persons who experience non-death losses such as the loss of a job.

Introduction

Since it first emerged in Wuhan, China in 2019, the Coronavirus, generally known as COVID-19 or SARS-CoV-2, has spread rapidly. As I write this chapter there are near 45 million cases worldwide and over a million deaths. The United States has a large share of these cases with over eight million cases and over 225,000 deaths. Even beyond the deaths, the Coronavirus has created widespread social disruption as nations placed restrictions on travel and imposed quarantines. Businesses, schools, entertainment and restaurants have closed – leading to significant job losses as well as increased isolation. As restrictions begin to ease in the United States and other parts of the world, there is considerable debate as to whether there will be a second wave of cases.

While there may be debate as to whether there will be a surge in the number of people infected, there is little doubt that one consequence of this pandemic will be a pandemic of complicated forms of grief. Such a pandemic of grief will not only be the result of the numbers of people infected but also the very nature of this pandemic.

In this chapter then we explore the special issues for grief that will likely be aroused within this pandemic. The very nature of the pandemic will not only influence the grief of individuals who experience the death of a loved one but also families of friends of those who die from other causes in the midst of the pandemic. Moreover, it will likely affect the medical staff that cares for such patients. In addition, there will be other persons – grieving non-death loss such as the loss of employment.

I begin the chapter by exploring some of the unique issues that complicate grief within the pandemic. Then, explore the populations at risk – offering interventive strategies to assist those who are bereaved. Finally, I consider the ways societies as a whole may be changed by this encounter with this new disease.

COVID-19 in context

Though medical science has made great strides in identifying the Coronavirus, there is still much that is unknown – generating both uncertainty and anxiety. We do know that the virus is highly contagious. Yet the effect of infection leaves a great deal of uncertainty. Some are likely to be asymptomatic though possibly carriers while others may have cold or flu symptoms. In other cases, the effects might be more severe and in anywhere from 2% to 5% of the cases, death might ensue especially if there are other factors affecting health. Another problem is that symptoms can suddenly increase in severity. Thus, a patient may seem to be stable or even improving prior to rapid decline, and possibly, death. In addition, the symptoms are often non-specific including fever, cough, respiratory difficulties, diarrhoea, aches and fatigue – so that almost any illness may lead to anxiety that one has been infected by the Coronavirus. Moreover, there is little known about long-term effects of the disease. There is, for example, no assurance that testing positive for antibodies to the disease offers future immunity nor do we know whether the virus may, at least in some infected individuals, result in other health problems later in life.

This anxiety is exacerbated by the disruption of routine that most people experienced during the collective quarantine and the phased reopening. Aside from those deemed essential workers, most individuals have had to work from home or have been furloughed from work. Students have seen their schools closed and have had to adjust to online learning. Sports, films and other forms of entertainment (aside from television) have been cancelled or limited. Even children's camps and sports have been cancelled or restricted. The effects of this imposed social isolation are not yet known but may include increased rates of alcoholism, domestic abuse, depression and anxiety (Sherman and Crunk, 2020; Hong 2020) – all of which complicate grief.

Most importantly, the COVID-19 Pandemic is a traumatic event. By that it is meant that the pandemic has challenged our assumptive world –

meaning we no longer see the world as safe, predictable or benevolent (Janoff-Bulman, 1992). This adds another complicating layer to grief as the world now is experienced as more dangerous and unexpected than believed. Thus, we not only deal with the death of an individual but the loss of the world as once experienced leading to increased anxiety and depression.

Populations at risk for grief in the pandemic

Persons mourning COVID-19 deaths

Obviously, families and friends – those in the intimate network – of individuals who have died as a result of COVID-19 infection are highly at risk for complicated grief reactions. These reactions can include a variety of complications including anxiety and somatic distress, depression and post-traumatic stress (Chew et al., 2020).

This is unsurprising as a death from COVID-19 has a number of significant risk factors. First, as stated earlier, it is a new disease, highly contagious, and rapidly spreading. As such, it is by nature a traumatic event that challenges our assumptive world – making it feel less safe, predictable and benevolent.

Deaths from COVID-19 are also relatively sudden and unpredictable. Most deaths occur in less than three weeks after the onset of symptoms. The death rates from the disease are generally low – less than 3% at the time of writing and generally older persons – especially those with other health issues – are most at risk. Yet, these statistics may mask the reality that though rare, other populations too – not generally in the risk categories – may experience fatalities as well. Moreover, there can be deaths, yet uncounted, related to the pandemic such as suicide.

Other factors too complicate grief. The disease often presents multiple symptoms that can easily be attributed to other illnesses generating guilt that a diagnosis and medical assistance was not proffered earlier. In addition, the highly contagious nature of the disease may evoke other sources of guilt. For example, persons may experience survivor guilt in that one person died while others survived. In some cases, there may be death causation guilt where individuals blame themselves for infecting another who died of the disease.

Moreover, during the pandemic, persons may experience multiple losses. These include not only the deaths of others but other losses such as the loss of income, employment and other opportunities. Because of these multiple losses, persons may be forced to relocate or make significant changes in their lifestyles. Both multiple losses and concurrent crises are factors that complicate grief (Worden, 2018). In addition, the COVID-19 Pandemic challenges our sense of the assumptive world adding an element of trauma – further complicating grief (Worden, 2018; Rando, 1993).

COVID-19 deaths can also raise deep spiritual issues. It may be difficult to find some sense of meaning in a disease that seems so capricious. In other cases, there may be moral guilt – perceiving this new plague as a punishment for sins committed by the individual or collectively by the society. Still others may have a cosmic anger – blaming the world or a deity for the death.

Then too, the process of dying may complicate grief. For example, generally the dying process can be a time for saying goodbye, offering final care, reminiscing and validating the life of the dying person, and finishing unfinished business. Yet restrictions on visiting can inhibit this process – forcing restricted or virtual visits. The result is that persons may die alone. That not only impairs the dying process but also complicates grief (Doka, 2016).

In addition, there may be ethical issues that complicate grief. Even in the brief period surrounding death of COVID-19, there may be significant ethical issues as to whether to place someone on a respirator or remove individuals from a respirator. Such decisions can cause familial conflict and cause significant moral distress that can complicate subsequent grief (Doka, 2005).

Finally, travel restrictions, limitations on assembly, and quarantines limit the efficacy of rituals. Research has clearly demonstrated that while meaningful funerals can facilitate the funeral process, problematic funerals can complicate grief. (Doka, 1984; 2016). During the pandemic, funerals are often restricted in numbers and often expressions of intimacy such as hugging are inhibited possibly leading to less meaningful rituals that subsequently complicate grief.

Persons dying of the pandemic from other causes

Yet it is not only deaths from COVID-19 that may place survivors at risk. Any death during the pandemic can create conditions and factors that exacerbate the grieving process. Many of these are the conditions discussed in the last section. Here too families may be suffering the multiple losses engendered by the pandemic including loss of employment, movement and routine. This may cause losses of income that create concurrent crises – complicating grief. And once again, there is the overlay of trauma due to the loss of the assumptive world.

And as with COVID-19 deaths, individuals may have limited opportunity to be with the dying person – troubling bereavement. Here, too, rituals may be restricted and many who would normally attend such rituals may be unable or unwilling to do so.

Yet, while many of the factors complicating bereavement in COVID-19 deaths can exacerbate grief in non-COVID-19 deaths, there are other problematic factors as well. In deaths that are not due to the coronavirus, survivors may feel disenfranchised (see Doka, 2002). In this case, the disenfranchisement is due to the fact that with all attention given to the COVID-19 deaths, deaths from other causes may not seem to get the same attention, focus or support. This then may intensify feelings of anger and isolation.

Grief experienced by medical/health personnel

Medical and health personnel also are at risk for significant grief reactions in COVID-19 Pandemic. It is well recognised that the medical and mental health staff can be vicariously traumatised by and grieve the deaths of patients (Papadatou, 2000; Katz and Johnson, 2016). In the COVID-19 Pandemic there are a variety of factors that make many deaths in this period especially problematic. First, given the relative absence of family members caused by either the quarantine or travel restrictions can lead to medical staff becoming more attached to patients as they try to fill the social and emotional void left by loved ones who are unable to visit.

Second, staff too are feeling the sense of trauma as their own assumptive world is challenged on so many levels. They are now coping with a new disease – offering care in the absence of clearly defined guidelines. They are seeing patients' dying alone, perhaps seven enforcing policies that inhibit visitation. In addition, they may carry their own fears about the illness – afraid that they may be carrying the virus to those whom they love.

Moreover, the nature of the death can create moral distress in staff. Jameton (1984, 1993) defined *moral distress* as the inner conflicts experienced by healthcare professionals when they experience personal, professional, spiritual or ethical dilemmas in the provision of patient care. Here facing a disease that is new, seeing patients alone and isolated, have conflict over ethical issues such as whether a patient should be placed on a respirator, overworked, deprived of needed resources, and facing their own fears about infection all contribute to a sense of moral distress in staff that can add both to compassion fatigue and a general demoralisation of staff.

Non-death losses

There is one more group that is likely to have significant grief reactions – those experiencing non-death losses. In the past few decades, there has been increased attention to the non-death losses that can generate grief (Doka, 1989, 2002, 2016; Harris, 2011, 2020). Yet in many ways the recognition of grief to non-death losses goes back to Freud's (1917) epochal paper, Mour*ning and Melancholia* that really begins the contemporary study of grief. Freud's illustrative case not of a grieving parent or spouse but rather a bride abandoned at the altar – reinforcing the idea that grief is about loss – not just death.

And losses loom large and significant in this pandemic. As stated earlier, we have all experienced a loss of an assumptive world. While we have experienced other new viral diseases such as SARS, MERS or Ebola, none have been as contagious and as widespread as COVID-19. Neither have they caused the widespread economic and social disruption associated with the COVID-19 Pandemic. Though may respond to the trauma in different ways and varying levels of intensity, the loss of an assumptive world – including the unpredictability and inability to plan for the future with any degree of certainty – is a universal loss created by the pandemic.

Other non-death losses may be more tangible. Loss of opportunities such as educational, travel and sports opportunities as travel restrictions are in place, schools and gyms close, events are cancelled, and athletic leagues cancel seasons. Others might have lost jobs and income. Thus, while the death rate of COVID-19 seems to be under 5%, most people have experienced some sense of loss as a result of the pandemic.

Coping with grief

Grief can be defined as a type of stress reaction; a set of highly personal and subjective responses that individuals experience in connection with real, perceived, or anticipated losses. Grief reactions may occur in any loss situation, whether the loss is physical or tangible, such as a death, significant injury, or loss of property, or symbolic and intangible such as the loss of a dream. The intensity of grief will vary, dependent upon many variables such as the meaning of that given loss to the individuals experiencing it. Because of the nature of COVID-19, a number of populations identified in the prior section may experience grief reactions of varying intensity for a variety of different losses including tangible losses due to death, residues of illness, loss of employment and income as well as intangible losses including the loss of an assumptive world. Individuals can experience grief in varied ways. These can include physical, affective, cognitive, spiritual, and behavioural manifestations. Recent approaches have emphasised that grief does not follow a predictable and linear course, stressing instead that it often proceeds in a roller-coaster-like pattern, full of ups and downs, times when the grief reactions are more or less intense. Some of these more intense periods are predictable – holidays, anniversaries, or other significant days – but other times may have no recognisable trigger.

Current work on grief has moved away from the concept of universal stages stressing the highly individual nature of loss (Doka, 2016). For example, J. William Worden (2018) described four tasks to grief: recognising the reality of the loss, processing the pain of grief (dealing with expressed and latent feelings), adjusting to a world without the deceased, and finding ways to remember the deceased while embarking on the rest of one's journey through life. Therese A. Rando (1993) suggested that grieving individuals need to complete six 'R' processes: recognise the loss, react to the separation, recollect and re-experience the deceased and the relationship, relinquish the old attachments to the deceased and the old assumptive world, readjust to the new world without forgetting the old, and reinvest. These and other similar models reaffirm the very individual nature of grief, acknowledging that these tasks or processes are not necessarily linear and that any given individual may have difficulty with one or more processes or tasks.

Stroebe and Schut (1999) describe a 'Dual-Process Model' model of grief. Here individuals who are bereaved oscillate or move between two core processes – adjusting to the loss of a significant attachment and restoration – that is learning to adjust to life in a world without the deceased's physical presence. To Stroebe and Schut, the key process is oscillation – moving between these two basic processes. If one becomes fixed on simply coping with the loss, there is the danger that grief can become chronic. Similarly, if the bereaved individual's only focus is restoration – attempting to live life without focusing on the loss – grief can be inhibited, absent or delayed.

Another prominent model of the grief process is suggested by Neimeyer (2001). Neimeyer focuses on meaning reconstruction as the key process of grief. Here one's life narrative now has to encompass the loss of a significant attachment. This loss may affect not only the individual's sense of self but also their assumptions about the world, philosophy and spirituality. The key question now becomes: *In the face of this loss who am I now and what do I/can I believe about the nature of the world?*

The critical point to remember is that the course of grief is not linear. Nor is there any inherent timetable to grief. Grief reactions can persist for considerable time, gradually losing intensity after the first few years. Recent research as well emphasises that one does not 'get over the loss'. Rather, over time, the pain lessens, and the grief becomes less disabling as individuals function at levels comparable to (and sometimes better than) pre-loss levels. Bonds and attachments to the lost object continue, however, and periods of intense grief can occur years after the loss (Klass, Silverman and Nickman, 1996). For example, the birth of a grandchild can trigger an experience of grief in a widow who wished to share this event with her now-deceased spouse.

The unfortunate truth is that the very nature of the COVID-19 pandemic is that it encompasses many factors that are likely to complicate grief in both deaths from the new virus as well as other deaths, from other causes that are occurring during the pandemic. First is sheer numbers. As I write this in June 2020, The Center for Disease Control and Prevention has identified over 2 million cases in the United States with over 100,000 deaths. Moreover, the Coronavirus also creates a sense of underlying anxiety as we are now forced to cope with a new disease that has unpredictable effects. The disease seems very random in its effects – some seem asymptomatic, others experience symptoms much like a cold or flu while still others die.

One of the most difficult aspects of the pandemic is that those who are dying in hospitals or nursing homes are often dying alone – the very antithesis of our image of a good death. Not only does the company of others ease dying but it also facilitates the subsequent grief of survivors. It offers family and friends the opportunities to say goodbye, finish business and share memories. For dying persons, the presence of these significant others validates their life, allows them to say final words, and offers the comfort and care that family and friends offer.

Moreover, quarantines, travel restrictions and limits on gatherings impair the rituals surrounding dying and death. Chaplains and other clergy may be unable to be present to offer deathbed rituals such as prayers or last rights – again complicating images of a good death. We may not be able to have the funeral rituals we desired and feel the comfort of the presence of family and friends. And even if we seek out support from counsellors or support groups, it is likely to be offered online – missing, to some degree, that critical human connection.

Then too, survivors may be coping with concurrent crises – factors that complicate grief. Because of the disruption of life caused by the pandemic, grieving individuals may be coping with multiple losses – of others they know, of jobs or income, or any other loss created by the pandemic.

For those who have died of the COVID-19 virus, there are other factors that complicate loss. As stated earlier the disease itself is both sudden and unpredictable. Some may die with little warning. Family members may struggle with spiritual issues – wondering why this disease emerged and why it killed someone they loved.

There may be survivor guilt – raising the question of how one died while the mourner survived – especially if both were infected. There can also be death causation guilt arising from the thought or suspicion that the mourner was the source of infection.

For non-COVID-19 deaths, there may be anger that the emergence of the disease affected both the death and funeral of a loved one. Mourners may feel disenfranchised – perceiving that those who died of the virus receive acknowledgement and support while their losses are neglected.

Interventive approaches

While the process of grief counselling is beyond the scope of this chapter, I refer readers to Worden's (2018) classic book on grief counselling and grief therapy. However, it is important to highlight a few critical issues for grief counsellors that are likely to arise during the pandemic.

Validation

Validation is often the heart of grief counselling. Validation means that the grief counsellor empathically acknowledges the importance and value of the loss to the bereaved client. In the COVID-19 pandemic, validation can be critical in a number of reasons as certain losses may be disenfranchised. Two populations most at risk are healthcare professionals and persons with non-death losses.

First are those with non-death losses. Such losses are often ignored and disenfranchised (Doka, 2002; Harris, 2020). Yet these losses, including the loss of a job, traditional schooling, routine, or income, as well as the traumatic loss of the assumptive world deeply affect many. Persons experiencing these losses may even disenfranchise their own losses – feeling these losses pall compared to the death of a loved one.

Second, healthcare professionals often ignore and disenfranchise their own losses (Doka, 2002; Papadatou, 2000). While healthcare professionals may struggle with losses of patients in many situations, the isolation imposed by the pandemic on both patients with COVID as well as those struggling with other illnesses may intensify bonding between patients and their caregivers. In fact, Fulton (1987) suggested that the relationship between patients and professional caregivers at the end-of-life is conducive to the conditions that underlie the Stockholm Syndrome. Fulton notes that the syndrome associated with captives identifying with captors really is part of a larger issue that bonding is intensified in crisis situations.

While these two populations are likely to respond positively to validation, it is an essential aspect of grief counselling in all situations. Even those populations struggling with the death from COVID-19 will benefit from validation. In addition, it is always critical for bereaved clients to identify secondary losses – or losses associated with the primary loss. For example, the loss of a parent who is the primary breadwinner may cascade into a series of secondary losses as income falls, families have to move, and treasured activities may no longer be affordable. These losses too need to be named and validated.

Grief issues likely to result as an aspect of the pandemic

While grief counselling is as individualised as grief reactions and influenced by many factors such as the relationship with the deceased, the nature of the attachment, the type of death, personality and mental health of the deceased, amount of social support and multiple other variables (see Worden, 2018), there are some issues that are likely to arise during the pandemic. First, survivors may have issues related to meaning-making and spiritual distress. The very fact that COVID-19 is a new disease with unpredictable outcomes can exacerbate the process of meaning-making as bereaved persons struggle with understanding why one person died from the virus while others have minimal or no symptoms of infection. The very onset of a worldwide pandemic can raise questions of meaning that, in some cases, can lead to spiritual distress – with perceptions of a world no longer benign or of a vengeful deity.

As mentioned earlier, guilt, blame and anger can also be aroused in grief.

Underlying these emotions can be feelings of survivor guilt where grievers ponder why they remain alive as another died and death causation guilt where one believes that they passed on the virus to another who died from the infection.

It is also important to assess the degree of social support bereaved individuals may have. Given the sense of social isolation they may be experiencing due to the quarantine and travel restrictions. In addition, given restrictions of hospitals, nursing homes and other healthcare facilities, the isolation of the dying individual may lead to bereaved individuals struggling with issues such as unfinished business or guilt at the inability to be by the side of dying relatives or friends.

Finally, it may be important to review the funeral ritual. While rituals can be powerfully therapeutic events, they can also complicate grief when the rituals are poorly performed (Doka, 1984). Again, quarantines, physical distancing and travel restrictions may impair the value of the ritual. Bereaved individuals may benefit from designing other rituals – later in the grieving process – such as an Anniversary Mass or an Unveiling of the Gravestone. Most faiths offer such traditions that can allow a public acknowledgement of loss. In addition, individuals can create their own private rituals that mark moments in their grief journey (see Doka, 2002, 2016).

Conclusion

In an earlier work, I described two types of dreaded diseases (see Doka, 1997). One of the types was diseases that stigmatised infected individuals – such as leprosy. Others were great pandemics such as influenza. Certainly, the COVID-19 Pandemic has become one of those diseases. Even though the mortality rate is relatively low, the widespread morbidity, the economic and social disruption it has created, and the rapid spread of the disease has wrecked considerable havoc and fear.

One result is a likely pandemic of complicated grief. All of the factors previously mentioned – the emergence of a new, highly infectious disease, the social isolation and economic disruption, the sudden nature of death and the traumatic loss of our assumptive world – complicate grief. The nature of the pandemic then is likely to leave host of psychological issues ranging from hypochondrias, anxiety and all the varied forms of complicated grief. Even a rapid vaccination while preventing new cases, may complicate the grief of those mourning the deceased. There issues of 'if only' – that 'if only the vaccine were developed two months ago' – may exacerbate the mourning process.

Where there is grief though, there is the possibility of growth. Past pandemics have led to improvements in health care and public health. Perhaps this pandemic will lead to greater understanding of how animal viruses evolve enabling them to infect humans. Perhaps it will enable new procedures that can quickly identify, control, and even set procedures to limit opportunities for viruses to so adapt. The isolation may create new appreciation of family and community. Certainly, it has already changed the nature of commerce and given a significant boast to telemedicine and even remote forms of offering therapy. That this pandemic will leave a mark is inevitable. We can only hope that the legacy will be more than a body count or broken bereaved survivors.

References

Chew, Q., Wei, K., Vasoo, S., Chua, H. and Sim, K., 2020. Narrative synthesis of psychological coping responses towards emerging infectious disease outbreaks in the general population: practical considerations for the COVID-19 Pandemic. *Singapore Medical Journal, (prepublication.* doi.org/10.11622/smedj.202046).

Doka, K., 1984. Expectation of death, participation in planning funeral rituals and grief adjustment. *Omega: Journal of Death and Dying*, 15, pp. 119–130.

Doka, K. (ed.), 1989. *Disenfranchised grief: recognizing hidden sorrow*. Lexington, MA: Lexington Books.

Doka, K., 1997. *AIDS, fear and society: challenging the dreaded disease*. Washington, DC: Taylor & Francis.

Doka, K. (ed.), 2002. *Disenfranchised grief: new directions, challenges, and strategies for practice*. Champaign, IL: Research Press.

Doka, K., 2005. Ethics, end-of-life decisions and grief. *Mortality*, 10, pp. 83–90.

Doka, K., 2016. *Grief is a journey: finding your path through loss*. New York: Atria Press.

Freud, S., 1917. Mourning and Melancholia. *Standard Edition*, v. XIV. London: Hogarth.

Fulton, R., 1987. *Anticipating grief*. Keynote Presentation to the Association for Death Education and Counseling, April.

Harris, D. (ed.), 2011. *Counting our losses: reflecting on change, loss and transition in everyday life*. New York, NY: Routledge.

Harris, D. (ed.), 2020. *Non-death loss and grief: context and clinical implications*. New York, NY: Routledge.

Hong, N. and Handal, P., 2020. Science, religion, government, and SARS-CoV-2: a time for synergy. *Journal of Religion and Health*, 59(2020), pp. 2263–2268. Doi: 10-1007/s10943-020-01047-y.

Jameton, A., 1984. *Nursing practice: the ethical issues*. Englewood Cliffs, NJ: Prentice Hall.

Jameton, A., 1993. Dilemmas of moral distress: moral responsibility and nursing practice. *AWHONNS Clinical Issues in Perinatal and Women's Health Nursing*, 4, pp. 542–551.

Janoff-Bulman, R., 1992. *Shattered assumptions: toward a new psychology of trauma*. New York, NY: The Free Press.

Katz, R. and Johnson, T., 2016. *When professionals weep: emotional and countertransference responses in palliative and end-of-life care*. New York, NY: Routledge.

Klass, D., Silverman, P. and Nickman, S., 1996. *Continuing bonds: new understandings of grief*. Bristol, PA: Taylor and Francis.

Neimeyer, R. (ed.), 2001. *Meaning reconstruction and the experience of loss*. Washington, DC: American Psychological Association.

Papadatou, D., 2000. A proposed model of health professionals grieving process. *Omega: Journal of Death and Dying*, 41, pp. 59–77.

Rando, T.A., 1993. *Treatment of complicated mourning*. Champaign, Il: Research Press.

Sherman, L. and Crunk, E., 2020. Fear and psychopathology during the COVID-19 crisis: Neuroticism, hypochondriasis, reassurance-seeking, and coronaphobia as fear factors. *Omega: Journal of Death and Dying*, In publication. Doi: 10.1177/0030222820949350.

Stroebe, M. and Schut, H., 1999. The dual process model of coping with bereavement: rationale and description. *Death Studies*, 23, pp. 273–289.

Worden, J.W., 2018. *Grief counseling and grief therapy: a handbook for the mental health practitioner*. New York, NY: Springer.

3 Apocalypse now: COVID-19 and the crisis of meaning

Robert A. Neimeyer, Evgenia Milman, and Sherman A. Lee

Key points

- Given the prevalence of fear and anxiety in response to the global contagion, the *Coronavirus Anxiety Scale* (CAS) serves as a valid and efficient screener for functional impairment and other worrisome psychological consequences.
- As the incidence of COVID mortality surges in many countries, a shadow pandemic of dysfunctional grief follows in its wake, which can be assessed by the carefully validated *Pandemic Grief Scale* (PGS) to identify bereaved survivors at heightened risk of substance abuse and suicide.
- The impact of both direct COVID stressors (e.g. diagnosis, death) and indirect COVID stressors (e.g. unemployment, loss of childcare) on mental health outcomes is mediated by meaning, as in the challenge to core beliefs in predictability and control as well as meaning making about the pandemic.
- Psychological intervention can be informed by people's responses to both the CAS and PGS, helping to target key symptoms and struggles, as well as by engaging those systems of meaning that have been shaken or shattered by the death and non-death losses resulting from the pandemic.

With the global pandemic of COVID-19 that has swept the planet has come the loss of a world of once familiar routines, relationships and resources that previously conferred on our lives a sense of security and meaning. In a matter of weeks, the citizens of nearly every nation were confronted by a radical transformation of their habitual activities, social networks and workplaces, as the threat posed by the rapidly spreading coronavirus jeopardized not only their ways of living, but also life itself. Our goal in the present chapter is to review evidence bearing on the psychological consequences of this apocalyptic threat to human existence, focusing particularly on the anxiety it has engendered in nearly all communities, as well as the profound grief left in the wake of multiple surges of mortality from COVID-19 in those nations contending with the highest rates of infection. In doing so we will also summarize our successful efforts to construct and validate effective and efficient screening measures for both coronavirus anxiety and dysfunctional grief following COVID bereavement, including as appendices both scales for the use of readers interested in adopting them in research or practice contexts. Finally we will review the substantial evidence suggesting that the psychological distress triggered by the pandemic can be explained by its assault on the world of meaning of people most affected by it, and conclude with a consideration of the implications of these findings for psychological support and treatment during and following the current crisis.

Anxiety in the context of COVID-19

Within one month after COVID-19 was declared a global pandemic, people were beginning to show serious signs of anxiety. A poll taken early in the pandemic revealed that more than 80% of Americans were worried about coronavirus infection (ABC News, 2020). In fact, anxiety was so high that new prescriptions for anti-anxiety medications increased by an alarming 37.7% from the month before the start of the pandemic (Express Scripts, 2020). Another sign that anxiety was quite prevalent in the beginning of the pandemic came from internet use. Ayers and his colleagues (2020) analyzed terms used in internet searches and discovered a 52% increase in searches that were indicative of acute anxiety a couple of weeks into the pandemic. Many people continued to experience heightened levels of anxiety through the early months of the pandemic, with nearly 30% of Americans reporting anxiety symptoms at clinical levels, a rate 21.7% higher than the previous year's pre-pandemic statistic of 8.1% (Centers for Disease Control and Prevention, 2020). Six months into the pandemic, when the global COVID-19 death rate neared one million, the vast majority of people continued to report concerns over the coronavirus (Bycoffe, Groskopf and Mehta, 2020).

Fear and anxiety over the coronavirus, which we will refer to as *coronavirus anxiety (CA)*, is more than just an emotional reaction. Rather, it is an important variable that has influenced people's mental health through the pandemic by its links to a host of psychological and behavioral issues. For example, CA has been found to be correlated with feelings of extreme hopelessness, suicidal ideation, negative religious coping, depression, generalized anxiety, health anxiety, death anxiety, substance abuse, rumination, loneliness, low vitality, low well-being, traumatic stress, violation of core beliefs and functional impairments (Ahmed et al., 2020; Arslan, Yildirim and Aytaç, 2020; Choi, Lee and Lee, 2020; Gaeta and Brydges, 2020; Lee, 2020a; Lee and Crunk, 2020; Lee et al., 2020a; Lee et al., 2020b; Milman, Lee and Neimeyer 2020a; Mora-Magaña et al., 2020; Skalski et al., 2020). Perhaps the most troubling connection found was between CA and suicide deaths. Specifically, in an analysis of 69 reported cases of suicide in India during the pandemic, the most prominent causal factor of suicide deaths was fear of COVID-19 (Dsouza et al., 2020).

Not unlike other pandemics in the past (see Taylor, 2019), some individuals during the COVID-19 crisis appear to be more vulnerable to elevated fear and anxiety regarding the coronavirus than others. For example, those who have been infected with the coronavirus reported greater anxiety over the virus than those who have not been infected (Lee, 2020a; Lee et al., 2020b), while high exposure healthcare workers (e.g. emergency room workers) showed higher levels of CA than their low exposure peers (Mora-Magaña et al., 2020). Similar to the trend found among anxiety disorders, women tend to report greater CA than men (Ahmed et al., 2020; Choi et al., 2020; Lee et al., 2020b; Mora-Magaña et al., 2020). It is important to note, however, that some studies have shown an opposite effect (Lee and Crunk, 2020; Lee et al., 2020a), while others showed no gender effect (Choi et al., 2020; Lee, 2020a; Skalski et al., 2020) in CA. There have also been age differences found whereby younger adults tend to have greater CA than older adults (Choi et al., 2020; Lee, 2020a; Lee et al., 2020a; Lee et al., 2020b). Research has also shown that certain personality traits are risk factors for CA. For example, individuals who have a generalized tendency to experience negative emotional states (i.e. high neuroticism; Lee and Crunk, 2020), do not recover from stress well (i.e. low stress resiliency; Labrague and De los Santos, 2020), and have trouble controlling their impulses (i.e. low ego resiliency; Skalski et al., 2020), tend to experience higher levels of CA than their counterparts.

Coronavirus Anxiety Scale (CAS)

Given the psychological toll that COVID-19 has taken on the mental health and well-being of people living through the pandemic, it is vital that mental health professionals efficiently screen-and-treat those suffering from a mental disorder and pandemic-related anxiety (Taylor, 2019). For example, in a study of 61 million people's health records in the US, individuals with a psychiatric condition were found to be more likely to catch COVID-19 and die from the disease than those without a mental health disorder (Wang, Xu and Volkow, 2020). In addition to these health risks, anxiety is also a particular concern among those living with a psychiatric condition. For example, individuals with eating disorders reported a worsening of anxiety since pre-pandemic times and they expressed greater concerns regarding the impact of the pandemic on their mental health compared to their physical health (Termorshuizen et al., 2020). In another study, individuals with anxiety or mood disorders reported being more negatively affected by the pandemic than those with no psychiatric condition (Asmundson et al., 2020). In addition, those with anxiety disorders reported more traumatic stress and fear about coronavirus contamination and danger than any other group in the study (Asmundson et al., 2020). This finding was consistent with a study by Lee et al. (2020a) who discovered higher levels of CA among those with a history of anxiety disorder compared to those who did not have a history of that condition. Thus, these findings highlight the need to identify and treat individuals suffering from mental disorders and high levels of CA during this global health crisis.

The *Coronavirus Anxiety Scale* (CAS; Lee, 2020a) is a mental health screening tool derived from a principal components analysis of a larger set of candidate items bearing on cognitive, behavioral, emotional and physiological symptoms of anxiety originating in the psychological literature (American Psychiatric Association (APA), 2013; Barlow, 1991; Cosmides and Tooby, 2000; Ekman, 2003; Ohman, 1993). Administering this set of items to 775 American adults at the outset of the COVID-19 pandemic, Lee (2020a) identified five items that captured somatic, physiological symptoms of fear and anxiety that are triggered by thoughts or information about the coronavirus (e.g. 'I felt paralyzed or frozen when I thought about or was exposed to information about the coronavirus') that demonstrated high factorial and construct validity. The original CAS (Lee, 2020a) measures symptoms across a two-week time span, while the newly created CAS 2.0 (Milman, Lee and Neimeyer, 2020b) measures symptoms across a one-week period, in view of the rapidly changing course of the epidemic marked by recurrent surges and associated spikes of concern about the adequacy of mitigation and treatment efforts. The diagnostic ability of the CAS to correctly distinguish individuals with clinically dysfunctional levels of anxiety from those without that level of distress are comparable to other psychiatric screening tools, such as the widely used GAD-7 (Spitzer et al., 2006), for example (Lee, 2020a; Lee et al., 2020b). Although total CAS scores of 9 and higher were found to best classify adults as having (76% to 90% sensitivity) or not having (85% to 90% specificity) dysfunctional levels of anxiety and associated impairment in work and social functioning (Lee, 2020a; Lee et al., 2020b), later research has suggested that this cut score may be too conservative. For example, some studies have proposed more optimal cut-scores ranging from 8 and higher (Mora-Magaña et al., 2020) to as low as 5 and higher (Lee, 2020b).

In addition to demonstrating its value as a mental health screener, numerous studies have also shown that the CAS screener meets and often exceeds psychometric standards of reliability and validity. For instance, studies demonstrate that the CAS has strong test-retest reliability (rs from .76 to .88), excellent internal consistency reliability (αs from .85 to .92), and contains items that statistically cohere (comparative fit indices > .95) around a single-latent coronavirus anxiety construct (Ahmed et al., 2020; Akkuzu et al., 2020; Choi et al., 2020; Lee, 2020a, 2020b; Lee et al., 2020b; Skalski et al., 2020). Research shows that the CAS is valid across the demographic groups of age, gender and race (Ahmed et al., 2020; Franco-Jimenez, 2020;

Lee et al., 2020b) and has been successfully adapted for use with a variety of cultural groups. For example, adapted versions of the CAS from Bangladesh (Ahmed et al., 2020), Peru (Franco-Jimenez, 2020), Poland (Skalski et al., 2020), Mexico (Mora-Magaña et al., 2020), South Korea (Choi et al., 2020), and Turkey (Evren et al., 2020), have all demonstrated solid properties of reliability and validity.

Although the CAS has strong support for its construct validity, as shown by its correlations with various indicators of distress and well-being, the most impressive psychometric attribute of this instrument is its evidence of incremental validity. Specifically, the CAS has repeatedly demonstrated its ability to predict depression, generalized anxiety, and social and work adjustment, beyond demographics, personality traits, and COVID-19 factors (Lee and Crunk, 2020; Lee et al., 2020a; Nikčević and Spada, 2020). Thus, the CAS is available as a valid and reliable measure of CA that can be used as a screener in all health and mental health settings, as well as a brief measure of a highly relevant clinical construct in ongoing research with adult populations around the world. At the level of psychological practice, it also has been found to correlate highly with such important symptoms as spiritual struggles, hopelessness, drug and alcohol coping and suicide ideation. A copy of the CAS 2.0 (Milman et al., 2020b) with scoring instructions appears in Table 3.1, and has been entered into the public domain to promote its use without cost or special permission, simply with appropriate citation of its original publication.

Grief in the time of corona

As the death toll from COVID-19 surges in many countries in the world, the spreading infection brings with it a second *shadow pandemic* in the wake of the first, a pandemic of bereavement under complicating circumstances. Decades of research have established numerous evidence-based risk factors for clinically impairing intense and complicated grief reactions, such as social isolation of the bereaved, unexpectedness of the death, challenges to the mourner's attachment bond to the deceased, spiritual struggles in bereavement, inability to make sense of the loss, socioeconomic and educational disadvantage of the mourners, and a lack of institutional support for families in the care facilities in which the deaths take place (Neimeyer and Burke, 2017). Notably, *every one* of these factors characterizes the circumstances in which COVID-19 deaths occur. Social isolation policies limit both available social support and meaningful engagement of families in end of life care. Vulnerable patients can decline precipitously even with medical support, as families experience helplessness in being unable to tend to their loved ones in the final weeks and days of life. Places of worship are shuttered during the pandemic as mourners may doubt God's beneficence and people's assumptive worlds are assaulted by unpredictable events beyond their prediction and control. Marginalized communities are at disproportionate risk

Table 3.1 Coronavirus Anxiety Scale 2.0 (Milman, Lee and Neimeyer, 2020a)

How often have you experienced the following activities over the last week?	Never	Rarely, 1–2 days	Sometimes, 3–4 days	Often, 5–6 days	Every day
1. I felt dizzy, lightheaded, or faint, when I read or listened to news about the coronavirus.	0	1	2	3	4
2. I had trouble falling or staying asleep because I was thinking about the coronavirus.	0	1	2	3	4
3. I felt paralyzed or frozen when I thought about or was exposed to information about the coronavirus.	0	1	2	3	4
4. I lost interest in eating when I thought about or was exposed to information about the coronavirus.	0	1	2	3	4
5. I felt nauseous or had stomach problems when I thought about or was exposed to information about the coronavirus.	0	1	2	3	4
Column Totals	___ +	___ +	___ +	___ +	___ +

Total Score:

Note. The CAS 2.0 is placed in the public domain to encourage its use in clinical assessment and research. No formal permission is therefore required for its reproduction and use by others, beyond appropriate citation of the original article. [*Reprinted with permission.*]

of mortality, and family engagement and education are abandoned by hospitals and eldercare facilities seeking to protect both vulnerable patients and healthcare professionals themselves from contagion (Menzies, Neimeyer and Menzies, 2020). Thus, the psychological toll of bereavement is likely to be particularly severe in the COVID era, just as demographic researchers warned at the very outset of the pandemic in the Western world (Verdery and Smith-Greenway, 2020). The scant research that has been done to date reinforces concerns that grief due to a COVID-19 death is indeed more severe than that resulting from other forms of loss, such as death through natural causes (Eisma et al., 2020). This finding is particularly concerning given that an acute grief reaction in the early months of mourning is a further risk factor for prolonged grief disorder (Boelen 2020), recognized by the World Health Organization (2019) *International Classification of Disease* as a unique condition requiring assessment and intervention.

Pandemic Grief Scale (PGS)

Given the burgeoning death toll to coronavirus around the world and the high risk of complications in bereavement that it entails, Lee and Neimeyer (2020) undertook the development of the Pandemic Grief Scale (PGS), following essentially the same procedures involved in the psychometric validation of the Coronavirus Anxiety Scale. First, a pool of over three dozen candidate items derived from the Persistent Complex Bereavement Inventory (PCBI; Lee, 2015; cf. American Psychiatric Association APA, 2013) and additional symptoms unique to the threat of the coronavirus (e.g. 'I felt guilty about not being able to be there for the deceased before he/she died') was generated to assess potentially severe and disabling responses to COVID loss. These were then rated by 831 American adults bereaved by a COVID death of a family member or close associate on a 4-point Likert type scale of frequency experienced over the preceding two weeks, an interval commonly adopted to assess the greater stability of grief relative to anxiety states. Significantly, over 40% of this sample reported seeking professional help for their grief, and nearly as many had tested positive for COVID-19.

Principal components analysis followed by confirmatory factor analysis identified five items with high reliability ($\alpha = 0.86$), sensitivity (87%) and specificity (71%) in diagnosing impairment in work and social functioning, with item content reflecting a wish to die in order to be with the deceased, identity confusion, apathy, difficulty reminiscing, and emptiness and meaninglessness (see Table 3.2). Moreover, the PGS was shown to measure dysfunctional grief symptoms in conceptually similar ways across age, gender and race, demonstrating measurement invariance. Scores on this brief screener also correlated substantially more highly with suicide ideation and use of substances as a means of coping with the loss than did a measure of Persistent Complex Bereavement Disorder (American Psychiatric Association APA, 2013) in past research (Lee, 2015), providing further evidence of its validity and clinical utility as a screener for dysfunctional grief. Most impressively, the PGS displayed strong evidence of its incremental validity, explaining 18% more of the variance in functional impairment resulting from COVID bereavement beyond that accounted for by measures of general anxiety and depression. It therefore should prove effective and efficient in screening for clinically significant grief in the pandemic, with a cut score of 7 or above identifying those who are struggling to a disabling extent with their loss. As with the CAS, we have placed the PGS into the public domain to encourage its use in research and practice without cost or special permission beyond citation of its original publication.

Alarmingly, Lee and Neimeyer (2020) found that *over 66% of 831 COVID-bereaved adults in their sample scored in the clinical range* of the PGS, underscoring concerns about a shadow pandemic of dysfunctional grief resulting from the coronavirus. The high incidence of clinically elevated grief in this cohort is unsurprising given the numerous risk factors for intense and preoccupying

Table 3.2 Pandemic Grief Scale (PGS; Lee and Neimeyer, 2020)

Over the last 2 weeks, how often have you experienced the following thoughts, feelings, or behaviors related to your loss?	Not at all	Several days	More than half the days	Nearly everyday
1. I wished to die in order to be with the deceased.	0	1	2	3
2. I experienced confusion over my role in life or felt like my identity was diminished because of the loss.	0	1	2	3
3. Nothing seemed to matter much to me because of this loss.	0	1	2	3
4. I found it difficult to have positive memories about the deceased.	0	1	2	3
5. I believed that without the deceased, life was either meaningless, empty, or could not go on.	0	1	2	3
Column Totals	____ +	____ +	____ +	____ +

Total Score: ____

Note. The PGS is placed in the public domain to encourage its use in clinical assessment and research. No formal permission is therefore required for its reproduction and use by others, beyond appropriate citation of the original article. Total scores of 7 or above on this measure represent clinically dysfunctional levels of pandemic grief. [*Reprinted with permission.*]

bereavement symptomatology and unfinished business that result directly or indirectly from the global outbreak of COVID-19, as noted above. This concern is further reinforced by the finding that PGS scores showed no reduction across the 6 months of bereavement represented in the Lee and Neimeyer (2020) sample, raising the prospect of enduring distress and impairment. However, just what percentage of those who are contending with clinical complications in the early months of their loss ultimately will meet criteria for Prolonged Grief Disorder (American Psychiatric Association (APA), 2021; World Health Organization, 2019) can only be determined by future research, inasmuch as criteria for this diagnosis require marked and persistent dysfunction for 6 to 12 months beyond the death.

Finally, this initial study using the PGS also suggests that some groups in this American sample are more likely to experience profound and perturbing grief in the wake of COVID bereavement than others. Specifically, black respondents and men seemed more vulnerable to maladaptive mourning than other ethnicities and genders, just as they are also more vulnerable to

COVID mortality. Those who were themselves diagnosed with COVID and who had sought professional services for their grief likewise were more likely to score highly on the measure, as were mourners who had lost partners or immediate family. Health systems and providers extending services to these groups would do well to evaluate not only the level of their distress, but also to be alert to the specific clinical issues suggested by those PGS items that they are strongly endorsing. Using these items (i.e. a death wish, erosion of personal identity, apathy toward life, difficulty accessing comforting memories of the deceased, and emptiness and meaninglessness) as 'conversation starters' could help professionals identify targeted therapeutic interventions ranging from careful assessment of suicide risk through specific foci for grief therapy, a topic to which we will turn below. First, however, it is important to explore a salient mechanism that accounts for much of the psychological distress stemming from the current apocalypse: disruptions in the systems of meaning of those most impacted by the pandemic.

Pandemic distress and the mediating role of meaning

To slow the spread of COVID, unprecedented measures have been taken to limit in-person contact, including social distancing, cessation of long-distance travel and sheltering-in-place by avoiding non-essential movement outside the home. Such socially facilitated means of curbing COVID transmission appear to reduce rates of infection, but they are also associated with substantial secondary stressors, including disruption of social support networks, daily routines, childcare, financial stability and employment. Despite these apparent burdens of social isolation, research has found that socially isolating is significantly associated with *lower* levels of CA (Milman, Lee and Neimeyer, 2020c). Lending support to this counterintuitive finding, surveys have found that social isolation policies are experienced positively by most North Americans, with nearly half of Canadians preferring to continue working from home (ADP Canada and Angus Reid Forum, 2020), 81% of Americans indicating that social distancing should continue even at the expense of the economy (Morning Consult and Politico, 2020), and two thirds of Americans reporting discomfort with returning to work (Nielsen, 2020). Crucially, research has also offered insight into the mechanism mediating the positive psychological impact of social isolation during the pandemic, highlighting meaning as a central factor. Such research has focused on two meaning-related variables in particular: core belief violation and meaning made of the pandemic.

Research suggests that people possess a set of largely implicit core beliefs which collectively convey the sense that we are worthy individuals who live in a just world where our experiences are the result of our actions, affording us agency to influence our lives with relative certainty regarding the future (Cann et al., 2010; Park and Kennedy, 2017; Park et al., 2016; Janoff-Bulman, 1989). Such research also describes how stressful or traumatic events, such as the pandemic, can violate our core beliefs, leaving us at a loss in a world rendered unfamiliar (Currier, Holland and Neimeyer, 2009; Currier et al., 2008; Schwartzberg and Janoff-Bulman, 1991). According to this perspective, the destructive nature of the pandemic lies in its capacity to substantially challenge the foundational beliefs upon which we build our system of personal meanings – key 'world assumptions' presuming the predictability of events, our control of relevant outcomes, and our self-agency, choice and movement toward valued goals. When circumstances such as the pandemic threaten us with loss of security, safety, relationships, jobs and futures, we are thrown into a process of reviewing, revising or reaffirming our pre-pandemic beliefs and assumptions (Neimeyer, 2019; Gillies, Neimeyer and Milman, 2015; Gillies, Neimeyer and Milman, 2014). Optimally, a productive meaning making process would result in more nuanced and useful beliefs that accommodate the reality of the pandemic while restoring a sense of meaning.

In the context of the pandemic, we found that participants who engaged in social isolation reported significantly less core belief violation and significantly greater meaning made of the pandemic (Milman et al., 2020b). In turn, those whose core beliefs were less violated by the pandemic or who made more meaning of the pandemic reported significantly lower CA. These findings suggest that compliance with social isolation guidelines lowers CA in at least two ways: (1) by bolstering core beliefs, thereby preventing a crisis of meaning and (2) by facilitating meaning making, thereby allowing recovery in cases where a violation of meaning has occurred. The foundational work of Victor Frankl offers insight into how meaning might be supported by the choice to isolate during the pandemic (Frankl, 1961; Frankl, 1985). Drawing on his experiences in concentration camps during the Holocaust, Frankl described how meaning can emerge from self-empowerment, proposing that the capacity to choose our response to the most harrowing of circumstances allows us find meaning in those same circumstances. Perhaps then, the choice to socially distance is the foundation for preserving agency and thereby making meaning of the pandemic.

Of note, contrary to the mental health benefits of social isolation, using exclusively non-social precautionary measures, such as handwashing and mask-wearing, as a standalone method of preventing COVID transmission was associated with *higher* levels of CA (Milman et al., 2020b). This finding might reflect the social nature of meaning making, which is understood to occur in coordination with social support networks and broader society through a collective negotiation of the meaning of stressful events, such as the pandemic (Neimeyer, Klass and Dennis, 2014). According to this perspective, fully participating in the precautionary measures recommended in the media, both social and non-social, may help individuals to feel a sense of solidarity with the prevailing culturally held meaning attributed to the pandemic in broader society, thereby allowing for a sense of existential grounding that relieves CA. Indeed, grief research has shown that experiencing social invalidation of meaning making, through perceived critique or judgment of the meaning that one attributes to a loss, is more detrimental to mental health outcomes than lacking access to social networks altogether (Bellet, Holland and Neimeyer, 2018). Applying this research to the pandemic suggests that noncompliance with social policies for reducing COVID exposure could elicit social invalidation of meaning making, and in turn may exacerbate CA.

Further research has offered a striking elaboration of the finding that meaning buffers the devastating psychological impact of the pandemic. Specifically, while the preservation of core beliefs and facilitation of meaning making appear to mediate lower CA (Milman et al., 2020b), the violation of core beliefs and disrupted meaning making appear to mediate poorer mental health outcomes including higher CA, depression and general anxiety (Milman et al., 2020a). In fact, core belief violation and disrupted meaning making explained people's severity of mental health symptoms to a greater degree than did demographics (gender, age, ethnicity and education), and multiple, substantial COVID stressors, including indirect COVID stressors (unemployment, loss of childcare and increased living costs) and even direct COVID stressors (diagnosis of the respondent and death of someone in their network). Crucially, the effects of each of these pandemic stressors on mental health were mediated by core belief violation and disrupted meaning making. Specifically, each stressor was associated with increased core belief violation and decreased meaning making. In turn, those whose core beliefs were more violated by the pandemic and those who made less meaning of the pandemic experienced greater depression, general anxiety and CA. These findings suggest that even the most devastating and direct pandemic circumstances, such as COVID diagnosis or death, impact mental health to the extent that they violate core beliefs. The mediating role of disruptions in core beliefs and meaning making is even more influential in the case of indirect COVID stressors, such as loss of employment, income or childcare, where they literally account for *all* of the variance in CA attributed to these factors.

To illustrate the clinical and public health implications of these findings, the violation of core beliefs in life's predictability, one's sense of control, and one's sense of self-agency seem to be mitigated by compliance with responsible social mitigation policies, such as social distancing. This finding not only has practical value, suggesting its use in messaging regarding the mental health benefits of such procedures, but it also is of theoretical interest, suggesting that engagement in a *behavior* (complying with social mitigation protocols) carries *cognitive* implications (conserving core beliefs), which in turn predicts *physiological* outcomes (the physiological disruption measured by the CAS).

In cases where the pandemic deals a crippling blow to one's belief system, making meaning may prove an insurmountable task, thereby exacerbating depression, general anxiety and CA. Alternatively, if making meaning of one's experience of the pandemic entails a substantial but manageable revision of violated beliefs, then such circumstances, while distressing, appear to result in lower mental health symptomatology. For example, although the surging threat of COVID may challenge one's sense of stability and security, making meaning of this reality nonetheless may result in a belief that life must be cherished and lived fully precisely because stability and security are not guaranteed. Similarly, a COVID job loss could violate achievement-oriented definitions of self-worth, but also foster new sources of self-worth such as perseverance despite setbacks. In these ways, the pandemic may violate core beliefs, but meaning making can give rise to new life-affirming sources of significance.

Taken together this research highlights a potential *crisis of meaning* and the recovery from such a crisis as a final, common pathway mediating the impact of the pandemic on mental health, both in terms of the protective function of social isolation and in terms of the adverse impact of diverse pandemic stressors (Milman et al., 2020a; Milman et al., 2020c; Milman et al., 2020b). Similar findings have been demonstrated in grief research, where a variety of loss-related stressors, ranging from violent death to low post-loss social support, have been found to predict contemporaneous and subsequent mental health symptoms by undermining survivors' capacity to make meaning of their loss (Milman et al., 2019a; Milman et al., 2018; Rozalski, Holland and Neimeyer, 2017; Boelen, de Keijser and Smid, 2015; Milman et al., 2019b).

Perhaps then, as is the case with grief and stress-coping more generally, adapting to the challenges posed by the pandemic depends substantially on one's ability to find or reconstruct meaning in the face or wake of these challenges. In other words, as suggested by the work of Victor Frankl, it may be that we are 'ready and willing to shoulder any suffering' as long as we can 'see a meaning in it' (Frankl, 1961). We conclude with a few practical prescriptions for psychiatrists, clinical and counseling psychologists, clinical social workers and other psychotherapists working with clients struggling with coronavirus anxiety and dysfunctional grief in the midst or wake of the pandemic.

From screening to meaning: prescriptions for practice

The research reviewed here carries practical implications for professionals working in health care settings, and especially for those psychologists, counselors and social workers who encounter clients contending with debilitating anxiety and grief in their clinical practice. Some of the following recommendations are straightforward and fall within the scope of practice of most therapists regardless of their discipline or theoretical perspective, whereas others, as noted, will require more specialized training that goes beyond graduate school and internship experiences. For this reason, we will begin with the former and progress to the latter, bulleting our points for brevity and impact.

- *Screen for suffering and symptomatology.* Although the strong psychometric properties displayed by both the CAS and PGS fully justify their use as impressively reliable and valid measures in future research, they were specifically constructed to serve as efficient and effective screeners for dysfunctional expressions of COVID-related anxiety and grief in health and mental health settings. We, therefore, advocate the inclusion of these simple 5-item measures as means of identifying those persons struggling with debilitating symptoms that pose risk for numerous worrisome clinical sequelae, as well as demonstrable functional impairment of a relational and occupational kind. Once identified, outreach and referral services can be better implemented with those in highest need, rather than overstretching professional resources by reaching out indiscriminately to those individuals more likely to respond resiliently to the losses and stressors stemming from the pandemic.

- *Develop a dialogue.* For those persons who are offered professional therapy or bereavement support for clinically elevated scores on either measure, therapists would do well to invite the personal narratives that underpin the numerical results on the CAS or PGS, sensitively shifting focus from assessment to intervention. One means of doing so is using items to which a client has responded with high ratings as 'conversation starters' for a deeper engagement and mutual consideration of possible interventions. For example, a counselor glancing at the CAS ratings by a client might begin by asking, 'You shared that you often have trouble sleeping because you keep thinking about the coronavirus. Can you say more about what keeps running through your mind at those times, and what you've tried to do to deal with that?' Likewise, a therapist scanning a client's PGS might prompt, 'You note here that it's really hard for you to reminisce about your husband and recover positive memories of him since his death. Can you give me an example of a recent time that you experienced that, and the feelings that arose for you then?' In each case, a few minutes of exploration could help build the therapeutic relationship by contributing to the therapist's accurate empathy for the client's specific suffering, and assist with the construction of targeted interventions (Chung et al., 2018, Eisma et al., 2015) or continuing bonds work or legacy projects (Klass and Steffan, 2017; Neimeyer and Lichtenthal, 2017)) in the second.

- *Promote emotion regulation.* A priority with both elevated coronavirus anxiety and dysfunctional grief is affecting regulation, the development of 'self capacities' to modulate arousal, self-soothe, and release emotional and physical tension. A wide range of techniques and practices can promote this goal, from simple breath work and progressive relaxation in the therapist's office through aerobic (e.g. running, biking) and anaerobic (e.g. Tai Chi, gardening) physical activity implemented in the client's daily life. More elaborate practices such as yoga, Mindfulness-Based Stress Reduction (Grossman et al., 2004), and special adaptations of mindfulness for the bereaved (Stang,

2015) not only ameliorate immediate sources of distress, but also build a foundation for greater self-compassion and emotion processing over time.

- *Surmount the limits of language.* Especially given the wordless, somatic quality of coronavirus anxiety and the ineffable separation distress at the heart of grief, arts-assisted practices can help give form or voice to both conditions, as well as foster their transformation. For example, expressive and creative writing can help clients name and claim elusive emotions and losses, as well as explore sources of resilience based on a clearer recognition of their needs (e.g. Neimeyer and Young-Eisendrath, 2012). Likewise, a cornucopia of clinical tools and techniques derived from the visual arts, music, and even movement and performance can be integrated into grief counseling to good effect, complementing and bridging to more conventional talk therapy (Thompson and Neimeyer, 2014).
- *Function as a secure base for client reflection and action.* Much of the power of therapy to provide a 'container' for distressing client experiences owes to the therapist's functioning as a *secure base* for the client, offering an optimal blend of *caring* and *daring*, that is, allowing a client to feel supported enough to introspect about sources of distress and challenged enough to respond to them actively (Van Wielink, Wilhelm and van Geelen-Merks, 2019). Serving as a reliable transitional attachment figure for the client may be especially valuable in bereavement, when the client is struggling with the threat imposed by the loss of the physical attachment to a loved one and is attempting to reconstruct a non-material bond (Kosminsky and Jordan, 2016). Like the emotional modulation that it also supports, this grounding sense of therapist presence (Neimeyer, 2012b) is foundational for many of the specific techniques that might then be introduced, whether these take the form of behavioral activation (Papa et al., 2013) or imaginal dialogues with the deceased (Neimeyer, 2012a).
- *Focus therapy on intervening in meaning.* Both the pandemic in general and COVID bereavement specifically pose serious challenges to pre-pandemic belief systems predicated on the sense that life is predictable, outcomes are controllable, the universe is just, and we as human beings exercise considerable agency in choosing how we live our lives. In the wake of the plenitude of death- and non-death losses stemming from the coronavirus crisis, all such beliefs are revealed to be fragile illusions, or at best far more humbly held than the world assumptions on which we once relied. Thus, most clients contending either with the lurking threat of COVID or their anguished grief in its aftermath need to review and revise their foundational beliefs about life. Furthermore, the losses of work, relationships and people are irreversible, whatever vaccination programs ultimately return some semblance of normality to the lives of survivors. In an important sense, then, counselors and therapists cannot change the harsh realities that their clients have suffered – but they can

work with that which *is* malleable by *intervening in meaning*, helping them make sense of what they have been through, find significance in a changed bond with the deceased, and re-learn themselves and their lives in the aftermath. In the presence of the pandemic, encouraging prudent compliance with social distancing and other socially responsible agentic acts can help preserve or restore people's sense of a meaningful and manageable world, as noted above. And in the context of grief therapy, both trauma-informed perspectives that help people revisit and repair their relationship with their loved one (Rubin, Malkinson and Witztum, 2012) and meaning-oriented interventions to process the *event story* of the loss and the *back story* of the connection with the deceased (Neimeyer, 2019) hold great promise for restoring a viable web of beliefs and bonds that reaffirm client resilience. A plenitude of practices supports these goals (Neimeyer, 2012c; Neimeyer, 2016).

Coda

The apocalyptic arrival of the coronavirus on the global scene signaled a sea change in modernity, one that stressed or shattered human hubris that presumed our freedom to work, play, travel and mingle as we like. With this unsettling reality came a seemingly endless train of losses – of security, closeness, roles, communities, recreation, rituals and even of the lives of friends and family that no vaccine will return. We, therefore, have tried to make a modest contribution to the widespread need to identify and serve the vulnerable survivors of such losses through the careful construction and diffusion of screening measures for both coronavirus anxiety and dysfunctional pandemic grief. Reviewing the findings of our studies to date, we further have proffered a few research-based recommendations regarding how we as helping professionals might best support the most affected survivors in their adaptation. We hope that these instruments and ideas will be of use to those readers who join us in this effort.

References

ABC News, 2020. A survey of the American general population (ages 18+). Available at: https://www.ipsos.com/sites/default/files/ct/news/documents/2020-04/topline-abc-coronavirus-041020_.pdf (Accessed: 22 December 2020).

ADP Canada and Angus Reid Forum, 2020. Canadians have mixed feelings on working remotely during COVID-19. Available at: https://www.adp.ca/en/resources/articles-and-insights/articles/c/canadians-have-mixed-feelings-on-working-remotely-during-covid-19.aspx (Accessed: 22 December 2020).

Ahmed, O., Faisal, R.A., Sharker, T., Lee, S.A. and Jobe, M.C., 2020. Adaptation of the Bangla version of the COVID-19 Anxiety Scale. *International Journal of Mental Health and Addiction.* https://doi.org/10.1007/s11469-020-00357-2

Akkuzu, H., Yumuşak, F.N., Karaman, G., Ladikli, N., Türkkan Z. and Bahadır, E., 2020. The reliability and validity of Turkish version of Coronavirus Anxiety

Scale. *Cyprus Turkish Journal of Psychiatry and Psychology*, 2(2), pp. 63–67. Doi:10.35365/ctjpp.20.2.09

American Psychiatric Association (APA), 2013. *Diagnostic and statistical manual of mental disorders* (5th ed.; DSM 5). Author.

American Psychiatric Association (APA), 2021. *Diagnostic and statistical manual of mental disorders, Text Revision* (5th ed.; DSM 5-TR). Author.

Arslan, G., Yildirim, M. and Aytaç, M., 2020. Subjective vitality and loneliness explain how coronavirus anxiety increases rumination among college students *Death Studies*. Doi: https://doi.org/10.1080/07481187.2020.1824204

Asmundson, G.J.G., Paluszek, M.M., Landry, C.A., Rachor, G.S., McKay, D. and Taylor, S., 2020. Do pre-existing anxiety-related and mood disorders differentially impact COVID-19 stress responses and coping? *Journal of Anxiety Disorders*, 74, pp. 1–6. Doi: https://doi.org/10.1016/j.janxdis.2020.102271

Ayers, J.W., Leas, E.C., Johnson, D.C., Poliak, A., Althouse, B.M., Dredze, M. and Nobles, A.L., 2020. Internet searches for acute anxiety during the early stages of the COVID-19 Pandemic. *JAMA Internal Medicine*, 24, pp. 1–2. Doi: 10.1001/jamainternmed.2020.3305

Barlow, D.H., 1991. Disorders of emotion. *Psychological Inquiry*, 2(1), pp. 58–71. Doi: https://doi.org/10.1207/s15327965pli0201_15

Bellet, B.W., Holland, J.M. and Neimeyer, R.A., 2018. The social meaning in life events scale (SMILES): A preliminary psychometric evaluation in a bereaved sample. *Death studies*, 43(2), pp. 103–112. Doi: https://doi.org/10.1080/07481187.2018.1456008

Boelen, P.A., de Keijser, J. and Smid, G., 2015. Cognitive–behavioral variables mediate the impact of violent loss on post-loss psychopathology. *Psychological Trauma: Theory, Research, Practice, and Policy*, 7(4), pp. 382–390. Doi: https://doi.apa.org/doi/10.1037/tra0000018

Boelen, P.A. and Lenferink, L.I.M., 2020. Symptoms of prolonged grief, posttraumatic stress, and depression in recently bereaved people: symptom profiles, predictive value, and cognitive behavioural correlates. *Social Psychiatry and Psychiatric Epidemiology*, 55, pp. 765–777. Doi: https://doi.org/10.1007/s00127-019-01776-w

Bycoffe, A., Groskopf, C. and Mehta, D., 2020 (July 23). How Americans view the coronavirus crisis and Trump's response. Available at: https://projects.fivethirtyeight.com/coronavirus-polls/ (Accessed: 22 December 2020).

Cann, A., Calhoun, L.G., Tedeschi, R.G., Kilmer, R.P., Gil-Rivas, V., Vishnevsky, T. and Danhauer, S.C., 2010. The core beliefs inventory: a brief measure of disruption in the assumptive world. *Anxiety, Stress & Coping*, 23(1), pp. 19–34. Doi: https://doi.org/10.1080/10615800802573013

Centers for Disease Control and Prevention, 2020. *The Household Pulse Survey*. Available at: https://www.cdc.gov/nchs/covid19/pulse/mental-health.htm (Accessed: 22 December 2020).

Choi, E., Lee, J., & Lee, S.A., 2020. Validation of the Korean version of the obsession with COVID-19 Scale and the Coronavirus Anxiety Scale. *Death Studies*. Doi: https://doi.org/10.1080/07481187.2020.1833383

Chung, K.-F., Lee, C.-T., Yeung, W.-F., Chan, M.-S., Chung, E.W.-Y. and Lin, W.-L., 2018. Sleep hygiene education as a treatment of insomnia: a systematic review and meta-analysis. *Family Practice*, 35(4), pp. 365–375.

Cosmides, L. and Tooby, J., 2000. Evolutionary psychology and the emotions. In M. Lewis, Haviland-Jones, J.M. (eds.), *Handbook of emotions*. New York, NY: Guilford Press, pp. 91–115.

Currier, J.M., Holland, J.M., Coleman, R.A. and Neimeyer, R.A., 2008. Bereavement following violent death: An assault on life and meaning. In Stevenson, R.G. and Cox, G.R. (eds.), *Death, value and meaning series: Perspectives on violence and violent death*. Amityville, NY: Baywood Publlishing Co., pp. 177–202.

Currier, J.M., Holland, J.M. and Neimeyer, R.A., 2009. Assumptive worldviews and problematic reactions to bereavement. *Journal of Loss and Trauma*, 14(3), pp. 181–195.

Dsouza, D.D., Quadros, S., Hyderabadwala, Z.J. and Mamun, M.A., 2020. Aggregated covid-19 suicide incidences in india: fear of covid-19 infection is the prominent causative factor. *Psychiatry Research*, pp. 113–145. Doi: https://doi.org/10.1016/j.psychres.2020.113145

Eisma, M.C., Boelen, P.A., van den Bout, J., Stroebe, W., Schut, H.A., Lancee, J. and Stroebe, M.S., 2015. Internet-based exposure and behavioral activation for complicated grief and rumination: a randomized controlled trial. *Behavior Therapy*, 46(6), pp. 729–748.

Eisma, M.C., Tamminga, A., Smid, G.E. and Boelen, P.A., 2020. Acute grief after deaths due to covid-19, natural causes and unnatural causes: an empirical comparison. *Journal of Affective Disorders*, 278, pp. 54–56. Doi: 10.1016/j.jad.2020.09.049

Ekman, P., 2003. *Emotions revealed: recognizing faces and feelings to improve communication and emotional life* (2nd ed.). Toledo, OH: Owl Books.

Evren, C., Evren, B., Dalbudak, E., Topcu, M. and Kutlu, N., 2020. Measuring anxiety related to covid-19: a Turkish validation study of the coronavirus anxiety scale. *Death Studies*, pp. 1–7. Doi: https://doi.org/10.1080/07481187.2020.1774969

Express Scripts, 2020 (April 16). America's state of mind report. Available at: https://www.expressscripts.com/corporate/americas-state-of-mind-report (Accessed: 22 December 2020).

Franco-Jimenez, R., 2020. Translation and psychometric analysis of the Coronavirus Anxiety Scale (CAS) in Peruvian youth and adults. *Interactions*, 6(2), pp. 159. Doi: https://doi.org/10.24016/2020.v6n2.159

Frankl, V.E., 1961. Logotherapy and the challenge of suffering. *Review of Existential Psychology and Psychiatry*, 1(1), pp. 3–7.

Frankl, V.E., 1985. *Man's search for meaning*. New York, NY: Simon and Schuster.

Gaeta, L. and Brydges, C.R., 2020. Coronavirus-related anxiety, social isolation, and loneliness in older adults in northern california during the stay-at-home order. *Journal of Aging & Social Policy*, pp. 1–12. Doi: https://doi.org/10.1080/08959420.2020.1824541

Gillies, J.M., Neimeyer, R.A. and Milman, E., 2014. The meaning of loss codebook: construction of a system for analyzing meanings made in bereavement. *Death Studies*, 38(4), pp. 207–216. Doi: https://doi.org/10.1080/07481187.2013.829367

Gillies, J.M., Neimeyer, R.A. and Milman, E., 2015. The grief and meaning reconstruction inventory (gmri): initial validation of a new measure. *Death Studies*, 39(2), pp. 61–74. Doi: https://doi.org/10.1080/07481187.2014.907089

Grossman, P., Niemann, L., Schmidt, S. and Walach, H., 2004. Mindfulness-based stress reduction and health benefits: A meta-analysis. *Journal of Psychosomatic Research*, 57(1), pp. 35–43.

Janoff-Bulman, R., 1989. Assumptive worlds and the stress of traumatic events: applications of the schema construct. *Social Cognition*, 7(2), pp. 113–136. Doi: https://doi.org/10.1521/soco.1989.7.2.113

Klass, D. and Steffan, E. (eds.), 2017. *Continuing bonds in bereavement: New directions for research and practice.* New York: Routledge.

Kosminsky, P.S. and Jordan, J.R., 2016. *Attachment-informed grief therapy: The clinician's guide to foundations and applications.* New York: Routledge.

Labrague, L. and De los Santos, J.A., 2020. Covid-19 anxiety among front-line nurses: predictive role of organisational support, personal resilience and social support. *Journal of Nursing Management.* Doi: https://doi.org/10.1111/jonm.13121

Lee, S.A., 2015. The persistent complex bereavement inventory: a measure based on the dsm-5. *Death Studies*, 39(7), pp. 399–410.

Lee, S.A., 2020a. Coronavirus anxiety scale: a brief mental health screener for covid-19 related anxiety. *Death Studies*, 44(7), pp. 393–401. Doi: https://doi.org/10.1080/07481187.2020.1748481

Lee, S.A., 2020b. Replication analysis of the coronavirus anxiety scale. *Dusunen Adam: The Journal of Psychiatry and Neurological Sciences*, 33, pp. 203–205. Doi: https://dx.doi.org/10.14744/DAJPNS.2020.00079

Lee, S.A. and Crunk, E.A., 2020. Fear and psychopathology during the covid-19 crisis: neuroticism, hypochondriasis, reassurance-seeking, and coronaphobia as fear factors. *OMEGA-Journal of Death and Dying*, Doi: https://doi.org/10.1177/0030222820949350

Lee, S.A., Jobe, M.C., Mathis, A.A. and Gibbons, J.A., 2020a. Incremental validity of coronaphobia: Coronavirus anxiety explains depression, generalized anxiety, and death anxiety. *Journal of Anxiety Disorders*, 74. Doi: 10.1016/j.janxdis.2020.102268.

Lee, S.A., Mathis, A.A., Jobe, M.C. and Pappalardo, E.A., 2020b. Clinically significant fear and anxiety of covid-19: a psychometric examination of the coronavirus anxiety scale. *Psychiatry Research.* Doi: https://doi.org/10.1016/j.psychres.2020.113112

Lee, S.A. and Neimeyer, R.A., 2020. Pandemic grief scale: a screening tool for dysfunctional grief due to a covid-19 loss. *Death Studies*, pp. 1–11. Doi: 10.1080/07481187.2020.1853885

Menzies, R.E., Neimeyer, R.A. and Menzies, R.G., 2020. Death anxiety, loss, and grief in the time of covid-19. *Behaviour Change*, 37(3), pp. 111–115. Doi: https://doi.org/10.1017/bec.2020.10

Milman, E., Lee, A.S. and Neimeyer, R.A., 2020a. Modelling pandemic depression and anxiety: the mediational role of core beliefs and meaning making. *Journal of Affective Disorders Reports.* Doi: https://doi.org/10.1016/j.jadr.2020.100023

Milman, E., Lee, S.A. and Neimeyer, R.A., 2020b. Social isolation and the mitigation of coronavirus anxiety: The mediating role of meaning. *Death Studies*, pp. 1–13. Doi: https://doi.org/10.1080/07481187.2020.1775362

Milman, E., Lee, S.A. and Neimeyer, R.A., 2020c. Social isolation as a means of reducing dysfunctional coronavirus anxiety and increasing psychoneuroimmunity. *Brain, Behavior, and Immunity.* Doi: https://doi.org/10.1016/j.bbi.2020.05.007

Milman, E., Neimeyer, R.A., Fitzpatrick, M., MacKinnon, C.J., Muis, K.R. and Cohen, S.R., 2018. Prolonged grief symptomatology following violent loss: the mediating role of meaning. *European Journal of Psychotraumatology*, 8(6), p. 1503522. Doi: 10.1080/20008198.2018.1503522

Milman, E., Neimeyer, R.A., Fitzpatrick, M., MacKinnon, C.J., Muis, K.R. and Cohen, S.R., 2019a. Prolonged grief and the disruption of meaning: establishing a mediation model. *Journal of Counseling Psychology*, 66(6), p. 714. Doi: https://doi.org/10.1037/cou0000370

Milman, E., Neimeyer, R.A., Fitzpatrick, M., MacKinnon, C.J., Muis, K.R. and Cohen, S.R., 2019b. Rumination moderates the role of meaning in the development of prolonged grief symptomatology. *Journal of Clinical Psychology*, 75(6), pp. 1047–1065. Doi: https://doi.org/10.1002/jclp.22751

Mora-Magaña, I., Lee, S.A., Maldonado-Castellanos, I., Jiménez-Gutierrez, C., Mendez-Venegas, J., Maya-Del-Moral, A., Rosas-Munive, M.D., Mathis, A.A. and Jobe, M.C., 2020. Coronaphobia among healthcare professionals in mexico: a psychometric analysis. *Death Studies*, pp. 1–10. Doi: https://doi.org/10.1080/07481187.2020.1808762w

Morning Consult and Politico, 2020. National tracking poll. Available at: https://www.politico.com/f/?id=00000171-7b47-ddd3-a173-ffd7a63d0000 (Accessed: 22 December 2020).

Neimeyer, R., 2019. Meaning reconstruction in bereavement: development of a research program. *Death Studies*, 43(2), pp. 79–91. Doi: https://doi.org/10.1080/07481187.2018.1456620

Neimeyer, R.A., 2012a. Chair work. In Neimeyer, R.A. (ed.), *Techniques of grief therapy: creative practices for counselling the bereaved*. New York, NY: Routledge, pp. 266–273.

Neimeyer, R.A., 2012b. Presence, process, and procedure: a relational frame for technical proficiency in grief therapy. In Neimeyer, R.A. (ed.), *Techniques of grief therapy: creative practices for counselling the bereaved*. New York, NY: Routledge, pp. 23–31.

Neimeyer, R.A., 2012c. *Techniques of grief therapy: creative practices for counseling the bereaved*. New York, NY, Routledge.

Neimeyer, R.A., 2016. *Techniques of grief therapy: assessment and intervention*. New York, NY: Routledge.

Neimeyer, R. and Burke, L., 2017. What makes grief complicated? Risk factors for complications in bereavement. In Doka, K. and Tucci, A. (eds.), *Living with loss: when grief is complicated. Washington, dc: Hospice foundation of America*. Washington, DC: Hospice Foundation of America.

Neimeyer, R.A., Klass, D. and Dennis, M.R., 2014. Mourning, meaning, and memory: individual, communal, and cultural narration of grief. In Batthyany, A. and Russo-Netzer, P. (eds.), *Meaning in positive and existential psychology*. New York, NY: Springer, pp. 325–346.

Neimeyer, R.A. and Lichtenthal, W.G., 2017. The presence of absence: the struggle for meaning in the death of a child. In Cox, G. and Stephenson, R. (eds.), *Children, adolescents, and death: Questions and answers*. Amityville, NY: Baywood, pp. 247–260.

Neimeyer, R.A. and Young-Eisendrath, P., 2012. Virtual dream stories. In Neimeyer, R.A. (ed.), *Techniques of grief therapy: creative practices for counseling the bereaved. New York*: Routledge, pp. 187–189.

Nielsen, L., 2020. *Is america ready to return to work and get back to business?* Available at: https://www.qualtrics.com/blog/covid-19-back-to-work/ (Accessed: 22 December 2020).

Nikčević, A.V. and Spada, M.M., 2020. The covid-19 anxiety syndrome scale: development and psychometric properties. *Psychiatry Research*, 292, pp. 113322. Doi: https://doi.org/10.1016/j.psychres.2020.113322

Ohman, A., 1993. Fear and anxiety: evolutionary, cognitive and clinical perspectives. In Lewis, M. and Haviland-Jones, J.M. (eds.), *Hand-book of emotions* (2nd ed.). New York, NY: Guilford, pp. 573–593.

Papa, A., Rummel, C., Garrison-Diehn, C. and Sewell, M.T., 2013. Behavioral activation for pathological grief. *Death Studies*, 37(10), pp. 913–936.

Park, C. and Kennedy, M., 2017. Meaning violation and restoration following trauma: conceptual overview and clinical implications. In Atmeier, E.M. (ed.), *Reconstructing meaning after trauma*. Elsevier, pp. 17–27.

Park, C.L., Riley, K.E., George, L.S., Gutierrez, I.A., Hale, A.E., Cho, D. and Braun, T.D., 2016. Assessing disruptions in meaning: development of the global meaning violation scale. *Cognitive Therapy and Research*, 40(6), pp. 831–846.

Rozalski, V., Holland, J.M. and Neimeyer, R.A., 2017. Circumstances of death and complicated grief: indirect associations through meaning made of loss. *Journal of Loss and Trauma*, 22(1), pp. 11–23. Doi: https://doi.org/10.1080/15325024.2016.11 61426

Rubin, S.S., Malkinson, R. and Witztum, E., 2012. *Working with the bereaved: Multiple lenses on loss and mourning*. Abingdon: Taylor & Francis.

Schwartzberg, S.S. and Janoff-Bulman, R., 1991. Grief and the search for meaning: exploring the assumptive worlds of bereaved college students. *Journal of Social and Clinical Psychology*, 10(3), pp. 270–288.

Skalski, S., Uram, P., Dobrakowski, P. and Kwiatkowska, A., 2020. The link between ego-resiliency, social support, sars-cov-2 anxiety and trauma effects. Polish adaptation of the coronavirus anxiety scale. *Personality and Individual Differences*. Doi: https://doi.org/10.1016/j.paid.2020.110540

Spitzer, R.L., Kroenke, K., Williams, J.B. and Löwe, B., 2006. A brief measure for assessing generalized anxiety disorder: the gad-7. *Archives of Internal Medicine*, 166(10), pp. 1092–1097. Doi: https://doi.org/10.1001/archinte.166

Stang, H., 2015. *Mindfulness and grief: With guided meditations to calm the mind and restore the spirit*. New York, NY: CICO Publishing.

Taylor, S., 2019. *The psychology of pandemics: preparing for the next global outbreak of infectious disease*. Newcastle upon Tyne, UK: Cambridge Scholars Publishing.

Termorshuizen, J.D., Watson, H.J., Thornton, L.M., Borg, S., Flatt, R.E., MacDermod, C.M., Harper, L.E., van Furth, E.F., Peat, C.M. and Bulik, C.M., 2020. Early impact of covid-19 on individuals with eating disorders: a survey of ~1000 individuals in the united states and the netherlands. *International Journal of Eating Disorders*. Doi: https://doi.org/10.1002/eat.23353

Thompson, B.E. and Neimeyer, R.A., 2014. *Grief and the expressive arts: Practices for creating meaning*. New York, NY: Routledge.

Van Wielink, J., Wilhelm, L. and van Geelen-Merks, D., 2019. *Loss, grief, and attachment in life transitions: a clinician's guide to secure base counseling*. New York, NY: Routledge.

Verdery, A.M. and Smith-Greenway, E., 2020. Covid-19 and family bereavement in the united states. *Applied Demography Newsletter*, 32, pp. 1–2.

Wang, Q., Xu, R. and Volkow, N.D., 2020. Increased risk of covid-19 infection and mortality in people with mental disorders: analysis from electronic health records in the united states. *World Psychiatry*. Doi: https://doi.org/10.1002/wps.20806

World Health Organization, 2019. *Prolonged grief disorder*. Available at: https://icd.who.int/browse11/l-m/en#/http://id.who.int/icd/entity/1183832314 (Accessed: 22 December 2020).

4 Physically distant but socially connected: streaming funerals, memorials and ritual design during COVID-19

Stacey Pitsillides and Jayne Wallace

> **Key points**
>
> - Digital memorials continue to be key in supporting people's bereavement following a death.
> - A range of simple technologies is being used and appropriated sensitively and creatively by funeral directors to support the bereaved and show dignity to the dead.
> - The technologies to create a more embodied presence at occasions like funerals exist but are not widely available.
> - Designers looking to contribute should focus on simple, accessible and meaningful interfaces that are specific to death and dying, embedding cultural values and supporting the agency of the bereaved.

Make do and mending: the technologies and memorials of COVID-19

In the 21st century a diverse range of approaches to using digital technologies in relation to death and grieving already exist. Online memorialisation is perhaps one of the most recognised of these. Memorials online are now an established part of building community between bereaved persons and for continued interactions with the dead (Roberts and Vidal, 2000; Refslund Christensen and Gotved, 2015). Researchers have commented on their role in increasing ties between the bereaved and connecting disparate networks of the deceased (Walter, 2015). Social media has often been the site of these memorials, introducing a range of impromptu practices that support memorialisation and moving grieving practices from private to public forums (Brubaker, Hayes and Dourish, 2013; Moore et al., 2019; Sofka, 2020). Part of their success in this context is through providing intuitive and practical ways to access the deceased after death, often becoming the centre of community thought, wishes and reflection (Roberts, 2012), as well as the means to enact continuing bonds (DeGroot, 2012; Klass and Steffen, 2017). Memorialisation gives permission for public expressions of grief that, historically, were socially hidden along with enfranchising otherwise illegitimate loss (Getty et al., 2011). It also supports the creation of social norms (Giaxoglou and Döveling, 2018) and netiquette, which includes an increased awareness of the role of the bereaved in policing sites for trolling and voyeurism (Pennington, 2013; Riechers, 2013; Sabra, 2017).

The nature of online memorials has shifted over time from simple image and text-based guest books, e.g. Virtual Memorial Gardens (Roberts, 2004), to increasingly creative practices that have given rise to new perspectives on memory and legacy (Walter et al., 2012; Lagerkvist, 2013). Memorialisation practices have always been interwoven with technology and often play with boundaries of the agency of the dead and their role in the lives of the living (Peters, 2000). However, during a global pandemic the lack of physical access to ritual practices has left a deep rift, that technology has been expected to fill. And although technologies that would make the experience of connection more embodied like telepresence, haptic interfaces, virtual and augmented reality exist, their usage is minimal. Instead, the technologies that have been used are mostly freemium services on computers and mobile phones like live-streaming, voice recording and video conferencing. These services have been appropriated hastily to fill the gaps in a 'make do and mend' approach to solving issues of presence and access around hospital visitation and attendance of funerals.

These swift technological improvisations share qualities with the 'make do and mend' ethos, which originated during WW2, where the British public was asked to be frugal and inventive with what they had in order to survive a time period of great turmoil (Hackney, 2006). Today, the UK governments' statements about their National Health Services (NHS) being on the *front line* and shortages of core equipment echo this mindset of using what comes to mind and hand, with the caveat that unlike in WW2 the government could and arguably should be better prepared in this current pandemic. That aspect aside, the positivity within the ethos of 'make do and mend' highlights the place of intuition and creativity within busy palliative care wards, where small acts of kindness, like playing a specific song or writing poetry are able to relieve some aspects of pain and suffering (Gunaratnam, 2007). This is similar to what we have seen where frantic NHS staff show care by pausing to hold a mobile phone for a patient to record final messages to their family, with some considering themselves to hold the important role of being proxies for loved ones (Hawkins, 2020; Siddique and Marsh, 2020). It is worth noting though, that although COVID-19 is a global pandemic it is not felt in the same way across the world, digital inequalities and vulnerabilities have increased as a result of the pandemic (Beaunoyer, Dupéré and Guitton, 2020). Debates around the use of technology in this chapter refer to places and sites that have relatively low levels of digital poverty and illiteracy. Having said this, in the UK 1.9 million households have no access to the internet and tens of millions more are reliant on pay-as-you-go services which limit their access (Kelly, 2020). Donations of mobile phones and tablets have been crucial to NHS wards during COVID with staff at times acting as core technical support.

This shift in the prevalence of death, dying and disease in the media and our own lives has created a unique understanding of the fragility of our medical, economic and political systems, alongside a deep global need for exploring how we can be physically distant but remain socially connected. Perhaps we can learn from cultures living in a diaspora where virtual communal practices embed traditional values (Carlson and Frazer, 2015; O'Carroll, 2014), creating an online counterpart for rituals. The use of digital memorials in disasters or crisis also sheds light on the relationship between the need to mourn and what we have to hand, where people turn to mobile technologies to create selfies-as-eulogies that nimbly share personal stories of loss, creating different forms of intimacy within a networked public (Cumiskey and Hjorth, 2017). The virtualisation of rituals is also becoming increasingly relevant for countries with land scarcity for burials and events like the Qingming Festival, where people in China visit gravesites to honour ancestors (tomb sweeping) have seen an increase in phone and online rituals (Kong, 2016) where death itself is being seen as somewhere in between the physical and the non-physical, developing the concept of spatial transcendence that may be used as a design prompt for considering an embodied response to technology-enabled rituals.

These approaches sit in stark contrast with visions of immortality and reanimation. For example, a recent documentary, launched in 2020 just prior to COVID-19 showcases the use of AI to enable a Korean mother, through a VR headset, to poignantly interact with her dead child (MBClife, 2020), while MIT Media Lab has been exploring futures where we may create digital heirs (Rahnama, n.d.) and most recently Kim Kardashian's (29 October 2020) video of her deceased father's hologram shared on Twitter[1] that she received as a 40th birthday present. These memorials show how technological developments are used to promote legacy and immortality. They support continuing interactions and perhaps even continuing bonds with the deceased but are not culturally specific in their form or accessible to wider publics. With the potential for creative bereavement weighed up against deep ethical concerns around the use of technologies to reanimate the dead and how their responses are scripted. COVID-19 has shown that rather than focusing on technological innovation as a form of immortality it is the specific experience of memorials and funerals that have mattered, alongside the collective presence of community and ability to honour the dead.

A current memorial project that has considered these factors is Unfinished Farewell. Jiabao Li and Laobai Wu (2020) used interaction design, sound, movement and fragmentation to embody the concept of engaging with and honouring the dead. By pressing the *farewell* button, you enter a digital version of a 3D room where the music changes and you are surrounded by cascading memorial statements that give the sensation of being amongst the dead. This memorial is not only sentimental but aims to document this experience of death in a pandemic collectively, particularly for those who were not included in the formal death count and may be forgotten. There is also a political aspect to the memorial whereby it aims to capture the 'information [people] posted before they passed away, which [the artists considered as] evidence they left to this era' (Figure 4.1).

The link between political agency, communication and memorialisation is well established (Schwartz, 2015) but this pandemic has shown how techno-political systems problematise this further. A prominent example of this is Dr Li Wenliang, the Wuhan doctor who became known as the COVID-19 whistle-blower. He was transformed into an icon, symbolising the political tensions in China when he died from COVID on 30 December 2019. His Sina Weibo[2] account swiftly became a virtual space for shared commemoration, conversation and critique, likened by the media to a Wailing Wall (Chenkuang, 2020) and a place for netizens to continue bonds that strike a balance between grief, political commentary and everyday encounters like referencing the Dr's love of fried chicken. However, the intangibility of digital tributes also left them vulnerable to censorship and inspection by the government. Four months after his death, the comments began to vanish, creating public outcry with 19 censored keyword combinations associated with Wenliang's account, focusing on combinations of his name with words like virus, central government or confirmed infections (Ruan, Knockel and Crete-Nishihata, 2020).

Figure 4.1 Unfinished Farewell. Concept and Direction Jiabao Li, Laobai Wu (https://www.farewell.care/?lang=en)

As this removal was done via a keyword search the comments need not be political to be removed and this left visceral gaps in chat conversations on the platform that may be deeply felt or remain undetected. The combination of Li Wenliang's identity as a whistle-blower, and the significance of citizens' contributions to his memorial, makes this contested space symbolic of the challenges of meaning making through ad-hoc memorials. However, re-purposing spaces to remember crises and make meaning is not only done through memorials or public figures. For example, the GitHub Diaries creates a repository to archive individual stories of the Chinese experience during the COVID–19 pandemic. GitHub is a code sharing platform/ social media space for programmers which was repurposed as a set of diaries that tell individual stories during COVID–19, particularly during the early stages in Wuhan (https://github.com/jiayiliujiayi/2020nCov_individual_archives) which had limited media coverage. As this is not a memorial nor linked to any famous figure it is able to weave together stories, which include encounters with the dead, to provide momentary snippets of what it was like to be at the centre of where the pandemic began.

Funeral Directors' creative uses of communication technologies and presence

Although it is clear that online memorials have found a place in our digital culture, these memorials have mostly been shown to augment rather than replace other forms of ritualisation, like a funeral, unless the bereaved only knew the person online (Haverinen, 2014; Elliot, 2020). COVID-19 has changed this by removing much of the in-person contact, limiting access to funerals and human touch. In contrast to memorials, live-streaming funerals have been less readily taken up prior to COVID-19. Some funeral homes have been reticent to introduce technologies into their establishments seeing the web-casting of funerals as challenging the traditional importance placed on presence (Nansen et al., 2017) despite the fact that organisations like the International Cemetery, Cremation and Funeral Association (https://iccfa.com/) have historically shown their support for webcasting, asserting in 2010 that this offering should be seen as best practice (De Vries and Moldaw, 2012). During the pandemic, social media has been used by funeral directors to share transparent reflections with the community on how COVID-19 has changed their practice. Louise Winter, founder of Poetic Endings (https://www.poetic-endings.com/) and Hasina Zamin, co-founder and CEO of Compassionate Funerals (https://www.compassionatefunerals.co.uk/) are two examples of this. Their use of live reflection spaces on Facebook is important as they reach a wide audience and allow people to ask questions within the live stream that provide public education and support on UK funerals during COVID.

Louise Winter[3] and Joanna Shears's Facebook live discussion (14 May 2020) focused on how the dead can be honoured in new ways during COVID-19 and the shifting role of celebrants as less, or no family are able to be physically present at a funeral, with celebrants becoming powerful proxies and mediators (Turner and Caswell, 2020). Some of the themes covered include: how using *mobile technologies* with the bereaved can feel isolating due to the lack of body language; the shifting landscape of *guidance and restrictions* where critical questions of whose role it is to police these events, e.g. venue, funeral director or police come into play; and managing the *emotions* of family members many of whom last saw their loved ones being collected by an ambulance. With no viewings, washing or dressings they describe the profound effect on the bereaved, leaving people questioning the reality of death and even struggling to believe who is being put into the grave, showing how strongly corpses are material signifiers of memory and identity (Hallam and Hockey, 2001). Funerals are often the time for the bereaved to take back control after a death but limitations during the pandemic mean that expectations of involvement and participation have been forced to shift.

In terms of design, Poetic Endings have focused on simplifying funerals in order to stop the family planning in one reality only for policy to change. Therefore, ceremonies must be small and meaningful, with a focus on distilling the essence of the person and creative approaches like setting a place at the funeral for people who are not there, led by family members. There is a distinct lack of prominent death-styles (Davies, 2015), with no limos and people struggling to get flowers in the early stages of the pandemic. In a similar response to a lack of technologies described in the previous section a lack of flowers led to people bringing a single bloom from their garden or to creating something handmade out of paper to adorn the coffin. Showing how thoughtfulness and creativity can remain at the core, when other forms of consumerism are absent (Cann, 2017). Objects also begin to play a key role for absent family, for example, in Winter and Shears's funeral preparations during the live-stream personal letters, apples, rosemary and roses were put within the grave by celebrants.

Facebook was also used to share experiences of Muslim funeral director Hasina Zaman[4] during COVID: (15 October 2020). She describes the challenges of having to sharply increase capacity from 10–12 funerals a month to around 60 enquiries, resulting in 10–15 phone calls a day with the newly bereaved. Compassionate Funerals also had to shift their business, becoming predominantly a mortuary space in the early stages of the pandemic. Despite the swift changes, the mortuary space was essential to upholding the Muslim values of caring for the dead in a respectful manner. Burials were conducted with care but also in haste, in order to provide space for new bodies and to support the needs of the community. Similar to Poetic Endings, there were challenges and sacrifices to be made; these included no open coffins, washing or shrouding. Another sacrifice was having no contact with clients, only via Whatsapp, Zoom or telephone. This was supplemented with ad-hoc practices like live-streaming of the deceased's face with people crying on the phone as they viewed the person who had died. This was particularly important for the bereaved as many struggled to find their loved ones in the bureaucratic systems – with funeral directors collaborating with medical staff, coroners, and the police to swiftly locate the bodies for family – who worried that they had been cremated due to policy-led discussions about mandatory cremation (Kartal, 2020).

A follow-up discussion[5] was conducted with Zaman, where she describes in more depth how shifts during the pandemic required the team to consider how to balance restrictions, while still retaining their core value of compassion and the ways that technology has enabled them to do this. Firstly, the pandemic created a demand for live-streaming that was not previously there. Compassionate Funerals explored a range of streaming services including Google Meet, Facebook Live and Zoom, which were used to record and live-streamed via phone. Although these services were free and easy to use there was no guarantee about the quality of recording, sound or stability of wi-fi. Therefore, they began experimenting with a range of paid services, some of which were also unreliable or unsuitable. For example, she recounts one occasion where an employee recording the service was dressed inappropriately and did not understand the nuances of the funeral sector. Following this experience, the team decided to preference services that have been designed sensitively for this sector, e.g. https://www.funeralstreaming.co.uk/, which allow the bereaved to have a picture and send in eulogies among other customisable features, but which comes with a cost of around £800–£1000. However, with privacy concerns and personal touches on people's mind most clients that could afford it did opt for this.

The cremation services companies Obtius (https://www.obitus.com/) and Wesley Media (https://www.wesleymedia.co.uk/) are both established players within many crematoriums, due to their music licensing business, but during the pandemic shifted the core of their offering to webcasting services which support high-quality audio-visual set-ups. Design-wise, it is easier to record in crematoria than in churches that have large echoey spaces and burial grounds which are outdoors and have challenges with wi-fi. Something worth emphasising in relation to the make-do and mend approach, within the context of *funeral technology*, is how difficult and heartbreaking it can be for the family when the live-streams do not work. The usability of these services also emphasises issues of technological access and digital inequalities (Beaunoyer, Dupéré and Guitton, 2020). This is why there is a trend within many funeral services in the pandemic towards professional live streaming and recording (Thorp, 2020), particularly when it occurs across continents and a lot of technical support is required. An example of this from Compassionate Funerals is in August 2020 when a family connected across all continents, with six children in distributed spaces sending in eulogies via a file which were then played on a large screen and the bereaved were able to view themselves on the live-stream giving their eulogies. This double viewing helps to support the bereaveds' need for meaning making during COVID funerals. As stated by Burrell and Selman

(2020, p.32) 'the benefit of after-death rituals including funerals depends on the ability of the bereaved to shape those rituals and say goodbye in a way which is meaningful for them, and on whether the funeral demonstrates social support for the bereaved' and in this section we can see how technology is both able to support and hinder this.

Free services can also be used in ways that do not require streaming. Zaman has found the use of Whatsapp to be key in showing the bereaved, the body in the morgue and sharing videos instead of a traditional viewing. Attendees of these viewings use this to perform rituals where they are shown the person's face (if the casket is open) and are able to send prayers. There have also been funerals where people would drive in to hold their phones out and record the service from a distance at public cemeteries. In cases where families cannot afford professional live-streaming services sometimes they will do the streaming themselves, but this is challenging unless someone finds meaning in having that role and a sense of agency in the process of communicating with the rest of the family. Having said this the available services do sometimes have unexpected benefits for the bereaved with poignant descriptions of Facebook Live funerals, which allowed the family to have a parallel commentary to the service, creating a very different type of connection to one that would take place in a traditional ceremony, where the use of mobile phones would be seen as disrespectful. This experience allowed the family to feel more collective then in real time and may be one of the principles we can use when thinking about the design of services. This use of social media as a real time connection through death can be a way for isolated individuals to take care of themselves and others as 'a network of obligations and services to the soul' (Foucault, 1988, p. 27). In addition to more formal routes of recording and sharing there are also personal sharings of the funerals via twitter and Instagram stories used for those at a distance. Examples of the things typically captured include images of eating cake; flowers; or an image of the person with the casket. In response to the lack of reception that typically follows the funerals, there has been an increase of food and drink being consumed at the graveside, which supports the inclusion of the person being buried into these rituals. The team at Compassionate Funerals are also exploring how the pandemic will change the future of their services, aware that young people are keen on the use of these technologies and would like to use this experience to invest in the future of recorded funerals which they believe are here to stay.

What could technology do?

Expanding the context, beyond memorialisation and experiencing funerals digitally, online environments provide new opportunities for coping with grief (Getty et al., 2011; Kasket, 2019). There are many examples of how social media sites are used as ways to journal grief journeys (Marshall, 2020) or make sense of feelings in grief (Say_goodbye_and_cry, 2020) as well as ways to offer personal support to others (Chaney, 2020), to normalise grief (Thegriefgang, 2020), or to build wider forums for bereavement support (Thegriefpad, 2020; Thegriefcase, 2020; Communitygriefsupport, 2020). Gurrieri and Drenten (2019) highlight that in countries where traditional social support structures break down many people turn to social media sites to seek comfort, advice, emotional support and use it as a way to externalise and share lived experiences.

Digital technologies can, of course, be utilised in more broad, physical and embodied ways. Some of the most seemingly meaningful examples in the context of death and bereavement have arisen from serendipitous use of digital technologies. Player Two (Wikstrom, 2016), for example, is a short film based on the real-life experience of 00WARTHERAPY00 (username) who commented on a YouTube video about whether videogames can be a spiritual experience (PBS Game/Show 2014):

> Well, when I was 4, my dad bought a trusty XBox. you know, the first, ruggedy, blocky one from 2001. We had tons and tons and tons of fun playing all kinds of games together – until he died, when I was just 6. I couldn't touch that console for 10 years.
> But once I did, I noticed something.
> We used to play a racing game, Rally Sports Challenge, actually pretty awesome for the time it came.
> And once I started meddling around... I found a GHOST.
> Literally.
> You know, when a time race happens, that the fastest lap so far gets recorded as a ghost driver? yep, you guessed it – his ghost still rolls around the track today.
> And so I played and played, and played, until I was almost able to beat the ghost. until one day I got ahead of it, I surpassed it, and...~
> I stopped right in front of the finish line, just to ensure I wouldn't delete it.
> Bliss.
> 00WARTHERAPY00 2014 https://www.youtube.com/watch?v=vK91 LAiMOio

Inadvertently the Xbox enabled 00WARTHERAPY00 to experience the co-presence of their father again, but perhaps more significantly, beyond facilitating embodied memories of playing the game together the ghost car supported an enlivened, new, dynamic experience. It enabled a new exchange akin to a form of dialogue for 00WARTHERAPY00 with their father from the vantage point of being ten years older, and all the emotions and intentionality that comes with that. The fact that 00WARTHERAPY00 chose not to beat their father's best time in order to keep his ghost car active testifies to the value they perceived in what the game was affording.

Echoes of this story can be seen in the reports of a bereaved brother finding a rare example of a Pokémon – Pikachu – on the grave of his younger brother when playing Pokémon Go (Tan, 2016) in 2016. The perceived significance of this was heightened for the bereaved brother because Pikachu had been his sibling's favourite figure and childhood character. There is internet speculation as to the validity of this story, but regardless of this it is an example of how technology can create layered and meaningful experiences for the bereaved connecting digital content to embodiments of the deceased and acting as proxies as well as providing suggestions of messages or symbols from or of the deceased.

Picking up on the questioned validity of the Pokémon story above we wanted to mention an example where technology has not needed to be 'working' in order to provide people with a means to feel a profound connection to deceased people, the mere suggestion and symbolism of a technology has come to embody and enable connectivity. The Wind Telephone in Otsuchi, Japan made by Itaru Sasaki in 2010 (Cuddon and Galer, 2019). Atlas Obscura (2020) after the death of a relative is a replica of a telephone booth housing a disconnected black rotary telephone. Located in his hilltop garden it was something he made for himself initially as a means to speak to his dead relative and to help him with his own grief. In 2011, Japan experienced an earthquake, tsunami and nuclear power plant disaster causing widespread death and 10% of the inhabitants of Otsuchi died. Thousands of people used the disconnected phone to dial a relative's number and speak to them. There is no trickery involved, the phone cable sits by its side and is clearly not connected. Nevertheless, people continue to use it and find comfort from speaking into it. The Wind Telephone exemplifies how powerful technology can be in symbolising or embodying connectivity to such an extent that people relate to the poetry and possibility of that and suspend their disbelief in order to gain comfort and feel a closeness to the people they are grieving.

There have also been purposeful examples of creative and sensitive pieces of academic research from Design and HCI fields that offer nuanced and rich ways to engage in practices around death and bereavement. Examples include design for looking back and on physical/digital memorials (Banks, 2011; Odom et al., 2018; Graham et al., 2015; Massimi and Baecker, 2010; Moncur and Waller, 2010; Moncur et al., 2015; Uriu and Okude, 2010; Walter, 2015; Jarvis, 2009), technology heirlooms (Kirk and Banks, 2008; Odom et al., 2012; Banks, Kirk and Sellen, 2012), mixed reality and narratives between the bereaved and the deceased in cemetery locations (Dow et al., 2005); new forms of legacy for the dead (Pitsillides, 2019; Moncur and Kirk, 2014), time loss and change in relation to new media (Schorr, 2014), design perspectives on phases of letting go (Odom et al., 2010; Sas, Whittaker, and Zimmerman, 2016; Sas, 2020), photographs and living on (Graham, 2015), thanatosensitivity (Massimi and Charise, 2009) and the value of continuing bonds (Getty et al., 2011; Ataguba, 2018; Wallace et al., 2018; Wallace et al., 2019; Wallace et al., 2020a; Wallace et al., 2020b).

Noteworthy examples in relation to the COVID-19 context are Fenestra (Odom et al., 2018) and Cremation Vessels (Jarvis, 2009). Fenestra offers an example of what a digital home altar could be, exemplifying how digital photos could support everyday practices of honouring the dead and how personal rituals can mesh physical (the flickering of a candle) and digital materials in sensitive ways. In the context of COVID-19 such designs, networked across family members could provide the aesthetic and human dimension to digital interfaces that people have struggled to find through laptop screens. Jarvis' non-digital proposals speak to embodiment and materiality in fascinating and poetic ways, whether finding ways to engage with 'letting go' through her sculptural bird feeders that are made from bird food and cremated human remains to allow the deceased to return to nature over time and to provide sustenance to other beings along that journey, or her pencil boxes that house pencils made from a person's remains (approx. 240 pencils) – the use of the pencils offering a form of cherishing the person and slowly letting them go as you write and the pencil box housing a sharpener that catches all of the shavings becoming an urn once all of the pencils have been used. In the context of COVID-19, where there have been enforced cremations, distancing from the deceased's body and lack of physicality in general often leading to difficulties in accepting the death, design ideas such as these could offer gentle and poetic ways to bring the body of the deceased back into the home and personal space of the bereaved. The challenge here is that these ideas and design artefacts are not productised and not available to the public to experience and the reality within the COVID-19 pandemic has been one of utilising the digital devices and apps that are commonplace.

Conclusion: design directions for COVID-19

COVID-19 has forced people to confront death while simultaneously upending all the usual ways we process loss, the paradox being that people 'are more aware of death and grieving, yet less available to help others through it' (Ohlheiser, 2020). We have been dealt a design challenge that shows a lack of simple, accessible and specific interfaces for supporting a meaningful death and bereavement during a pandemic. This can be seen as a call to action to develop accessible and affordable technologies and social systems that include appropriate netiquette built into their core communities (Sofka, 2020). It shows the role of design researchers in the field of thanatosensitive design (Massimi, 2014) is to investigate the ways that these technologies blend within people's homes and personal experiences of loss in ways that are not dominated by market needs. By focusing on providing opportunities for meaning making through bespoke objects and experiences, we consider how the pandemic has created new opportunities to evaluate the role of technologies at the end of life. Grief during the pandemic has made us face fundamental questions of how to live with trauma and face mortality and how the arts and humanities can be the driving force that helps us to make sense of the world again (Yancy, 2020). The use of communication technologies in settings like churches, burial grounds and crematoriums also offer design spaces and evolving business models that could provide more embodied encounters with the dead when physically distant.

Notes

1 Original tweet: https://twitter.com/KimKardashian/status/1321955644736303104?ref_src=twsrc%5Etfw%7Ctwcamp%5Etweetembed%7Ctwterm%5E1321955644736303104%7Ctwgr%5Eshare_3&ref_url=https%3A%2F%2Fwww.bbc.co.uk%2Fnews%2Fentertainment-arts-54731382 last accessed 10 Nov 2020.
2 Sina Weibo is one of the largest microblogging platforms in China with 430 million active users a month in 2018 (https://www.nytimes.com/2018/11/19/fashion/china-social-media-weibo-wechat.html).
3 Permission has been granted to share this link to the Facebook recorded conversation: https://www.facebook.com/misslouisewinter/videos/2963599540420422 and for it to be used within this research.
4 Permission has been granted to share this link to the Facebook recorded conversation: https://www.facebook.com/groups/104742819300/permalink/10159261195804301 and for it to be used within this research.
5 The discussion was conducted via Zoom (22 Oct 2020) and instigated by Hasina Zamin based on the author's request to use the material from Facebook. The content has been paraphrased from this conversation and approved by the interviewee prior to publication.

References

Ataguba, G., 2018. Towards an evaluation of mobile life logging technologies and storytelling in socio-personal grieving spaces. In Proceedings of the 2018 ACM International Joint Conference and 2018 International Symposium on *Pervasive and Ubiquitous Computing and Wearable Computers* (pp. 5–8).
Atlas Obscura, 2020. Wind Telephone. Available at: https://www.atlasobscura.com/places/wind-telephone#:~:text=Sasaki%20opened%20his%20kaze%20no,pilgrimage%20from%20around%20the%20country (Accessed: 21 October 2020).
Banks, R., 2011. *The future of looking back* (Microsoft Research). Unterschleissheim, Germany: Microsoft Press.
Banks, R., Kirk, D. and Sellen, A., 2012. A design perspective on three technology heirlooms. *Human–Computer Interaction*, 27(1–2), pp. 63–91.
Beaunoyer, E., Dupéré, S. and Guitton, M.J., 2020. COVID-19 and digital inequalities: reciprocal impacts and mitigation strategies. *Computers in Human Behavior*, 111, p. 106424.
Brubaker, J.R., Hayes, G.R. and Dourish, P., 2013. Beyond the grave: Facebook as a site for the expansion of death and mourning. *The Information Society*, 29(3), pp. 152–163.
Burrell, A. and Selman, L.E. 2020. How do funeral practices impact bereaved relatives' mental health, grief and bereavement? A mixed methods review with implications for COVID-19. *OMEGA-Journal of Death and Dying*. Doi: 10.1177/0030222820941296.

Cann, C.K., 2017. Buying an afterlife: mapping the social impact of religious beliefs through consumer death goods. *Religions*, 8(9), pp. 167–180.

Carlson, B. and Frazer, R., 2015. "It's like Going to a Cemetery and Lighting a Candle": Aboriginal Australians, Sorry Business and social media. *AlterNative: An International Journal of Indigenous Peoples*, 11(3), pp. 211–224.

Chaney, A. (2020) Instagram. Available at: https://www.instagram.com/deathmidwifeabby/ (Accessed: 13 November 2020).

Chenkuang, H., 2020. 'Online wailing wall': How Chinese netizens continue to honor Li Wenliang, COVID-19 whistleblower. SupChina. Available at: https://supchina.com/2020/03/31/chinese-netizens-continue-to-honor-li-wenliang-covid-19/ (Accessed: 5 November 2020).

Communitygriefsupport, 2020 Instagram. Available at: https://www.instagram.com/communitygriefsupport/ (Accessed: 13 November 2020).

Cuddon, S. and Galer, S.S., 2019. BBC. Japan's phone to the dead. Available at: https://www.bbc.co.uk/programmes/p07cj0h3 (Accessed: 21 October 2020).

Cumiskey, K.M. and Hjorth, L., 2017. *Haunting hands: mobile media practices and loss*. New York: Oxford University Press.

Davies, D.J., 2015. *Mors Britannica: lifestyle & death-style in Britain Today*. Oxford: Oxford University Press.

Degroot, J.M., 2012. Maintaining relational continuity with the deceased on Facebook. *OMEGA-Journal of Death and Dying*, 65(3), pp. 195–212.

De Vries, B. and Moldaw, S., 2012. Virtual memorials and cyber funerals: contemporary expressions of ageless experiences. In Sofka, C., Gilbert, K. and Noppe, I., (eds.), *Dying, death, and grief in an online universe. For counselors and educators*. New York, NY: Springer Publishing Company, pp. 135–148.

Dow, S., Lee, J., Oezbek, C., MacIntyre, B., Bolter, J.D. and Gandy, M., 2005. Exploring spatial narratives and mixed reality experiences in Oakland Cemetery. In Proceedings of the 2005 ACM SIGCHI International Conference on *Advances in computer entertainment technology* (pp. 51–60).

Elliot, K.J., 2020. 'Final Fantasy' gamers hold online funeral for player who died of COVID-19. Global News. Available at: https://globalnews.ca/news/6832247/coronavirus-video-game-funeral/ (Accessed: 5 November 2020).

Foucault, M., 1988. Technologies of the Self. In Martin, L., Gutman, H. and Hutton, P. (eds.), *Technologies of the Self: a seminar with Michel Foucault*. Amherst, Massachusetts: University of Massachusetts Press.

Getty, E., Cobb, J., Gabeler, M., Nelson, C., Weng, E. and Hancock, J., 2011. I said your name in an empty room: grieving and continuing bonds on facebook. In Proceedings of the SIGCHI Conference on *human factors in computing systems* (pp. 997–1000).

Giaxoglou, K. and Döveling, K., 2018. Mediatization of emotion on social media: forms and norms in digital mourning practices. *Social Media+ Society*, 4(1), p. 2056305117744393.

Gotved, S., 2014. Research review: death online-alive and kicking!. *Thanatos*, 3(1/2014). pp. 112–126.

Graham, C., 2015. The photograph reaches out: uses of photographs of the dead in China. *Mortality*, 20(4), pp. 351–374.

Graham, C., Arnold, M., Kohn, T. and Gibbs, M.R., 2015. Gravesites and websites: a comparison of memorialisation. *Visual Studies*, 30(1), pp. 37–53.

Gunaratnam, Y., 2007. Where is the love? Art, aesthetics and research. *Journal of Social Work Practice*, 21(3), pp. 271–287.

Gurrieri, L. and Drenten, J., 2019. Visual storytelling and vulnerable health care consumers: normalising practices and social support through Instagram. *Journal of Services Marketing*, 33(6), pp. 702–720.

Hackney, F., 2006. 'Use Your Hands for Happiness': home craft and make-do-and-mend in British Women's Magazines in the 1920s and 1930s. *Journal of Design History*, 19(1), pp. 23–38.

Hallam, E. and Hockey, J., 2001. *Death, memory and material culture*. Oxford: Berg Publishers.

Haverinen, A., 2014. In-game and out-of-game mourning: on the complexity of grief in virtual worlds. In Christensen, D. and Sandvik, K. (eds.), *Mediating and re-mediating death and dying*. Surrey: Ashgate Publishing Limited, pp. 155–174.

Hawkins, J., 2020. NHS staff lend their phones to dying coronavirus patients to say final goodbyes. Mirror. Available at: https://www.mirror.co.uk/news/uk-news/nhs-staff-lend-phones-dying-21828361 (Accessed: 6 November 2020).

Jarvis, N., 2009. Nadine Jarvis: challenging post mortem traditions. The Daily Undertaker. Available at: http://www.dailyundertaker.com/2009/02/nadine-jarvis-post-mortem.html (Accessed: 13 November 2020).

Kartal, A.G., 2020. COVID-19:UK's faith groups react to mandatory cremation. Anadolou Agency. Available at: https://www.aa.com.tr/en/europe/covid-19uks-faith-groups-react-to-mandatory-cremation/1776042 (Accessed: 9 November 2020).

Kasket, E., 2019. *All the ghosts in the machine: illusions of immortality in the digital age*. London, UK: Robinson.

Kelly, A., 2020. Digital divide 'isolates and endangers' millions of UK's poorest. The Guardian. Available at: https://www.theguardian.com/world/2020/apr/28/digital-divide-isolates-and-endangers-millions-of-uk-poorest. (Accessed: 9 December 2020).

Kirk, D. and Banks, R., 2008. On the design of technology heirlooms. In *SIMTech'08*. Microsoft Research, Cambridge 20–21 Nov 2008.

Klass, D. and Steffen, E.M. (eds.), 2017. *Continuing bonds in bereavement: new directions for research and practice*. New York, NY: Routledge.

Kong, L., 2016. No-place, new places: death and its rituals in urban Asia. In Waghorne, J. (ed.), *Place/no-place in urban Asian religiosity*. Singapore: Springer, pp. 49–70.

Lagerkvist, A., 2013. New memory cultures and death: existential security in the digital memory ecology. *Thanatos*, 2(2), pp. 1–17.

Li, J. and Wu, L., 2020. *Unfinished Farewell*. Available at: https://www.farewell.care/?lang=en. (Accessed: 8 December 2020).

Marshall, N., 2020. Instagram #GriefAndGrace Available at: https://www.instagram.com/nicolamarshall.griefandgrace/?hl=en (Accessed: 13 November 2020).

Massimi, M., 2014. Stories from my thanatosensitive design process. *Interactions*, 21(1), pp. 47–49.

Massimi, M. and Baecker, R.M., 2010. A death in the family: opportunities for designing technologies for the bereaved. In Proceedings of the SIGCHI Conference on *Human Factors in computing systems* (pp. 1821–1830).

Massimi, M. and Charise, A., 2009. Dying, death, and mortality: towards thanatosensitivity in HCI. In CHI'09 Extended Abstracts on *Human Factors in Computing Systems* (pp. 2459–2468).

MBClife, 2020. [VR휴먼다큐멘터리 - 너를 만났다] 세상 떠난 딸과 VR로 재회한 모녀 | '엄마 안 울게. 그리워하지 않고 더 사랑할게' (ENG/SPA subbed). YouTube. Available at: https://www.youtube.com/watch?v=uflTK8c4w0c&t=176s (Accessed: 6 November 2020).

Moore, J., Magee, S., Gamreklidze, E. and Kowalewski, J., 2019. Social media mourning: using grounded theory to explore how people grieve on social networking sites. *OMEGA-Journal of Death and Dying*, 79(3), pp. 231–259.

Moncur, W. and Kirk, D., 2014. An emergent framework for digital memorials. In Proceedings of the 2014 conference on *Designing interactive systems* (pp. 965–974).

Moncur, W. and Waller, A., 2010. Digital inheritance. In Proceedings of the RCUK Digital Futures Conference, ACM, Nottingham, UK.

Moncur, W., Julius, M., Van Den Hoven, E. and Kirk, D., 2015. *Story Shell: the participatory design of a bespoke digital memorial.* In Proceedings of 4th Participatory Innovation Conference (pp. 470–477).

Nansen, B., Kohn, T., Arnold, M., van Ryn, L. and Gibbs, M., 2017. Social media in the funeral industry: On the digitization of grief. *Journal of Broadcasting & Electronic Media*, 61(1), pp. 73–89.

O'Carroll, A.D., 2014. Kanohi kit e kanohi – A thing of the past? Examining the notion of "virtual" ahikā and the implications for kanohi kit e kanohi. *Pimatisiwin: A Journal of Aboriginal & Indigenous Community Health*, 11(3). pp. 441–455.

Odom, W., Harper, R., Sellen, A., Kirk, D. and Banks, R., 2010. Passing on & putting to rest: understanding bereavement in the context of interactive technologies. In Proceedings of the SIGCHI Conference on *Human Factors in computing systems* (pp. 1831–1840).

Odom, W., Banks, R., Kirk, D., Harper, R., Lindley, S. and Sellen, A., 2012. Technology heirlooms? Considerations for passing down and inheriting digital materials. In Proceedings of the SIGCHI Conference on *Human Factors in computing systems* (pp. 337–346).

Odom, W., Uriu, D., Kirk, D., Banks, R. and Wakkary, R., 2018. Experiences in designing technologies for honoring deceased loved ones. *Design Issues*, 34(1), pp. 54–66.

Ohlheiser, A., 2020. The lonely reality of Zoom funerals. MIT Technology Review. Available at: https://www.technologyreview.com/2020/04/13/999348/covid-19-grief-zoom-funerals/ (Accessed: 9 November 2020).

PBS Game/Show, 2014. Youtube. Available at: https://www.youtube.com/watch?v=vK91LAiMOio (Accessed: 21 October 2020).

Pennington, N., 2013. You don't de-friend the dead: an analysis of grief communication by college students through Facebook profiles. *Death Studies*, 37(7), pp. 617–635.

Peters, J.D., 2000. *Speaking into the air: a history of the idea of communication.* Chicago: University of Chicago Press.

Pitsillides, S., 2019. Digital legacy: designing with things. *Death Studies*, 43(7), pp. 426–434.

Rahnama, H., n.d. Project Overview ‹ Augmented Eternity and Swappable Identities –. MIT Media Lab. Available at: https://www.media.mit.edu/projects/augmented-eternity/overview/ (Accessed: 10 November 2020).

Refslund Christensen, D. and Gotved, S., 2015. Online memorial culture: an introduction. *New Review of Hypermedia and Multimedia*, 21(1–2), pp. 1–9.

Riechers, A., 2013. The persistence of memory online: digital memorials, fantasy, and grief as entertainment. In Maciel C. and Pereira V. (eds.), *Digital legacy and interaction: post-mortem issues*. Cham: Springer, pp. 49–61.

Roberts, P., 1999. Tangible sorrow, virtual tributes: cemeteries in cyberspace. In deVries, B. (ed.), *End of life issues: interdisciplinary and multidisciplinary perspectives*. New York: Springer, pp. 337–358.

Roberts, P. and Vidal, L.A., 2000. Perpetual care in cyberspace: a portrait of memorials on the web. *OMEGA-Journal of Death and Dying*, 40(4), pp. 521–545.

Roberts, P., 2004. The living and the dead: community in the virtual cemetery. *OMEGA-journal of Death and Dying*, 49(1), pp. 57–76.

Roberts, P., 2012. '2 people like this': mourning according to format. *Bereavement Care*, 31(2), pp. 55–61.

Ruan, L., Knockel, J. and Crete-Nishihata, M., 2020. Censored contagion: how information on the Coronavirus is managed on Chinese social media. The Citizen Lab. Available at: https://citizenlab.ca/2020/03/censored-contagion-how-information-on-the-coronavirus-is-managed-on-chinese-social-media/ (Accessed: 5 November 2020).

Sabra, J.B., 2017. "I hate when they do that!" Netiquette in mourning and memorialization among Danish Facebook users. *Journal of Broadcasting & Electronic Media*, 61(1), pp. 24–40.

Sas, C., Whittaker, S. and Zimmerman, J., 2016. Design for rituals of letting go: An embodiment perspective on disposal practices informed by grief therapy. *ACM Transactions on Computer-Human Interaction (TOCHI)*, 23(4), pp. 1–37.

Sas, C., 2020. Thanatosensitive design exemplars for embodied experience of non-attachment. Available at: https://enablingongoingness.com/Workshop-Papers (Accessed: 13 November 2020).

Say_goodbye_and_cry, 2020. Instagram. Available at: https://www.instagram.com/say_goodbye_and_cry/ (Accessed: 13 November 2020).

Schorr, S., 2014. The Bereavement Project: picturing time and loss through photographs in the landscape of new media. In Christensen, D. and Sandvik, K. (eds.), *Mediating and remediating death and dying*. Surrey: Ashgate Publishing Limited, pp. 75–91.

Siddique, H. and Marsh, S., 2020. Coronavirus: Britons saying final goodbyes to dying relatives by videolink. The Guardian. Available at: https://www.theguardian.com/world/2020/mar/24/britons-saying-final-goodbyes-to-dying-relatives-by-videolink-covid-19 (Accessed: 6 November 2020).

Sofka, C.J., 1997. Social support "internetworks," caskets for sale, and more: thanatology and the information superhighway. *Death Studies*, 21(6), pp. 553–574.

Sofka, C., 2020. Netiquette regarding digital legacies and dealing with death, tragedy, and grief. Available at: https://www.siena.edu/files/resources/netiquette-social-media-and-grief.pdf. (Accessed: 21 December 2020).

Schwartz, M., 2015. *Dead matter: the meaning of Iconic corpses*. Minneapolis, MN: University of Minnesota Press.

Tan, A., 2016. Mashable. Available at: https://mashable.com/2016/07/14/pikachu-on-grave/?europe=true (Accessed: 21 October 2020).

Thegriefcase, 2020. Instagram. Available at: https://www.instagram.com/thegriefcase/ (Accessed: 13 November 2020).

Thegriefgang, 2020. Instagram. Available at: https://www.instagram.com/thegriefgang/ (Accessed: 13 November 2020).

Thegriefpad, 2020. Instagram. Available at: https://www.instagram.com/thegriefpad/ (Accessed: 13 November 2020).

Thorp, A., 2020. Coronavirus: 'I used to film weddings but now I film funerals'. BBC News. Available at: https://www.bbc.co.uk/news/av/uk-england-leicestershire-54292982 (Accessed: 9 November 2020).

Turner, N. and Caswell, G., 2020. A relative absence: exploring professional experiences of funerals without mourners. *OMEGA-Journal of Death and Dying.* Doi: 10.1177/0030222820959960.

Uriu, D. and Okude, N., 2010. ThanatoFenestra: photographic family altar supporting a ritual to pray for the deceased. In Proceedings of the 8th ACM Conference on *Designing Interactive Systems* (pp. 422–425).

Wallace, J., Thomas, J., Anderson, D. and Olivier, P., 2018. Mortality as framed by ongoingness in digital design. *Design Issues*, 34(1), pp. 95–107.

Wallace, J., Koulidou, N., Duncan, T., Lawson, S., Trueman, J., Craig, C., Fisher, H., Morrissey, K., Montague, K. and Welch, D., 2019. 'Blueprints' physical to digital: curation of media to support ongoingness. RTD2019.

Wallace, J., Montague, K., Duncan, T., Carvalho, L.P., Koulidou, N., Mahoney, J., Morrissey, K., Craig, C., Groot, L., Lawson, S., Olivier, P., Trueman, J. and Fisher, H., 2020a. ReFind: design, lived experience and ongoingness in bereavement. In Proceedings of the 2020 CHI Conference on *Human Factors in Computing Systems* (pp. 1–12).

Wallace, J., Odom, W., Montague, K., Koulidou, N., Sas, C., Morrissey, K. and Olivier, P., 2020b. HCI at End of Life & Beyond. In Extended Abstracts of the 2020 CHI Conference on *Human Factors in Computing Systems* (pp. 1–8).

Walter, T., Hourizi, R., Moncur, W. and Pitsillides, S., 2012. Does the internet change how we die and mourn? Overview and analysis. *OMEGA-Journal of Death and Dying*, 64(4), pp. 275–302.

Walter, T., 2015. New mourners, old mourners: Online memorial culture as a chapter in the history of mourning. *New Review of Hypermedia and Multimedia*, 21(1–2), pp. 10–24.

Wikstrom, J., 2016. Youtube. Available at: https://www.youtube.com/watch?v=gCtSgb-b7zg (Accessed: 21 October 2020).

Yancy, G., 2020. Judith Butler: Mourning Is a Political Act. Available at: tinyurl.com/y87vqa59 (Accessed: 13 November 2020).

5 Social death in 2020: Covid-19, which lives matter and which deaths count?

Jana Králová

Key points

- The UK's government in/actions during the Covid-19 pandemic impose social death on some individuals, groups and populations. Some of whom will die because of social causes of death, that is social death. This may, or may not, be accompanied by the Covid-19.
- Social death theory challenges the definition of *avoidable mortality* of the Organisation for Economic Co-operation and Development (OECD). Its conceptual robustness is called into the question due to lack of its capacity to encompass social realities of avoidable deaths.
- The use of the International Classification of Disease (ICD) for classifying causes of death is called into question due to its lack of capacity to encompass social realities of death and dying. This includes its use by the UK Office of National Statistics (ONS) and raises the broader question of how mortality is measured.
- To expose considerable analytical power of social death theory the three major schools of thought slavery, death studies and genocide are introduced along with their exceptions. Together, they reveal social causes of death, the social death.
- Impact of inadequate UK governmental policy on Black, Asian and minority ethnic and on the residents of care homes during the Covid-19 pandemic are used as examples of 'death by social causes', the social death.
- The chapter is conceptual; its interpretations may be challenged and will benefit from empirical testing in the future.

Introduction

Eventually, when comprehensive data about the acute respiratory syndrome coronavirus 2 (SARS-CoV-2, henceforth Covid-19) will be available, it will become apparent that many individuals, groups and populations died not only due to the virus itself (although some have), but also due to *social death*. That is due to the inadequacy and in/actions of the UK governmental policy and its impact on specific individuals, groups and populations.

We may question the reliability of sources suggesting that Sagrada Família's architect Antoni Gaudí died unnecessarily due to being mistaken for a beggar and consequently receiving basic care usually reserved for the poorest of the poor (Tarragona, 2014). However, we should not doubt that the *perceived value of the human being* determines the quality of life they are able to achieve and quality of care they may receive (Moller, 2004). Human value can be reduced by, for example, structural violence (Farmer et al., 2004; Hamed et al., 2020), social suffering (Renault, 2010; Rylko-Bauer and Farmer, 2016), compromised resilience (Dagdeviren, Donoghue and Promberger, 2016) and inconsequential agency (Gilleard and Higgs, 2011; Weissbrodt and Divine, 2015; Wrenn, 2014).

Social death, in the context of this argument and further supported by following evidence, is defined as vital relational harm caused to the individual, or group, or population which has a lasting and adverse impact on their ontology and as such, poses a direct threat to their social vitality. It may be achieved through impairments on a combination of the core components of social death: social identity, social connections, legal identity, wealth and the body. This has a lasting and at times cross-generational effect on their relationality and their structural possibility.

Worldwide, deaths in relation to Covid-19 are quantified, by counting the deaths of people who test positive (before or after their death), the deaths of people suspected to have Covid-19 (based on symptoms or those that are epidemiologically linked), or excess deaths, that is additional deaths compared with those in the same weeks in previous years (Comas-Herrera et al., 2020).

In 2017 an Organisation for Economic Co-operation and Development (OECD) working group aimed to define *avoidable mortality*. The group defines avoidable mortality through two key terms, 'preventable mortality' and 'treatable or amendable mortality' (Organisation for Economic Co-operation and Development, 2019). The cause of death in preventable mortality *can be prevented through public health prevention*, that is prior to the onset of the disease through primary preventions and interventions and is the focus of the following debate. In the case of treatable and amendable mortality, can be avoided mainly through medical treatment including secondary prevention and health care intervention. The OECD uses the International Classification of Disease (ICD) for its categorisation of causes of death. Following the outbreak of the pandemic, Covid-19 had been given an emergency code as part of ICD-10, while the 11th version of the ICD will come to an effect on 1 January 2022.

In December 2019, the UK Office of National Statistics (ONS, 2019) sought users' views on implementation of the OECD definition of avoidable mortality and concluded that respondents were overall supportive of it, apart from the restricting of avoidable mortality to those under 75 years old which is discussed later. Additionally, in July 2020 ONS (Office for National Statistics, 2020) reported on socioeconomic inequalities in avoidable mortality in England in 2018. The same report focuses on diseases of the circulatory and respiratory systems (Covid-19 was not included at the time), alcohol and drug-related deaths and injuries. Conclusively, the proportion of avoidable death in 2018 in England is substantially larger in the most deprived areas of the country. The lesser an area's deprivation, the generally decreased rate of avoidable death. This raises a question whether how we approach the idea of preventable mortality *reflects lived social reality*. Given that the data clearly shows that mortality is greatest in the most deprived areas, should social deprivation be considered a cause of death?

'On 30 March 2017, during a meeting in the UK Parliament about cuts to welfare payments (benefits) and sanctions, a minute's silence was held to remember all those who died as a result of the welfare cuts and austerity measures that have become part of the UK policy landscape since the 2007–2008 financial crisis' (Mills, 2018, p. 303). The point that 'dead people don't claim' captures the essence of suicides resultant from dire social circumstance and raises the question of accountability for these deaths (Mills, 2018, p. 302).

It is evident that preventable mortality is hindered by socioeconomic inequalities hand in hand with social processes such as structural violence, racism, dehumanisation, et alia. This raises the question whether the ICD is an appropriate tool for identifying causes of death, or whether instead, its use omits the social reality of death and dying. The critique of the medicalisation of mortality is long-standing and so is the invitation to include social, sociological, philosophical as well as socio-economic dimensions of death and dying into measures of mortality (Erikson and Torssander, 2008; Hallam, Hockey and Howarth,1999; Howarth, 2007; Kellehear, 2008; Borgstrom, 2015, 2017). It is therefore necessary to include 'social diseases' and 'social causes of death', hence: *the social death* into the conceptualisation of avoidable and more specifically, preventable mortality. Whether this can be achieved through the ICD remains unexplored.

It is argued that Covid-19 in and of itself does not *cause* inequality. Instead, I propose that Covid-19 *exacerbates* long-standing inequalities, discriminations, dehumanisations, and injustices and brings them to the forefront of societal attention, not least due to its scale and impact. In doing so, it leaves some individuals, groups and populations unprotected and exposed to *inhumane* treatment.

The three major schools of thought in social death theorising will be introduced. Following on from that, their exceptions will be elaborated. Social death theory is used to portray not only individuals, groups and populations which are most vulnerable, but also expose the processes by which they remain so. Consequently, the social death inflicted on Black, Asian and minority ethnic communities and on care home residents during the Covid-19 pandemic is drawn. The conclusion suggests that social causes of death, or social death, be included in the OECD's conceptualisation of avoidable mortality, more specifically of preventable mortality. This is to incorporate the social reality of death and dying into how mortality is measured.

'Archaeology' of social death: three schools of thought

Some level of predictability of death exists among populations defined as socially dead. These are not however accounted for in any contemporary mortality measures despite being embedded in the UK End of life care policy (Borgstrom, 2015). There are three major schools of thought regarding social death: Patterson's (1982), Card's (2002, 2010) and the literature deployed in death studies (Goffman, 1959, 1961; Glaser and Strauss, 1965; Sudnow, 1967; Kalish, 1968; Sweeting and Gilhooly, 1991). Approaches that do not adhere to these three schools of thought will be discussed later.

The first school of thought is based on Patterson's (1982) work on slavery and is internationally cited as a seminal work on social death that is not necessarily limited to the context of slavery. Google Scholar (December 2020) lists over 5,500 citations. Unlike other conceptualisations, Patterson firmly roots social death in black ontology and consequently offers a black epistemological framework. This fact requires serious attention in relation to how we may wish to re-conceptualise inequality and social injustice more broadly. Studies of slavery (Rooke, 1990; Jamieson, 1995; Mason, 2003; Brown, 2009; Brace, 2014), racialised imprisonment (Gordon, 2011; Bery, 2013; Guenther, 2013), racially motivated lack of legal and social protection (Cacho, 2012) racially motivated discrimination (Loyd and Burridge, 2007) along with genocide (Card, 2002, 2010) credit Patterson for introducing the concept of social death.

These authors use Patterson's (1982) conceptualisation of social death as a springboard for exposing complexities of systemic, systematic, intersectional, symbolic, physical, racially motivated, interrelational, emotional, political, economic and other violence. Furthermore, Patterson's (1982) conceptualisation of social death has influenced LGBTQI+ studies (Backus, 1993; Richardson, 2012), comparative family studies (Peter, 2010) and refugee studies (Limbu, 2009). Hence it emerges that the social death framework has much more to offer then may be initially apparent. The common denominator among the studies implementing Patterson's (1982) conceptualisation is the manifest recognition that, although groups and individuals have some ability to exercise agency, resistance, and resilience, under the weight of severe oppressions, their agency remains largely inconsequential.

The second school of thought represents interdisciplinary death studies which suggest different origins of the social death concept. Here, we find Goffman (1961), Glaser and Strauss (1965), Sudnow (1967), Kalish (1968) cited as founders of the social death concept (Mulkay and Ernst, 1991; Timmermans and Sudnow, 1998; Norwood, 2009). More recent studies (McColgan, Valentine and Downs, 2000) also refer to Sweeting and Gilhooly's (1991) influential literature review of social death in sociology and nursing.

Goffman's (1961) analysis of dehumanising practices involved in institutionalising mental health hospital patients is seminal. He has been heavily criticised, however, for his comparing the hospital setting with concentration camps (Siegler and Osmond, 1971), the criticism being that patients, unlike prisoners in concentration camps, have rights and duties and so do their families. This, however, is contestable in that it assumes that the patient's actions are legally and practically consequential and that they have social connections. This may not be the case for all.

Interestingly, in a footnote, Sudnow (1967) credits Goffman (1961) for the notion of social death, though the purpose for which he is employing the term differs from Goffman's. This difference is however not sufficiently explored or otherwise explained, leaving readers to make their own judgement as to how these two conceptualisations may be related. Also, since Goffman (1961) does not use the term 'social death' explicitly, it is hard to judge what parts of Goffman's work Sudnow (1967) are referring to. Following ethnographic exploration of the treatment of 200 dying patients in two US hospitals, Sudnow (1967) spelled out the differences: between 'clinical death', announced by the 'death signs'; 'biological death', the ending of all of the biological functions; and 'social death', conducted through the actions of others, where the person is treated as already deceased, although still clinically and biologically alive.

Likewise, Glaser and Strauss (1965) observed interactions between the dying person and their surrounding social networks in six hospitals over a period of six years. From this resulted the middle range theory of the 'awareness context'. The authors classify the level of awareness of forthcoming death between the patient and their social surrounding and the interplay of social processes that help to navigate interactions leading up to the person's death. For the theorisation of the social death concept, however, the key contribution of this work lies in its recognition of 'categorical discounting'. This is a specific behaviour that occurs during interaction with patients whose awareness is being disregarded due to their condition. In such a situation 'staff members may act without taking awareness into account' (Glaser and Strauss, 1965, p. 107). This means treating the patient as if they were dead or not present because the person concerned, due to lack of practically consequential agency, cannot challenge such treatment.

Kalish (1968) theorises death as: (a) physical, in the biological and clinical senses, (b) psychological, based on self-awareness, (c) social, both self-perceived and other-perceived; in the former case a person believes that they are as good as dead, in the latter case it is others who think so; (d) sociological, tied to the status of an individual in the community which also includes legal death, implying loss of legal protection. Notably, upon psychological death the person 'not only does not know *who* he is – he does not know *that* he is'. (Kalish, 1968, p. 253, emphasis in the original). Also,

> any given individual is socially dead for those people who once knew him as alive and who now think of him as being, for all practical purposes, dead or non-existent. He is socially dead to any given person to the degree that that person perceives him as dead (Kalish, 1968, pp. 254–255).

Yet, Kalish (1968, p. 255) also notes that 'some basically socially dead individuals will create meaning for themselves in their more limited environment and continue to function with reasonable effectiveness'. In other words, despite being considered socially dead by others, it is possible for a person to create meaningful life, perhaps here the idea of spiritual vitality may apply (Card, 2010; Johnson, 2013).

Sweeting and Gilhooly (1991) comprehensively reviewed social death literature in sociology and nursing, seeing it as a transition from life to death. Notably, they identified *personhood* and *worthwhile life* as concepts related to social death and observed that while in the modern western world social death is mostly viewed negatively, in traditional societies it has been perceived as inherent in the dying process. What they omit, however, is the recognition of the disengagement theory which 30 years earlier proposed at times controversially, that older people's withdrawal from society towards the end of their lives may be functional, welcome and mutual (Cumming and Henry, 1961). Conceivably, by 'making space' for younger populations.

In their theoretical exploration, Sweeting and Gilhooly (1991) consider three empirical examples; those in the final stages of terminal illness, the very old, and those with dementia or in a coma. From these instances, the authors identified several features that are likely to be related to the onset of social death in Western societies. This conceptualisation of social death as an accompaniment to impending physical death is common among medical anthropologists (Borgstrom, 2015, 2017). However, it would benefit from taking into an account social processes revealed above: where social death is practically a substitute for death (Patterson, 1982) and may at times be worse than physical death, since 'being deprived of life may not be a worse harm for the person who is tortured' (Card, 2010, p. 236). Here, torture may be conceived of broadly as social suffering (Renault, 2010; Rylko-Bauer and Farmer, 2016) and/or biographical pain (Johnson, 2013).

The common denominator among these studies of death and dying revolves around loss and maintenance of social identity, of social connections, of legal identity and agency. It further raises the questions of preservation of human value, meaning of life mostly at the end of it, and includes institutionalised living and dying.

The third school of thought is represented by genocide scholars who are largely unaware of the other two schools and cite philosopher Claudia Card (2002, 2010, 2012) as seminal. Several scholars have developed her proposal in various directions, yet all in support of including social death in the UN definition of genocide (Abed, 2006; Crook and Short, 2014; Schott, 2011a, 2011b; Short, 2010; Žalec, 2013). These efforts may be broadly summarised as: (a) genocide as a consequence of damage to an environment, (b) genocide as a consequence of the breakdown of interpersonal and cross-generational relationships, (c) genocide as a consequence of assaults on a group's culture.

Card's (2002, 2010) work, *The Atrocity Paradigm,* is a secular theory of evil, positioned between classic utilitarian and stoic perspectives. While recognising atrocities as paradigms of evil, it neither defines evil actions simply by their damaging consequences nor reduces them to the perpetrators' wickedness. Evils are 'reasonably foreseeable intolerable harms produced by *inexcusable* wrongs' (Card, 2010, p. 16, emphasis in the original). Card (2010) pays homage to Patterson's (1982) notion of natal alienation (referring to cross-generational harm in slavery and genocide) which forms an important building block in her argument. Card's life-long aim of including social death into the UN definition of genocide is yet to materialise.

To conclude, each of the three schools of thought offer different qualities. The first, Patterson's (1982), is mostly utilised for its ability to depict domination and for its analysis of intrusive and extrusive social death. Intrusive social death is where the slave 'intrudes' into the community, coming from the outside in. Extrusive social death afflicts those who have 'fallen out' of their community due to economic or legal failure. It is of great importance that Patterson's (1982) social death offers a black onto-epistemological framework which may serve as fruitful base for analysis which moves beyond the narrative of 'inclusion' and instead *is intrinsically humane.*

The second school of thought represented by interdisciplinary death studies offers a range of micro-universes of relational dynamics pertaining to maintenance or loss of social and legal identity as well as social connections and agency, along with embodied experiences of death and dying with some references to the role of socio-economic inequality. From this school, we may derive specific ways by which human beings may be enabled or prevented from sustaining meaningful life, self-worth, dignity and quality of life in the circumstances of profound vulnerability and exposure.

The third school of thought is represented by genocide scholars focuses on the community level and teaches us much about preservation of the group's identity and social vitality across generations in the context of the degradation of their physical environment, their cultural heritage, and of futures which will no longer be possible.

Taken together, I hope that the above discussion facilitates interdisciplinary exchange across the fields of study which typically and historically do not collaborate, yet which share a common interest in theorising social death.

The exceptions

The exceptions to the above three schools of thought of social death theory are worth examining in greater detail because their contributions are theoretically unique, and they further enable the following analysis.

The works of Van Gennep (1960) and Turner (1967) are cited in relation to social death's conceptualisation (Patterson, 1982; Robins, 2006; Borgstrom, 2015, 2017). It is Turner's (1967) elaboration of the liminal period in Van Gennep's (1960) rites of passage which is of interest here. Turner (1967, p. 97) notes that the socially dead 'are neither living nor dead from one aspect, and both living and dead from another' which makes them *'structurally invisible'* (Turner, 1967, p. 99, emphasis mine). This notion of 'structural invisibility' is especially pertinent. Hence, that which is named: *social death*, can be foreseen and can thus be measured and prevented.

It seems likely that Mulkay and Ernst (1991) first made the connection between social death's conceptualisation in the first (slavery) and the second (death studies) schools of thought. Yet, the significance of their interdisciplinary linking continues to be overlooked. Mulkay and Ernst (1991) describe the changing profile of social death in the light of demographic changes, specifically age and gender. Firstly, they offer critical analyses of Goffman (1961), Glaser and Strauss (1965) and Sudnow (1967) and their respective uses of social death before introducing their own theoretically enhanced conceptualisation of social death, applied to the older people, women and children. Specifically, Mulkay and Ernst (1991) use Patterson's (1982) point that slaves were able to create social life among themselves even under the most severe domination, to critique what they perceive as Sudnow's (1967) narrow anthropological interpretation of social death. This question of the gravity of the impact of social death and its relation to agency, or the lack of it, reoccurs in the debates and remains contested.

Studies concerned with reduced agency due to ageing or brain injury (Birchley et al., 2016; Gilleard and Higgs, 2015; Kitzinger, Kitzinger and Cowley, 2017) as well as absent agency due to dementia (Gilhooly et al., 1994; Gilleard and Higgs, 2011) provide examples of situations where agency may be very limited or not present at all. Furthermore, there are some agents who may not be part of research samples or debates. The 'structurally invisible' (Turner 1967) may include hard to reach populations (Kellehear, 2009) or those who live and die alone (Seale, 1996; Caswell and O'Connor, 2015). That does not imply, however, that dying alone necessarily means social death or lack of agency; for some it may, for others, not (Visser 2018, Turner and Caswell 2020). Furthermore, how to identify suicides among those who die alone, is yet to be established. Additionally, exercising agency may have grave consequences for undocumented migrants (Weissbrodt and Divine, 2015) or

North Korean defectors (Son et al., 2019). From this, and if further impacted by structural violence (Farmer et al., 2004; Hamed et al., 2020) and compromised resilience (Dagdeviren, Donoghue and Promberger, 2016), we may conclude that although agency is intrinsically present to human beings (Hallam, Hockey and Howarth, 1999), under the circumstances of severe oppression, structural or otherwise, it may become practically inconsequential (Cacho, 2012; Giroux, 2011; Wrenn, 2014).

Lovell's (2011) anthropological study of New Orleans Charity Hospital after its damage by Hurricane Katrina credits Biehl (2004) for the origin of the concept of social death. Biehl's ethnographic account of Vita, a southern Brazilian community of severally impoverished people without any access to social protection, captures vividly how structural violence fuels structural invisibility and how agency can become practically inconsequential (Biehl 2004). However, Lovell's (2011) argument that the enforcement of 'stratified reproduction' resulted in a diminished 'social body' of African-Americans, although well evidenced, would be better supported by Card's (2010) social death, because it would enable Lovell (2011) to make claims to genocide. Further, Patterson (1982) would add gravity and a black onto-epistemological framework to the analysis.

Despite this, Lovell (2011, p. 476) refers to people who have been left '*with death*'. Lovell builds here on Biehl's (2004) reference to Mauss (1979) for social death's conceptualisation, specifically, to Mauss' essay *The physical effect on the individual of the idea of death suggested by the collectivity* (1979, p. 80, emphasis in the original), in which he explores 'those cases where the subject who dies does not believe or know himself to be ill, *he only believes, for precise collective causes, that he is in a state close to death*'. Mauss (1979) suggests that it is the fact that a person's death is wished for the individual by their community, and that the excluded person is fully aware of this desire, that may lead to their physical death. Henceforth, we can see why Lovell (2011) was able to implement this notion in relation to a community's devastation. Mauss (1979), however, makes links to Durkheim's (1951) anomic suicide, the kind committed due to societal disorder, which remains pertinent.

Hage's (2003) contribution towards theorising social death is also important and relates to the above-presented debates about agency. Hage (2003) argues that Palestinian suicide bombing may be interpreted as a form or resistance and 'survival' that is aimed at acquiring *meaning of life* within the severe constraints of Israeli colonial occupation and violence. That is,

> the suicide bombers become a sign that Palestinians have not been broken. They are a sign of life. For what better sign of life is there, in such violent conditions, than the capacity to hurt despite the greater capacity of the other to hurt you (Hage, 2003, p. 74).

Thus, we may suggest that in the extremist, agency in the attempt to resist social death may amount to physical death. This ability, however, is hindered by the unequal distribution of symbolic as well as economic power which, when lacking, deprives people of their social recognition and profoundly limits their life chances. Hence, Palestinian youth for whom 'nothing symbolizes social death like this inability to dream a meaningful life' (Hage, 2003, p. 79), turns to the culture of martyrdom to derive a meaning of their life *from* death. Recalling earlier Sweeting and Gilhooly's (1991) point about *worthwhile life*, we may suggest that when a person/s perceive their life as worthless they may find meaning in death. More recently, Norwood (2009) provided evidence suggesting that social death in The Netherlands may be prevented through conversation about possibility of undergoing euthanasia, to maintain life. Consequently, the debate revolving around assisted suicide would be apt, alas beyond the scope of this contribution.

Moreover, Giroux's (2011) concept of 'the social death of social state' is firmly rooted in an extensive study of Zygmunt Bauman. Giroux (2011) cites eight of Bauman's works to demonstrate how since the 1980s, neoliberal politics, economies and public pedagogy endanger 'true democracy': one that considers social welfare an inalienable right and will not tolerate moral negligence. Contrary to this,

> shame is now used to wage a war on the poor rather than poverty, on young people rather than those economic and political forces that undermine their future, and on those considered other rather than on the underlying structures and ideologies of various forms of state and individual racism (Giroux, 2011, p. 597).

What makes Giroux's 'social death' unique is its application to political economy and the implication of moral responsibility derived from Bauman's work. Not only is it made clear that inflicting social death on the most vulnerable populations is profoundly wrong, but it further implies moral responsibility and accountability not only of those causing it but also of those who are not actively opposing it. This is illustrated especially clearly in Bauman's study of the Holocaust (1989), which Giroux does not cite, but which closely resembles Card's (2010) position regarding the culpability for doing evil which includes failure to prevent it.

Crucial, Guenther (2013) employs social death's *relational* dimension in her phenomenological analysis of solitary confinement. Guenther (2013) credits Patterson (1982) for the origin of the social death concept, but also includes the additional concept of civil death which enables her to address issues of legal identity and of its lack in the context of supermax prisons. Guenther's (2013, p. 123) questions are universally applicable across the social death debate, since she asks what happens when an intercorporeal living being such as this is confined for a prolonged period of time to a small, enclosed space, isolated from other living beings and from an open-ended relation to the world? What are the ethical, political, and even ontological implications of such confinement?

The ontological dimension and the analytical depth that Guenther's social death comprises is pivotal.

Equally important is Judith Butler's (2010) theorising, who uses the term social death to describe 'ungrievable' lives and deaths. Suggesting that certain lives and deaths although utterly dehumanised, make up for the crucial workings of the politics of war. This is because they are exploitable, yet structurally invisible. Thus, 'specific lives cannot be apprehended as injured or lost if they are not first apprehended as living. If certain lives do not qualify as lives or are, from the start, not conceivable as lives within certain epistemological frames, then these lives are never lived nor lost in the full sense'. (Butler, 2010, p. 1). It is my understanding that Butler (2010) refers to *ontology which is not reduced but 'incomplete'*. It never had a chance to become fully ontologically recognised (or 'framed', to use Butler's descriptor) due to externally imposed limits.

The exceptions to the above introduced three schools of thought of social death theory draw our attention to structural similarities of social death's conceptualisation across different areas of expertise while pointing out micro, mezzo and macro presence of social death across societal structures. Moreover, something of a philosophical base of social death is introduced suggesting that ontology plays key role in social death debate. Furthermore, specific groups of individuals and populations, vulnerable to social death, have been mentioned but my list is not exhaustive, not least because human worth and value are repeatedly being called into question and that the 'register of social death' 'authorizes the lives of some while disallowing the lives of others' (Biehl, 2004, p. 476) and whoever is not on the register today, may well be there tomorrow.

This section has presented evidence that some individuals and populations remain structurally invisible, dehumanised, unprotected and without the recourse to legal representation, public funds and as such their agency and resilience, although more or less present, remain for all practical and legal purposes inconsequential. The following section explores social death imposed on Britain's Black, Asian and minority ethnic communities in the context of the Covid-19 pandemic, along with a discussion of the impact of inadequate UK's governmental policy on residents of care homes and how these two instances illustrate death by social causes, the social death. The conceptual suitability of the OECD's (2019) avoidable mortality and specifically the notion of preventable mortality is thus called into question. Social death as a concept is offered as a way of accounting for social causes of death.

Covid-19: which lives matter and which deaths count?

This section aims to demonstrate the analytical potential of social death theory to capture multi-dimensional, dynamic, structural and intersectional complexities associated with the impact of social causes of death on the UK's most vulnerable populations during the Covid-19 pandemic. It indicates an analytical frame for including the 'structurally invisible', those affected by social causes of death, the socially dead, into the vocabulary of social policy and measures of mortality.

The question to what extent public health policies succeeded or failed in preventing avoidable mortality in the context of Covid-19 will be discussed for many decades to come. The focal point of the following discussion is the *preventable mortality* which may be avoided through public policy (Organisation for Economic Co-operation and Development, 2019). Social death scholarship suggests that preventable and foreseeable harms are evil (Card, 2010, 2012), social welfare an inalienable right (Cacho, 2012; Giroux, 2011; Wrenn, 2014), moral negligence intolerable (Bauman 1989) and all lives thus endangered grievable (Butler 2010). I shall apply these elementary philosophical points to the Covid-19 pandemic.

Black, Asian, and minority ethnic communities

Although it has been repeatedly evidenced that Covid-19 disproportionately impacts Black, Asian and minority ethnic (henceforth BAME) communities (Public Health England 2020), the UK government has remained slow to offer specifically tailored support. Yet, the likelihood of testing positive and the consequent risk of being admitted to ICU for COVID-19 are greater in all ethnic minority groups in the UK compared with whites. Relevant factors may include poverty, education, household size, population density and geographical location (Martin et al., 2020; Mathur et al., 2020b; Niedzwiedz et al., 2020; Verhagen et al., 2020). Likewise, referrals to palliative care for BAME patients, especially women, take longer compared to White ethnic patients (Chidiac et al., 2020). Still, the UK government's Race Disparity Unit, despite publishing the first quarterly report on progress to address Covid-19 health inequalities, omits any discussion of the impact of structural violence and racism in dealing with the pandemic (Butt, 2020).

Beginning with the *first school of thought,* Patterson's (1982) *social death*, we are reminded that social death can result from domination, racial violence, or an assault on black lives and deaths via cross-generational physical, symbolic and structural violence. We also recall that social death is a substitute for physical death (Patterson 1982). The slow coming social policy that would effectively protect BAME communities and the delay in referrals along with the lack of effective strategies may for some lead to death. This is not necessarily due to the virus itself, though it will inevitably play part, but more so to a lack of effective social infrastructure, welfare and other measures to protect BAME communities. Such deaths are preventable and occurring more, due to *social* rather than medical factors.

The second school of thought represented by the interdisciplinary studies of death reminds us of dehumanising practices through which a person's value is diminished and consequently impacts on the perceived worth of their life and/or their death (Goffman, 1961; Glaser and Strauss, 1965; Sudnow, 1967; Kalish, 1968). In other words, some lives are perceived as deserving of being saved, while others are not. For example, resuscitation efforts, their vigour and duration are determined by the person's perceived social value; how perceived social value (for persons without home, or those using substances, older people or people with disability) lead to lesser resuscitative efforts and greater probability of death (Timmermans and Sudnow, 1998). Equally, we may also appreciate that social death disproportionately impacts women and older people (Mulkay and Ernst, 1991).

Furthermore, social death's impact on BAME communities in the Covid-19 pandemic amounts to a 'racialised rightlessness and the criminalisation of the unprotected' (Cacho, 2012). Whereby the only recognisable personhood is conditioned by whiteness and underpinned by a neoliberal political philosophy (Giroux, 2011; Guenther 2013; Wrenn, 2014). Conversely, those who do not fulfil these criteria remain outside the frames of recognition and are left to most inhumane misfortunes (Butler, 2010).

Given that the Covid-19 pandemic is a global phenomenon and therefore impacts BAME communities world-wide, *the third school of thought* represented by genocide scholars may assist in asking whether, in the extreme, the lack of effective and protective social policy may be in its consequence, genocidal. This would not be dissimilar to the instance presented above in the context of post-Katrina New Orleans (Lovell, 2011).

Furthermore, we may recall the key points arising from the above-mentioned *theoretical exceptions*. Notably, the concept of structural invisibility (Turner, 1967) and exploitability of ungrievable deaths (Butler, 2010) to which some populations are more exposed than others (Mulkay and Ernst 1991; Cacho 2012; Hage, 2003). This, in the UK takes place within the context of the neoliberal political philosophy which is at the best of times hard to hold to an account (Giroux, 2011), and at its worse, kills (Cederstrom and Fleming, 2012). Thus, raising once again the question of agency and the lack therefore, in terms of its in/consequential impact within the constraints of structural violence.

Thus, apart from death by the Covid-19, the BAME communities are dying due to social causes that is by lack of effective pro-black, pro-social-social-policy, access to health care, welfare and efficient community support. Recalling the definition of preventable mortality, which *can be avoided through public health prevention*, and congruent with the urgent call for actions and policies to address COVID-19 among UK ethnic minorities (Mathur et al., 2020a) policy action is required. It remains to be tested, however, whether the OECD's (2019) avoidable mortality is conceptually robust enough to encompass social realities of avoidable deaths, inclusive of death by social causes, the social death.

Care home residents

The policy response to Covid-19 in the care homes provides an additional example of a situation where deadly consequences of inadequate social policy, and resultant deaths could have been prevented. It is likely that the distinction between the deaths caused by Covid-19, and the deaths brought about by social as well as physical consequences of inadequate social policy and associated social causes, will remain hard to statistically distinguish for a while yet. However, this distinction must be noted to improve the theoretical robustness of 'avoidable mortality' (Organisation for Economic Co-operation and Development, 2019). Equally, restricting the definition of avoidable mortality to those under 75 years old, is likely to continue raising questions (Office for National Statistics, 2019). This is due not least to recognised demographic changes of growing into the fourth age (Laslett, 1994; Gilleard and Higgs, 2011, Higgs and Gilleard, 2020; Johnson 2013). It is similarly important to differentiate between deaths of care home residents, some of whom may die in hospital, from deaths that take place in the care homes (Comas-Herrera et al., 2020).

The issues pertaining to preventable mortality of care home residents (Organisation for Economic Co-operation and Development, 2019) include the underreporting of Covid-19 death in care homes in first eight weeks of the pandemic, the estimate of 25,000 patients discharged from hospitals to care homes in England between 23 March 2020 and 15 April 2020, with an unknown number of patients discharged to care homes later and the inadequate testing of all involved (Daly, 2020; Mitha 2020; Oliver, 2020). Although the idea of freeing beds in hospitals may have been well intended, the deaths that resulted from this decision, although appearing under the code of Covid-19 of the International Classification of Disease (ICD) in the context of preventable mortality (Organisation for Economic Co-operation and Development, 2019), were in fact deaths by social causes, the social deaths, ensuing from an inadequate social policy and underpinned by the diminished value of elderly lives and deaths (Higgs and Gilleard, 2020).

Thus, in relation to care home residents, the *first school of thought,* Patterson's (1982) *social death*, reminds us that social death is cumulative and intersectional. Therefore, not only are care home residents vulnerable due to age, and due to residing in a care home, but some also are Black, Asian or minority ethnic and are therefore even more vulnerable to white supremacy (Bery, 2013; Cacho, 2012). Further, Patterson's (1982) notions of intrusive and extrusive social death are not to be forgotten. This is because the first may remind us that some residential settings are still not quite as culturally sensitive as they could be, while the second may prompt us to consider that the disadvantage is not only intersectional, but also cumulative. Whereby, the 'falling out' of the society may also happen not only due to socio-economic 'failure' or 'criminalisation' as discussed above, but occurs still, even at the old age.

The second school of social death thought revolves around loss of social identity and loss of social roles, loss of legal identity as well as arising issues of poverty all of which may be part of the experience of moving into the residential setting (Rosenberg, 1982; Mulkay and Ernst, 1991; Sweeting and Gilhooly, 1991; Howarth, 2007; Kellehear, 2007; Foster and Woodthorpe, 2013). The ongoing debate about loss, maintenance and absence of agency among older people presented as part of *theoretical exceptions* is especially fruitful and its considerations should not be dismissed lightly. For example, we may ask to what extend where residents with or without dementia and those living with frailty and comorbidities, able to exercise their agency during the Covid-19 pandemic (Laslett, 1994; Gilleard and Higgs, 2011, Higgs and Gilleard, 2020; Johnson, 2013)? Inseparable from these considerations are also questions pertaining to meaning of life at the end of it (Sweeting and Gilhooly, 1991; Hage, 2003).

A further issue, especially applicable in the context of Covid-19 pandemic, is the loss of social connections and resultant social isolation (Seale, 1996; Buch, 2015). In terms of *theoretical exceptions* at this point, we may recall Guenther's (2013) phenomenological analysis which offers a comprehensive explanation of the impact of prolonged physical isolation and lack of social contact. Consider, the spatial constraints of a typical care home bedroom, especially under the conditions of no visiting by relatives. A connection with social death in solitary confinement seems pertinent. Likewise, the detrimental impact of the isolation due to Covid-19 governmental guidance pertaining to 'shielding' amongst clinically vulnerable (Department of Health and Social Care, 2020), has been reported (Baker and Clark, 2020; Brooks et al., 2020). All the while, the awareness of the fact that our community wishes us dead (Mauss, 1979), connected with possible functionality of this process (Cumming and Henry, 1961) may amount to additional social causes of death. That said, we shall also recall those who do live and die alone by choice (Kellehear, 2009; Turner and Caswell, 2020). Further still, the mortality resulting from cuts to social care funding has been evidenced (Giroux, 2011; Daly, 2020; Mills, 2018; Mitha, 2020; Oliver, 2020).

The third school of social death thought represented by genocide scholars is useful for articulating the antithesis of social death, the *social vitality* which

> exists through relationships, contemporary and intergenerational, that create contexts and identities that give meaning and shape to our lives. Some of those relationships are with kin, friends, and co-workers. Others are less personal and mediated by basic social institutions – economic, political, religious, educational, and so on. Loss of social vitality comes with the loss of such connections (Card, 2010, p. 237).

Furthermore, 'social vitality is *interpersonal*. An individual can experience social death without others experiencing it, too. But for an individual to have social vitality, others must have it' (Card, 2010, p. 262). Notably, 'vital interests can be transgenerational and thus survive one's death' (Card, 2007, p. 20). Thus, we may recall the need for *worthwhile life* as opposed to social death (Sweeting and Gilhooly, 1991).

This helps us to appreciate possible social causes of death of care home residents which may move beyond social isolation into the realm of cross-generational losses. This includes lost interactions with grandchildren and their parents who are prevented from visiting, and lost connections with the local community. Equally, we may recognise the loss of sense of belonging, the lost connections with communities of faith, along with the cultural institutions. Given the current dependence on technology for maintenance of social connection, digital poverty and/or digital illiteracy are likely to be a contributing factor.

Collective social vitality is compromised by the impact of Covid-19 and mirrors the general demoralisation of the population at large. Henceforth, it is likely that care home residents are aware of the inadequacy of social policy and of its impact on their lives and potential deaths. Consequently, we may recall that awareness of a community's death wish may lead to a person's physical death (Mauss, 1979). Thus, we cannot but question how we think about causes of deaths. The debate regarding suicides resulting from societal disorder, to which the Covid-19 pandemic undoubtedly belongs, is beyond the scope of this chapter, but is certainly worth attending to (Durkheim, 1951).

Concluding remarks

The above-presented analysis applies three schools of social death theory and their exceptions to two examples of 'death by social causes', the social death. The first instance considered is the impact of inadequate UK government policy on BAME communities, and the second instance considered the impact of inadequate governmental policy on care homes residents during the Covid-19 pandemic. The principal aim of this analysis was to demonstrate the considerable analytical power of social death theory which may serve as a starting point for including social causes of death into mortality measures. Specifically, I aimed to challenge the conceptualisation of *avoidable mortality* of the OECD which uses the ICD to categorise causes of death and thus omits from its conceptual frame 'social causes of death', the social death. Specifically, preventable mortality, which *can be prevent through public health measures,* was the focus of the analysis. This exposed the impact of inadequate policy and in/action on the most vulnerable populations, thus inflicting social death which is yet to be included into the semantic, policy and legal frames of recognition to better reflect the social reality of death and dying.

Consequently, the greater question arises as to how we may change our approach to inequalities, injustices, exclusions and oppressions and move beyond established sociological categories to enable those who remain 'not to be seen and not to be there' to become structurally visible, accounted for and protected?

References

Abed, M., 2006. Clarifying the concept of genocide. *Metaphilosophy*, 37(3–4), pp. 308–330.

Backus, M.G., 1993. Judy Grahn and the lesbian invocational elegy: testimonial and prophetic responses to social death in "a women is talking to death". *Signs*, 18(4), pp. 815–837.

Baker, E. and Clark, L.L., 2020. Biopsychopharmacosocial approach to assess impact of social distancing and isolation on mental health in older adults. *British Journal of Community Nursing*, 25(5), pp. 231–238.

Bauman, Z., 1989. *Modernity and the Holocaust*. Cambridge: Polity Press.

Bery, S., 2013. Imprisoned imaginaries: whiteness and nation of Islam. *Borderlands*, 12(2), pp. 53–79.

Biehl, J., 2004. Life of the mind: the interface of psychopharmaceuticals, domestic economies, and social abandonment. *American Ethnologist*, 31(4), pp. 475–496.

Birchley, G., Jones, K., Huxtable, R., Dixon, J., Kitzinger, J. and Clare, L., 2016. Dying well with reduced agency: a scoping review and thematic synthesis of the decision-making process in dementia, traumatic brain injury and frailty. *BMC Medical Ethics*, 17(1), p. 46.

Borgstrom, E., 2015. Social death and English end of life care policy. *Contemporary Social Science*, 10(3), pp. 272–283.

Borgstrom, E., 2017. Social Death. *QJM: International Journal of Medicine*, 110 (1), pp. 5–7.

Brace, L., 2014. Bodies in abolition: broken hearts and open wounds. *Citizenship Studies*, 18(5), pp. 485–498.

Brooks, S.K., Webster, R.K., Smith, L.E., Woodland, L., Wessely, S., Greenberg, N. and Rubin, G.J., 2020. The psychological impact of quarantine and how to reduce it: rapid review of the evidence. *The Lancet*. [online]. Available at: Psychological impact of social isolation_LANCET.pdf (Accessed: 16 December 2020).

Brown, V., 2009. Social death and political life in the study of slavery. *American Historical Review*, 114(5), pp. 1231–1249.

Buch, E.D., 2015. Postponing passage: doorways, distinctions, and the thresholds of personhood among older Chicagoans. *Ethos*, 43(1), pp. 40–58.

Butler, J., 2010. *Frames of war: when is life grievable?* London, UK: Verso Books.

Butt, J., 2020. Racism and covid-19—a matter of life and death. *The British Medical Journal* [online]. Available at: https://blogs.bmj.com/bmj/2020/10/28/jabeer-butt-racism-and-covid-19-a-matter-of-life-and-death/ (Accessed: 20 December 2020).

Cacho, L.M., 2012. *Social death: racialized rightlessness and the criminalization of the unprotected*. New York, NY: New York University Press.

Card, C., 2002. *The atrocity paradigm: a theory of evil*. Oxford: Oxford University Press.

Card, C., 2007. Genocide and social death. In: Card, C. and Marsoobian A.T. (eds.), *Genocide's aftermath: responsibility and repair*. Oxford: Blackwell Publishing, pp. 10–26.

Card, C., 2010. *Confronting evils: terrorism, torture, genocide*. Cambridge: Cambridge University Press.

Card, C., 2012. Surviving long-term mass atrocities. *Midwest Studies in Philosophy*, 36(1), pp. 35–52.

Caswell, G. and O'Connor, M., 2015. Agency in the context of social death: dying alone at home. *Contemporary Social Science*, 10(3), p. 249.

Cederstrom, C. and Fleming, P., 2012. *Dead man working*. London, UK: John Hunt Publishing.

Comas-Herrera, A., Zalakaín, J., Lemmon, E., Henderson, D., Litwin, C., Hsu, A.T., Schmidt, A.E., Arling, G. and Fernández, J.-L. (2020). *Mortality associated with COVID-19 in care homes: international evidence*. Article in LTCcovid.org, International Long-Term Care Policy Network, CPEC-LSE, 14 October. Available at: International Long Term Care Policy Network_Mortality-associated-with-COVID-among-people-living-in-care-homes-14-October-2020-5.pdf (Accessed: 5 December 2020).

Chidiac, C., Feuer, D., Flatley, M., Rodgerson, A., Grayson, K. and Preston, N., 2020. The need for early referral to palliative care especially for Black, Asian and minority ethnic groups in a COVID-19 pandemic: findings from a service evaluation. *Palliative Medicine*, 34(9), pp. 1241–1248.

Crook, M. and Short, D., 2014. Marx, Lemkin and the genocide-ecocide nexus. *International Journal of Human Rights*, 18(3), pp. 298–319.

Cumming, E. and Henry, W.E., 1961. *Growing old*. New York: Basic Books

Dagdeviren, H., Donoghue, M. and Promberger, M., 2016. Resilience, hardship and social conditions. *Journal of Social Policy*, 45, pp. 1–20.

Daly, M., 2020. COVID-19 and care homes in England: what happened and why? *Social Policy & Administration*, 54(7), pp. 985–998.

Department of Health and Social Care, 2020. Clinically extremely vulnerable receive updated guidance in line with new national restrictions. Available at: https://www.gov.uk/government/news/clinically-extremely-vulnerable-receive-updated-guidance-in-line-with-new-national-restrictions#:~:text=The%20clinically%20extremely%20vulnerable%20group,such%20as%20cystic%20fibrosis. (Accessed: 7 December 2020).

Durkheim, E., 1951. *Suicide: a study in sociology*. New York, NY: The Free Press.

Erikson, R. & Torssander, J., 2008. Social class and cause of death. *European Journal of Public Health*, 18(5), pp. 473–478.

Farmer, P., Bourgois, P., Fassin, D., Green, L., Heggenhougen, H.K., Kirmayer, L., Wacquant, L. and Farmer, P., 2004. An anthropology of structural violence. *Current Anthropology*, 45(3), pp. 305–325.

Foster, L. and Woodthorpe, K., 2013. What cost the price of a good send off? The challenges for British state funeral policy. *Journal of Poverty and Social Justice*, 21(1), pp. 77–89.

Gilhooly, M.L., Sweeting, H.N., Whittick, J.E., McKee, K., 1994. Family care of the dementing elderly. *International Review of Psychiatry*, 6(1), pp. 29–40.

Gilleard, C. and Higgs, P., 2011. Frailty, disability and old age: a re-appraisal. *Health*, 15(5), pp. 475–490.

Gilleard, C. and Higgs, P., 2015. Social death and the moral identity of the fourth age. *Contemporary Social Science*, 10(3), p. 262.

Giroux, H., 2011. Neoliberalism and the death of the social state: remembering Walter Benjamin's Angel of history. *Social Identities*, 17(4), pp. 587–601.

Glaser, B.G. and Strauss, A.L., 1965. *Awareness of dying*. London, UK: Weidenfeld and Nicolson.

Goffman, E., 1959. *The presentation of self in everyday life*. London: Penguin.

Goffman, E., 1961. *Asylums: essays on the social situation of mental patients and other inmates*. London, UK: Penguin.

Gordon, A.F., 2011. Some thoughts on haunting and futurity. *Borderlands*, 10(2), pp. 1–21.

Guenther, L., 2013. *Solitary confinement: social death and its afterlives*. Minneapolis, MN: University of Minnesota Press.

Hage, G., 2003. "Comes a time we are all enthusiasm": Understanding Palestinian suicide bombers in times of exighophobia. *Public Culture*, 15(1), pp. 65–89.

Hallam E., Hockey J. and Howarth G., 1999. *Beyond the body: death and social identity*. London, UK: Routledge.

Hamed, S., Thapar-Björkert, S., Bradby, H. and Ahlberg, B.M., 2020. Racism in European health care: structural violence and beyond. *Qualitative Health Research*, 30(11), pp. 1662–1673.

Higgs, P. and Gilleard, C., 2020. The ideology of ageism versus the social imaginary of the fourth age: two differing approaches to the negative contexts of old age. *Ageing & Society*, 40(8), pp. 1617–1630.

Howarth, G., 2007. Whatever happened to social class? An examination of the neglect of working class cultures in the sociology of death. *Health Sociology Review*, 16(5), pp. 425–435.

Jamieson, R.W., 1995. Material culture and social death: African-American burial practices. *Historical Archaeology*, 29(4), pp. 39–58.

Johnson, M., 2013. Biography and generation: spirituality and biographical pain at the end of life in old age. In Silverstein, M. and Giarrusso, R. (eds.), *Kinship and cohort in an ageing society: from generation to generation*. Baltimore: JHU Press, pp. 176–190.

Kalish, R.A., 1968. Life and death: dividing the indivisible. *Social Science and Medicine*, 2(3), pp. 249–259.

Kellehear, A., 2007. *A social history of dying*. Cambridge: Cambridge University Press.

Kellehear, A., 2008. Dying as a social relationship: a sociological review of debates on the determination of death. *Social Science and Medicine*, 66(7), pp. 1533–1544.

Kellehear, A., 2009. Dying old: and preferably alone? Agency, resistance and dissent at the end of life. *International Journal of Ageing and Later Life*, 4(1), pp. 5–21

Kitzinger, J., Kitzinger, C. and Cowley, J., 2017. When 'sanctity of life'and 'self-determination'clash: Briggs versus Briggs [2016] EWCOP 53 – implications for policy and practice. *Journal of Medical Ethics*, 43(7), pp. 446–449.

Laslett, P., 1994. The third age, the fourth age and the future. *Ageing & Society*, 14(3), pp. 436–447.

Lovell, A.M., 2011. Debating life after disaster: Charity Hospital babies and bioscientific futures in post-Katrina New Orleans. *Medical Anthropology Quarterly*, 25(2), pp. 254–277.

Limbu, B., 2009. Illegible humanity: the refugee, human rights, and the question of representation. *Journal of Refugee Studies*, 22(3), pp. 257–282.

Loyd, J.M. and Burridge, A., 2007. La Gran Marcha: anti-racism and immigrants rights in Southern California. *ACME: An International Journal for Critical Geographies*, 6(1), pp. 1–35.

Martin, C.A., Jenkins, D.R., Minhas, J.S., Gray, L.J., Tang, J., Williams, C., Sze, S., Pan, D., Jones, W., Verma, R. and Knapp, S., 2020. Socio-demographic heterogeneity in the prevalence of COVID-19 during lockdown is associated with ethnicity and household size: Results from an observational cohort study. *EClinicalMedicine*, 25, p. 100466.

Mason, J.E., 2003. *Social death and resurrection: slavery and emancipation in South Africa*. Charlottesville: University of Virginia Press.

Mathur, R., Bear, L., Khunti, K. and Eggo, R.M., 2020a. Urgent actions and policies needed to address COVID-19 among UK ethnic minorities. *The Lancet*, 396(10266), pp. 1866–1868.

Mathur, R., Rentsch, C.T., Morton, C., Hulme, W.J., Schultze, A., MacKenna, B., Eggo, R.M., Bhaskaran, K., Wong, A.Y., Williamson, E.J. and Forbes, H., 2020b. Ethnic differences in COVID-19 infection, hospitalisation, and mortality: an Open SAFELY analysis of 17 million adults in England. MedRxiv.

Mauss, M., 1979. The physical effect on the individual of the idea of death suggested by the collectivity. In Littlewood, R. and Dein, S. (eds.), *Cultural psychiatry and medical anthropology: an introduction and reader*. London, UK: Bloomsbury Publishing, pp. 79–92.

McColgan, G., Valentine, J. and Downs, M., 2000. Concluding narratives of a career with dementia: accounts of Iris Murdoch at her death. *Ageing and Society*, 20(1), pp. 97–110.

Mills, C., 2018. 'Dead people don't claim': a psychopolitical autopsy of UK austerity suicides. *Critical Social Policy*, 38(2), pp. 302–322.

Mitha, S., 2020. UK COVID-19 Diary: Policy and Impacts. *National Tax Journal*, 73(3), pp. 847–878.

Moller, D.W. (2004). *Dancing with broken bones: portraits of death and dying among inner-city poor*. Oxford: Oxford University Press.

Mulkay, M. and Ernst, J., 1991. The changing profile of social death. *Archives Européennes de Sociologie*, XXXII(1), pp. 172–196.

Niedzwiedz, C.L., O'Donnell, C.A., Jani, B.D., Demou, E., Ho, F.K., Celis-Morales, C., Nicholl, B.I., Mair, F.S., Welsh, P., Sattar, N. and Pell, J.P., 2020. Ethnic and socioeconomic differences in SARS-CoV-2 infection: prospective cohort study using UK Biobank. *BMC Medicine*, 18, pp. 1–14.

Norwood, F., 2009. *The maintenance of life: preventing social death through euthanasia talk and end-of-life care: lessons from the Netherlands*. Durham, Carolina Academic Press.

Office for National Statistics, 2019. Consultation Response: Review of Avoidable Mortality Definition (December 2019). Available at: https://consultations.ons.gov.uk/health-and-life-events/avoidable-mortality-definition/ (Accessed: 10 December 2020).

Office for National Statistics, 2020. Socioeconomic inequalities in avoidable mortality in England: 2018. Available at: https://www.ons.gov.uk/peoplepopulationandcommunity/birthsdeathsandmarriages/deaths/bulletins/socioeconomicinequalitiesinavoidablemortalityinengland/2018#:~:text=The%20absolute%20inequality%20in%20the,with%20the%20least%2C%20in%202018 (Accessed: 15 December 2020).

Oliver, D., 2020. David Oliver: Let's not forget care homes when covid-19 is over. *British Medical Journal* (online), 369. Available at: https://www.bmj.com/content/3 69/bmj.m1629.full

Organisation for Economic Co-operation and Development, 2019. Avoidable mortality: OECD/Eurostat lists of preventable and treatable causes of death (November 2019 version). Available at: Avoidable-mortality-2019-Joint-OECD-Eurostat-List-preventable-treatable-causes-of-death.pdf (Accessed: 01 December 2020).

Patterson, H.O., 1982. *Slavery and social death: a comparative study*. Cambridge: Harvard University Press.

Peter, K.B., 2010. Transnational family ties, remittance motives, and social death among Congolese migrants: a socio-anthropological analysis. *Journal of Comparative Family Studies*, 41(2), pp. 225–243.

Public Health England, 2020. Beyond the data: understanding the impact of COVID-19 on BAME groups. Available at: https://assets.publishing.service.gov.uk/government/uploads/system/uploads/attachment_data/file/892376/COVID_stakeholder_engagement_synthesis_beyond_the_data.pdf (Accessed: 15 December 2020).

Renault, E., 2010. A critical theory of social suffering. *Critical Horizons*, 11(2), pp. 221–241.

Richardson, M., 2012. 'My father didn't have a dick': social death and Jackie Kay's Trumpet. *Journal of Lesbian and Gay Studies*, 18(2–3), pp. 361–379.

Robins, S., 2006. From "rights" to "ritual": AIDS activism in South Africa. *American Anthropologist*, 108(2), pp. 312–323.

Rooke, P., 1990. Slavery, social death and imperialism – the formation of a Christian black élite in the West Indies, 1800–1845. In Mangan, J.A. (ed.), *Making imperial mentalities – socialisation and British imperialism*. Manchester: Manchester University Press, pp. 23–45.

Rosenberg, E., 1982. Athletic retirement as social death: concepts and perspectives. *Sport and the Sociological Imagination*, pp. 245–258.

Rylko-Bauer, B. and Farmer, P., 2016. Structural violence, poverty, and social suffering. In Brady, D., and Burton, L., (eds.), *The Oxford handbook of the social science of poverty*. Oxford: Oxford University Press, pp. 47–74.

Schott, R.M., 2011a. War rape, natality and genocide. *Journal of Genocide Research*, 13(1–2), pp. 5–21.

Schott, R.M., 2011b. War rape, social death and political evil. *Development Dialogue*, 55, pp. 47–62.

Seale, C., 1996. Living alone towards the end of life. *Ageing and Society*, 16(1), pp. 75–91.

Short, D., 2010. Cultural genocide and indigenous peoples: a sociological approach. *International Journal of Human Rights*, 14(6), pp. 833–848.

Siegler, M. and Osmond, H., 1971. Goffman's model of mental illness. *The British Journal of Psychiatry*, 119(551), pp. 419–424.

Son, S., Bielefeld, D., Yang, H., Lee, H., Oh, S., Stevens, S., Choi, Y., Shin, E., Yoon, D. and Olesen, C., 2019. *Mapping the fate of the dead: Killings and burials in North Korea*. Seoul, Korea: Transitional Justice Working Group.

Sudnow, D., 1967. *Passing on*. Englewood Cliffs, NJ: Prentice Hall.

Sweeting, H.N. and Gilhooly, M.L., 1991. Doctor, am I dead? A review of social death in modern societies. *Omega: Journal of Death and Dying*, 24(4), pp. 251–269.

Tarragona, J.M., 2014. The deadly accident of Gaudí. Available at: http://www.antonigaudi.org/the-deadly-accident-of-gaudi-1138.html (Accessed: 1 November 2020).

Timmermans, S. and Sudnow, D., 1998. Social death as self-fulfilling prophecy: David Sudnow's Passing On revisited. *Sociological Quarterly*, 39(3), pp. 453–472.

Turner, V.W., 1967. *The forest of symbols: aspects of Ndembu ritual*. London, UK: Cornell University Press.

Turner, N. and Caswell, G., 2020. Moral ambiguity in media reports of dying alone. *Mortality*, 25(3), pp. 266–281.

Van Gennep, A., 1960. *The rites of passage*. London, UK: Routledge.

Verhagen, M.D., Brazel, D.M., Dowd, J.B., Kashnitsky, I. and Mills, M.C., 2020. Forecasting spatial, socioeconomic and demographic variation in COVID-19 health care demand in England and Wales. *BMC medicine*, 18(1), pp. 1–11.

Visser, R., 2018. Homemaking, temporality and later life. *Home Cultures*, 15(3), pp. 289–307.

Weissbrodt, D. and Divine, M., 2015. Unequal access to human rights: the categories of noncitizenship. *Citizenship Studies*, 19(8), pp. 870–891.

Wrenn, M.V., 2014. Agency and neoliberalism. *Cambridge Journal of Economics*, 39(5), pp. 1231–1243.

Žalec, B., 2013. Genocide as social death: a comparative conceptual analysis. *Anthropological Notebooks*, 19(2), pp. 57–74.

Part II
Institutional care and Covid-19

6 End-of-life decision-making in the context of a pandemic

Natalie Pattison and Lucy Ryan

Key points

This chapter aims to delineate issues pertaining to the unique nature of decision-making in the COVID-19 pandemic situation. Theories and literature are presented in relation to decision-making, core principles of shared decision-making and how patient conditions affect decision-making processes, framing these within a healthcare utilisation context. A description of best principles for practice is outlined, alongside description of the nuanced nature of decision-making and the complexity of end-of-life decisions in a pandemic. In this chapter the following key points are addressed:

- The urgency of decision-making in a pandemic (including societal pressures, clinical and government pressures and the influence of media).
- Healthcare rationing and utilisation drawing on notions of Utilitarianism, Principalism and Resource-based views, using the UK National Health Service response as an exemplar.
- Decision-making processes, including shared-decision making principles and communication applied to COVID-19, and particularly in the context of frailty.
- Achieving best practice principles for decision-making in highly-pressured pandemic situations.

End-of-life decisions – a global rationing context

The global pandemic COVID-19 (also referred to as SARS Cov-2) has heightened awareness around end-of-life decision-making; there is a unique sense of urgency at times of global crisis that need to be addressed. The pressure for hospital beds was unprecedented in the 21st-century and significant adjustments were made to free up critical care and hospital beds across the UK and the world. This unique situation led to debates as to whether there should be consideration of who received potentially scarce resource. This was in light of reported outcomes in relation to COVID-19 in particular patient groups, such as older and/or frail people (Yang et al., 2020; Zhou et al., 2020; Miles et al., 2020). However, this has become a shifting landscape with new evidence emerging week by week and a need for decision-making that is responsive and dynamic in relation to this new evidence.

Across the world, there have been discussions and plans established around surge criteria and management, with input from the World Health Organisation, and countries' own military sources to support prioritisation of those in greatest need and a rapid expansion of hospital (and in particular critical care services). In the UK, we saw the emergence of Nightingale hospitals, and across the rest of the world, temporary 'field' hospitals were commonplace. As the numbers of cases surged globally, and evidence from China and Italy emerged, questions began to surface around the appropriateness and feasibility of offering all healthcare treatments to all people with COVID-19.

Clinical ethics committees have been rapidly convened to help support the difficult decisions about treatment preferences and goals of care with patients during COVID-19. These committees, comprising of legal, ethical and clinical expertise, are present in many hospitals in the UK (Fritz et al., 2020), with similar models globally. Pandemic preparations for COVID-19 saw the resurrection of arguments for reverse triaging, that had emerged in previous pandemics such as Severe Acute Respiratory Syndrome (SARS), H1N1 (2009 influenza) and H5N1 (avian influenza), deciding who and who should not receive critical care treatments (Pollaris and Sabbe, 2016; Christian et al., 2006).

Rationing resources: a necessary evil during COVID-19?

At the time of writing a third wave of the COVID-19 pandemic is upon us in the UK and other parts of Europe (Cacciapaglia, Cot and Sannino, 2020; BBC News, 2020), with potentially further devastating consequences beyond the current deaths of nearly two million worldwide, and nearly half a million death in Europe (European Centre for Disease Prevention and Control, 2020; Johns Hopkins University and Medicine, 2021).

The concept of rationing medicine has been around since time immemorial, and again has emerged during this pandemic. At the outset of the surge in the UK, the English National Health Service (NHS) and National Institute for Health and Clinical Excellence (NICE) developed guidance on managing patients and admissions to critical care services, specifically the use of the Rockwood Clinical Frailty Scale to guide decisions around levels of critical care support (National Institute for Health and Care Excellence

(NICE), 2020a; Rockwood et al., 2005). Within days, patient groups had lobbied for amendments (National Institute for Health and Care Excellence (NICE), 2020b), suggesting that using a simplistic score with people with learning disabilities and stable long-term conditions would place them at a significant disadvantage (National Institute for Health and Care Excellence (NICE), 2020b), resulting in immediate update (National Institute for Health and Care Excellence (NICE), 2020a). NHS England have since been clear this guidance was never intended as a triage tool (NHSE, 2020).

This example demonstrated the heightened awareness of the impact of COVID-19 resource decisions, and emphasising the importance of, and need for, robust and individualistic decision-making in health care (Faculty of Intensive Care Medicine, 2020; Bosslet et al., 2015). However, in the context of disaster situations, such as pandemics, it becomes more difficult to advocate for individual autonomy as the premise for decision-making, as there are limited resources, and ethical frameworks shift. Utilitarianism is sometimes cited as a bioethical principle during pandemics (Morris, 2015; Savulescu, Persson and Wilkinson, 2020; Robert et al., 2020), with the concept of greatest good, or 'right' action, for the greatest number (Mills, 1987) underpinning resource allocation. In the UK, this culminated in an early decision in the first wave to stop all elective surgery to be able to provide an effective, rapid response with finite NHS resources (NHS England and NHS Improvement, 2020). Utilitarianism within pandemics has been outlined in terms of length and quality of life, numbers of lives saved, and the moral equivalence of withholding or withdrawing treatments, social benefit, moral responsibility and avoidance of bias (Savulescu, Persson and Wilkinson, 2020). However, this is met with criticism (Savulescu, Persson and Wilkinson, 2020) around the rights of individuals, particularly those who are marginalised, such as the chronically ill and those with learning and/or physical disabilities. Medicine has historically been underpinned by a deontological approach, the patient-physician relationship is a private transaction and person-centred (Garbutt and Davies, 2011), however, resource constraints present a challenge with a shift to a societal, or utilitarian view. From a resource perspective, rationing emerges as a frequent source of debate. The ethical arguments that centre on rationing in relation to the pandemic are varied, with a call for clarity around implicit and explicit rationing (Spector-Bagdady et al., 2020). Explicit rationing refers to set criteria, and using resources, and budgeting against established or set priorities, and implicit rationing has been described as 'muddling through', where values that guide decisions emerge without being stated overtly (Ham and Coulter, 2001). These approaches to rationing can be viewed at the macro, or policy, level, or at the meso level, with health board, authorities and commissioners choosing how to discharge those set priorities (Ham and Coulter, 2001).

The NICE example of early guidance on managing COVID patients and admissions, outlined above (National Institute for Health and Care Excellence

(NICE), 2020b), emphasised how there has to be public engagement and involvement with priority-setting and policy (Ham and Coulter, 2001; Robert et al., 2020). A social media outcry on Twitter (Bloomer, 2020) led to these rapid amendments, and demonstrated insufficient public involvement in determining policy, which perhaps was not seen as feasible in a pandemic by NICE initially, but with subsequent realisation that it was not only feasible but essential.

A resource-based view of healthcare emphasises the need for rare and distinct resources to be considered in developing a competitive edge in healthcare management (Kash et al., 2014). While this is not necessarily the best approach in a pandemic where a collective response is paramount to advancing treatments and care in the pandemic (World Health Organization, 2020), recognising how external factors, such as COVID-19, need to be considered against the internal resource perspective in health care organisations is warranted. This can help to support an agile health care system that can deal with the pressures of COVID-19, and potentially support local decisions that take into account all the resources available. The development of large field hospitals globally, in order to support the rapidly expanding need for acute care beds, was one example of this. The idea being that healthcare during COVID-19 would be available to all those in need. However, this had to be balanced against decisions about the amount of support (such as critical care services or ventilators) that would be available, and with the emerging evidence that certain groups were likely to have much worse outcomes if they fell critically ill. This prompted widespread discussion about whether to admit patients to hospital and what kind of support people would receive if admitted (British Medical Association, 2020; National Institute for Health and Care Excellence (NICE), 2020a; Cesari and Proietti, 2020; Ierson, 2020). The rationing of equipment made the headlines, with a worldwide scramble to procure enough ventilators to support the breathing of these critically ill people (CNN, 2020), with car and vacuum manufacturers working to develop basic ventilators, alongside debates about who should receive resources such as critical care and artificial ventilation (Truog, Mitchell and Daley, 2020; Emanuel et al., 2020).

Agility of healthcare systems has been seriously tested across the world, and decision-making is one aspect of this that has received significant attention (Rubin et al., 2020). The British Medical Association published guidance around COVID-19 and decision-making, emphasising the notion of respect, individualism, and fairness, crucially stating that flexibility during the pandemic was key (British Medical Association, 2020). Models of decision-making that have the ability to be agile are described shortly.

Transparency is a crucial element of robust decision-making (British Medical Association, 2020). Novel ways to try to address inequality and ensure sound, and morally just decisions have been developed, such as the use of clinically-based artificial intelligence and machine learning to create algorithms to inform decisions (Vaishya et al., 2020; Debnath et al., 2020). However, a criticism levelled at artificial intelligence, increasingly used outside pandemic to inform health care decisions, policy and develop the evidence base, is that transparency is lacking (Tzachor, Whittlestone and Sundaram, 2020). Equally, Tzachor et al. (2020) also suggest that current government-led mechanisms are equally opaque and we have a societal responsibility to address this opacity.

The emotive nature of end-of-life decision-making, and the desire to do what is deemed morally right, coupled with the threat of litigation has compounded some of the issues usually associated with EOL decisions. In the context of a global pandemic there is an urgency to these decisions that is not usually present, and with resources concentrated on providing at-scale health care responses to COVID-19. So how are these urgent decisions negotiated within systems and, most importantly, at an individual level?

Previous pandemics, like SARS, H1N1, H5N1 and MERS, have laid the ground for decision-making considerations, but these are time, legally, culturally and context dependent (Robert et al., 2020; Christian et al., 2006), and in the case of US policy in H5N1, not always underpinned by robust ethical frameworks (Thomas, Dasgupta and Martinot, 2007). Thomas et al. (2007) argue that in pandemics, policy decisions about resources should be guided by several principles, including:

- Recognising that an ethical dimension exists,
- Identifying specific ethical issues,
- Identifying guidelines and tools for ethical reasoning,
- Deciding who is responsible for which ethical decisions,
- Preparing responsible parties to engage in ethical decision-making,
- Putting the decided plans into action, and
- Evaluating whether the action achieved the intended result (Thomas et al., 2007, p. S26).

More recently, Jeffrey (2020) in his discussion of relational ethics in COVID-19, specifically cites access to resources as an ethical challenge, suggesting that in a pandemic, health care professionals have to shift away from duty-based, Kantian principles of individualism towards more of a collective response that includes society (Jeffrey, 2020). This aligns with a utilitarian approach. Again, there is the need to engage with public fora to understand how acceptable this (Robert et al., 2020), and what the alternatives and consequences might be of following this route.

Factors that influence health care decisions at the end of life: application to COVID-19

Frailty emerged as an important predictor of mortality outcome in COVID-19 in an early observational study across Europe, the COPE study (Hua et al.,

2016), however, as Maltese et al. (2020) pointed out in a scoping review of frailty in COVID-19, frailty was only investigated in regard to overall mortality, hospital contagion, intensive care unit admission rates, and disease phenotypes, rather than in relation to interventions or responsiveness to treatment. A comprehensive frailty assessment, such as that used with older people the comprehensive geriatric assessment has been suggested (Lewis et al., 2020). The British and American Geriatric Societies (Farrell et al., 2020; American Geriatrics Society, 2020) have both issued position statements on the importance of early decision-making to support a proactive approach to manage their illness and anticipate any care needs.

As the COVID-19 pandemic saw the need for a strategic approach to assessing patient's vulnerability, and the UK prepared for the possibility of finite resources across the NHS, a simple clinical assessment was required to aid decision-making. Frailty assessments were adopted to support escalation plans and avoid age discrimination (Swiss Society Of Intensive Care, 2020; SIAARTI, 2020). There is growing evidence towards the use of frailty assessments and indices as important factors for consideration, in the appropriate context, for reliable clinical assessment in COVID-19, and to open up advance care planning discussions (Baker et al., 2020; Aw et al., 2020). Patients with severe frailty have already been identified as having serious adverse outcomes during critical illness (Bagshaw et al., 2015; Bagshaw et al., 2014; Muscedere et al., 2017). These outcomes include an increase in mortality, decreased respiratory function, and the requirement for intensive rehabilitation (De Silva et al., 2018; Bagshaw et al., 2014; Muscedere et al., 2017). More recently in relation to the current SARS-CoV-2 virus, frailty has been directly linked with the prediction of poor prognosis, even more so than the identification of comorbidities (Ma et al., 2020).

Frailty assessments have been well validated in the older population, and there is significant evidence to support this notion (De Silva et al., 2018). The Clinical Frailty Score (CFS) was directly referred to in the NICE COVID-19 rapid guideline: critical care in adults (NG159) (National Institute for Health and Care Excellence (NICE), 2020b). Evidence suggests that the CFS is a reliable predictor of outcome, but is only validated in patients over 65 years of age, and should be used as an adjunct to a patient-centred approach. This premise underpins the notion of good decision-making.

Whilst there have been arguments around the generic use of frailty assessments during the COVID- 19 pandemic, with Moug et al. (2020) warning us about practical applicability of the tool when face to face conversations are limited, we are beginning to see an increase in applicability. Tempering this application with the concept of individualism presents a challenge in how these blunt tools are applied to such important decisions. However, there is a growing body of evidence that supports the use of frailty assessments in older inpatients that are being treated for COVID-19 (National Institute for Health and Care Excellence (NICE), 2020b; Baker et al., 2020; Hewitt et al., 2020; Leclerc et al., 2020; Lewis et al., 2020; Ma et al., 2020; Maltese et al., 2020; Miles et al., 2020; Moug et al., 2020). With an independent correlation between a high frailty score and increased mortality in relation to COVID-19, the use of the frailty assessment is one element to consider in helping optimise and promote the process of decision-making and advance care planning for these patients, as long as the principle of individualism, and balancing of each person's situation, is also considered.

Decision-making principles in COVID-19

Notions of decision-making, while sitting within legal frameworks, are shaped by many cultural and individual influences. Principles that underpin Western concepts of decision-making include autonomy, non-maleficence, beneficence and justice, however, in a time of pandemic these are challenged by utilitarian principles that are juxtaposed against individualism. An example of this is access to ventilators and critical care. At a service level, outside a pandemic situation, elective and non-elective surgical cases comprise almost 50% of admissions to adult critical care services in the UK. In the COVID-19 pandemic, services needed to be prioritised to free up critical care beds, facilities, staff and ventilators. At the height of the first wave of the pandemic, when it became clear the NHS was at risk of being overwhelmed by COVID cases, NHS England took the decision to cancel or postpone all elective surgery, focussing efforts on emergency services and the response to COVID (NHS England and NHS Improvement, 2020). Anaesthetics machines were repurposed into ventilators, and proposals were mooted to share ventilators in the US in the advent of severe shortage (Beitler et al., 2020; White and Lo, 2020). In Australia, similar discussions about who should have access to the finite resource of ventilators were also raised (Simpson, Milnes and Steinfort, 2020). Shifting sands in relation to the evidence in relation to COVID-19 persist, however as the bodies of evidence grow and consolidate what is known, confidence in decisions grow. The COVID-19 pandemic presented a new challenge to public health decision-making, how to convey clear information to protect the public in the absence of clear evidence or in the face of ever-changing evidence? Public health policy is underpinned by similar principles to those in clinical practice. Ferrinho et al. (2020) outlined how Principalism informed the public health debate, and how these can be applied to COVID-19. These can be summarised as:

- The harm principle (restricting individual rights or liberty to protect others);
- The principle of the least restrictive or coercive means (using the least amount of force to impose said restrictions);
- The reciprocity principle (society, or the state, has a duty to support

individuals who have to comply with public health measures – e.g. through supporting lost income);
- The transparency principle (clear accountable, equal contributions from all stakeholders);
- The precautionary principle (applying public health measures in the absence of clear scientific evidence);
- The equity principle (the effects of applying measures should not result in disadvantage to a particular group);
- The principle of robust scientific evidence (in the absence of this, measures are applied to allow generation of that evidence).

During the COVID-19 pandemic, particularly at the outset where there was very little evidence, large-scale lockdowns have been imposed on an almost global scale, underpinned by the precautionary principle. As evidence for lockdowns was generated through sophisticated modelling, public health clinicians had to balance this against equity principles, and this has been a political challenge ever since. In the UK, generation of robust evidence occurred through government commissioning and funding of large-scale COVID-19 research and relaxation of data transfer laws to facilitate the rapid generation of an evidence base.

As we emerged out of the first wave in the UK, concern about legal challenges being mounted against the government, or healthcare providers, for prioritising one health condition (COVID-19) over others, such as ophthalmology and cancer (Campbell, 2020). In the US, concern was also raised over legal challenges around limited access to resources (Cohen, Crespo and White, 2020). Balancing these resource-based arguments is a significant challenge. Collectivism, the concept that the collective interest overrides an individual interest, trumped Individualism at the outset, but as the second wave of COVID-19 approached globally this view was increasingly challenged. For people who were frail, had co-morbidities and were older, global evidence emerged delineating how the mortality from COVID-19 was disproportionately higher, and outcomes were predicted to be very poor in these groups, as outlined earlier. This evidence undoubtedly informed decisions about who should access the finite resources to treat COVID-19 in acute care.

Individual decisions are based on the premise that each decision is weighed against the balance of burdens and benefits for that person, guided by what they feel is in their best interests. Where a person cannot contribute to those decisions, best interest decisions take place. Best interest decisions involve reaching transparent decisions where an individual does not have capacity to contribute, by establishing what would have been an individual's wishes (using family views to inform) and taking these into account, to make a decision (Macfarlane et al., 2019; Faculty of Intensive Care Medicine, 2019; Faculty of Intensive Care Medicine, 2020; Mental Capacity Act, 2005).

Shared decision-making, the principle there should be no decisions without involving those whom the decision affects, was, and continues to be also challenged in COVID-19. At the time of writing, the UK is in the midst of the third wave with nearly three million cases reported (Johns Hopkins University and Medicine, 2021), and over 86 million cases worldwide. While only a proportion of these require hospital and, in turn, critical care services, The benefits and burdens of a prolonged stay in critical care and hospital, as a result of COVID-19, needs to be balanced against individual preferences and goals of treatments, and where these views are absent due to lack of mental capacity (from unconsciousness or critical illness for example), the views of those closest to the individual should be sought (Faculty of Intensive Care Medicine, 2019; Faculty of Intensive Care Medicine, 2020; Mental Capacity Act, 2005). How to enact this principle that all decisions must involve affected individuals, or their legal representatives, presented a new challenge; in-depth discussions with individuals or family were hampered by family not being allowed to visit hospitals (NHS, 2020), impaired communication and lack of visual cues because of Personal Protective Equipment (PPE), time and bed pressures. These conversations increasingly took place over telephone or videocalls (Pattison, 2020; Rose et al., 2020 (submitted)). Every effort to include patients in these decisions, and elicit wishes, is important, and strategies for managing conflict in decision-making (which can be intra-professional, family and patient, or patient-professional, family-professional) is crucial (Faculty of Intensive Care Medicine, 2019; Faculty of Intensive Care Medicine, 2020). Usual communication skills, known to enhance shared decisions at end of life and as a consequence reduce acute and critical care interventions at end of life (Orford et al., 2019), were significantly diminished in these circumstances. Rapid, easy-access, user-friendly and nationally approved guidance, building on existing guidance emerged in the UK to support clinicians in practice to have these conversations, and make decisions that followed best interests, and best practice (Faculty of Intensive Care Medicine, 2019; Faculty of Intensive Care Medicine, 2020; British Medical Association, 2020; Parry, Mannix and Pattison, 2020).

The care home situation, where care homes in UK were overwhelmed with COVID-19 cases, not helped by an initial focus on acute hospital services, and prioritisation of PPE supply chains to acute hospitals as a result of temporary PPE shortages. Those responsible for medical decisions in care homes were required to make rapid decisions about the appropriateness of admission to hospital, sometimes in the absence of family contributions (British Geriatric Society, 2020). There were accusations of blanket decision-making around Do Not Attempt Cardio-Pulmonary Resuscitation (DNACPR) policies in the UK for frail and older people in the first wave of the pandemic, resulting in a national inquiry (https://www.theguardian.com/world/2020/oct/12/inquiry-begins-into-blanket-use-in-england-of-COVID-do-not-resuscitate-orders) (Booth, 2020), with reports of groups of people (such as care home residents) having DNACPR policies applied, and vulnerable people receiving letters from GPs outlining they were no longer for DNACPR. These allegations may have arisen as a result of perceived and misplaced attempts to alleviate potential pressures on the NHS, in order for COVID-19 to be the focus on acute healthcare. This presented a direct threat to notions of individualism, and was quickly challenged with the UK regulator, the Care Quality Commission, issuing stark reminders that this was unacceptable (Care Quality Commission, 2020). However, the fact that these situations arose, suggested confusion and ill-preparation for managing healthcare decisions in the advent of a pandemic.

Since then, the pandemic response has yielded a large volume of information regarding potential in many different patient populations, supported by large scale intelligence from studies such as the International Severe Acute Respiratory and Emerging Infection (ISARIC) global consortium, with the aim of proving a platform to share data, and help delineate aspects of the disease such as clinical characterisation to inform treatment across 132 countries (https://isaric.tghn.org/). The ISARIC 4C algorithm (https://isaric4c.net/risk/), intended for clinicians to augment with decision-making, can now predict with a high degree of accuracy which patients admitted to hospital with COVID-19 are likely to die, presenting an individual mortality score. Clinical teams have to sensitively navigate how to convey this information to individual patients and families, and take this into account when deciding how to use the information in a clinical setting.

Decision aides and shared decision-making

Supportive tools have been proposed in many studies as a mechanism to enhance patient and family involvement in decisions (Oczkowski et al., 2016b; Oczkowski et al., 2016a). As outlined earlier shared decision-making is an approach increasingly adopted in Western healthcare. There is controversy over whether shared decision-making approaches actually impact end of life outcomes, in terms of communication, conflict, trust, satisfaction and quality of dying, not least because of the heterogeneity in how outcomes are measured (Hajizadeh et al., 2016). However, one systematic review highlighted that where shared decision-making has been applied, outcomes tended towards improved affective-cognitive outcomes for patients and families (specifically, knowledge, attitudes and emotions) (Shay and Lafata, 2015). Phillips et al. systemic review of decision aides identified that while the aim of many aides was to foster inclusion in shared decisions, the design of the aides ran counter to this (Phillips et al., 2019), with a large proportion insufficiently addressing patient needs, specifically in relation to the extent in which patients wanted to take part in shared decision-making (and their views of how much families and health professionals should participate), inconsistent acknowledgement, elicitation and documentation of how individual patient needs varied, and level of information (Phillips et al., 2019).

However, developing a sense of connection and interaction is mitigated through a culture of facilitating involvement, by encouraging partnering in care activities (Mitchell et al., 2016). This emphasises how a shared approach and co-design is important, as is the focus on which part of the process, and which outcome, is of most pertinence to patients and families.

Components of shared decision-making have been outlined as (Hajizadeh et al., 2016; Faculty of Intensive Care Medicine, 2019; Faculty of Intensive Care Medicine, 2020):

- Patient/family or caregiver involvement in the decision-making process
- Level/volume information about prognosis/underlying condition/disease process
- Eliciting values, goals and preferences for treatment
- Understanding decision-making role preference (autonomous, active, shared, passive)
- Transparent and understandable clinician recommendations in the context of the decision
- Consideration patients' informed values and goals
- Opportunity for wider consultation
- Assessing understanding of information
- Providing information about treatment choices, and risks and benefits of choices

What is not factored into these principles is how to navigate this in unprecedented situations where resources are challenged, such as the COVID-19 pandemic situation, and where establishing goals and preferences for treatment may not be achievable in the same way. The thorny issue of deontological, or individualistic, practices is set against utilitarian, societal views, and how this in turn affects the ability to achieve person-centred decision-making. We saw how consultation processes and communication were diminished as outpatient and general practitioner (GP) appointments were cancelled, and moved to online formats, where the nuanced interactions in face-to-face appointments about highly emotive and sensitive subjects were lost. Opportunities for wide consultation is lessened as services are restricted to essential services, and although a patient might articulate preferred treatments and a clinician may strive for person-centred decisions, these may not be possible (such as admission to critical care for 'trials' of critical care (Lecuyer et al., 2007; Vink et al., 2018) in a time of surge and crisis.

Advanced Care Planning in a pandemic

The level of preparation also needs to account for receptiveness on both an individual and wider socio-cultural level regarding uptake of end-of-life decisions in the context of a pandemic. In non-pandemic times, UK studies have consistently shown poor uptake and engagement in both community and hospitalised patients (Knight et al., 2020; Sharp et al., 2013; Butler et al., 2015; Kitzinger and Kitzinger, 2016), with similar findings elsewhere in the world (Jimenez et al., 2018), influenced by institutional, legislative as well as cultural drivers. Advanced Care Planning (ACP) offers people the chance to take control and communicate their priorities and preferences for care and treatment options. The current pandemic has highlighted the importance of the concept of ACP as a basis to understand a person's prognosis and support shared decisions. Emergency admissions for patients who are frail or with multiple co-morbidities present risks for both patients and services (NHS England South, 2014; The Kings Fund, 2010; Craswell et al., 2016), including overwhelming services with avoidable admissions and placing vulnerable patients at high risk from hospital-acquired harms through unnecessary admissions. Managing patients in the community to reduce avoidable admissions is one way of preventing an emergency admission (NHS England South, 2014). Understanding a patient's prognosis based on their own health, and the evidence of how a disease may affect certain patient populations is an integral part of an inclusive decision-making process.

Discussions exploring potential outcomes in individual cases, could prevent unwanted admissions/treatment, or in some cases help identify patients' preferences for critical care treatments before an acute onset of any illness such as COVID-19. Shared decision-making should be a collaborative approach in order to combine the expertise and experience of clinicians with the patient's own beliefs and preferences (Faculty of Intensive Care Medicine, 2019).

Understanding a disease process can enable these conversations to be constructive, with sensitive transparency key to this, and information based on the most up-to-date evidence around treatments, symptom management and prognostics. COVID-19 raised feelings of uncertainty for many professionals as many questions around this novel disease continue to be unanswered. This uncertainty creates barriers and may reduce patient satisfaction during a shared decision conversation (Abrams et al., 2020). Addressing uncertainty in shared decision-making requires honesty, acknowledgement of hope, willingness to readdress/revisit, being open to emotions, respecting decisions, being reconciled to the prospect of non-decisions, clarifying goals and coordination of care (Berger, 2015). Exploring a person's prognosis in relation to personal frames of reference, goals for treatment, identifying what outcomes are important to them, in the context of possible pre-existing co-morbidities, and the effect these may have on likely outcomes, allows a realism to be portrayed.

Adapting the process of shared decision-making interactions has been imperative during the course of the pandemic, and in order to breakdown the new barriers faced such as PPE, virtual consultations and the reduction in non-COVID services, all of which have affected interpersonal communication and have presented significant challenges (Montgomery et al., 2020). These challenges have highlighted how, in a pandemic, principles of inclusive or shared decision-making can be disrupted given the rapidity, novelty and enormity of the situation.

Achieving best practice principles

Aiming for person-centred or shared decision-making, framed through individualistic or deontological lenses, is infinitely more achievable in non-pandemic situations. The test comes when there are unforeseen external factors, like COVID-19, that apply enormous pressures to often already creaking health care systems. There are several considerations at play.

What is the resource available to support best practice in decision-making in a pandemic? This includes:

- The human resource of staff available to have those discussions, at the right point in a person's illness trajectory (e.g. clinician and/or ethicist availability);
- The support for training to ensure best practice;
- The infrastructure to support decisions, such as institutional and healthcare policy (e.g. institutional clinical ethics committees, organisational/national guidance or mandates);
- The societal orientation towards those decisions, such as rationing of healthcare;
- The tools available for staff to use to support decision-making, such as structured communication tools, family conferencing;
- The practical, on-the-ground, resources such as communication aides (e.g. videoconferencing to support decisions with families in the absence of family visiting).

Balancing these resources against what people need to make autonomous decisions is a significant ask in a pandemic, as COVID-19 has demonstrated, and the risk and benefits of each approach has to be carefully considered, alongside the consequences. Consequentialism arguments that might usually prevail about outcomes based on what is the right course of action, are challenged in the face of the pandemic as there will be poor outcomes for many based on actions at all levels, governmental, institutional, unit and individual level. The unenviable task rests with all of those who have a stake in the decisions and cannot be abstracted out easily.

On a practical level, the notion of fostering inclusion is paramount. By focussing on how to best include people in decisions that directly and indirectly affect them, and at the same time being honest and transparent about the limits to those decisions, as a consequence of the pandemic, the principle of individualism can be maintained. In these unusual circumstances of the COVID-19, best practice has to centre on maintaining honest communication, transparency, moral balancing and maintaining a good understanding of ethics (both clinical and virtue) to clearly convey stances, inclusion by optimising and addressing potential barriers (such as seeking alternatives to the lack of face-to-face appointments with virtual appointments supported by training on how best to communicate in virtual settings) and seeking individual preferences for treatment that are consistent with what is possible in a constrained healthcare system, and balancing these against societal needs. Decision-making has to be a shared endeavour at all levels of society and the individual, with structures in place to enhance engagement and involvement; through these means we can strive for best decisions in a difficult time.

References

Abrams, E.M., Shaker, M., Oppenheimer, J., Davis, R.S., Buckstein, D.A. and Greenhawt, M., 2020. The challenges and opportunities for shared decision making highlighted by COVID-19. *Journal of Allergy and Clinical Immunology: In Practice*, 8, pp. 2474–2480.

American Geriatrics Society, 2020. American Geriatrics Society policy brief: COVID-19 and nursing homes. *Journal of the American Geriatrics Society*, 68(5), pp. 908–911.

Aw, D., Woodrow, L., Ogliari, G. and Harwood, R., 2020. Association of frailty with mortality in older inpatients with Covid-19: a cohort study. *Age and Ageing*, 49(6), pp. 915–922.

Bagshaw, S.M., Stelfox, H.T., Johnson, J.A., McDermid, R.C., Rolfson, D.B., Tsuyuki, R.T., Ibrahim, Q. and Majumdar, S.R., 2015. Long-term association between frailty and health-related quality of life among survivors of critical illness: a prospective multicenter cohort study. *Critical Care Medicine*, 43(5), pp. 973–982.

Bagshaw, S.M., Stelfox, H.T., McDermid, R.C., Rolfson, D.B., Tsuyuki, R.T., Baig, N., Artiuch, B., Ibrahim, Q., Stollery, D.E., Rokosh, E. and Majumdar, S.R., 2014. Association between frailty and short-and long-term outcomes among critically ill patients: a multicentre prospective cohort study. *CMAJ*, 186(2), pp. E95–E102.

Baker, K.F., Hanrath, A.T., van der Loeff, I.S., Tee, S.A., Capstick, R., Marchitelli, G., Li, A., Barr, A., Eid, A., Ahmed, S. and Bajwa, D., 2020. COVID-19 management in a UK NHS Foundation Trust with a High Consequence Infectious Diseases centre: a detailed descriptive analysis. *medRxiv*. Doi: 2020.05.14.20100834.

BBC News, 2020. Covid: UK seeing second wave, says Boris Johnson. Available at: https://www.bbc.co.uk/news/uk-54212654 (Accessed: 6 January 2021).

Beitler, J.R., Mittel, A.M., Kallet, R., Kacmarek, R., Hess, D., Branson, R., Olson, M., Garcia, I., Powell, B., Wang, D.S. and Hastie, J., 2020. Ventilator sharing during an acute shortage caused by the COVID-19 pandemic. *American Journal of Respiratory and Critical Care Medicine*, 202(4), pp. 600–604.

Berger, Z., 2015. Navigating the unknown: shared decision-making in the face of uncertainty. *Journal of General Internal Medicine*, 30(5), pp. 675–678.

Bloomer, A., 2020. COVID-19: NICE clarifies use of frailty score in new rapid guidance. *Geriatric Medicine Journal*. Available at: https://www.gmjournal.co.uk/covid-19-nice-clarifies-use-of-frailty-score-in-new-rapid-guidance (Accessed: 6 January 2021).

Booth, R., 2020. Inquiry begins into blanket use in England of Covid 'do not resuscitate' orders. *The Guardian*. Available at: https://www.theguardian.com/world/2020/oct/12/inquiry-begins-into-blanket-use-in-england-of-covid-do-not-resuscitate-orders (Accessed: 6 January 2021).

Bosslet, G.T., Pope, T.M., Rubenfeld, G.D., Lo, B., Truog, R.D., Rushton, C.H., Curtis, J.R., Ford, D.W., Osborne, M., Misak, C. and Au, D.H., 2015. An official ATS/AACN/ACCP/ESICM/SCCM policy statement: responding to requests for potentially inappropriate treatments in intensive care units. *American Journal of Respiratory and Critical Care Medicine*, 191(11), pp. 1318–1330.

British Geriatric Society, 2020. COVID-19: Managing the COVID-19 pandemic in care homes for older people. Available at: https://www.bgs.org.uk/resources/covid-19-managing-the-covid-19-pandemic-in-care-homes (Accessed: 6 January 2021).

British Medical Association, 2020. COVID-19 – ethical issues. A guidance note. Available at: https://www.bma.org.uk/media/2360/bma-covid-19-ethics-guidance-april-2020.pdf (Accessed: 6 January 2021).

Butler, J., Binney, Z., Kalogeropoulos, A., Owen, M., Clevenger, C., Gunter, D., Georgiopoulou, V. and Quest, T., 2015. Advance directives among hospitalized patients with heart failure. *JACC: Heart Failure*, 3(2), pp. 112–121.

Cacciapaglia, G., Cot, C. and Sannino, F., 2020. Second wave COVID-19 pandemics in Europe: a temporal playbook. *Scientific Reports*, 10(1), pp. 1–8.

Campbell, D., 2020. Man plans to sue NHS after cancer surgery delayed due to coronavirus. *The Guardian*. Available at: https://www.theguardian.com/society/2020/jul/11/man-plans-to-sue-nhs-after-cancer-surgery-delayed-due-to-coronavirus (Accessed: 6 January 2021).

Care Quality Commission, 2020. Joint statement on advance care planning. Available at: https://www.cqc.org.uk/news/stories/joint-statement-advance-care-planning (Accessed: 6 January 2021).

Cesari, M. and Proietti, M., 2020. COVID-19 in Italy: ageism and decision making in a pandemic. *Journal of the American Medical Directors Association*, 21(5), pp. 576–577.

Christian, M.D., Hawryluck, L., Wax, R.S., Cook, T., Lazar, N.M., Herridge, M.S., Muller, M.P., Gowans, D.R., Fortier, W. and Burkle, F.M., 2006. Development of a triage protocol for critical care during an influenza pandemic. *CMAJ: Canadian Medical Association Journal*, 175(11), pp. 1377–1381.

CNN, 2020. The world is scrambling to buy ventilators in the Covid-19 pandemic. One country has only four of them – for 12 million people. Available at: https://edition.cnn.com/2020/04/18/africa/covid-19-ventilator-shortage-intl-scli/index.html (Accessed: 7 January 2021).

Cohen, I.G., Crespo, A.M. and White, D.B., 2020. Potential legal liability for withdrawing or withholding ventilators during COVID-19: assessing the risks and identifying needed reforms. *JAMA*, 323(19), pp. 1901–1902.

Craswell, A., Marsden, E., Taylor, A. and Wallis, M., 2016. Emergency Department presentation of frail older people and interventions for management: Geriatric Emergency Department Intervention. *Safety in Health*, 2(1), p. 14. Doi: 10.1186/s40886-016-0049-y

De Silva, T.R., Theou, O., Vellas, B., Cesari, M. and Visvanathan, R., 2018. Frailty screening (FRAIL-NH) and mortality in French nursing homes: results from the incidence of pneumonia and related consequences in nursing home residents study. *Journal of the American Medical Directors Association*, 19(5), pp. 411–414.

Debnath, S., Barnaby, D.P., Coppa, K., Makhnevich, A., Kim, E.J., Chatterjee, S., Tóth, V., Levy, T.J., d Paradis, M., Cohen, S.L. and Hirsch, J.S., 2020. Machine learning to assist clinical decision-making during the COVID-19 pandemic. *Bioelectronic Medicine*, 6(1), pp. 1–8.

Emanuel, E.J., Persad, G., Upshur, R., Thome, B., Parker, M., Glickman, A., Zhang, C., Boyle, C., Smith, M. and Phillips, J.P., 2020. Fair allocation of scarce medical resources in the time of Covid-19. *The New England Journal of Medicine*. Available at: https://www.nejm.org/doi/full/10.1056/NEJMsb2005114 (Accessed: 7 January 2021).

European Centre for Disease Prevention and Control, 2020. COVID-19 situation update worldwide, as of 27 September 2020. Available at: https://www.ecdc.europa.eu/en/geographical-distribution-2019-ncov-cases (Accessed: 28 September 2020).

Faculty of Intensive Care Medicine, 2019. *Care at the end of life: A guide to best practice, discussions and decision-making in and around critical care*. London: FICM.

Faculty of Intensive Care Medicine, 2020. *Decision Making for Critical Care in the context of Covid-19. Background to the NICE Guidance*. London: FICM.

Farrell, T.W., Ferrante, L.E., Brown, T., Francis, L., Widera, E., Rhodes, R., Rosen, T., Hwang, U., Witt, L.J., Thothala, N. and Liu, S.W., 2020. AGS Position Statement: Resource Allocation Strategies and Age-Related Considerations in the COVID-19 Era and Beyond. *Journal of the American Geriatrics Society*, 68, pp. 1136–1142.

Ferrinho, P., Sidat, M., Leiras, G., Passos Cupertino de Barros, F. and Arruda, H., 2020. Principalism in public health decision making in the context of the COVID-19 pandemic. *The International Journal of Health Planning and Management*, 35(5), pp. 997–1000.

Fritz, Z., Huxtable, R., Ives, J., Paton, A., Slowther, A.M. and Wilkinson, D., 2020. Ethical road map through the covid-19 pandemic. *BMJ*, 369, p. 2033.

Garbutt, G. and Davies, P., 2011. Should the practice of medicine be a deontological or utilitarian enterprise? *Journal of Medical Ethics*, 37(5), pp. 267–270.

Hajizadeh, N., Uhler, L., Herman, S.W. and Lester, J., 2016. Is shared decision making for end-of-life decisions associated with better outcomes as compared to other forms of decision making? A systematic literature review. *MDM Policy & Practice*, 1(1), p. 2381468316642237.

Ham, C. and Coulter, A., 2001. Explicit and implicit rationing: taking responsibility and avoiding blame for health care choices. *Journal of Health Services Research & Policy*, 6(3), pp. 163–169.

Hewitt, J., Carter, B., Vilches-Moraga, A., Quinn, T.J., Braude, P., Verduri, A., Pearce, L., Stechman, M., Short, R., Price, A. and Collins, J.T., 2020. The effect of frailty on survival in patients with COVID-19 (COPE): a multicentre, European, observational cohort study. *The Lancet Public Health*, 5(8), pp. e444–e451.

Hua, F., Xie, H., Worthington, H.V., Furness, S., Zhang, Q. and Li, C., 2016. Oral hygiene care for critically ill patients to prevent ventilator-associated pneumonia. *Cochrane Database of Systematic Reviews*, 10, Cd008367.

Ierson, K.V., 2020. Healthcare ethics during a pandemic. *The Western Journal of Emergency Medicine*, 21(3), pp. 477–483.

Jeffrey, D.I., 2020. Relational ethical approaches to the COVID-19 pandemic. *Journal of Medical Ethics*, 46, pp. 495–498.

Jimenez, G., Tan, W.S., Virk, A.K., Low, C.K., Car, J. and Ho, A.H.Y., 2018. Overview of systematic reviews of advance care planning: summary of evidence and global lessons. *Journal of Pain and Symptom Management*, 56(3), pp. 436–459.
Johns Hopkins University and Medicine, 2021. COVID-19 Dashboard by the Center for Systems Science and Engineering (CSSE) at Johns Hopkins. Available at: https://coronavirus.jhu.edu/map.html (Accessed: 7 January 2021).
Kash, B.A., Spaulding, A., Gamm, L.D. and Johnson, C.E., 2014. Healthcare strategic management and the resource based view. *Journal of Strategy and Management*, 7(3), pp. 251–264.
Kitzinger, C. and Kitzinger, J., 2016. Increasing the awareness and uptake of Advance Decisions in Wales. Available at: https://www.wcpp.org.uk/wp-content/uploads/2018/04/PPIW-Report-Increasing-the-awareness-and-uptake-of-Advance-Decisions.pdf (Accessed: 7 January 2021).
Knight, T., Malyon, A., Fritz, Z., Subbe, C., Cooksley, T., Holland, M. and Lasserson, D., 2020. Advance care planning in patients referred to hospital for acute medical care: results of a national day of care survey. *E-Clinical Medicine*, 19, p. 100235.
Leclerc, T., Donat, N., Donat, A., Pasquier, P., Nicolas, L., Schaeffer, E., D'aranda, E., Cotte, J., Fontaine, B., Perrigault, P.F. and Michel, F., 2020. Prioritisation of ICU treatments for critically ill patients in a COVID-19 pandemic with scarce resources. *Anaesthesia Critical Care & Pain Medicine*, 39, pp. 333–339.
Lecuyer, L., Chevret, S., Thiery, G., Darmon, M., Schlemmer, B. and Azoulay, É., 2007. The ICU trial: a new admission policy for cancer patients requiring mechanical ventilation. *Critical Care Medicine*, 35(3), pp. 808–814.
Lewis, E.G., Breckons, M., Lee, R.P., Dotchin, C. and Walker, R., 2020. Rationing care by frailty during the COVID-19 pandemic. *Age and Ageing*, 50(1), pp. 7–10.
Ma, Y., Hou, L., Yang, X., Huang, Z., Yang, X., Zhao, N., He, M., Shi, Y., Kang, Y., Yue, J. and Wu, C., 2020. The association between frailty and severe disease among COVID-19 patients aged over 60 years in China: a prospective cohort study. *BMC Medicine*, 18(1), pp. 1–8.
Macfarlane, M., Shayler, S., Nelms, L. and Willis, D., 2019. Tracey judgement and hospice DNACPR orders: steady as she goes or seismic change? *BMJ Supportive & Palliative Care*, 9(4), pp. e34–e34.
Maltese, G., Corsonello, A., Di Rosa, M., Soraci, L., Vitale, C., Corica, F. and Lattanzio, F., 2020. Frailty and COVID-19: a systematic scoping review. *Journal of Clinical Medicine*, 9(7), p. 2106.
Mental Capacity Act, 2005. UK: HMSO. Available at: https://www.legislation.gov.uk/ukpga/2005/9/contents (Accessed: 7 January 2021).
Miles, A., Webb, T.E., Mcloughlin, B., Mannan, I., Rather, A., Knopp, P. and Davis, D., 2020. Outcomes from COVID-19 across the range of frailty: excess mortality in fitter older people. *European Geriatric Medicine*. Doi: 10.1007/s41999-020-00354-7
Mills, J.B., 1987. *Utilitarianism and other Essays*. London, UK: Penguin.
Mitchell, M.L., Coyer, F., Kean, S., Stone, R., Murfield, J. and Dwan, T., 2016. Patient, family-centred care interventions within the adult ICU setting: An integrative review. *Australian Critical Care*, 29(4), pp. 179–193.
Montgomery, C.H., Sturdy, S., McCulloch, C., Doherty, A., Pattison, N. 2020. Critical care work during COVID-19: a sociological analysis of staff experiences. Available at: https://ssrn.com/abstract=3741243 *or* http://dx.doi.org/10.2139/ssrn.3741243 (Accessed: 7 January 2021).

Morris, A.C., 2015. Triage during pandemic influenza: seeking absolution in numbers? *British Journal of Anaesthesia*, 114(6), pp. 865–867.

Moug, S., Carter, B., Myint, P.K., Hewitt, J., McCarthy, K. and Pearce, L., 2020. Decision-making in COVID-19 and Frailty. *Geriatrics*, 5(2), p. 30. Doi: 10.3390/geriatrics5020030

Muscedere, J., Waters, B., Varambally, A., Bagshaw, S.M., Boyd, J.G., Maslove, D., Sibley, S. and Rockwood, K., 2017. The impact of frailty on intensive care unit outcomes: a systematic review and meta-analysis. *Intensive Care Medicine*, 43(8), pp. 1105–1122.

National Institute for Health and Care Excellence (NICE), 2020a. COVID-19 rapid guideline: critical care in adults. Available at: https://www.nice.org.uk/guidance/ng159/resources/covid19-rapid-guideline-critical-care-in-adults-pdf-66141848681413 (Accessed: 7 January 2021).

National Institute for Health and Care Excellence (NICE), 2020b. NICE updates rapid COVID-19 guideline on critical care. Available at: https://www.nice.org.uk/news/article/nice-updates-rapid-covid-19-guideline-on-critical-care (Accessed: 7 January 2021).

NHS, 2020. Visiting healthcare inpatient settings during the COVID-19 pandemic: principles. Available at: https://www.england.nhs.uk/coronavirus/wp-content/uploads/sites/52/2020/03/C0751-visiting-healthcare-inpatient-settings-principles-131020_.pdf (Accessed: 7 January 2021).

NHS England and NHS Improvement, 2020. Next steps on NHS response to COVID-19: Letters from Sir Simon Stevens and Amanda Pritchard. Available at: https://www.england.nhs.uk/coronavirus/publication/next-steps-on-nhs-response-to-covid-19-letter-from-simon-stevens-and-amanda-pritchard/ (Accessed: 7 January 2021).

NHS England South, 2014. Safe, compassionate care for frail older people using an integrated care pathway: practical guidance for commissioners, providers and nursing, medical and allied health professional leaders. Available at: https://www.england.nhs.uk/wp-content/uploads/2014/02/safe-comp-care.pdf (Accessed: 7 January 2021).

NHSE, 2020. NHS and other professional bodies' response to the Sunday Times, 25 October 2020. Available at: https://www.england.nhs.uk/2020/10/nhs-and-other-professional-bodies-response-to-sunday-times/ (Accessed: 6 January 2021).

Oczkowski, S.J., Chung, H.O., Hanvey, L., Mbuagbaw, L. and You, J.J., 2016a. Communication tools for end-of-life decision-making in ambulatory care settings: a systematic review and meta-analysis. *PloS One*, 11(4), p. e0150671.

Oczkowski, S.J., Chung, H.O., Hanvey, L., Mbuagbaw, L. and You, J.J., 2016b. Communication tools for end-of-life decision-making in the intensive care unit: a systematic review and meta-analysis. *Critical Care*, 20(1), p. 97.

Orford, N.R., Milnes, S., Simpson, N., Keely, G., Elderkin, T., Bone, A., Martin, P., Bellomo, R., Bailey, M. and Corke, C., 2019. Effect of communication skills training on outcomes in critically ill patients with life-limiting illness referred for intensive care management: a before-and-after study. *BMJ Supportive & Palliative Care*, 9(1), pp. e21–e21.

Parry, R., Mannix, K. and Pattison, N., 2020. How to have urgent conversations about withdrawing and withholding life-sustaining treatments in critical care–including phone and video calls. Available at: https://www.realtalktraining.co.uk/app/uploads/2020/04/How-to-have-urgent-conversations-about-withdrawing-and-withholding-life-sustaining-treatments-in-critical-care-Full-post.pdf (Accessed: 7 January 2021).

Pattison, N., 2020. End-of-life decisions and care in the midst of a global coronavirus (COVID-19) pandemic. *Intensive & Critical Care Nursing*, 58, p. 102862.

Phillips, G., Lifford, K., Edwards, A., Poolman, M. and Joseph-Williams, N., 2019. Do published patient decision aids for end-of-life care address patients' decision-making needs? A systematic review and critical appraisal. *Palliative Medicine*, 33(8), pp. 985–1002.

Pollaris, G. and Sabbe, M., 2016. Reverse triage: more than just another method. *European Journal of Emergency Medicine*, 23(4), pp. 240–247.

Robert, R., Kentish-Barnes, N., Boyer, A., Laurent, A., Azoulay, E. and Reignier, J., 2020. Ethical dilemmas due to the Covid-19 pandemic. *Annals of Intensive Care*, 10(1), pp. 1–9.

Rockwood, K., Song, X., MacKnight, C., Bergman, H., Hogan, D.B., McDowell, I. and Mitnitski, A., 2005. A global clinical measure of fitness and frailty in elderly people. *CMAJ: Canadian Medical Association Journal*, 173(5), pp. 489–495.

Rose, L.Y., Casey, L., Cook, A., Metaxa, V., Pattison, N., Ramsay, P., Rafferty, A., Xyrichis, A. and Meyer, J., (Submitted). Communication and virtual visiting for families of patients in intensive care during COVID-19: a UK national survey. *Critical Care*. Doi: 10.1513/AnnalsATS.202012-1500OC.

Rubin, E.J., Harrington, D.P., Hogan, J.W., Gatsonis, C., Baden, L.R. and Hamel, M.B., 2020. The urgency of care during the Covid-19 pandemic—learning as we go. *New England Journal of Medicine*, 382, pp. 2461–2462.

Savulescu, J., Persson, I. and Wilkinson, D., 2020. Utilitarianism and the Pandemic. *Bioethics*, 34, pp. 620–632.

Sharp, T., Moran, E., Kuhn, I. and Barclay, S., 2013. Do the elderly have a voice? Advance care planning discussions with frail and older individuals: a systematic literature review and narrative synthesis. *British Journal of General Practice*, 63(615), pp. e657–e668.

Shay, L.A. and Lafata, J.E., 2015. Where is the evidence? A systematic review of shared decision making and patient outcomes. *Medical Decision Making*, 35(1), pp. 114–131.

SIAARTI, 2020. *Clinical ethics recommendations for the allocation of intensive care treatments in exceptional resource-limited circumstances.* Italy: SIAARTI.

Simpson, N., Milnes, S. and Steinfort, D., 2020. Don't forget shared decision-making in the COVID-19 crisis. *Internal Medicine Journal*, 50(6), pp. 761–763.

Spector-Bagdady, K., Laventhal, N., Applewhite, M., Firn, J.I., Hogikyan, N.D., Jagsi, R., Marks, A., McLeod-Sordjan, R., Parker, L.S., Smith, L.B. and Vercler, C.J., 2020. Flattening the rationing curve: the need for explicit guidelines for implicit rationing during the COVID-19 Pandemic. *The American Journal of Bioethics*, 20(7), pp. 77–80.

Swiss, S.O.I.C.M., 2020. Recommendations for the admission of patients with COVID-19 to intensive care and intermediate care units (ICUs and IMCUs). *Swiss Medical Weekly*, 150, p. w20227.

The Kings Fund, 2010. *Avoiding hospital admissions. What does the research evidence say?* London, UK: The Kings Fund.

Thomas, J.C., Dasgupta, N. and Martinot, A., 2007. Ethics in a pandemic: a survey of the state pandemic influenza plans. *American Journal of Public Health*, 97(Supplement_1), pp. S26–S31.

Truog, R.D., Mitchell, C. and Daley, G.Q., 2020. The toughest triage—allocating ventilators in a pandemic. *New England Journal of Medicine*, 382(21), pp. 1973–1975.

Tzachor, A., Whittlestone, J. and Sundaram, L., 2020. Artificial intelligence in a crisis needs ethics with urgency. *Nature Machine Intelligence*, 2(7), pp. 365–366.

Vaishya, R., Javaid, M., Khan, I.H. and Haleem, A., 2020. Artificial Intelligence (AI) applications for COVID-19 pandemic. *Diabetes & Metabolic Syndrome: Clinical Research & Reviews*, 14, pp. 337–339.

Vink, E.E., Azoulay, E., Caplan, A., Kompanje, E.J. and Bakker, J., 2018. Time-limited trial of intensive care treatment: an overview of current literature. *Intensive Care Medicine*, 44(9), pp. 1369–1377.

White, D.B. and Lo, B., 2020. A framework for rationing ventilators and critical care beds during the COVID-19 pandemic. *JAMA*, 323(18), pp. 1773–1774.

World Health Organization, 2020. COVID-19 latest updates: media briefing on COVID-19. Available at: https://www.who.int/emergencies/diseases/novel-coronavirus-2019/media-resources/press-briefings (Accessed: 7 January 2021).

Yang, X., Yu, Y., Xu, J., Shu, H., Liu, H., Wu, Y., Zhang, L., Yu, Z., Fang, M., Yu, T. and Wang, Y., 2020. Clinical course and outcomes of critically ill patients with SARS-CoV-2 pneumonia in Wuhan, China: a single-centered, retrospective, observational study. *The Lancet Respiratory Medicine*, 8(5), pp. 475–481.

Zhou, F., Yu, T., Du, R., Fan, G., Liu, Y., Liu, Z., Xiang, J., Wang, Y., Song, B., Gu, X. and Guan, L., 2020. Clinical course and risk factors for mortality of adult inpatients with COVID-19 in Wuhan, China: a retrospective cohort study. *The Lancet*, 395, pp. 1054–1062.

7 NHS values, ritual, religion, and Covid19 death

Douglas Davies

Key points

Of paramount importance to the major British response to the Covid19 global pandemic was a dramatic intensification of the pre-existing significance of the National Health Service as the prime carrier of the core cultural value of life itself. A theoretical model accounting for how emotions generate 'values' and belief-like constructs from otherwise ordinary 'ideas', in a process embracing notions of identity and even of destiny, parallels innovative popular responses that ritualised gratitude to self-sacrificing health-care workers. This applause from countless doorsteps, along with daily medical-scientific-political bulletins, and a distinctive address from the Queen, generated both a diffuse and highly focused ritualization of British society, all at a time when major religious buildings were actually closed.

This worldview approach to the British National Health Service (NHS) during the Covid19 period of cultural trauma deploys the anthropological-sociological concepts of sacralisation of identity, and dual-sovereignty, to analyse forms of ritual-symbolic behaviour that intensify pre-existing features of British cultural belief and practice. Driven by anxiety over viral infection and fear of bereavement and death, mortality emerges from culturally marginal to sharp public focus in the NHS as bearer of Britain's core cultural values of healthcare fostered through its distinctive curation of 'life'.

Worldview, ideas-identity-destiny

The worldview model offers an increasingly valuable and inclusive perspective upon cultural values, religion, spirituality, secularity and the like, with relevant intellectual roots in social and psychological traditions (Weber, [1922] 1965; Freud, [1932] 1973; Droogers and van Harskamp,

2014; Taves and Asprem, 2018; THEOS, 2020). Of direct relevance is my own, Droogers' influenced, analysis of mortality in Britain, formulated 'as a contribution to world-view studies'; setting the NHS alongside the Monarchy, military, and media, as British institutions constituting its 'Establishment' (Davies, 2015, p. 373). Little did I think, when writing it, how germane its worldview framing of 'lifestyle and death-style in Britain today' would prove under Covid19.

Intensified through national-political media, this pandemic period brings problems of existence to the fore through sickness, death, bereavement and severe constraints upon ordinary life. Captured in idioms of lockdown and shielding, the government-imposed constrained lifestyle was legitimated as saving life and protecting the NHS. This coalescing of 'life and NHS' by enjoining members of society to restrict their activities triggered widespread emotional responses, including that of public-private ritualisation. To analyse these behavioural dynamics I deploy a theoretical scheme embracing emotions and identity, grounded in the hypothesis that if some idea is pervaded by an emotion it is transformed into a value, that when such values help constitute a sense of identity they constitute *beliefs* and if, beyond that, some beliefs foster and frame a sense of destiny, they can be regarded as religious beliefs or destiny factors (Davies, 2017, pp. 5–8, p. 54). Of thousands of ideas only a minority attract emotionally significant commitments and affinities to metamorphose into *values*, and fewer still feed our very sense of identity to constitute beliefs. This formulaic hypothesis allows us to differentiate between degrees of intensity of commitment between values, beliefs, and religious beliefs (or destiny factors), and also accounts for those reckoning themselves 'spiritual but not religious', whose identity is fostered through many emotion-laden values but in terms of the hope-laden condition of devotees of explicit religious traditions whose eschatological dynamics confer a sense of our own destiny or life-path.

As for this schema and the NHS, under the constraints of the Covid19 Crisis period two issues coincide, one personal and one communal. At the personal level, practically all Britons have direct experience of the NHS through local general practitioners, medical centres, and hospitals whose Accident and Emergency Departments were, until the Covid19 outbreak, increasingly overloaded by self-directed individuals. Similarly, from antenatal classes to the hospitalisation of terminally sick relatives, the NHS became a cradle to grave institution, with millions having positive private NHS memories that do not make *news*. These are invariably emotion-saturated, whether through accidents, anxiety over neo-natal and infant illnesses, the anguish over mid-life diagnoses demanding operating or medication, or in worrying chronic conditions. Then, with the onset of maladies in old age, terminal illness, hospitalisation, and bereavement and its attendant flows of grief, NHS systems frame events and transforming the bare name of the NHS into the emotion-pervaded value. For a few, the NHS even contributes to a person's identity.

Communally, the Covid19 period has both intensified and aggregated such personal *values* not only into a collective *values* set but also, I propose, into a form of identity-linked *belief*. Both the NHS and British society have, since its immediate post-war formation, undergone a variety of developments affecting people's expectations, sometimes even to the point of dependency on the Welfare State. This has, however, sometimes involved negative episodes evincing blame, as when some babies' body parts were retained without parental knowledge or permission (Redfern, 2001), and Dr Harold Shipman murdered over 200 of his otherwise appreciative patients, a phenomenon best depicted as 'cultural betrayal' (Davies, 2015, pp. 21–22, pp. 140–141). Some malaise over more routine procedures and, very occasionally, miss-diagnoses and treatment, also occur and over a couple of pre-Covid19 decades both formal and personal concerns over increased managerial bureaucratisation had erupted (Francis, 2010; Rothery, 2013). These factors echo aspects of the relationship between the individual and the state marked in the *Beveridge Report* of 1942 and already accounted for in my *Mors Britannica* study (Beveridge, [1942] 1966; Davies, 2015, pp. 98–103).

Ritual-symbolism and Covid19 NHS

However, not until now has the NHS become the absolute focus of social and cultural preoccupation in a media intensified spotlight uniting individual and communal emotional dynamics. Singled out by political leaders as in need of *saving*; motifs of *Save our NHS* or *Save the NHS* became emphatic mottos, notably daily political-medical-scientific briefings broadcast from 10 Downing Street. Here ritual-symbolism combined medical-political messages. Three lecterns, variously occupied by the Prime Minister, Health Minister, other leading politicians, Chief and Assistant Medical Officers, and some key scientific advisors were bordered by Union Flags in a wood-panelled room. Such flags are relatively unusual ritual objects in most non-military British ceremonial, certainly when compared with the US and its omnipresent Stars and Stripes. The lecterns, as viewed on television screen from left to right, carried the statements *Stay Home, Protect the NHS, Save Lives*. The verbal messages given there, as exhibited in many public contexts, combined personal-domestic and national interests through the pivotal call to *Protect the NHS, Save the NHS*, or *Save Our NHS*. This *saving* of the NHS had its centre of gravity in the widespread government fear that Intensive Care Units (ITUs) would be overcome by the numbers of the very sick. The Downing Street briefings and their timing framed this anxiety in its rite-like event of the key personnel processing from *backstage* to the lecterns. Later, a television monitor with questions posed by the media or even members of the general public was included as the heart of government was aligned with personal and community concerns. Here, then, a scenario involved in which personal-individual values were extended to identity-enhancing *beliefs* embedded in national concerns. These performances of *state* officials, closely observed, repeated, and commented upon by media, emerged as belief-rooted behaviour whose daily repetition soon afforded its own form of ritual.

Applause

One of the most symbolic NHS interfaces between the private-domestic *values* and public-communal *beliefs* arising over a ten-week period from early March until May 2020 involved people being enjoined to stand at the threshold of their homes, albeit socially distanced from their neighbours, and clap each Thursday evening at 8:00 p.m. This informally generated action became widely adopted, most especially in urban contexts of appropriate numbers of people. Some banged saucepans played musical instruments, in a concerted sound to appreciate the work of the *front-line* medical staff, another term reminiscent of military activity. This echoes the anthropological notion of *communitas* or the shared emotional experience of those in a *liminal* or transitional state occurring in a rite of passage. By etymological accident, *liminal* happens to be derived from the Latin *limen* or threshold, literally doorstep. Victor Turner developed *communitas* to add an emotional dimension to Arnold van Gennep's original *liminality* and its preoccupation with social status. While both were concerned with more formal rites of passage as vehicles for transition in social status, something inapplicable to doorstep applause, there does seem to be a degree of family resemblance between them, especially if we see this doorstep behaviour more in Turner's notion of celebratory liminoid activity in modern societies (Davies, 2002, pp. 126–127, p. 132). Here there is much to ponder in terms of the NHS, core cultural values, and public performance in the light of Turner's view that '*communitas* is the primal ground, the *urgrund* of social structure' (1975, p. 23).

Other symbolic accompaniments of this period include the drawing and display of rainbows, small and large, these often carried *Thank You NHS* messages. Whether or not many were aware of the ancient Near-Eastern symbolic significance of the rainbow, as in the biblical sign of divine promise with Noah following the great flood, when God reaffirmed a covenant with humanity, or not we do not know (Genesis 9: 12–17). Still, there is a colourful and ease of production of this semi-circular design, especially by younger children, and thousands were displayed in house windows. I was given one, through the letterbox, drawn in coloured pencil by the infant daughter of neighbours and, personally speaking, found it an emotionally touching *thought*, not least when the same family offered to do shopping in the event of personal isolation. Something many experienced.

Monarch, old soldier, and cultural treasure

While the Queen and other members of the Royal family participated in the practice of applause, her prime ritual-symbolic presence was captured, especially, in two events – one an investiture, another a speech- whose dynamic significance integrated historical values with the crisis. On Friday 17 July 2020 Her Majesty Queen Elisabeth II knighted Captain Thomas Moore at Windsor Castle. As a centenarian this former soldier had undertaken to walk some one hundred lengths of his garden as a charitable support of the NHS. This captured public attention and, through social and press media, led to 'The Captain Tom Foundation' whose webpage allowed for donations (www.captaintom.org). The Foundation speaks of 'Captain Tom and his family' engaged in 'Combating loneliness, Supporting hospices, Helping those facing bereavement'. It raised more than thirty million pounds, with a motto expressed as 'Inspiring hope where it is needed most'. Among other events, he published an autobiography, *Tomorrow will be a Good Day*, and a picture book for children. He was given the Freedom of the City of London in a virtual ceremony. In other contexts, the military provided its own actual ritual frame for his later garden-walking. His Knighthood too was aligned with the NHS, and the fact that Queen Elisabeth appeared in person for its ceremonial event was stressed by the media as her first public appearance since the cultural lockdown, a period she otherwise spent at Windsor Castle. For she, too, clearly belonged to Captain Tom's generation of those who were being *shielded* at home from the virus. In some ways this can be seen as complementing her formal address to the nation given on 5 April 2020, itself a rite-like event whose words were powerfully enhanced as coming from the Queen.

This timely speech, with extensive media coverage, was remarkable for the rarity of her public addresses, largely limited to her traditional Queen's Speech on Christmas Day. Its text adopted a rite-like form, speaking of *an increasingly challenging time* involving *disruption in the life of our country*, as well as of *grief, financial difficulties*, and *enormous changes to the daily lives of us all*. The very second sentence pinpoints 'everyone on the NHS frontline, as well as care workers' and all essential role providers. Here the *frontline*, military-like motif marks the overarching cultural sense of embattlement with the Covid19 virus. When talking of *tackling this disease* she hoped that in the future people would look back and 'take pride in how they responded to this challenge', an expression that older people probably saw as an echo of the popular semi-jocular idiom 'what did you do in the war Daddy?' But now there was no sense of a jest. The war-reference was obvious as she went on to say that those who come after us will say the Britons of this generation were *as strong as any*. Its resonance with war conditions was reinforced when she spoke of her first broadcast made in 1940, during that War when, helped by her sister, she spoke 'to children who had been evacuated from their homes and sent away for their own safety'. Here the theme of 'safety' and 'homes' ran alongside 'challenge' and 'common endeavour'. Moving towards its conclusion she coupled 'the great advances of science' with 'our instinctive compassion to heal' as she used a double reference to 'succeed' and 'success'. The final three sentences of the speech are especially telling and merit full quotation for a very particular ritual- focused reason.

> *We should take comfort that while we may have more still to endure, better days will return. We will be with our friends again. We will be with our families again. We will meet again. But for now, I send my thanks and warmest good wishes to you all.*

Unlike Christmas speeches which always carry some explicit Christian reference, there is none here for this Covid19 address is distinctively different for, analytically speaking, it expresses a strongly implicit form of *cultural blessing* inherent in those final sentences and their liturgy-like three-fold, 'We will be', 'We will be', and 'We will meet'. The object of this future-directed comfort lies in *friends* and *family*. Whether friends coming first was intended to embrace wider society before the immediacy of family remains a moot point. What is clear is that the 'We will meet again' idiom echoes the familiar Second World War song, 'We'll meet again, don't know where, don't know when, but I know we'll meet again some sunny day'. That 1939 song was made famous by Vera Lynn, often called 'The Forces' Sweetheart'. A 'national treasure' in herself, she died on 18 June 2020 and was cremated on 10 July at the Woodvale Crematorium, East Sussex. This death was, itself, ritually serendipitous for this crisis period. Her coffin, covered by the Union Jack, and its hearse had a military escort through her town before it moved to the Brighton crematorium, passing through crowds reported as having spontaneously sung 'We'll meet again'. At the service her bearers were drawn from the army, navy, air force and her own honours-insignia were laid on it. There was, in this, some echo of the public framing of the 1997 funeral procession of Diana Princess of Wales.

Earlier that day, Sir Tom Moore paid tribute to her. While hundreds lined the town's streets and sang, a spitfire fly-past took place. The day before her funeral an enormous portrait of her was projected onto the White Cliffs of Dover – a visual evocation of her war-time song on that very topic, and above which the Battle of Britain was fought by the Royal Air Force. These events linking the Queen, Sir Tom, and Dame Vera Lynne show how a tradition-laden British culture, highly publicised through many media outlets, able and willing to integrate diverse and 'accidental' events in a ritual-symbolic tapestry of cultural identity-enhancement under stress, evoking war-resilience through an old-soldier's endeavour, honoured by the Monarch in a society where *honours* are generally prized. It would be difficult to artificially stage such a multi-vocal symbolic collage. In this we do not encounter a ritual in the sense of a repeated event, but a unique dramatic collocation of mutually evocative symbolic units whose separate elements fused in culture-laden affinities, with the NHS and national survival at its heart.

Time passing and 'destiny'

On the wider public stage reflected in the media, by end of October there has emerged much discussion as to whether popular support for government-imposed rules of social distancing can be sustained for long periods of time.

Wales reinstated a strict regime from late October 2020, as did Scotland and Northern Ireland, all at the very time when the Westminster Parliament raised the possibility of a shorter period of isolation for those reacting positive to Covid19 tests, after a week of intense politics between central government and senior metropolitan leaders of Northern English cities over funding the pinpointing of places such as Blackpool and Manchester as in need of much tighter control than some South and South-East English areas. A similar argument arises over the funding of free school meals for poorer schoolchildren over impending holiday periods. The distinctive high-profile leadership of the well-known footballer Marcus Rushford in fostering financial support was in October 2020 widely supported by other volunteers to fill this apparent gap in provision. All this suggested tensions between English political dynamics and the very large populations of these Northern areas, unlike the smaller populations of other UK countries. So too with party political division which had, over the early crisis period showed some unity of purpose. Still, even though some politically aligned sense of *communitas* seemed to wane, concerns over the NHS remained steady, as though it was a distinctive entity of its own.

What then of the NHS, not only as an identity conferring institution motivating cultural 'belief' but also, perchance as a signpost for cultural destiny? While the category of 'destiny' is far from easy to define, the fact that it is often associated with explicit religious traditions and, arguably, also with committed political ideologies makes it potentially problematic within a liberal democracy. Yet, it is worth pressing this point for no other institution embraces the entire population with something like an existential and ontological property, albeit but an ethic of care for all at their point of need in sickness and mortality. Put tersely, it is the very notion of *life* itself, its preservation and terminal care within a Welfare State that, arguably, has come to constitute Britain's core cultural value. Moreover, this preoccupation with vitality-mortality rooted welfare is sustained and increasingly fostered by all political parties as an evolving scheme of national development. This contrasts sharply with the US where the 'American Dream' and its 'Manifest Destiny', espouses no similar health programme, rather it prompts political division, as when 'Obama-care' is deeply opposed by President Trump. Recent decades have witnessed all UK politicians affirm that the 'NHS is safe in our hands'. Mantra-like, this claim gained considerable significance when Prime Minister, Boris Johnson, was hospitalized with Covid19: almost ironically, he was now *safe* in NHS hands, a case reminiscent of the notion of the wounded healer's capacity to benefit other sufferers, an idiom seemingly rejected by President Trump's Covid19 episode (Davies 2002, p. 147).

NHS and 'religion'?

Significantly, the evolving NHS has also paralleled both increasing multi-culturalism and increased secularisation of the British public arena, and while the Church of England in its inclusive mode of faith is accepting of other denominations and religions and, in some ways, even speaks for them, 'religion' no longer has a singular attraction for all, not least for the growing number for whom indifference matches or outweighs faith commitment. It is especially potent to witness the governmental closure of all places of worship at the height of the Covid19 crisis. Whereas many cathedrals have served extensively as prime sites of gathering, memorial, and ceremony following crises in recent decades, this was now impossible. Along with many places of worship across most religious traditions now went online, and while there are reports of more people engaging in prayer, the clear social fact is that 'religion' was now, more clearly than ever, located in the private sphere of online choice. This will, in due course, provide much debatable material for the sociologists of secularisation.

These issues encourage consideration of the NHS as a religion-like focus of deep human concern, perhaps even of 'ultimate concern' – a phrase redolent of theological interest – 'The object of theology is what concerns us ultimately' (Tillich, 1953, p. 15). Although such a discussion cannot be pursued here, I do raise the theme of the NHS as potentially expressing a 'soft destiny' in the UK, an appropriate stance for a modern liberal democracy where 'destiny' embraces the idea of meaning and purpose to life pursued through shared practical ethics. That engages both separate religious traditions possessing their own 'harder' destiny factors, and religiously indifferent or secular folk who also desire 'significance' and ultimacy. Here further theoretical analysis can be brought to bear on the ritualising of the NHS, in that ritual seldom accompanies empty categories or a meaning-bereft cultural acts. It is because the NHS carries core British cultural values that the government could adopt it as the prime medium of attack upon the Covid19 crisis and the general public easily respond. To purse the 'saving' and 'protecting' of the NHS we now turn to a pair of concepts that may help explain that challenge.

Sacralisation of identity, dual sovereignty and spirituality

While the two conceptual foci adopted here represent relatively ignored elements of social theory, they carry a distinctive relevance for the position already discussed on matters of identity, emotion, religion and spirituality in healthcare.

Sacrality and NHS

The notion of 'the sacred' relates to the history, theology, and social science of religions. Sociologically, the Durkheimian tradition argued for the sacred being a quality of group experience that strengthened devotees and elicited a sense of respect through ritual events (Durkheim, 1915, pp. 205–239). The Dutch sociologist Hans Mol, separately developed the 'respect' element in terms of identity theory, arguing that phenomena contributing to a person or group's sense of identity are, in turn, viewed as above reproach, and accorded respect – even awe. He spoke of the commitment associated with institutions ensuring safe identities as anchoring 'a system of meaning in the emotions' that 'given time, develops into awe which wraps the system in 'don't touch' sentiments' (1976, p. 12). Such identity conferral is often found in religion, family, profession, hobby and volunteering, I propose that within the UK it is the NHS that has also acquired this capacity on a grand scale. To what Mol saw as a sacralising processes occurring 'with time', we can add the elements of crisis, sickness and death as speeding up the mutually interactive process of the sacralisation of identity and of institution. These elements enter into the process of 'intensification' whereby ordinary behaviour is transformed into ritually potent activity (Davies, 2008).

Though it merits much more extensive analysis than be provided here, and with both Durkheim and Mol in mind, future researchers might also be considering Roy Rappaport's extensive analysis of ritual to explore the very phrase 'NHS' in terms of his key concept of 'ultimate sacred postulate' (Rappaport, 1999, pp. 326–328). Interestingly, for an anthropologist, he also found Tillich's theological engagement with 'ultimate concern' worth his attention (Rappaport, 1999, pp. 284–284). Provisionally, given that the abstract notions of 'life', 'care' and 'death' are concretely allied with sickness, protective clothing, corpses and funerals, one might consider 'NHS' as an ultimate sacred postulate in which these 'most abstract of conceptions are bound to the most immediate and substantial of experiences' (Rappaport, 1999, p. 405).

In many Covid19 visual and narrative contexts, often media broadcast, the intensive therapy unit (ITU) assumed primacy of hospitalised space, along with concern over a sufficiency of ITU beds, medical protective clothing, apparatus and staff. The provision of seven regional Nightingale Hospitals was rapidly made, an emergency response aided by military logistics, though not as necessary as originally anticipated. Still, at the time of writing in October 2020 some may yet be required as a resurgence of infection occurs. Even their naming after Florence Nightingale (1820–1910), celebrated nursing innovator during the Crimean War (1853–1856), struck a militaristic motif of fighting the virus. Filmed reports from ITUs dramatically depicted personal protective equipment (PPE), with PPE becoming a rapidly acquired abbreviation of protective need. So too with ventilators, as diverse manufacturers directed output to this commodity. Both ITU and PPE provision pinpoints the core cultural value of 'life' curated by the NHS and reinforces our understanding of 'clapping for the NHS' discussed earlier. The other perspective illuminating the NHS role in culturing care and sustaining core values lies in the notion of dual sovereignty.

Dual sovereignty

I derive this relatively unfamiliar concept from Rodney Needham's anthropological model of Dual Sovereignty while also being alert to Guenon's similar approach (Needham, 1980; Guenon, [1929] 2001). Needham pursues two complementary forms of authority in society, the Jural or Legal, and the Mystical. While jural-legal factors are self-explanatory, 'mystical' factors may sound confusing, fuzzy, or implicitly religious. That, however, is misguided, for mystical authority refers to things that foster and enhance identity and cause people to flourish. This model proposes that an institution or social group is favoured when possessing balanced and complementary forms of this authority. We might even see British society itself as containing strong features of both, ever complementing and checking each other in the total 'Establishment' of society (Davies, 2015, pp. 46–48, pp. 272–274).

All groups require an organisation for survival, embracing bureaucratic procedures consonant with the wider law of the land. Similarly, organisations succeed to the degree that they balance the established rationale for their existence with innovative adaptation to its social environment. As, historically, with many religious groups, some fail, merely survive, or flourish. Finance and legality are fundamentally important here since economic 'capital' fosters or hinders other group goals. The Covid19 period has, dramatically, witnessed a Conservative Government's jural authority inundating crisis contexts with unheard of levels of expenditure for peacetime needs: massive economic capital being vital to sustain 'cultural capital'. Jural authority – the rule of law – is prized by democratic societies and maintained through parliament, judiciary, police and the military, with the monarch finally embodying that rule, traditionally speaking, under God. Moreover, both forms of authority often come to formal expression in and through ritual events in Courts of Law, Investitures, and many other civic and religious contexts, the outcome of hard-won political and religious changes, civil and world wars, as well as cultural innovations. Amidst complex social-cultural dynamics the jural-mystical balance brings justice and causes people to flourish.

The perfect conceptual bridge between jural and mystical authority lies in the 'duty of care'. While its legal dimension largely concerns employment law, more mystical elements are expressed in valuing employees, as also in 'good-wishes', 'goodwill' and people saying they are 'thinking of you'. During the Covid19 Crisis the phrase 'Keep Safe' achieved this goal. At times of personal trouble or crisis this terminology often takes the more religious form of 'praying for' someone. This language of personal support enhances our sense of self when troubled just as in more ordinary circumstances we are encouraged by 'a kind word'. In so doing our mystical capital increases and our sense of identity enhanced. Mystical authority is often found in sincere friend, beloved parent, mentor, or teacher, or world leaders, public figures and celebrities who 'do good' and 'serve as examples'. These 'benefit' us, enhancing our sense of self. National events such as *Children in Need* or even *The Great North Run*, typify this sense of care and charity, with the Covid19 period eliciting many such events, including that of Major Tom discussed earlier.

By contrast the experience of 'identity depletion' follows betrayal, bullying, and abuse (Davies, 2011, pp. 68–94). The cyber-bullying of children even to the point of suicide marks the fragility of our identity and need for succour. During the Covid19 crisis numerous online scams to cheat the unwary out of money have been publicised. Blessing and cursing are the two faces of mystical authority – one positive and one negative. When justice is done and 'seen to be done' mystical authority is enhanced. When justice is 'felt' not to be done people sense some kind of 'loss'. Indeed, an individual may even 'feel sick' when pillars of society – those who should balance Jural and Mystical Authority – fail (Davies, 2011, pp. 186–211). Though sometimes associated with NHS misdiagnosis or treatment, over the crisis period the overwhelming spotlight fell on its 'life-saving' nature.

NHS, spirituality paradox

Here the language of mystical authority overlaps with ideas of 'spirituality', something reflecting life's complex meaningfulness through things that enhance a person's sense of identity. Spirituality encompasses links with others, the past, present and hopes for the future. Whereas 'spirituality' has often been used by mainstream religious traditions to describe the quality and the 'feel' of life pursued by believers, recent decades have witnessed its popularity in healthcare contexts, quite apart from religious overtones. The prevalence of books on secular and atheist, as well as healthcare and wellbeing forms of spirituality, frees the word for bringing people together on issues of care who might, otherwise, be divided by religious-political differences (Compte-Sponville, 2007; Cook, Powell and Sims, 2009). For example, The National Council for Palliative Care's *Finding the Missing Piece Conference* in March 2010 pinpointed 'spirituality' as that 'piece'; though they also intended the allusion to 'peace' (NCPC, 2012). Such events often align spirituality with end of life care and issues of dignity – itself an idea now invested not only with emotion to generate a value, but also aligned with our sense of identity and, beyond that even with a sense of our destiny. Though problematic for the NHS and politicians, such dignity over end of life care and death itself had already become a key issues of social life, especially as many people are living into older old age all before Covid19 elevated 'Care Homes' and their elderly as the most susceptible to the virus and in need of greatest protection – on this the debate continues.

Conclusion

These provisional reflections, hostages to fortune for future research, portray the NHS as an evolving British institution, born of mid-20th-century post-war reconstruction, but intensified in its social-political focus as the prime vehicle of cultural values through the Covid19 Pandemic. All at a time when the Church of England, the symbolic base of UK religion, was closed for business in its parish churches yet striving to minister 'online'. As a worldview approach to one complex society and its popular ritual responses to lifesaving work this discussion invites further debate on values, beliefs and destiny and their dynamic fostering whether in traditional religion or the NHS.

References

Beveridge, W., [1942]/1966. *The report on the Inter-Departmental Committee on social insurance and allied services.* London, UK: HMSO.
Compte-Sponville, A. (transl. Nancy Huston), 2007. *The book of atheist spirituality: an elegant argument for spirituality without God.* London, UK: Bantam Books.
Cook, C., Powell, A. and Sims, A. 2009. *Spirituality and psychiatry.* London, UK: RC Psych Publications.
Davies, D.J., 2002. *Anthropology and theology.* Oxford: Berg.
Davies, D.J., 2008. Cultural intensification: a theory for religion. In: Day, A. (ed.), *Religion and the individual.* Aldershot: Ashgate, pp. 7–18.
Davies, D.J., 2011. *Emotion, identity, and religion: hope, reciprocity and otherness.* Oxford: Oxford University Press.
Davies, D.J., 2015. *Mors Britannica: lifestyle and death-style in Britain today.* Oxford: Oxford University Press.
Davies, D.J., 2017. *Death, ritual and belief* (3rd ed.). London, UK: Bloomsbury.
Droogers, A., with van Harskamp, A., 2014. *Methods for the study of religious change: from religious studies to worldview studies.* Sheffield: Equinox.
Durkheim, E. (transl. Joseph Ward Swain), 1915. *The elementary forms of the religious life.* London, UK: George Allen and Unwin Ltd.
Francis, R., 2010. *Independent inquiry into patient care provided by the Mid-Staffordshire NHS Foundation, January 2005–March 2009.* London, UK: HMSO.
Freud, S., [1932]/1973. The Question of a *Weltanschauung.* In: Strachey, J. (ed.), with Richards, A., *New introductory lectures on psychoanalysis.* Harmondsworth, Middlesex: Penguin Books, pp. 193–219.
Guenon, R., [1929]/2001. *Spiritual authority and temporal power.* Hillsdale. NY: Sophia Perrenis.
Mol, H., 1976. *Identity and the sacred.* Oxford: Blackwell.
Needham, R., 1980. *Reconnaissences.* Toronto: University of Toronto Press.
NCPC, 2012. Definitions: what do we mean by spiritual support. In: The National Council for Palliative Care, *The missing piece: meeting people's spiritual needs in end of life care.* The National Council for Palliative Care, p. 4.
Rappaport, R., 1999. *Ritual in the making of humanity.* Cambridge: Cambridge University Press.

Redfern, M., 2001. *The Royal Liverpool Children's Inquiry*. London, UK: Stationery Office.

Rothery, S., 2013. *The Times*. Letters. London. March 12th.

Taves, A. and Asprem, E., 2018. Scientific worldview studies: a programmatic proposal. In: Petersen, A.K., Gilhus, I.S., Martin, L.H., Jensen, J.S. and Sørensen, J. (eds.), 2018. *Evolution, cognition, and the history of religion: A New Synthesis*. Leiden: Brill.

THEOS, 2020. Worldviews in Religious Education. Available at: https://www.theosthinktank.co.uk/research/2020/10/21/worldviews-in-religious-education (Accessed: 22 November 2020).

Tillich, P., 1953. *Systematic theology (vol.1)*. Digswell Place: James Nesbit & Co. Ltd.

Turner, V., 1975. *Revelation and divination in Ndembu ritual*. Ithaca, NY: Cornell University Press.

Weber, M. (transl. Ephraim Fischoff), [1922]/1965. *The sociology of religion*. London, UK: Methuen.

8 Non-COVID-19 related dying and death during the pandemic

Wai Yee Chee, Samuel S.Y. Wang, Winnie Z.Y. Teo, Melissa Fong, Andy Lee, and Woon Chai Yong

---

Key points

- Covid-19 has had a devastating impact upon the provision of palliative care services.
- Strict quarantine measures have contributed to psycho-social isolation, limiting the effectiveness of current palliative care services.
- Patients their families and healthcare professionals experience grief and ethical dilemmas when faced with managing terminal care during the COVID-19 pandemic.
- Healthcare professionals should focus on mitigating the risk of maladaptive grief contributed by the pandemic by attempting to facilitate the family members participation throughout the illness trajectory of their loved ones.

COVID-19, the disease caused by the Severe Acute Respiratory Syndrome Coronavirus 2 (SARS-CoV-2), has resulted in unprecedented global upheaval since early 2020. Its destructive ripples have altered every fabric of our society, constantly challenging every system and infrastructure that had previously kept our world going. Having taken away at least 900,000 lives as of September 2020, the pandemic has also crippled economies and deepened existing woes of humanitarian crises.

Restrictions ranging from quarantine orders to citywide lockdowns were ubiquitous globally, making dying in the community extremely challenging. In this chapter, we will examine the repercussions of COVID-19 in Singapore on non-COVID-19 deaths through two anecdotes. Both cases will illustrate how the pandemic influenced treatment decisions, aggravated bereavement and generated ethical concerns for families and caregivers. Case 1 highlights the grief and bereavement experience of a mother who lost her son during the pandemic period in Singapore a cosmopolitan city state while Case 2 describes how funerary constraints due to Singapore's countermeasures, eventually led to overtreatment in a non-COVID-19 palliative case.

Case 1   The effects of COVID-19 on a non-COVID-19 related, hospitalised palliative patient during the pandemic: dying, death and grieving in a foreign land

In March 2020, a 65-year-old widow, Madam Lee, flew from China to Singapore, after receiving news that her only son, Richard, was dying from leukaemia in the intensive care unit (ICU) of a local acute hospital. When she arrived, Madam Lee had to stay in self-isolation for 14 days as per local quarantine policies. In addition, the hospital did not allow any physical contact between Madam Lee and the ICU unit, where the healthcare workers and other patients in the non-COVID-19 ICU had to be kept 'safe' in the looming coronavirus outbreak.

The care team provided daily updates to Madam Lee through virtual meetings. She was very anxious about Richard's condition and questioned whether care for non-COVID-19 patients would be compromised as she assumed more healthcare resources would be diverted to COVID-19 related patients.

Throughout her time in Singapore, Madam Lee stayed in Richard's apartment. One of Richard's friends would deliver and leave the groceries at the doorstep without making physical contact with Madam Lee. Two of Richard's friends would take turn to help Madam Lee link up virtually with Richard through video calls and facilitate updates from the ICU team. A community social worker was arranged by the hospital to support Madam Lee. The social worker had to comply with stipulated precautions to don mask and gloves to see Madam Lee, observe safe distancing and limit her duration of contact. In her first week in Singapore, Madam Lee attempted to appeal for exceptions to the rules, explaining that Richard was not a COVID-19 patient and she had requested for swabbing to exempt her from the stipulated self-isolation. She was frustrated and felt helpless. Richard died within a week of Madam Lee's arrival. The hospital team arranged for Madam Lee to be with Richard in his final hours, in an isolation room outside of the ICU unit. Richard was cremated in Singapore after a 3-day wake was held. During this period, a limit of no more than 10 persons was allowed to attend funerals. Hence, only a few close friends were allowed to attend. Some of his colleagues were ambivalent about attending the funeral. Relatives from China could not fly to Singapore. Arrangement was made for Madam Lee to return to China with his remains, to be kept in her home during the period when she had to observe another 14 days of self-isolation.

Discussion

Impact of the pandemic on the grief of non-COVID-19 deaths

In the span of two weeks, Madam Lee had to cope with Richard's sudden deterioration, his death and funeral. Her grief experience across the timeframe was influenced by the interplay of pandemic related factors as well as non-pandemic related factors which might have been amplified because of the context.

Care factors unique to the COVID-19 pandemic

The level of separation distress and emotional pain associated with child loss predispose bereaved parents to a higher risk of prolonged grief disorder, especially mothers (Zhou et al., 2020). In the case of Madam Lee, the separation distress was compounded by the forbidding measures in place due to the pandemic that prevented her from being by the side of her dying son. Faced with the prospect of Richard's impending death, her anticipatory grief was heightened. Madam Lee's emotional pain was intensified by the sudden severance of her role as a protective and nurturing mother, when Richard would have needed her most. Restrictions on visiting policies of the dying family member were cited as an example of a risk factor for prolonged grief disorder related to death during COVID-19 (Goveas and Shear, 2020). Her stress level would inevitably be high when Richard was dying and also after his death, as she appraised the situation as more demanding than the resources available to her to deal with it (Lazatus and Folkman, 1984). Her acute grief reactions included anger directed at the care team, Richard, the community social worker and herself. She could not sleep and wanted to 'shut out the world' while dealing with her anxiety and guilt.

At a time when the healthcare system was overwhelmed, the role of the family in supporting the dying was minimised. This double jeopardy was especially difficult for patients requiring intensive care not related to COVID-19 infection. Family members might be further anguished by their inability to ascertain if adequate care was provided to their loved ones, given the mainstream focus on re-deployment of healthcare resources for COVID-19 related care.

Communication barriers – language and mode

Circumstances surrounding death is a risk factor for complications in the grieving process (Stroebe, Schut and Stroebe, 2007). While Madam Lee received routine updates from the care team through virtual meeting, the lack of access to seeing Richard and to engage members of the care team in person might be perceived as a lack of institutional support for Richard's care. It did not help that the medical team was not fluent in her native language and she was handicapped in the working language of the team. Hence, meeting Madam Lee's information need and facilitating her involvement in Richard's care would be paramount in mitigating her risk of developing any complications resulting from the unusual circumstances.

Disenfranchised grief – Covid overshadowing non-COVID losses

In times of crisis, deaths associated with the pandemic took prominence and overshadow other types of losses. Madam Lee's grief was relatively muted, without the usual social and cultural rituals. Isolation in bereavement, when grief cannot be socially supported, constitutes as disenfranchised grief (Doka, 1999). Relatives and friends, overseas and local, either could not attend the funeral or were ambivalent about attending a funeral during a pandemic, more so with the prevailing regulations imposed on the limited number of people allowed at any one time. Madam Lee's earlier perception of Richard not being provided with adequate care had extended to him not given a proper send off. She wondered if she had done any wrong in her life for Richard to be dealt such an unjustified fate. Self-blame and shame, in addition to regrets, disappointments and anger were evident in her narrative for the days following his death. She made attempts to restore peace within herself and with Richard although her cognitive effort was thwarted by the uncertainties of whether she could make a difference to ensure Richard's well-being in the afterlife, without the usual traditions and customs. She resorted to 'talking' to Richard and explaining all the inadequacies and improvisation given the pandemic, in her search for a legitimate space to hold her grief, to assert her love for Richard.

Social isolation – impact on the bereaved

Social isolation compounds difficulty in adjustment for the bereaved (Stroebe, Schut and Stroebe, 2007). Madam Lee was in a foreign land, without any next of kin by her side as she faced Richard's death. She would speak with her younger sister through video calls whenever she felt up to it. The regulations on safe distancing impeded Richard's friends from visiting her, although some semblance of social connection was provided through virtual meetups with two of his close friends. Madam Lee had to spend most of her 14 days in the confine of Richard's apartment, with little human touch, except for home visits conducted by the community social worker. Her perception of whether she was socially connected or isolated would predict if the experience would complicate her bereavement. While she needed the support from the various sources, she was also ambivalent about receiving it as she tried to stay in control in the face of Richard's sudden departure. If she had found the experience positive, she would be able to find a 'silver lining' in the death event of Richard and be encouraged to reach out to others for help in adjusting to life without him, while believing that she could still maintain her agency. Else, her sense of isolation might compromise her ability to find any 'saving grace' in her predicament and threaten her sense of safety in a world without Richard, resulting in a heightened sense of vulnerability.

Making meaning of non-COVID-19 related death during the pandemic

Culture-specific factors that influence the grief experience of bereaved Chinese parents include the ideology of filial piety, the concept of destiny and perceived stigma of losing a child (Shi et al., 2019). Madam Lee raised the question of why Richard had to die of leukaemia in a Coronavirus pandemic when he was at the peak of his career and life. In the process of making sense of the loss, the pandemic outbreak would inevitably be weaved into the narrative as the destiny of the deceased and/or the bereaved, which might help to downplay or accentuate the role constrain of Madam Lee and her ability to control the circumstances of his death.

Attempts to mitigate the risk of maladaptive grief in a non-COVID-19 related death

Appointing a community social worker to support Madam Lee had facilitated her participation in the care and decision-making for Richard. The social worker conducted home visits to join Madam Lee in the virtual meetings with the medical team, and to process the information with her after the meetings so that she could form a coherent impression of the chronological events related to Richard's condition and treatment. The companionship and availability of the social worker was perceived as helpful support, to mitigate the sense of isolation and as an anchor for Madam Lee.

In the final hours for Richard, after prompting Madam Lee to bring along some of Richard's personal items, the social worker arranged with the hospital and escorted Madam Lee in the middle of the night to see him. At the mortuary, Madam Lee managed to express her love, appreciation, forgiveness (Byock, 2014) towards Richard and to bid him farewell. She later reported she was at peace that she could do something for Richard – to shave him, comb his hair, wash his face and apply his favourite lotion on his hands. She was convinced she should let him go after she saw the state of his body while dressing him. She later thanked the social worker for guiding her when she was at a loss not knowing what she could do when she finally could see Richard. Her participation in care in the final hours had enabled her to appraise her experience more positively, a protective factor in her adaptation to the loss (Zhai and Du, 2020).

Madam Lee was allowed to attend Richard's funeral, after an application was made to the regulatory officer, on compassionate grounds. She was consulted to make key decisions in the planning of Richard's funeral. For friends and colleagues who could not attend, they were invited to share photographs and videos they had of Richard and a montage was produced by one of his friends as a tribute to Richard and played during his funeral. It was a symbolic object representing of Richard (Sas and Coman, 2016) and a source of comfort for Madam Lee, who discovered other aspects of Richard's life in Singapore.

Case 2   The effects of COVID-19 on the care plans of a non-COVID home palliative patient during the pandemic: overtreatment, ethical concerns and funerary constraints

Madam AY, a centenarian patient, suffered from foot gangrene which was not responsive to antibiotics administered in a government hospital. Lacking mental capacity to make a decision for herself due to underlying cognitive impairment, her doctors decided against surgical intervention in the form of an amputation after discussing with her family members. The family believed an amputation will prevent her from entering the afterlife with all her body parts intact – a culturally common phenomenon in the Chinese context.

She was referred for home palliative care on 16 April 2020, about a week since the 'Circuit Breaker' period. On the first visit, her proxy had clearly expressed the family's wish to prolong her life as much as possible until the 'Circuit Breaker' was over. This was in a bid to honour Madam AY's previously stated wish to have a grand funeral which they knew was not possible in during the circuit breaker, as funerals were limited up to ten people and ostentatious display of funerary rites were impossible (Ministry of Health, 2020a).

Indebted to their mother who went through much hardship to raise them up, her children were very keen to materialise this extravagant last rite to pave the way to her afterlife. This resolution saw the family engaging expensive maggot therapy and negative wound pressure therapy at home in a bid to delay the deterioration of the foot infection. Subsequently, Madam AY was admitted to the private hospital's ICU due to her worsening foot infection and severe chest infection. Over the next three weeks, she had intravenous drips and life-prolonging trials of antibiotics which unfortunately, did not help to improve her condition. A peripherally inserted central catheter and nasogastric tube were also inserted during this period to support the treatment measures being administered. The poor prognosis was reiterated to the family by the vascular surgeon in charge. As the family mooted a discharge back home for terminal care, a private physician was engaged to look at trials of further treatment at home.

Madam AY was eventually discharged back home on 29 May 2020. However, she remained on multiple intravenous fluid replacement regime, high flow oxygen therapy and continuous 24-hour monitoring at home. Her deterioration despite the intensive therapies saw a build-up of tension and disagreement within the closely knitted family. A subsequent discussion regarding a proposed pleural effusion drainage at home threw the family into even more disarray.

The light at the end of the tunnel for Madam AY finally emerged on 15 June 2020 when the Singapore government announced further relaxation on the public health measurements on movement and gathering restrictions including those for funerals. With this, the family, in consultation with the private home care physician and home palliative care team, decided not to proceed with a pleural effusion tap at home and halted all intravenous therapies. Madam AY passed on peacefully at home on the same day.

Probing deeper, we found out that if not for the circuit breaker that had hindered Madam AY's last wish, they would certainly have opted against readmission and aggressive treatments in the last phase of Madam AY's life.

Discussion

The effects of COVID-19 are certainly profound. Through this anecdote, we see how COVID-19 impacts non-COVID deaths in the community, impacting several tenets of cultural and health beliefs that centre round sickness and death.

Resource allocation

Palliative care and hospice practices have been deeply impacted by COVID-19 in numerous ways. Undoubtedly, COVID-19 had crippled much of the work done over time to improve equitable allocation of healthcare and palliative care resources especially for marginalised populations globally (Rodin et al., 2020). Severe drug shortages, including opioids, ensued because of supply chain and production disruptions from lockdowns (Shuman, Fox and Unguru, 2020). Prior to COVID-19, access to opioids for pain management was already a major concern (Knaul et al., 2018). The pandemic aggravated this shortage, further reducing its access especially in impoverished regions around the world (Singh, Deodhar and Chaturvedi, 2020).

Although drug shortages did not significantly impact on healthcare in Singapore, the potential concerns with surge of cases and potential intensive care beds shortages were considered. The public healthcare system was overwhelmed before the establishment of community isolation facilities. In this instance, postponement of inevitable death using high resource settings may pose concerns especially with potential resource limitations. In additions, some of the treatments were invasive, and may result in harm for patient, including worsening the symptoms control.

Ethical concern: moral distress

A pandemic like COVID-19 can potentially precipitate moral conflicts and, even accentuate existing moral distress and moral uncertainty that plague the healthcare scene daily. Moral distress (Jameton, 1984) occurs when a nurse knows the right thing to do, but institutional constraints make it nearly impossible to pursue the right course of action (Jameton, 1984). In refining Jameton's ethical frameworks on moral distress, moral dilemma and moral constraints, Fourie had proposed a broader definition, in contrast to Jameton's narrow definition, of moral distress in 2015, that is, 'Moral distress is a psychological response to morally challenging situations such as those of moral constraint or moral conflict, or both' (Fourie, 2015, p. 93).

Various situations have evoked a sense of moral distress, in the healthcare settings, during the pandemic. In Case 2, moral distress was induced within the palliative homecare team. The root cause triggering moral distress is largely traced to the issue of over-treatment in order to honour patient's wishes. While it was certain that there were minimal chances to increase curability in Madam AY's situation and that aggressive treatment might have inflicted more suffering in her plight, yet this was a bid to prolong Madam AY's life so that her ultimate wishes could be honoured. Although this decision was definitely not congruent with the philosophy of palliative care, it was the only option the family could undertake in view of the severe constraints that resulted from the various public health measures against COVID-19. What then, was the best decision to undertake?

Madam AY's situation is but one of the many ethically challenging circumstances that healthcare staff had to navigate through during COVID-19. Like wadding in murky waters, healthcare staff are pressurised to respond and make judicious decisions in a very short span of time, prioritising conflicting public health, institutional and individual level needs on a daily basis. For example, while patients were awaiting their COVID-19 swab results, hospital staffs were not allowed to stay vigil by their bedside until the swab test comes back as negative. This may result in patients dying in isolation leading to hospital staff feeling regretful not being able to spend the last moments with a dying patient.

Dying in Isolation

Dying alone has always been antithetical to the philosophy underpinning palliative care, which advocates that no one should die alone as much as possible (Radbruch et al., 2020). However, due to the stringent measures undertaken by hospitals, it necessitated that all patients with respiratory symptoms, palliative cases or not, had to be swabbed and isolated. This protocol resulted in many patients, both COVID-positive and non-COVID patients, dying in isolation. Staff are not allowed to keep vigil by the bedside while families who could only watch helplessly from afar in the wards. In Case 1, while exceptions were eventually allowed, it was clearly demonstrated that the pandemic inflicted many additional bureaucratic barriers that had to be overcome before Richard's mother could be granted permission to catch a final glimpse of her son, even though he was a non-COVID patient, for the last time.

In Case 2, while Madam AY was fortunate to pass away at home, her family was concerned that her funerary rites may be lonely and isolated, not as ostentatious as Madam AY may have desired. This brings us to the next point: The effects of COVID-19 on funerary rites.

Funerary restrictions and constraints

In Singapore, as in most countries worldwide in the same period, visitors were not allowed to enter other households during the circuit breaker. Extended families were unable to spend quality moments with their loved ones who were already at the end of life. All voluntary, allied health and spiritual-support services were all suspended. Home palliative care providers could only provide basic medical attention to palliative patients who might have complex palliative needs. This was often limited to providers providing medical advice over the phone due to visitation restrictions. As such, this may have led to visits to their nearest general practitioner or hospital when their medical needs could not be addressed by home palliative care providers, which may not have been in keeping with the patient's final wishes.

Funerals were limited up to ten people in Singapore in the initial period (Ministry of Health, 2020b). These restrictions disrupted long standing cultural norms and impeded the usual process of grief and mourning. In Case 2, Madam AY's family valued collective mourning and filial piety, therefore, death was postponed at the expense of patient's comfort.

Grieving other non-COVID-19 related deaths during the pandemic

There were also other unintended consequences of the coronavirus outbreak on the bereavement experience of others who lost their loved ones from non-covid-19 related causes.

Acceptance of early death

Not all bereaved were negatively impacted during the COVID-19 pandemic. A bereaved person who was attending professional counselling recounted how the pandemic has helped her to re-appraise the death of her loved one positively, a reframing that reflected her meaning-based coping (Folkman, 2001), applying the pandemic context. She took comfort that her spouse died just before the pandemic so that she was able to care for him, visit him and was by his side when he was dying. She was grateful that her husband loved her enough to choose to leave earlier, as it was unimaginable for her to have to deal with the restrictions during the pandemic should he have died during the virus outbreak.

Pandemic as a shield for acute grief reactions

Another widow had also found benefits in the pandemic to cope with her grief in the early days of losing her spouse through a heart attack. She was not ready to talk to anybody about her loss and the requirement to stay-at-home have helped to 'legitimise' her prolonged absence from social life. The pandemic had also prevented her son from making his overseas trip, and together with her daughter working from home, she was not left to grief alone.

Grief entrapped by the pandemic

The various levels of measures put in place to mitigate the pandemic across the world have a cascading effect that could derail the efforts of individuals to restore some normalcy and to effectively adjust to life without their loved ones (Goveas and Shear, 2020). A grieving mother could not settle the estate matters of her son without having to repeat her 'story' of losing her son to multiple agencies as different workers were rotated to attend to her, due to a change in on-site work arrangement. She would cry whenever she had to recount her circumstances to overseas stockbrokers and her level of anxiety escalated with the prolonged delays in processing her claims. She described herself as being 'stuck in a conspiracy' that prevented her from healing from her grief and to move forward in life without her son.

Public health priority limiting individual preferences

For one patient, the nursing home was akin to her home and she wished to stay there even when she has become sick with a pneumonia, but due to the Covid-19 strict public health measures requiring isolation of patients with acute respiratory illness. In nursing homes, stringent measures had to be put in place to curb the number of positive cases. Clinicians from home palliative care providers supporting nursing homes were prohibited from entering these institutions until clarifications were issued from the Agency of Integrated Care, a nationwide coordinating body for community care services. Any patient fulfilling the suspect criteria would also be immediately referred to a dedicated swabbing facility or acute hospital. This resulted in many hospital readmissions from homes and nursing homes, which might have even been unnecessary, regardless of previously expressed preferences of care.

Conclusion

When the impact of the larger context of a pandemic threatens to overwhelm the individual's grief experience, maladaptation in bereavement would be a likely outcome. People affected by non-COVID-19 dying and deaths are at risk of disenfranchised grief, in addition to the multiple demands and stressors that stretch their ability to cope. The COVID-19 pandemic is unprecedented. It brought with it multiple demands and stressors, that could challenge the pre-loss meaning structures of the bereaved, causing a dissonance that would drive the bereaved in a search for meaning (Gillies and Neimeyer, 2006). Health and community care professionals should focus on mitigating the risk of maladaptive grief contributed by the pandemic situation, by recognising the patient and the family as a unit of care, attempting to be the conduit to enable the participation of family members throughout the illness trajectory of their loved ones.

'How people die remains in the memory of those who live on'
– Dame Cicely Saunders

References

Byock, I., 2014. *The four things that matter most: a book about living*. New York, NY: Simon and Schuster.
Doka, K.J., 1999. Disenfranchised grief. *Bereavement Care*, 18(3), pp. 37–39.
Folkman, S., 2001. Revised coping theory and the process of bereavement. In Stroebe, M.S., Hansson, R.O., Stroebe, W. and Schut, H. (eds.), *Handbook of bereavement research: consequences, coping, and care*. Washington, DC: American Psychological Association, pp. 563–584.
Fourie, C., 2015. Moral distress and moral conflict in clinical ethics. *Bioethics*, 29(2), pp. 91–97.
Gillies, J. and Neimeyer, R.A., 2006. Loss, grief, and the search for significance: toward a model of meaning reconstruction in bereavement. *Journal of Constructivist Psychologist*, 19(1), pp. 31–65.
Goveas, J.S. and Shear, M.K., 2020. Grief and the COVID-19 pandemic in older adults. *The American Journal of Geriatric Psychiatry*, 28(10), pp. 1119–1125.
Jameton, A., 1984. *Nursing practice: the ethical issues*. Upper Saddle River, NJ: Prentice Hall.
Knaul, F.M., Bhadelia, A., Rodriguez, N.M., Arreola-Ornelas, H. and Zimmermann, C., 2018. The Lancer Commission on palliative care and pain relief – findings, recommendations, and future directions. *The Lancet Global Health*, 6, pp. S5–S6.
Lazatus, R.S. and Folkman, S., 1984. *Stress, appraisal, and coping*. New York, NY: Springer.

Ministry of Health, 2020a. Moving into phase two of re-opening. Available at: https://www.moh.gov.sg/news-highlights/details/moving-into-phase-two-of-re-opening (Accessed: 3 December 2020).

Ministry of Health, 2020b. Circuit breaker to minimise further spread of covid-19. Available at: https://www.moh.gov.sg/news-highlights/details/circuit-breaker-to-minimise-further-spread-of-covid-19 (Accessed: 3 December 2020).

Radbruch, L., De Lima, L., Knaul, F., Wenk, R., Ali, Z., Bhatnaghar, S., Blanchard, C., Bruera, E., Buitrago, R., Burla, C. and Callaway, M., 2020. Redefining palliative care – a new consensus-based definition. *Journal of Pain and Symptom Management*, 60(4), pp. 754–764.

Rodin, G., Zimmermann, C., Rodin, D., al-Awamer, A., Sullivan, R. and Chamberlain, C., 2020. COVID-19, palliative care and public health. *European Journal of Cancer*, 136, pp. 95–98.

Sas, C. and Coman, A., 2016. Designing personal grief rituals: an analysis of symbolic objects and actions. *Death Studies*, 40(9), pp. 558–569.

Shi, G., Wen, J., Xu, X., Zhou, N., Wang, J., Shi, Y., Liu, H., Wang, J. and Stelzer, E.M., 2019. Culture-related grief beliefs of Chinese Shidu parents: development and psychometric properties of a new scale. *European Journal of Psychotraumatology*, 10(1), p. 1626075.

Shuman, A.G., Fox, E. and Unguru, Y., 2020. Preparing for COVID-19 related drug shortages. *Annals of the American Thoracis Society*, 17(8), pp. 928–931.

Singh, A.G., Deodhar, J. and Chaturvedi, P., 2020. Navigating the impact of COVID-19 on palliative care for head and neck cancer. *Head & Neck*, 42(6), pp. 1144–1146.

Stroebe, M., Schut, H. and Stroebe, W., 2007. Health outcomes of bereavement. *The Lancet*, 370(9603), pp. 1960–1973.

Zhai, Y. and Du, X., 2020. Loss and grief amidst COVID-19: a path to adaptation and resilience. *Brain, Behavior, and Immunity*, 87, pp. 80–81.

Zhou, N., Wen, J., Stelzer, E.-M., Killikelly, C., Yu, W., Xu, X., Shi, G., Luo, H., Wang, J. and Maercker, A., 2020. Prevalence and associated factors of prolonged grief disorder in Chinese parents bereaved by losing their only child. *Psychiatry Research*, 284, p. 112766.

9 Covid-19 and care home deaths and harms: a case study from the UK

Alisoun J. Milne

> **Key points**
>
> - Care home residents experienced very high levels of excess deaths and harms during the first five months of the pandemic;
> - Families and care workers were also exposed to high levels of physical and psychological harm;
> - Many of these outcomes were preventable;
> - Care homes were poorly supported by agencies tasked with managing the pandemic;
> - In order for care home residents, their families and staff to be better protected in the future both short and long-term actions are required;
> - Long-term care needs to be radically reformed and become part of a universal integrated health and social care system

This chapter will explore the impact of Covid-19 on care homes in the UK. My focus is on the nature and extent of virus-related deaths and harms to residents, their families and staff. Most of the evidence is drawn from the first five months of the pandemic, between March and July 2020. Although this case study is from the UK, many of the issues raised will have wider resonance for care homes across Europe and beyond (Anand et al., 2021). I am not only arguing that many of the deaths and harms were preventable but that the causes constitute infrastructural and governmental neglect of some of our most vulnerable older citizens on a grand scale. The role played by ageism is also a defining feature of the scandal. These are the issues which I return below.

Care homes and care home populations in the UK

Firstly, by way of providing context for the chapter, it is instructive to remind ourselves what a care home is and the profile of care home residents.

Care homes are defined by Huber et al. (2009, p.84) as 'institutions and living arrangements where care and accommodation are provided jointly to a group of people residing in the same premises or sharing common living areas'. They tend to be regarded as the place of 'last resort' and are situated geographically and metaphorically 'off the public radar' (Dening and Milne, 2020).

Approximately 420,000 people live permanently in care homes in the UK. This figure represents about 4% of the total older population[1] (LaingBuisson, 2019). The majority of residents are aged 85 years or over, have complex co-morbid conditions and need help with activities of daily living. Although dementia is estimated to affect four fifths of residents, only two fifths receive specialist dementia care (Dening and Milne, 2020).

There are 15,487 care homes in the UK. Two fifths are nursing homes, i.e. homes that offer nursing care, whilst three fifths are residential homes, i.e. homes that offer care and support. Over the last 20 years care homes have increasingly been provided by private for-profit companies and care has been paid for by the individual[2] older person as opposed to homes being publicly provided and/or funded. Currently 75% homes are for-profit; half of residents are publicly funded[3] (LaingBuisson, 2019). The shift 'towards the private' reflects the influence of neoliberal market ideology embraced by the UK government; it is especially relevant to services for older people both in the community and in residential settings (Milne, 2020a; Walker, 2020). The care home sector – if indeed it can be described as one – is increasingly fragmented, atomised and outside the purview of policy makers and public sector agencies (Daly, 2020).

These issues are important to note as a number of systemic challenges facing care homes during the pandemic relate to how they are provided and funded and who is responsible for the funding and management of responses to the crisis (Milne, 2020a).

Covid-19 and deaths in care homes

The World Health Organisation estimates that up to 50% of *all* Covid-19 deaths have occurred among care home residents in Europe; this figure is 41% for the UK (World Health Organisation, 2020). Although the final death toll will not be known for some time, as of June 30th, 35,500 excess deaths have been linked to the virus in UK care homes (Comas-Herrera and Fernandez, 2020). Care homes in England recorded a 79% increase in excess deaths compared to 66% in Wales, 62% in Scotland and 46% in Northern Ireland (Bell et al., 2020). At least two thirds of all deaths are of people living with dementia. The Graph below illustrates the rise and rise of care home deaths in England between April and July (Figure 9.1).

Other data relating to care home deaths is also important. Covid-19 has been recorded in at least two fifths of care homes in England and three fifths in Scotland. In June, it was noted that 'between a quarter and third of

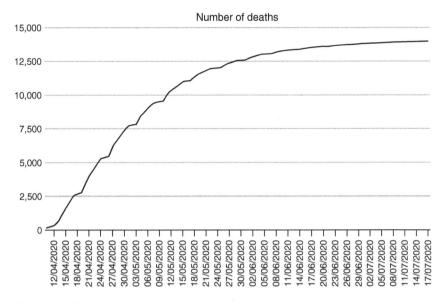

Figure 9.1 The cumulative number of care home residence deaths in care homes involving Covid-19 in England between April and July 2020
Source: Office for National Statistics, 2020. Available at: https://www.ons.gov.uk/peoplepopulationandcommunity/birthsdeathsandmarriages/deaths/articles/deathsinvolvingcovid19inthecaresectorenglandandwales/deathsoccurringupto12june2020andregisteredupto20june2020provisional (retrieved 28 November 2020).

residents dying in a single care home from coronavirus is not uncommon' (Comas-Herrera et al., 2020, p367). The speed with which deaths occurred is stark; dozens of residents died in a short period of time. It is not just the number of deaths that are a scandal it is also the manner of (some of) the deaths. Unverified results suggest that a third of excess deaths in UK care homes were a result of 'being left alone without adequate food, water' or access to pain relief (Comas-Herrera et al., 2020, p368).

There are a number of reasons for the excess deaths in care home. Although age related vulnerability is relevant, it does not explain the significant number of deaths, nor their frequency, especially in the early stages of the pandemic.

The UK's strategy of prioritising the protection of acute National Health Service (NHS) services at the expense of out of hospital 'at risk' populations, including care home populations, was a key driver. At least 25,000 older people were discharged from hospitals into care homes to free up beds between March and June 2020. This large group of patients were not routinely tested for Covid-19. As Dr Harwood, a Consultant Geriatrician, pointed out 'Care homes are always vulnerable, residents are frail and live communally

...' (Harwood, 2020). Those who had the virus brought it into care homes where it quickly spread creating, what the scientists call, *fatal cluster effects*. It was not until the 15 April 2020, after 5,700 patients had died in care homes or hospitals[4], that the government 'required' all patients discharged from hospital into a care home to be tested (Iacobucci, 2020).

The UK's Department of Health and Social Care (DHSC) was also slow to advise against visits from relatives, another obvious route of infection transmission; it did not act until early April. Agency staff – who often work across a number of care homes and who were relied on during the pandemic to provide cover for permanent staff who were ill or shielding – would also have been a primary source of transmission (Milne, 2020a).

Another major issue relates to lack of effective protection. Care homes were woefully unprepared to deal with the virus, in good part because they were not seen as a priority for receipt of Personal Protective Equipment (PPE) and/or testing. An 'action plan for care homes' was not published by the DHSC until April 15th: six weeks after the government's national 'coronavirus action plan' (which made no mention of care homes) and 3.5 weeks after the Prime Minister announced the (first) UK lockdown. On May 15th – a month after the care homes action plan – Age UK reported that 'many homes are struggling to access PPE and testing'. Even where testing is available it may not be local: in late May staff from a home in Derbyshire were obliged to travel for an hour to Grantham to get a test if they needed one (Carter, 2020). The Chairman of the Science and Technology Committee[5] wrote a letter to the Prime Minister in mid-May stating that the government's 'ability to make tests available to care homes has been inadequate' throughout the pandemic. He also accused Public Health England[6] (PHE) of 'abandoning care homes' in the first critical weeks.

One of the main reasons for this failure is confusion about which agency is responsible for overseeing and managing provision of PPE and testing to care homes. PHE, the Care Quality Commission (which inspects the quality of care homes, CQC) and the DHSC have given mixed and contradictory messages. Care homes report being told, *in the same day,* that it is CQC's responsibility and then subsequently that it is PHE's.

A key barrier to understanding what was happening regarding care home deaths was lack of data. The National Care Forum[7] (an independent care sector body) describes care homes as planning their response 'with their hands tied' because data about outbreaks were not published until the end of April. PHE had counted more than 4,500 Covid-19 outbreaks in care homes before it issued its findings. For many weeks the government did not include deaths in care homes in its official statistics. This underscores its lack of understanding of the risks care homes were facing and as the death toll rose, its reluctance to acknowledge its own role in contributing to these (Milne, 2020a).

Funding issues are also a contributory factor. In mid-May the Government released a £600m cash injection for care homes to help control infection.

English Councils have also been given £3.7bn 'crisis funding' to support the adult social care sector through the pandemic. These sums have been dismissed as 'derisory' by care home managers who consider it insufficient to cover the costs of PPE let alone the extra costs related to testing and the provision of additional staffing. Extra staff were needed to provide cover for sick (or shielding) colleagues and to be able to offer 1:1 'isolation care' to residents with the virus or those discharged from hospital. Some care homes have complained too that they have 'struggled' to gain access to the funds local authorities have been allocated.

It has also – shockingly – been reported that some General Practitioners have been asked to 'pressure care home residents into signing "do not attempt resuscitation order"' (DNAR) if they get Covid-19. The Care Quality Commission[8] also uncovered evidence that DNAR orders had been issued for whole groups of care home residents without consent having been sought from either the residents themselves or their families (Amnesty International, 2020). This appears to be particularly the case for groups of residents with dementia.

Not all care home deaths – during the first five months of the pandemic – related directly to Covid-19. It has been estimated that just under half the excess deaths were from 'other causes'. These include General Practitioners not being able to visit care homes and care homes being discouraged – or sometimes unable – to send residents to hospital for treatment for non-virus related health conditions (O'Dowd, 2020).

Residents are not the only group exposed to risk of death. At least 268 social care staff[9] have died from coronavirus in England and Wales between March and May. The ONS estimates that social care staff are twice as likely to die as healthcare workers (and members of the general population). Most are women working part time; they are also disproportionately from BAME backgrounds (Samuel, 2020). In its report, *As if Expendable: the UK government's failure to protect older people in care homes during the Covid-19 pandemic,* Amnesty International (2020) baldly states that 'There appears to have been a catastrophic failure to provide proper PPE and a failure to grapple with the alarmingly high death rate amongst BAME workers' (p29).

Covid-19 and harm

Death was not the only damage done. Since the beginning of the pandemic residents have been effectively trapped in their bedrooms with little interaction with visitors, even digitally or via phone (Milne, 2020b). One of the more common features of 'risk reduction' adopted by care homes – and subsequently 'advised' by government – was to completely stop, or severely restrict, visits by relatives.

Visits from relatives – and friends – are central to the care of residents, buffering against loneliness, anxiety and depression by providing continuity, advocacy and emotional support. Visiting can also provide residents with a sense of meaning, value and connectedness (O'Caoimh et al., 2020). For residents with dementia, lack of contact and social engagement can lead to deterioration of behavioural and cognitive symptoms such as wandering, agitation or aggression (Suarez-Gonzalez, 2020). During the pandemic there is an evidence of increased use of antipsychotics, hypnotics and other sedatives used to 'treat' these symptoms, ensure compliance with social distancing and cope with staff shortages (Velayudhan et al., 2020). The Alzheimer's Society (2020) reports that many residents with dementia are becoming withdrawn and depressed; they do not understand why loved ones are no longer visiting, they feel abandoned and are also losing cognitive and motor skills, including fundamental skills such as the ability to speak, eat or drink. Some have described their relative as 'disappearing'; one man told the Alzheimer's Society (2020) Helpine, 'I'm really fearful my wife won't recognise me at the end of this pandemic'.

There is reduced interaction with care workers too as they are required to prioritise 1:1 'isolation care' and/or may be absent for reasons noted above. Reduced attention from, often familiar, workers is not just about loss of communication and engagement, it is also about the loss of relationships, touch and comfort. Care homes are tactile environments where staff help residents with meals and personal care; they also offer familiarity, a kind touch and security.

Curtailment of visits also has a negative impact on relatives. It disrupts bonds, coping mechanisms and even their own sense of identity (Larkin and Milne, 2017). Recent research identifies spouses as experiencing high levels of anxiety and depression; for some, psychological symptoms are as severe as those prior to admission (O'Caoimh et al., 2020). The role of relatives as informal 'inspectors' of the quality of care is also important.

Another disturbing issue relates to end of life. There is evidence that residents' wishes regarding end-of-life were either not sought or were disregarded entirely (Brennan et al., 2020). Residents were also (often) dying alone without the presence of close relatives. Family members have not had the opportunity to say good-bye to their loved ones causing unimaginable levels of pain and distress to both the older person and their family.

A UK barrister suggests that one of the most profound examples of harmful treatment relates to care home residents who are the subject of Deprivation of Liberty Safeguards (DoLS)[10] (Lewis, 2020). Deprivation of Liberty Safeguards are used to ensure the safety of people who have limited mental capacity, for example older people living with advanced dementia. One of its key requirements is that 'it must be in the person's best interests to be detained ... (and that it is) *necessary to prevent harm*' (my emphasis). In the pandemic, it is challenging to argue that living in a care home is 'preventing harm'; in some instances, residents are being placed directly in the path of the virus. In the year ending 31 March 2019, 116,940 DoLS applications were granted in care homes or hospitals. Lewis suggests that the local authority – the public agency who makes the application for

DoLS – has an ongoing duty to ensure that detention remains in the person's 'best interests'; it is likely to be failing to do this in current circumstances.

The government also suspended regular oversight visits from the CQC during the pandemic. The decision to exclude both family and CQC visits contributes to care homes becoming (more) closed as institutions. It makes it less likely that residents gain access to health care (which we know happened, see above) and increases the risk of abuse and neglect not be identified, reported or investigated (Amnesty International, 2020; Mikelyte and Milne, 2016).

Care staff have also been exposed to harm. Workers – who called a whistleblowing helpline operated by Compassion in Care – described the 'horrendous' unsafe conditions they are facing over lack of PPE and the terrible impact this is having on their mental health and wellbeing (https://compassionincare.com/). Dealing with a high number of deaths, of people they have often come to know well, over a short period of time is hugely emotionally demanding. The fact that some died in pain without their family present would have amplified distress. Despair, PTSD and persistent complex grief are real risks; staff may experience guilt for not being able to do more to help a resident and if they learn – due to inadequate PPE and testing – that they may have been responsible for transmitting the virus to one or more residents, this can profoundly affect their mental health (Greenberg et al., 2020). Other emotional challenges include being unable to perform essential therapeutic roles such as dancing with a resident or giving them a hug and being obliged to provide personal care in a 'distanced way', i.e. wearing a mask and keeping a distance. Supervisory and peer support for addressing difficult emotional challenges are limited in care home settings, compounding the problem (Dening and Milne, 2020).

Staff have made many sacrifices during the pandemic period. Most notably, in order to protect residents and stop the virus spreading, some care workers made the decision to leave their family homes and move into the care home. This was the case at Beechside Home in Liverpool; there are many other examples.

In July, the Public Accounts Committee[11] (public finances oversight committee) described the government as having 'thrown care homes to the wolves' (House of Commons Public Accounts Committee, 2020). It expressed particular concern for care home staff who 'have endured the strain and trauma' of responding to the pandemic, with limited access to testing and PPE and at risk of becoming ill or even dying. Staff absences have been running at 10% to 20%. In a sector already facing a recruitment and retention crisis, managing the additional challenges of Covid-19 has created a serious workforce crisis. It has also, paradoxically, publicly exposed (some of) the complexities of care work and the vulnerability of staff; this is an issue to which I return below.

Discussion

It is clear that the pandemic has had devastating consequences for care home residents, their families and staff. It is also clear that the crisis was seriously (mis)managed; some would say it constitutes a violation of the human rights of both residents and staff (Amnesty International, 2020). It is important both to appreciate the nature of this failure and to locate it in its 'bigger picture'.

I have already outlined the specific ways in which care homes were marginalised – some would say ignored – for the first few months of the pandemic. In her review of deaths in UK care homes the author concludes that, 'care home residents are simply not considered to be important enough to justify the deployment of resources, to be protected or be included in pandemic planning' (Milne, 2020a). Even when care homes were, eventually, included in policy and public agency responses to the virus, these were of mixed quality, uneven and late in the day.

A number of commentators consider that the care home scandal was a crisis waiting to happen. Covid-19 has exposed serious inadequacies in the UK's care home system (Pollock, Clements and Harding-Edgar, 2020). It has made visible, and amplified, a pre-existing seam of governmental ignorance and indifference of catastrophic proportions. Very limited national attention is paid to care homes – and social care more widely – it is fragmented and infrastructurally weak and is conceptualised as the handmaiden to health care. The care home sector in the UK is among the most privatised in the Western world (Dening and Milne, 2020). Homes operate in the market and are driven by commercial principles; these shape their priorities and whilst there are many examples of excellent care, the quality of care overall is variable and vulnerable to the vicissitudes of investors and the stock market (Burton et al., 2020). Although care homes are regulated by the CQC they sit outside the purview of the public sector; they occupy a liminal once-removed status inside, and yet separate from, the care system. There is also an inherent conflict between care homes being a place of 'care' and a place of 'home' (Mikelyte and Milne, 2016).

Other causative dimensions include long term underfunding of the care home sector, 'light touch' inspection and oversight regimes and the profound lack of voice and power that older people who need care and support have, especially if they are frail and/or have dementia (Phillipson, 2020). Unprecedented recent cuts to public services have compounded funding issues. Since 2010 local authorities have been obliged to reduce their spending on social care for older people in real terms by 17%, despite rising demand. This has had a direct impact on the funding of long-term care for those older people who need financial support from their local authorities, compromising their 'choice' of care home and destabilising the care home market, especially in deprived areas (Health and Social Care Committee, 2020). There is an increasing division between those who pay their own care home fees and those who depend on local authority funding.

As older people are the majority users of care home services, Covid-19 has, by default, also made visible political, structural and societal ageism (Skoura-Kirk, 2020). Walker (2020) argues strongly that '... the woeful neglect of care homes, resulting in huge unnecessary loss of life, is the result of institutional ageism', affecting not only residents but staff as well. Despite the care home sector's dependence on its staff they have some of the worst working conditions of any workforce in the UK. Nearly a quarter of the 1.5 million people working in social care (residential[12] and community) are on zero hours contracts and in March 2019 around a quarter were being paid the national living wage of £7.83 (now £8.72) per hour (or less). It is noteworthy that staff on zero hours contracts do not receive sick pay. Whilst Covid testing has improved for care home staff in the last few months, the conditions that drive the need to go to work when ill have not. The fact that a number of care workers have died (see above), and many others have become ill in the line of duty, has helped to make visible the risks, both physical and psychological, that care home staff are routinely exposed to. It has also drawn attention to the complexity and skilled nature of care work, an issue that is widely underacknowledged (Dyer, 2020; Moriarty, Manthorpe and Harris, 2018).

The interdependencies between health and social care – and the inequalities between the two sectors – have also been highlighted by the crisis reinforcing the case for the development of a universal integrated health and social care system. Pollock et al. (2020) suggest that 'radical action is required to bring all (care) services and staff under government control in a national and publicly accountable system so that high quality care is delivered by a trained and properly equipped workforce with decent terms and conditions of service' (p2). What is needed, they argue – and what is so obviously lacking – is a plan of action to transform long term care, much like that for the NHS, which aims to reform the whole system, a system that routinely fails residents, their families and care workers and which 'shames us all'.

The last point relates to how the virus has been understood by key decision makers. Given the extent of the impact of the pandemic on care homes it is perhaps surprising that they are barely acknowledged in meetings of the Scientific Advisory Group for Emergencies (SAGE). Between January and May SAGE minutes mention care homes only twice. The fact that SAGE's membership does not include anyone from the social care community nor a clinician with ageing expertise further reinforces the sense that care homes have simply not been any part of the strategic national response to the crisis. SAGE would have been well served to pay attention to the evidence emerging from other European countries, exposed to the pandemic before the UK, upon which to base a plan. Both Spain and Italy had experienced significant numbers of care home deaths early in 2020: a pattern that we could have learned from.

Conclusion

It is difficult not to come to the conclusion that care homes were an afterthought during the first five months of the pandemic, not prioritised or even really considered in the UK context. The experiences discussed in this chapter are reflected in the rest of Europe and in North America too. Care homes, and those who live, visit and work in them, have been abandoned in most countries and by most states (Anand et al, 2021). The lessons to be drawn from the UK's care home scandal have clear relevance beyond our shores.

As we enter a second lockdown in early November 2020, one wonders what has changed. There is certainly greater recognition that care homes need more attention and increased funding and the scandal has been foregrounded in media reporting and by national and international agencies, including Amnesty International. The 60 member coalition that sent a letter to the Minister for Health and Social Care calling for visits to care homes to be permitted this time around and that relatives be treated as 'key workers' in terms of testing and PPE, is an example of a specific action (https://www.nursingtimes.net/news/social-care/government-urged-to-support-care-home-visiting-in-second-lockdown-02-11-2020/). Legal action is also being taken against the government regarding its failure to procure and distribute enough PPE to protect the lives of care workers and there are widespread calls for a public inquiry into the UKs response to the Covid-19 pandemic, including its management of care homes (Dyer, 2020).

There are, in essence, two levels of response to the care home crisis. One is short term and relates to responses to the issues outlined in this Chapter whilst the second is much longer term and relates to infrastructural and strategic change. David Oliver, Geriatrician and British Medical Journal columnist writes, '... perhaps with care homes getting more public attention than at any point during my (30 year) career, this will give us the impetus to provide some more meaningful, lasting and credible solutions to the funding and provision of care homes as was promised by the prime minister at the start of this parliament ...' (2020). If these largely preventable deaths and harms are to be avoided during the rest of the life of the current pandemic, and in future pandemics, then significant changes need to be made to the sector, both in the short and longer-term. The time to act is now given the level of public recognition and concern for care home residents' plight, families' anger and our reliance as a society on workers whose status and rights have for so long been in the shadows. It is not only a matter of human rights and of social justice; it is quite literally a matter of life and death.

Notes

1 Older is defined as 65 years and over.
2 Privately funded by the individual older person and/or their family.
3 If an older person requires care home admission and has no, or very limited,

access to private funds the local authority must pay the fees; in some circumstances the NHS will also pay full or part of the fee.
4 In England and Wales.
5 The Science and Technology Committee's role is to ensure that Government policy and decision-making are based on good scientific advice and evidence.
6 Public Health England exists to protect and improve the nation's health and wellbeing and reduce health inequalities.
7 NCF is the membership organisation for not-for-profit organisations in the care and support sector.
8 The Care Quality Commission regulates and inspects health and social care services in England.
9 These will not all be care home staff - some will be domiciliary care staff - but the majority will be.
10 DoLS ensures people who cannot consent to their care arrangements in a care home or hospital are protected if those arrangements deprive them of their liberty. Arrangements are assessed to check they are necessary and in the person's best interests.
11 The Committee of Public Accounts is a select committee of the British House of Commons. It is responsible for overseeing government expenditures and to ensure they are effective and honest.
12 650k people work in care homes in England.

References

Alzheimer's Society, 2020. *Thousands of people with dementia dying or deteriorating - not just from coronavirus as isolation takes its toll.* Available at: https://www.alzheimers.org.uk/news/2020-06-05/thousands-people-dementia-dying-or-deteriorating-not-just-coronavirus-isolation

Amnesty International, 2020. *As if expendable: the UK government's failure to protect older people in care homes during the Covid-19 pandemic.* Available at: https://www.amnesty.org.uk/files/2020-10/Care%20Homes%20Report.pdf

Anand, J., Donnelly, S., Milne, A., Nelson-Becker, H., Ayala-Deusdad, B., Sirotkina, R., Cellini, G., Vignare, E.-L. and Kinni, R.-L. (in press), 2021. The Covid-19 pandemic & care homes for older people in Europe - deaths, damage & violations of human rights. *European Journal of Social Work*, forthcoming.

Bell, D., Comas-Herrera, A., Henderson, D., Jones, S., Lemmon, E., Moro, M., Murphy, S., O'Reilly, D. and Patrignani, P., 2020. *COVID-19 mortality and long-term care: A UK comparison.* LTCcovid.org. International Long-Term Care Policy Network, CPEC-LSE. Available at: https://ltccovid.org/2020/08/28/covid-19-mortality-and-long-term-care-a-uk-comparison/[PP1]

Brennan, J., Reilly, P., Cuskelly, K. and Donnelly, S., 2020. Social work, mental health, older people and Covid19. *International Psychogeriatrics*, 32(10), pp. 1205–1209.

Burton, K., Bayne, G., Evans, C., Garbe, F., Gorman, D., Honhold, N., McCormick, D., Othieno, R., Stevenson, J.E., Swietlik, S., Templeton, K., Tranter, M., Willocks, L. and Guthrie, B., 2020. Evolution and impact of COVID-19 outbreaks in care homes: population analysis in 189 care homes in one geographic region, *BMJ Yale*. https://doi.org/10.1101/2020.07.09.20149583

Carter, R., 2020. Covid-19: the support UK care homes need to survive, *British Medical Journal*, 369, pp. m1858. Doi: https://doi.org/10.1136/bmj.m1858

Comas-Herrera, A. and Fernandez, J.-L., 2020. *Estimates of number of deaths of care home residents linked to the COVID-19 pandemic in England*. Available at: https://ltccovid.org/2020/05/12/estimates-of-mortality-of-care-home-residents-linked-to-the-covid-19-pandemic-in-england/

Comas-Herrera, A., Fernández, J.-L., Hancock, R., Hatton, C., Knapp, M., McDaid, D., Malley, J., Wistow, G. and Wittenberg, R., 2020. *COVID-19: implications for the support of people with social care needs in England*. Journal of Aging and Social Policy, 32(4–5), pp. 365–372.

Comas-Herrera, A., Zalakaín, J., Lemmon, E., Henderson, D., Litwin, C., Hsu, A.T., Schmidt, A.E., Arling, G. and Fernandez, J.-L., 2020. *Mortality associated with COVID-19 in care homes: international evidence*. Available at: https://ltccovid.org/wp-content/uploads/2020/10/Mortality-associated-with-COVID-among-people-living-in-care-homes-14-October-2020-3.pdf

Daly, M., 2020. COVID-19 and care homes in England: what happened and why? *Social Policy & Administration*, pp. 1–14. Doi: https://doi.org/10.1111/spol.12645

Dening, T. and Milne, A., 2020. Mental health in care homes for older people. In Dening, T., Thomas, A., Stewart, R. and Taylor, J.-P. (eds.), *Oxford Textbook of Old Age Psychiatry* (3rd ed.) London, UK: Open University Press, pp. 343–358.

Dyer, C., 2020. Covid-19: doctors make bid for public inquiry into lack of PPE for frontline workers. *British Medical Journal*, 369, pp. m1905. Doi: https://doi.org/10.1136/bmj.m1905

Greenberg, N., Docherty, M., Gnanapragasam, S. and Wessely, S., 2020. Managing mental health challenges faced by healthcare workers during covid-19 pandemic. *British Medical Journal*, 368, pp. m1211. Doi: https://www.bmj.com/content/368/bmj.m1211

Harwood, R., 2020. *Did the UK response to the COVID-19 pandemic fail frail older people?* Available at: https://www.bgs.org.uk/blog/did-the-uk-response-to-the-covid-19-pandemic-fail-frail-older-people

Health and Social Care Committee, 2020. *Social care: funding and workforce, House of Commons*. Available at: https://committees.parliament.uk/work/136/social-care-funding-and-workforce/

House of Commons Public Accounts Committee, 2020. *Readying the NHS and social care for the COVID-19 peak Fourteenth Report of Session 2019–21 Report*. Available at: https://committees.parliament.uk/publications/2179/documents/20139/default/

Huber, M., Rodrigues, R., Hoffmann, F., Gasior, K. and Marin, B., 2009. *Facts and figures on long-term care – Europe and North America*. Vienna: European Centre for Social Welfare Policy and Research.

Iacobucci, G., 2020. Covid-19: care home deaths in England and Wales double in four weeks. *British Medical Journal*, 369, pp. m1612. Doi: https://doi.org/10.1136/bmj.m1612

LaingBuisson, 2019. *Care homes for older people UK market report*. London, UK: Laing and Buisson.

Larkin, M. and Milne, A., 2017. What do we know about older former carers? Key issues and themes. *Health and Social Care in the Community*, 25(4), pp. 1396–1403.

Lewis, O., 2020. *Why social workers should be aiming to get residents out of care homes during the pandemic*. Community Care. Available at: https://

www.communitycare.co.uk/2020/04/21/social-workers-aiming-get-residents-care-homes-pandemic/

Mikelyte, R. and Milne, A., 2016. Exploring the influence of micro-cultures on the mental health and well being of older people living in long term care. *Special Issue of Quality in Ageing, Mental Health and Later Life*, 17(3), pp. 198–214.

Milne, A., 2020a. Notes on a scandal: coronavirus & care homes for older people. Social work 2020 under Covid-19 Magazine. Available at: https://sw2020covid19.group.shef.ac.uk/2020/06/03/notes-on-a-scandal-coronavirus-care-homes-for-older-people/

Milne, A., 2020b. *The impact of corona confinement on older people's mental health: some reflections*. Available at: https://ageingissues.wordpress.com/2020/07/01/the-impact-of-corona-confinement-on-older-peoples-mental-health-some-reflections/

Moriarty, J., Manthorpe, J. and Harris, J., 2018. *Recruitment and retention in adult social care services*. London, UK: Social Care Workforce Research Unit, Kings College.

O'Caoimh, R., Donovan, M.R., Monahan, M.P., O'Connor, C.D., Buckley, C., Kilty, C., Fitzgerald, S., Hartigan, I. and Cornally, N., 2020. Psychosocial impact of Covid-19 nursing home restrictions on visitors of residents with cognitive impairment: A cross-sectional study as part of the engaging remotely in care project. *Frontiers in Psychiatry*, https://doi.org/10.3389/fpsyt.2020.585373

O'Dowd, A., 2020. Covid-19: care home deaths in England and Wales rise sharply. *British Medical Journal*, 369, pp. m1727. Doi: https://doi.org/10.1136/bmj.m1727

Office for National Statistics, 2020. *The cumulative number of care home residence deaths in care homes involving Covid-19 in England*. Available at: https://www.ons.gov.uk/

Oliver, D., 2020. *Preventing more deaths in care homes in a second pandemic surge*. Available at: https://www.bmj.com/content/bmj/369/bmj.m2461.full.pdf

Office of National Statistics, 2020. Deaths involving COVID-19 in the care sector, England and Wales: deaths occurring up to 12 June 2020 and registered up to 20 June 2020 (provisional). Available at: https://www.ons.gov.uk/peoplepopulationandcommunity/birthsdeathsandmarriages/deaths/articles/deathsinvolvingcovid19inthecaresector-englandandwales/latest#main-points

Phillipson, C., 2020. Covid-19 and the crisis in residential and nursing home care. Available at: https://ageingissues.wordpress.com/2020/04/08/covid-19-and-the-crisis-in-residential-and-nursing-home-care/

Pollock, A.M., Clements, L. and Harding-Edgar, L., 2020. Covid-19: why we need a national health and social care service. *British Medical Journal*, 369, pp. m1465. Doi: https://doi.org/10.1136/bmj.m1465

Samuel, M., 2020. *Covid-19 deaths among social care staff far outstripping those in healthcare*. Community Care 12th May. Available at: https://www.communitycare.co.uk/2020/05/11/covid-19-deaths-among-social-care-staff-far-outstripping-healthcare/

Skoura-Kirk, E., 2020. Why make a fuss over some old people? Available at: https://sw2020covid19.group.shef.ac.uk/2020/05/18/320/

Suarez-Gonzalez, A., 2020. Detrimental effects of confinement and isolation in the cognitive and psychological health of people living with dementia during COVID-19: emerging evidence. *LTCcovid, International Long-Term Care Policy Network*. CPEC-LSE.

Velayudhan, L., Aarsland, D. and Ballard C., 2020. Mental health of people living with dementia in care homes during COVID-19 pandemic. *International Psychogeriatrics*, 32(10), pp. 1253–1254.

Walker, A., 2020. Institutional ageism and the pandemic. Available at: https://sw2020covid19.group.shef.ac.uk/2020/07/14/institutional-ageism-and-the-pandemic/

World Health Organisation, 2020. New WHO/Europe guidance shows more can be done to protect people in need of long-term care during the COVID-19 pandemic. Available at: https://www.euro.who.int/en/health-topics/Health-systems/pages/news/news/2020/5/new-whoeurope-guidance-shows-more-can-be-done-to-protect-people-in-need-of-long-term-care-during-the-covid-19-pandemic

10 Impact of Covid-19 on mental health and associated losses

Manju Shahul-Hameed, John Foster, Gina Finnerty, and Panagiotis Pentaris

---

Key points

- Reflection on the learning through the lens of publications, research, newspaper articles and social media;
- Explore how mental health is misbalanced in people's lives;
- Preventing loss of life due to COVID-19 lead to poor mental health outcomes, such as isolation, anxiety, depression, job loss and suicidal ideation;
- Providing policy recommendation and amendments to meet the needs, exacerbated by the pandemic for the people with mental illness.

Introduction

The Covid-19 pandemic and resulting economic downturn have negatively affected mental health and created new barriers for people already suffering from mental illness. Hospitals may have become mostly coronavirus receiving stations and patients with cancer, mental health patients and other health conditions were no longer a priority during the first few months of the pandemic. Many patients with these conditions have had their treatment rightly stopped and saw a wider scale rationing of services in the first few months of the pandemic, while medical or non-medical needs continue to be demanding, resulting in simultaneous impact.

The effect of Covid-19 on mental health has emerged as a matter of concern. A number of factors related to Covid-19 can adversely affect the mental health of individuals, with an even higher risk in those predisposed to psychological conditions. Being in quarantine or isolation for extended periods of time has been associated with depression, anger, anxiety, and suicide (Rossi et al., 2020). Similarly, uncertainty of economic recovery and loss of job security are important factors previously associated with neuropsychiatric perturbations (Bünnings, Kleibrink and Weßling, 2017; Mucci et al., 2016;

Nordt et al., 2015). Concerns have also been raised about increase in incidents of domestic violence and 'screen time' of individuals during the Covid-19 pandemic, which are known risk factors for the development or worsening of psychological conditions (Dhir et al., 2018). Furthermore, fear and paranoia of being infected with the virus and the stigma associated with manifesting symptoms such as cough or sneezing could negatively impact mental well-being (Chaturvedi, 2020). The fear of losing a loved one and the grief following a loss are other potential disturbances to mental health accompanying disease outbreaks (Morris et al., 2019; Elizarrarás-Rivas et al., 2010)

In addition to heightened risk of depression and anxiety for the general public, it has been predicted that the Covid-19 pandemic is likely to increase rates of substance use (Czeisler et al., 2020; Rolland et al., 2020), loneliness (Killgore et al., 2020), domestic violence and child abuse (Usher et al., 2020). These are all factors known to contribute to the development and worsening of psychiatric disorders.

Even with the challenges of Covid-19, though, some fantastic examples of integrated working have been driven to rapidly safeguard patients and support staff. In a matter of days, UK national bodies, like the Department of Health and Social Care, quickly removed/tackled legislative, policy and organisational barriers that have impacted upon the health and social care system for many years. Covid-19 has exposed deep gaps in how integrated care is being delivered. More people were dying in the care homes and people's homes than the hospitals (Pentaris et al., 2020). There is increasing evidence that the rapid discharge of people into the community without appropriate testing, when combined with the inadequate protection of staff, has potentially transferred the risk from hospitals to primary and social care and to the most vulnerable in society (Burke, 2020).

This chapter aims to understand the burden of mental health following the Covid-19 pandemic and the urgent need to continue the implementation of four decades of policy initiatives on integrated care to increase intervention and prevention efforts to address mental health conditions now and if there is a second wave.

Mental health pre Covid-19

Mental health is integral to living a healthy, balanced life (Tengland, 2001). Our mental health encompasses our psychological, emotional and social well-being. In other words, it impacts how we feel, think and behave each day. Our mental health also contributes to our decision-making processes; how we cope with stress; and how we relate to others in our lives. And yet, 792 million people are affected by mental health issues worldwide, placing mental disorders among the leading causes of ill-health and disability. According to the *Global Burden of Disease* study of the Institute for Health Metrics and Evaluation (2017), it is estimated that 970 million people globally have a mental or substance use disorder.

Mental, neurological and substance use disorders (MNS) are common, highly disabling, and associated with significant premature mortality (Charlson et al., 2015). One in four people in the world will be affected by mental or neurological disorders at some point in their lives. According to data by the World Health Organization (WHO, n.d.) for the period 2000–2012, mental disorders accounts for 30% of the non-fatal disease burden and 10% of the overall disease burden worldwide, including death and disability.

Mental health disorders include depression, bipolar, anxiety, schizophrenia and other psychoses, dementia, and eating disorders. Major depression is thought to be the second leading cause of disability worldwide and a major contributor to the burden of suicide and ischemic heart disease. Depressive disorders are already the fourth leading cause of the global disease burden. They are expected to rank second by 2020, behind ischemic heart disease but ahead of all other diseases (Morris, 2002).

Prevention programmes have been shown to reduce depression, both for children (e.g. through protection and psychological support following physical and sexual abuse) and adults (e.g. through psychosocial assistance after disasters and conflicts). Also receiving better, more joined up care in the community will benefit people with mental illness. The question 'What causes mental illness' remains unresolved, albeit the extensive work undertaken. Psychiatrists speak of a combination of risk factors and starting with the genes; in 2018, scientists pinpointed 44 gene variants that raise the risk of depression. As Ricardo Araya, director of the *Centre for Global Mental Health* at King's College, suggests, 'what you inherit is a certain vulnerability or predisposition, and if things happen on top of that then people would then be more likely to suffer from a mental problem'.

The impact of MNS on the social and economic well-being of individuals, families, and societies is large, underestimated and often ignored. Treatments are available, but nearly two-thirds of people with a known mental disorder never seek help from a health professional (World Health Organization, 2001; also see Magaard et al., 2017). Stigma, discrimination and negligence prevent care and treatment from reaching people with mental disorders, according to WHO (2016). Further, WHO claims that the responsibility for action lies with governments. Currently, more than 40% of countries have no mental health policy, over 30% have no mental health programme, and around 25% of countries have no mental health legislation. These are serious gaps in the care system and service provision.

The world was not set up to respond to the growing mental health crisis before Covid-19, and this remains the case. Prior to the Covid-19 outbreak, global statistics on mental health conditions were already bleak. The global economy loses more than US$ 1 trillion per year due to depression and anxiety (World Health Organization, 2016). Mental health conditions contribute to 25% of years lived with disability in the world. Depression is a leading cause of disability, affecting 264 million people. Around half of all mental health conditions start by age 14, and suicide is the second leading cause of death in young people aged 15–29 (WHO, 2020). Every 40 seconds someone dies by suicide. More than 1 in 5 people living in settings affected by conflict suffer from a mental health condition, and people with severe mental disorders die 10–20 years earlier than the general population. Despite the scale of the problems funding is woefully inadequate. Development assistance for mental health (DAMH) has never exceeded 1% of development assistance for health (DAH). Similarly, in low and middle-income countries (LMICs), less than 1.6% of national health budgets are spent on mental health.

Impact of Covid-19 on mental health

As the coronavirus pandemic rapidly sweeps across the world, it is inducing a considerable degree of fear, worry and concern in the population at large and among certain groups in particular, such as older adults, care providers and people with underlying health conditions. At the time of writing this chapter (November 2020), globally, we are experiencing an upsurge in Covid-19 cases, which is often discussed as the 'second wave'. All concerns that were initially expressed, are currently intensified with the reassurance that the pandemic is neither gone nor finished with its impact.

Globally, mental health is being challenged like never before. Whilst there are many uncertainties about how the current pandemic will progress, what is clear is that the impact on the mental health and psychosocial well-being of those most affected will be significant. This is a pivotal moment in the history of mental health. How the world tackles these challenges now will determine the well-being of a generation; it will impact the drive to successful recovery and building back societies stronger for the future.

Most countries have taken action to curtail the spread of the virus through measures such as lockdowns, social distancing (or physical distancing) and voluntary self-isolation, having an effect on people's usual activities, routines and/or livelihoods. Whilst necessary, such measures and the disease itself, may have an adverse impact on mental health, i.e. levels of loneliness, depression, harmful alcohol and drug use, and self-harm or suicidal behaviour are also expected to rise. More than two-thirds of adults in the UK (69%) report feeling somewhat or very worried about the effect Covid-19 is having on their life (Office for National Statistics, 2020b). The most common issues affecting wellbeing˙ are worry about the future (63%), feeling stressed or anxious (56%) and feeling bored (49%).

A cross-sectional electronic survey-based assessment of individuals above the age of 18 years was conducted among participants from diverse demographic groups across continents using standardized self-report scales to screen for general psychological disturbance, risk for PTSD, and symptoms of depression (Płomecka et al., 2020). The study anonymously screened individuals from the USA, Spain, Italy, France, Germany, the UK, Iran,

Turkey, and Switzerland for psychological symptoms related to Covid-19 pandemic. Female sex, pre-existing psychiatric condition, and prior exposure to trauma were identified as notable risk factors, whereas optimism, ability to share concerns with family and friends like usual, positive prediction about Covid-19, and daily exercise predicted fewer psychological symptoms.

What are the implications?

In addition to presenting new or enhanced stressors, the pandemic has diminished many of the mechanisms people typically use to cope with stress. The Health Foundation (2020) published material that suggests that the most popular coping mechanisms during lockdown have been staying in touch with friends and family and taking daily outdoor exercise, which has helped nearly half of the adults surveyed. Work has also been important, with the value for mental wellbeing extending beyond the financial benefits, but there are inequalities: job loss is socioeconomically patterned, some groups cannot get outdoors, and some are unable to remain digitally connected to friends and family. All of this increases the likelihood that the pandemic will increase mental health inequalities.

Impact on people with existing mental health illness

People suffering from mental health conditions may already experience poverty, chronic medical problems and social disparity (Ngui et al., 2010). Covid-19 is likely to adversely affect this population more acutely than the rest of the population. Those with existing poor mental health are facing a number of risks including increased rates of mental ill health and disruption to treatment, medications and the lifeline of support services. Studies are showing Covid-19 is likely to exacerbate existing mental health symptoms or trigger relapse among people with pre-existing mental health illness (e.g. Chatterjee et al., 2020). With reduced access to mental health services, there are fears people are staying away until they reach crisis point, which will result in a flood of exacerbated and untreated mental illness after the pandemic, and mental health providers are already reporting significant increases in demand and severity of new referrals (NHS Providers, 2020).

In an online survey in South Africa, of those with a prior diagnosed mental health condition, some 12% identified feelings of suicide as the main challenge, and 6% indicated substance use as a difficulty (www.sadag.org). In Buenos Aires, Argentina, a neurological institute reported an over 99% reduction in patient encounters since Covid-19 (Allegri and Sevlever, 2020). Community-based psychosocial support activities have also been severely impacted with many countries seeing groups, associations and community-based initiatives that brought people together regularly before the pandemic unable to meet for months. Demand for face-to-face mental health services has significantly decreased due to fear of infection, especially among older people (Khoury and Karam, 2020). Many services have had to switch to remote mental health care (e.g. The Collaborative, Talkspace or Mental Capacity Assessments), providing consultations through digital platforms or by phone to varying degrees of success. Some countries are investing in innovative digital and telecommunication solutions and the appointment of more mental health professionals. However, this does not negate the risks of digital poverty and/or digital illiteracy and how it is, subsequently, impacting on accessibility of mental health services among those who most need it under the circumstances of a pandemic.

On the frontline: impact on health workers

Frontline workers are playing a crucial role in fighting the outbreak and saving lives. But they are under exceptional stress and while deaths of health workers are rising, the mental ill health rates are rising faster still (Munawar and Choudhry, 2020). Frontline workers, especially healthcare workers, are at particularly high risk of mental ill health, including suicide attempts, the risk of burnout and stigmatisation. Preliminary data from Pakistan indicated that among health professionals working during this pandemic, 42% were likely to experience moderate psychological distress, with some 26% showing severe psychological distress (personal communication, 2020; unpublished data). In Canada, a survey reported that among health workers dealing with the Covid-19 crisis, 47% said they needed psychological support (Potloc, 2020). There have also been reports of stigmatisation toward those working with people with Covid-19, and the self-care and social support of staff is being compromised.

The importance of organisational and governmental support for healthcare workers in terms of provision of suitable equipment, personal protective equipment (PPE) and working conditions to ensure minimal mental health difficulties. Chile, Italy, Spain, Philippines, the UK and the US have introduced dedicated teams providing mental health support for health workers. Initiatives include the introduction of personal screening for stress and mental health illness involving an assessment of occupational exposure to Covid-19.

Impact on Covid-19 patients and their families

People who test positive for Covid-19 have to cope with fear, anxiety and uncertainty about their condition, as well as physical discomfort and separation from loved ones. A study among hospitalised patients in China showed that 34.7% of patients had symptoms of anxiety and 28.4% of depression (Kong et al., 2020). Similarly, Montauk and Kuhl (2020) argue that the current pandemic only exacerbates the traumatic experiences that intensive care unit families face when their loved one is in isolation. For those who have loved ones affected by Covid-19, they face worry and separation. People who experience the death of a family member often do not have the opportunity to be present in their last moments, or to hold funerals which can have a profound effect on grieving and impact mental health (Burrell and Selman, 2020), as Chapters 2, 3 and 4 in this volume argue.

Some Covid-19 patients may have experienced stigma, discrimination and intimidation (Imran et al., 2020). This can lead people to hiding the illness to avoid such discrimination, prevent people from seeking health care, and discourage them from adopting healthy behaviours, all of which undermines efforts to control the pandemic.

Impact on the elderly

Elderly people are at high risk of mental ill health – especially those with dementia – due to the anticipated long periods of social/physical distancing and the accompanying isolation and loneliness (Pentaris et al., 2020). There may be a worsening of cognitive decline in older people, who may be one of the last groups for whom lockdown measures are lifted. Older people fear infection from the virus, so are no longer accessing services. Italy has seen a 50% reduction in hospital admissions for stroke, while in Argentina visits to memory clinics almost completely stopped. There has also been a reduction in the workforce taking care of older people, as carers are diverted to work on Covid-19, and border closures – particularly in Europe – are preventing migrant workers who provide a large proportion of care for the elderly, from entering host countries (http://www.mhpss.net).

Impact on general populations

Results of initial studies confirm that fear, loneliness, sadness and anxiety are common as people are afraid of infection, dying, losing family members, losing their income or livelihoods, being socially isolated and separated from loved ones (also see Ornell et al. (2020)). These are risk factors not only for the short term, but also long-term mental health problems. One survey in the UK revealed 1 in 5 people are concerned about social isolation, and 1 in 10 have negative feelings or worries about finances, employment or the virus (Ipsos MORI, 2020). To deal with these stressors, people may use different coping mechanisms some of which are harmful including rising alcohol consumption which can exacerbate issues such as interpersonal violence, drugs, or spending more time on potentially addictive behaviours such as gaming and gambling. Statistics from Canada (https://www150.statcan.gc.ca/n1/pub/11–627-m/11–627-m2020029-eng.htm) indicate some 20% of the population aged 15–49 increased their alcohol consumption during the pandemic. Relationships are being tested as some family members are being forced to spend much more time together which, whilst for some, can strengthen relations, for others is adding additional strain (Goodwin et al., 2020).

There have, for example, been serious concerns about victims of domestic abuse being locked down with perpetrators (Usher et al., 2020; Bradbury-Jones and Isham, 2020). A report by UK MPs found 16 people – 14 women and 2 children – were killed in the first 3 weeks of lockdown, and calls to the national helpline *Refuge* were 49% higher than usual (BBC News, 2020).

Social connection is vital to well-being in humans, and whilst internet-based media and applications such as Zoom, Microsoft Teams, Skype, WhatsApp and FaceTime may allow for social interactions to continue, they do not replace the need for in-person human contact. Numbers of people volunteering, who offer alternatives to social connection, however, have halved during the pandemic. This may be because volunteers could be in at-risk groups, or their activities have been halted, potentially putting older or vulnerable individuals at additional mental health risk. There is likely to be increased vigilance by the statutory and third sector organisations towards cleanliness and hygiene, which when coupled with fears of infection and disease may lead to feeling more anxious than usual.

People's housing, their ability to afford housing and the quality of the housing are strong influences on mental health. People who rent have experienced greater financial impacts during the pandemic than those who own their homes (Office for National Statistics, 2020a); another example of a driver for poor mental health that is socioeconomically patterned. During lockdown, people have spent far more time than usual in their homes. Quality of housing and the opportunities it affords – including personal and outdoor space – are highly variable. For example, one in eight households (12%) in Great Britain have no access to a private or shared garden, and black people in England are nearly four times more likely than their white counterparts to have no access to outdoor space at home (37% versus 10%) (Office for National Statistics, 2020b).

Covid-19 and the digital divide

Billions of people are going online to stay in touch during the pandemic, but almost half of the world's population has no access to the internet. Covid-19 has exposed and intensified the digital divide (Ramsetty and Adams, 2020), which impacts women more than men and fewer than 1 in 5 people in the least developed countries are connected (World Economic Forum, 2020).

From schools setting coursework online to office staff working from home, the internet is the answer to many coronavirus lockdown problems. But what about the billions of people who can't get online? Globally, drawing on UNESCO (2019), only just over half of households (55%) have an internet connection. According to the same source, in the developed world, 87% are connected compared with 47% in developing nations, and just 19% in the least developed countries.

In total, 3.7 billion people have no internet access (UNESCO, 2019). The majority are in poorer countries, where the need to spread information about how to combat Covid-19 is most urgent and migrants and those in poverty being particularly vulnerable (World Economic Forum, 2020). South Africa has made access to its Covid-19 website free of charge, with no data or airtime required, and local broadband provider Telkom has done the same for educational websites and sites providing coronavirus updates, such as the National Institute for Communicable Diseases (WE Forum, 2020).

In spite of free access, there remains a significant digital gender divide (UNESCO, 2019). Globally, women are 23% less likely than men to use mobile internet[1]. The gap is wider in South Asia, followed by sub-Saharan Africa. Human connectivity is needed to close the digital divide.

Such gaps may exacerbate mental health issues as the use of the internet and information technologies during the pandemic are the answer to human proximity, closeness and communication with one another. Once the means to contact is not an option, whether this is because of lack of resources or digital poverty, mental health is further at risk.

Change, loss and bereavement

During the coronavirus outbreak people have been through enormous change and experienced loss of different types, including the death of loved ones. Other types of losses, though, should not be quickly dismissed. During the pandemic, there were changes brought about by loss of the personal freedom. This may be adjusting to the loss of not being able to go to places or coping with the loss of income or employment. Further, the valuable aspects of the social connections with others, that have been lost include hugs and handshakes, social activities and simply sharing the same physical space with friends and relatives. The loss of power and control over their lives is what people had to cope with, while coping with the Covid-19 pandemic itself.

Young people have had their lives turned upside down by the pandemic. Almost every young person has had to adjust to dramatic changes in their education, routine and home life, with lack of social connection, isolation and adjusting to online studies not always with adequate support available. This already had a huge impact on the young people's mental health, increased feelings of anxiety, isolation, a loss of coping mechanisms and a loss of motivation. Closure of day care centres and schools combined with restrictions on movement are limiting chances for children to interact and access learning opportunities all of which are taking a toll on their mental health. A study among Italian and Spanish parents (Orgilés et al., 2020) showed that 85.7% of parents perceived changes in their children's emotional state and behaviour during confinement at home. The same study showed that children were struggling to concentrate (76.6%), were irritable (39%), restless (38.8%, nervous (38%) and experiencing feelings of loneliness (31.1%).

Stress and social isolation are likely to affect brain health and development, with young children at risk of developing lifelong challenges by periods of prolonged exposure to toxic stress and by deprivation in nutrition, stimulation and health care which can affect brain health and development (Yoshikawa et al., 2020). Children are spending more time with families during lockdown and when there is already abuse in the family – or risk of it – this is even more likely to occur. Parents and carers need to make sure their children feel loved and secure. More than one billion children across the globe are currently locked out of classrooms because of quarantine measures, and albeit online classrooms, reasons like digital poverty and illiteracy keep many children away from their education for significant periods.

The Mental Health Foundation reports over a third of people in full-time work surveyed were concerned about losing their job, and mental health impacts on people who were unemployed were widespread and severe. A quarter reported not coping well with the stress of the pandemic (twice as many as those in employment), almost half were worried about not having enough food to meet basic needs, and one in five had experienced suicidal thoughts (Marshall, Bibby and Abbs, 2020).

Loss for women is higher compared to men as women are reporting greater levels of increased anxiety and depression than men in many cases. A survey on stress levels in the Indian population during the pandemic showed that 66% of women reported being stressed, compared to 34% of men (The Hindu, 2020). Similarly, in China, a study saw women report symptoms of anxiety and depression more commonly than men during the outbreak (Du et al., 2020). Increased stressful situations and lockdown can also result in increases in violence against women, with estimates that globally 31 million additional cases of gender-based violence can be expected to occur if lockdown continues for at least six months (UNFPA, 2020). Such domestic violence has mental health consequences including depression, anxiety and post-traumatic stress disorder (PTSD). It seems that governments are facing the need to prevent and redress any violence as a key part of response plans for Covid-19, including creating safe ways for victims and survivors to report violence safely or seek support.

Coping with the death of someone close can be compounded by not being able to be with them during their final hours due to the restrictions that have been placed on assembly as a result of the quarantine measures to prevent the spread of the virus. Bereavement can make people feel anxious, sad, angry, shocked, grief-stricken, withdrawn, in disbelief, guilty, sad and in denial. This will have an impact on sleep, concentration, appetite and making decisions. People can also experience physical pain, such as headaches and muscle pain, as well as less specific bodily reactions that are similar to feelings of anxiety.

New data has revealed that deaths of patients detained under the Mental Health Act are running at twice the rate of 2019, with half of the fatalities down to Covid-19 (Thomas, 2020). In UK, the Care Quality Commission

(CQC) stated that 112 patients detained under the Mental Health Act had died between 1 March and 1 May 2020. This compares to a total of 56 deaths during the same period of 2019, 61 deaths in 2018, and 70 deaths in 2017. These figures include both people who are detained in hospital and people subject to the Mental Health Act, but who are still in the community. Since 1 March 2020, 56 detained patients have died from either suspected or confirmed Covid-19.

Suicidal ideation

Social isolation, anxiety, fear of contagion, uncertainty, chronic stress and economic difficulties may lead to the development or exacerbation of stress-related disorders. Suicidality in vulnerable populations including individuals with pre-existing psychiatric disorders, low-resilient persons, individuals who reside in high Covid-19 prevalence areas and people who have a family member or a friend who has died of Covid-19 (Figure 10.1; Sher, 2020, p. 709).

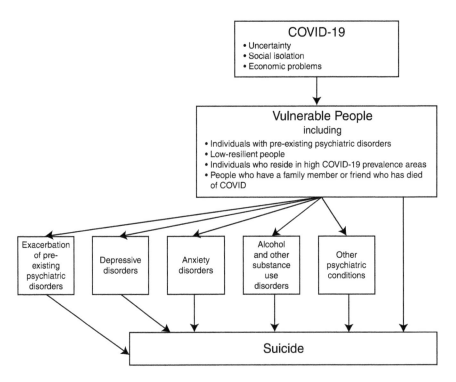

Figure 10.1 Suicidal behaviour in vulnerable populations in the COVID-19 era.
Source: *Sher, L. 2020. The impact of the Covid-19 pandemic on suicide rates. QJM: An International Journal of Medicine, 113(10), 707–712* doi:10.1093/qjmed/hcaa202, by permission of Oxford University Press.

For years America had been reeling from a steady rise in "deaths of despair," which are defined as deaths by suicide or associated with alcohol or drug use (Barna, 2020). Nearly 182,000 people died from those means in 2018. The Covid-19 outbreak has resulted significant economic disruption, job losses and many other challenging realities. Stress-related psychiatric conditions including mood and substance use disorders are associated with suicidal behaviour (Czeisler et al., 2020). The Covid-19 crisis may increase suicide rates during and after the pandemic (Sher, 2020). Mental health consequences of the Covid-19 crisis including suicidal behaviour are likely to be present for a long time and peak later than the actual pandemic. Multiple cases of Covid-19 related suicides in the US, the UK, Italy, Germany, Bangladesh, India and other countries have been reported in mass media and psychiatric literature, more of which is discussed in Chapter 15 of this book. For example, in Germany, a finance minister, Thomas Schaefe, committed suicide near Frankfurt in late March 2020. He reportedly felt despair over the economic impacts of the coronavirus pandemic.

The surge in demand to complete the suicide prevention programme – funded in part by the Department of Health and Social Care in the UK – is telling of how a charity called *Zero Suicide Alliance* reached a total of one million participants worldwide since its launch in 2017. The online training takes around 20 minutes and leads users through the skills they might need to help someone who may be considering suicide, tackling stigma and promoting open communication.

Using cases of Covid-19 related suicides in the US, Italy, the UK, Germany, Saudi Arabia, India, and Bangladesh, a study highlights that suicide risk associated to the coronavirus pandemic (Thakur and Jain, 2020). Four major risk factors that the authors identified are social distancing and isolation, economic recession stemming from Covid-19 lockdowns, healthcare professionals' stress, trauma, and stigma and discrimination. Tweets claiming that deaths by suicide have increased by 200% since lockdown spread on Twitter on 29 June 2020. The tweets, shared across the UK, do not specifically state in which region they are referring to, but in the body of one of the widely shared tweets, it references *Samaritans UK*. There are no official statistics or evidence to support the claim that the rates of suicide increased 200% during the period of lockdown (i.e. from 23 March to present), therefore the claim that the rate of suicides has increased 200% cannot be corroborated. The *Samaritans* echo this finding about the lack of reliable statistical data on suicide rates during the period of lockdown in their responses to many of the individual tweets on the issue: "There is currently no evidence of a rise in suicide rates. However, we know that many people are struggling with their mental health during this difficult time and we are here 24/7 for whoever needs us".

To assess mental health, substance use, and suicidal ideation during the pandemic, representative panel surveys were conducted among adults aged ≥18 years across the US during June 24–30, 2020 (Czeisler et al., 2020).

According to those surveys, during June 24–30, 2020, US adults reported considerably elevated adverse mental health conditions associated with Covid-19. The percentage of respondents who reported having seriously considered suicide in the 30 days before completing the survey (10.7%) was significantly higher among respondents aged 18–24 years (25.5%), minority racial/ethnic groups (Hispanic respondents [18.6%], non-Hispanic black respondents [15.1%]), self-reported unpaid caregivers for adults (30.7%), and essential workers (21.7%). Community-level intervention and prevention efforts, including health communication strategies, designed to reach these groups could help address various mental health conditions associated with the Covid-19 pandemic.

There is a briefing, which is commissioned by the Healthcare Quality Improvement Partnership (HQIP) on behalf of the NHS England. It describes the findings from real-time surveillance system (which was set up to respond to the Covid-19 pandemic) relating to child death by suicide in England during lockdown. This report finds, among the likely suicide deaths reported after lockdown, that restriction to education and other activities, disruption to care and support services, tensions at home and isolation appeared to be contributing factors.

Conclusion

From the outset it has been clear that the potential mental health effect of the Covid-19 pandemic and the associated quarantine measures were going to be one of the most important aspects of the crisis. Mental health and subjective wellbeing outcomes are important in their own right, and they are also risk factors for future physical health and longevity, so will be an indication of the future indirect health consequences of the pandemic. The impact of Covid-19 on mental health has been identified as an important area of research going forward, and a number of papers have pointed out that mental health considerations should be an important element of decisions regarding at what speed and in what way to lift the lockdown and physical distancing restrictions that have been imposed (in November 2020, many countries are facing a second national lockdown, or varied local lockdowns).

As yet there are no empirical data available relating to the mental health impact of contracting Covid-19. However, lessons from previous pandemic situations indicate that there is likely to be a risk of Covid-19 patients, who recover, developing symptoms of PTSD or depression. This is likely to be moderated by personal traits such as resilience, availability and quality of social support and the patient's own worries related to the illness and recovery.

Among the many inequalities exposed by Covid-19, digital poverty and the digital gender divide are of great importance. Telemedicine services are readily available to anyone owning a telephone or a computer and can be provided through video calls, phone call, text messaging and online forums. The current circumstances under which mental health services become available, systemically exclude parts of the population that either do not own (or cannot afford) the right electronic devices or lack the literacy to make use of them. Such and many other challenges that have been discussed in this chapter require ongoing attention, in light of the foreseeable long-term impact of Covid-19 on mental health.

Note

1 Also see https://broadbandcommission.org/Documents/SOBB-REPORT%20HIGHT LIGHTS-v3.pdf

References

Allegri, R. and Sevlever, G., 2020. Invited commentary: the elusive paradox: the woods behind the trees. Neurology blogs. Available at: https://blogs.neurology.org/covid-19-coronavirus/invited-commentary-the-elusive-paradox-the-woods-behind-the-trees/ (Accessed: 10 November 2020).

Barna, M., 2020. Experts fear suicide, deaths of despair will rise in wake of COVID-19: Mental health crisis. *The Nation's Health* (July), 50(5), pp. 1–10.

BBC News. 2020. UK lockdown: Calls to domestic abuse helpline jump by half. Available at: https://www.bbc.co.uk/news/uk-52433520 (Accessed: 3 December 2020).

Bradbury-Jones, C. and Isham, L., 2020. The pandemic paradox: The consequences of COVID-19 on domestic violence. *Journal of Clinical Nursing*, 29(13-14), pp. 2047–2049.

Bünnings, C., Kleibrink, J. and Weßling, J., 2017. Fear of unemployment and its effect on the mental health of spouses. *Health Economics*, 26(1), pp. 104–117.

Burke, C., 2020. Will covid-19 close the integrated care gap or widen it? *Health Service Journal*. Available at: https://www.hsj.co.uk/integration/will-covid-19-close-the-integrated-care-gap-or-widen-it/7027499.article (Accessed: 11 November 2020).

Burrell, A. and Selman, L.E., 2020. How do funeral practices impact bereaved relatives' mental health, grief and bereavement? A mixed methods review with implications for COVID-19. *OMEGA-Journal of Death and Dying*. Doi: 0.1177/003 0222820941296.

Charlson, F.J., Baxter, A.J., Dua, T., Degenhardt, L., Whiteford, H.A. and Vos, T., 2015. Excess mortality from mental, neurological and substance use disorders in the Global Burden of Disease Study 2010. *Epidemiology and Psychiatric Sciences*, 24(2), pp. 121–140.

Chatterjee, P., Nagi, N., Agarwal, A., Das, B., Banerjee, S., Sarkar, S., Gupta, N. and Gangakhedkar, R.R., 2020. The 2019 novel coronavirus disease (COVID-19) pandemic: a review of the current evidence. *Indian Journal of Medical Research*, 151(2), p. 147.

Chaturvedi, S.K., 2020. Covid-19, Coronavirus and Mental Health Rehabilitation at Times of Crisis. *Journal of Psychosocial Rehabilitation and Mental Health*, 7 (1-2), pp. 1–2.

Czeisler, M.É., Lane, R.I., Petrosky, E., Wiley, J.F., Christensen, A., Njai, R., Weaver, M.D., Robbins, R., Facer-Childs, E.R., Barger, L.K. and Czeisler, C.A., 2020.

Mental health, substance use, and suicidal ideation during the COVID-19 pandemic—United States, June 24–30, 2020. *Morbidity and Mortality Weekly Report*, 69(32), p. 1049.

Dhir, A., Yossatorn, Y., Kaur, P. and Chen, S., 2018. Online social media fatigue and psychological wellbeing—a study of compulsive use, fear of missing out, fatigue, anxiety and depression. *International Journal of Information Management*, 40, pp. 141–152.

Du, J., Dong, L., Wang, T., Yuan, C., Fu, R., Zhang, L., Liu, B., Zhang, M., Yin, Y., Qin, J. and Bouey, J., 2020. Psychological symptoms among frontline healthcare workers during COVID-19 outbreak in Wuhan. *General Hospital Psychiatry*. Doi: 10.1016/j.genhosppsych.2020.03.011

Elizarrarás-Rivas, J., Vargas-Mendoza, J.E., Mayoral-García, M., Matadamas-Zarate, C., Elizarrarás-Cruz, A., Taylor, M. and Agho, K., 2010. Psychological response of family members of patients hospitalised for influenza A/H1N1 in Oaxaca, Mexico. *BMC psychiatry*, 10(1), pp. 104–112.

Goodwin, R., Hou, W.K., Sun, S. and Ben-Ezra, M., 2020. Quarantine, distress and interpersonal relationships during COVID-19. *General psychiatry*, 33(6). Doi: 10.1136/gpsych-2020-100385

Imran, N., Afzal, H., Aamer, I., Hashmi, A.M., Shabbir, B., Asif, A. and Farooq, S., 2020. Scarlett letter: a study based on experience of stigma by COVID-19 patients in quarantine. *Pakistan Journal of Medical Sciences*, 36(7). Doi: 10.12669/pjms.36.7.3606

Institute for Health Metrics and Evaluation, 2017. *Global burden of disease. The Lancet: Latest global disease estimates reveal perfect storm of rising chronic diseases and public health failures fuelling COVID-19 pandemic*. Available at: http://www.healthdata.org/gbd/2019 (Accessed: 17 November 2020).

Ipsos MORI, 2020. *COVID-19 and mental wellbeing*. Available at: https://www.ipsos.com/ipsos-mori/en-uk/Covid-19-and-mental-wellbeing (Accessed: 11 November 2020).

Khoury, R. and Karam, G., 2020. Impact of COVID-19 on mental healthcare of older adults: insights from Lebanon. *International Psychogeriatrics*, *32*(10), pp. 1177–1180.

Killgore, W.D., Cloonen, S.A., Taylor, E.C. and Dailey, N.S., 2020. Loneliness: A signature mental health concern in the era of COVID-19. *Psychiatry Research*, p. 290. Doi: 10.1016/j.psychres.2020.113117

Kong, X., Zheng, K., Tang, M., Kong, F., Zhou, J., Diao, L., Wu, S., Jiao, P., Su, T. and Dong, Y., 2020. Prevalence and factors associated with depression and anxiety of hospitalized patients with COVID-19. *BMJ Yale*. Doi: 10.1101/2020.03.24.20043075.

Magaard, J.L., Seeralan, T., Schulz, H. and Brütt, A.L., 2017. Factors associated with help-seeking behaviour among individuals with major depression: a systematic review. *PloS One*, 12(5), pp. 1–17.

Marshall, L., Bibby, J. and Abbs, I., 2020. Emerging evidence on COVID-19's impact on mental health and health inequalities. Available at: https://www.health.org.uk/news-and-comment/blogs/emerging-evidence-on-covid-19s-impact-on-mental-health-and-health (Accessed: 3 December 2020).

Montauk, T.R. and Kuhl, E.A., 2020. COVID-related family separation and trauma in the intensive care unit. *Psychological Trauma: Theory, Research, Practice, and Policy*, 12(1), pp. 96–97.

Morris, B., 2002. World Health Report on mental disorders treatment. *International Journal of Health Care Quality Assurance*, 15(1), p. I.

Morris, K.L., Goldenberg, J.L., Arndt, J. and McCabe, S., 2019. The enduring influence of death on health: insights from the terror management health model. *Self and Identity*, 18(4), pp. 378–404.

Mucci, N., Giorgi, G., Roncaioli, M., Perez, J.F. and Arcangeli, G., 2016. The correlation between stress and economic crisis: a systematic review. *Neuropsychiatric Disease and Treatment*, 12, pp. 983–993

Munawar, K. and Choudhry, F.R., 2020. Exploring stress coping strategies of frontline emergency health workers dealing Covid-19 in Pakistan: a qualitative inquiry. *American Journal of Infection Control*, 49(3), pp. 286–292.

Ngui, E.M., Khasakhala, L., Ndetei, D. and Roberts, L.W., 2010. Mental disorders, health inequalities and ethics: a global perspective. *International Review of Psychiatry*, 22(3), pp. 235–244.

NHS Providers, 2020. The impact of COVID-19 on mental health trusts in the NHS. Available at: https://nhsproviders.org/media/689590/spotlight-on-mental-health.pdf (Accessed: 12 November 2020).

Nordt, C., Warnke, I., Seifritz, E. and Kawohl, W., 2015. Modelling suicide and unemployment: a longitudinal analysis covering 63 countries, 2000–11. *The Lancet Psychiatry*, 2(3), pp. 239–245.

Office for National Statistics, 2020a. *Personal and economic well-being in Great Britain: May 2020*. Available at: https://www.ons.gov.uk/peoplepopulationandcommunity/wellbeing/bulletins/personalandeconomicwellbeingintheuk/may2020 (Accessed: 11 November 2020).

Office for National Statistics, 2020b. *Coronavirus and the social impacts on Great Britain: 5 June 2020*. Available at: https://www.ons.gov.uk/peoplepopulationandcommunity/healthandsocialcare/healthandwellbeing/bulletins/coronavirusandthesocialimpactsongreatbritain/5june2020 (Accessed: 12 November 2020).

Orgilés, M., Morales, A., Delvecchio, E., Mazzeschi, C. and Espada, J.P. 2020. Immediate psychological effects of the COVID-19 quarantine in youth from Italy and Spain. PsyArXiv Preprints, available at: https://psyarxiv.com/qaz9w/ (Accessed: 26 November 2020).

Ornell, F., Schuch, J.B., Sordi, A.O. and Kessler, F.H.P., 2020. "Pandemic fear" and COVID-19: mental health burden and strategies. *Brazilian Journal of Psychiatry*, 42(3), pp. 232–235.

Pentaris, P., Willis, P., Ray, M., Deusdad, B., Lonbay, S., Niemi, M. and Donnelly, S., 2020. Older people in the context of COVID-19: a European perspective. *Journal of Gerontological Social Work*, 63(8), pp. 736–742. Doi: 10.1080/01634372.2020.1821143.

Płomecka, M.B., Gobbi, S., Neckels, R., Radziński, P., Skórko, B., Lazerri, S., ... Jawaid, A. 2020. Mental health impact of COVID-19: A global study of risk and resilience factors. *BMJ Yale*. Doi: https://10.3389/fpsyt.2020.581426.

Potloc, 2020. Potloc study: Canadian health workers share their insights from the front lines of the COVID-19 pandemic. Available at: https://potloc.com/blog/en/potloc-study-canadian-health-workers-insights-front-lines-covid-19-pandemic/ (Accessed: 17 November 2020).

Ramsetty, A. and Adams, C., 2020. Impact of the digital divide in the age of COVID-19. *Journal of the American Medical Informatics Association*, 27(7), pp. 1147–1148.

Rolland, B., Haesebaert, F., Zante, E., Benyamina, A., Haesebaert, J. and Franck, N., 2020. Global changes and factors of increase in caloric/salty food intake, screen use, and substance use during the early COVID-19 containment phase in the general population in France: survey study. *JMIR Public Health and Surveillance*, 6(3), p. e19630.

Rossi, R., Socci, V., Talevi, D., Mensi, S., Niolu, C., Pacitti, F., Di Marco, A., Rossi, A., Siracusano, A. and Di Lorenzo, G., 2020. COVID-19 pandemic and lockdown measures impact on mental health among the general population in Italy. *Frontiers in Psychiatry*, 11. Doi: doi.org/10.3389/fpsyt.2020.00790.

Sher, L., 2020. The impact of the Covid-19 pandemic on suicide rates. *QJM: An International Journal of Medicine*, 113(10), pp. 707–712.

Thakur, V. and Jain, A., 2020. COVID 2019-suicides: a global psychological pandemic. *Brain, Behavior, and Immunity*, 88, pp. 952–953.

Tengland, P.A., 2001. *Mental health: a philosophical analysis* (Vol. 9). Berlin & New York, NY: Springer Science & Business Media.

The Health Foundation. 2020. Emerging evidence on COVID-19's impact on mental health and health inequalities. Available at: https://www.health.org.uk/news-and-comment/blogs/emerging-evidence-on-covid-19s-impact-on-mental-health-and-health (Accessed: 17 January 2021).

The Hindu. 2020. With increased workload, women a stressed lot. Available at: https://www.thehindu.com/news/cities/chennai/with-increased-workload-women-a-stressed-lot/article31293591.ece (Accessed: 3 December 2020).

Thomas, R., 2020. Deaths of detained mental health patients double due to covid-19. Available at: https://www.hsj.co.uk/coronavirus/deaths-of-detained-mental-health-patients-double-due-to-covid-19/7027601.article (Accessed: 16 November 2020).

UNESCO. 2019. New report on global broadband access underscores urgent need to reach the half of the world still unconnected. Available at: https://en.unesco.org/news/new-report-global-broadband-access-underscores-urgent-need-reach-half-world-still-unconnected (Accessed: 3 December 2020).

UNFPA. 2020. New UNFPA projections predict calamitous impact on women's health as COVID-19 pandemic continues. Available at: https://www.unfpa.org/pcm/node/24174 (Accessed: 3 December 2020).

Usher, K., Bhullar, N., Durkin, J., Gyamfi, N. and Jackson, D., 2020. Family violence and COVID-19: Increased vulnerability and reduced options for support. *International Journal of Mental Health Nursing*, 29, pp. 549–552.

World Economic Forum. 2020. Coronavirus has exposed the digital divide like never before. Available at: https://www.weforum.org/agenda/2020/04/coronavirus-covid-19-pandemic-digital-divide-internet-data-broadband-mobbile/ (Accessed: 3 December 2020).

World Health Organization. n.d. *Health statistics and information systems: estimates for 2000–2012*. Available at: https://www.who.int/data/gho/data/themes/mortality-and-global-health-estimates (Accessed: 3 December 2020).

World Health Organization. 2001. The world health report 2001: Mental disorders affect one in four people. Available at: https://www.who.int/news/item/28-09-2001-the-world-health-report-2001-mental-disorders-affect-one-in-four-people (Accessed: 3 December 2020).

World Health Organization. 2016. Mental health and substance use. Available at: https://www.who.int/teams/mental-health-and-substance-use/mental-health-in-the-workplace (Accessed: 3 December 2020).

World Health Organization. 2020. *Suicide: key facts*. Available at: https://www.who.int/teams/mental-health-and-substance-use/mental-health-in-the-workplace (Accessed: 3 December 2020).

Yoshikawa, H., Wuermli, A.J., Britto, P.R., Dreyer, B., Leckman, J.F., Lye, S.J., Ponguta, L.A., Richter, L.M. and Stein, A. 2020. Effects of the global coronavirus disease-2019 pandemic on early childhood development: Short- and long-term risks and mitigating program and policy actions. *Journal of Pediatrics, 223*, pp. 188–193. Doi: 10.1016/j.jpeds.2020.05.020

11 Assisted dying and Covid-19

Theo Boer and Kevin Yuill

Key points

- The numbers of assisted deaths, shown by evidence from Canada and the Netherlands, look to be from 30 to 40% down during the three months from April to June 2020;
- Initially, assisted dying services closed down or were reduced to a minimum, suggesting that assisted dying is not an essential aspect of health care;
- This is despite the indications that the demand for assisted dying grew during the Covid-19 crisis;
- Loneliness, particularly through isolation, may have contributed to this higher demand for assisted dying;
- In several countries, Do Not Resuscitate orders were placed on mentally disabled people, underlining fears of those who oppose assisted dying that differential value is placed on entire categories of human lives.

Introduction

During Covid-19, what has happened in areas where some form of assisted dying – euthanasia or assisted suicide[1] – is legal? These practices are almost entirely facilitated by medical personnel, some of whom have also been engaged in a battle against Covid. This chapter examines various areas of the world where assisted dying is legal in order to understand how Covid has affected planned death. Though much of the data concerning assisted dying since Covid struck Europe, North America and Australia has yet to be made available, it is possible to see three emerging developments.

First, it is likely that numbers of assisted deaths in the first months of the Covid-pandemic will be down significantly compared to the same period a year back. Requests have risen amongst the 'worried well' in relation to Covid (though almost all practitioners agree that assisted dying is not appropriate for those suffering from Covid). However, as the lockdowns in the spring of 2020 progressed, others report that assisted-dying requests rose with the loneliness and isolation imposed by Covid (Munro, 2020). Second, the response of providers of assisted dying to the Covid-crisis has shone a harsh light on their claims that these procedures are the only effective means to alleviate unbearable suffering. Several physicians and nursing personnel abandoned their assistance in dying in order to concentrate on battling the virus and to avoid exposing themselves to unnecessary risk. Assisted dying is not as indispensable as some practitioners have argued. Third, the initial response of some medical authorities in the US and the UK, who placed do-not-resuscitate (DNR) notices on some patients and said they would not be allowed into hospitals if they showed symptoms of Covid, seemed to be to devalue the lives of some (Dyer, 2020; Boodman, 2020). This has underlined fears by disabled groups and elderly people that their lives are not regarded as equally worthy of protection and that, if assisted dying is made legal, they might be encouraged to take the option (Coleman, 2010, Finlay and George, 2011, Braddock, 2020).[2]

Legal developments

Though the devastation wrought by the pandemic – particularly in relation to the elderly – may have shown how every life is precious, it has not stopped the Dutch from announcing 'completed life' legislation giving healthy senior citizens access to an assisted death. Halted by a few months due to the pandemic, Spokesperson Pia Dijkstra of the liberal coalition party D66 announced a draft-bill giving any Dutch citizen 75 years and older a state-facilitated right to assistance in suicide (Bremmer, 2020). Many reactions to the law proposal were very emotional, especially given the ordeal of many elderly patients under the Covid-pandemic. Dutch journalist Hummie van der Tonnekreek sees continuity between what she considers the government's failure to protect elderly people in nursing homes from the virus, and the Completed Life Act: 'Under the watchful eye of the Minister of Health, the virus was allowed to take its course among the frail elderly.' She calls the proposed law 'yet another attack on the 70-plus generation' (Tonnekreek, 2020).

A related but separate story is the rising number of advance directives. Legal both in areas where assisted dying is legal and where it remains illegal, advance directives allow patients to direct, should they become incapacitated, that medical treatment in certain circumstances should either go ahead or not take place. With one notable exception – the Dutch Supreme Court ruled in May 2020 that an advance directive may form the basis for euthanasia in an incompetent patient – advance directives do not give license for assisted dying (no author, *Guardian*, 2020). The directive is simply an extension of the near-universal right to refuse medical treatment. Some feel that Covid-19 has made the advance directive much more imperative (Rowe, 2020).

The claim of campaigners for a change in the law in England and Wales that the Covid-crisis has exposed 'everything that is wrong with our relationship with dying' should lead to assisted-dying laws being re-examined as the country begins to recover. The chief executive of British pro-assisted dying organization, Sarah Wootton and staff member Lloyd Riley have authored a book that takes into account the Covid-crisis and calls for a change in the Suicide Act 1961 to allow assisted suicides. 'The coronavirus has thrust death and dying into the mainstream.' They note that '[w]e are now discussing our mortality more than ever'. 'There has never been a better time for an ambitious reform of dying in this country', they conclude (Wootton and Riley, 2020, p. 12, p. 11).

They may be wrong. In some cases, Covid seems to have diverted attention away from impending legislation to legalize assisted dying, albeit perhaps temporarily. Euthanasia is legal in Belgium, the Netherlands, Luxemburg, Colombia and Canada. With the exception of Colombia, assisted suicide is legal in all these countries, plus in a number of US states, starting in Oregon in 1997 and now including California, Colorado, Hawaii, Maine, New Jersey, Vermont and Washington, as well as the District of Columbia. A law permitting assisted suicide came into force in the Australian state of Victoria in June, 2020, and in Western Australia another such law is scheduled to go into effect in the near future. Most recently, a referendum allowing assisted suicide but not euthanasia has been successful in New Zealand.

Other bills were halted in their tracks by the Covid-crisis, belying the apparent urgent necessity of the legislation. Of all of the legislation tabled in the United States, only the Massachusetts bill remains active, but it, too, lies pending with all other 'non-emergency' bills for the state. None of the aid in dying bills the Arizona State Legislature considered in the 2020 legislative session advanced. The Connecticut state legislature did consider a death-with-dignity bill in 2020 but the legislature postponed all of its hearings, and the bill is unlikely to advance. In Florida, the first-ever aid in dying bill, SB 1800, the Death with Dignity Act, died in March 2020, indefinitely postponed and withdrawn from consideration. It is unlikely that similar legislative attempts in Georgia, Indiana, Iowa, Kentucky, Maryland, Minnesota, Maryland, New Hampshire, New York, Rhode Island, Utah and Wisconsin will progress any time soon. Montana remains in legal limbo as it has no statute prohibiting assisted suicide but no statute allowing it has successfully passed (Death With Dignity, 2020).

In Canada, the Quebec superior court ruled in September 2019 in the Truchon/ Gladu cases that the existing legal precondition for an assisted death – that the individual seeking it must face a 'reasonably foreseeable' natural death – is too restrictive and therefore unconstitutional. It ordered the legislation to be amended in line with their interpretation that the right to assisted dying is guaranteed by the Canadian constitution. The result, Bill C-7, was presented in February of 2020 and contains three major changes:

(1) a removal of the requirement for a reasonably foreseeable death, except for patients whose sole underlying condition is a mental illness; (2) assisted dying may even be available to patients who have lost the capacity to consent since deciding to do so through an agreement with a medical or nurse practitioner; and (3) a removal both of the 10-day 'reflection period' and of the requirement that a patient provide final consent (Bill C-7, Government of Canada, 2020). Thus, important safeguards meant to prevent abuse will be removed. However, due to the global pandemic's disruption of parliamentary proceedings, the federal government requested a delay in February 2020 to the requirement to legislate in the Truchon rulings. In June 2020, Justice Minister and Attorney General David Lametti filed a motion requesting another extension to December 18, 2020 (Harris, 2020).

Some may argue that these delays are not in any substantial way connected to shifting views on the morality of assisted dying. After all, Covid-19 has halted other legislative procedures as well, and the reasons may be practical rather than moral. However, as we will argue below, if assisted dying is as necessary and urgent as its advocates argue, why was it not granted a more urgent status in the legislation processes?

Practical developments

The same might be said about other implications in terms of practical applications of assisted dying. First, the pandemic has forced some procedures in Canada – where assisted dying is known as Medical Aid in Dying (MAID) – to be quicker. 'I have provided for MAID on the same day that I've met someone on certain occasions', said Dr. Stefanie Green, president of the Canadian Association of MAID Assessors and Providers. Though the mandatory period of reflection is normally 10 days, doctors may circumvent the law if two of them agree that the patient is at risk of losing their capacity, if the patient is expected to die sooner than ten days, or if the patient is 'about to die (immediately)'. The assisted dying procedure may thus be speeded up in order to prevent an impending death through Covid-19. However, Dr. Green indicates that 'often, in that kind of situation, the best care is probably good palliative comfort care' (McCue, 2020). In another interview, Dr Green related the story of one patient in Ontario, Canada, who had the procedure performed in a funeral home. 'After getting two "no's" in the first two calls, the patient's family found another funeral home that was certainly willing to do so,' said Dr Green. The patient was given a room and had their life ended with medical help on the premises. Since her life was terminated in a funeral home, the patient's funeral arrangements also took place there (Cullen, 2020).

Beyond the logistics involved in finding a place to deliver the procedure, physicians performing medically assisted deaths are facing the same problem faced by health professionals everywhere: shortages of the necessary equipment. Doctors are worried about shortages in the drugs used in medically assisted deaths. Some of those drugs are also used in patients placed on ventilators and in palliative sedation, which means the drugs are in high demand among health professionals caring for victims of the pandemic. Medical masks, gloves and glasses have often taken weeks to arrive (Expertisecentrum Euthanasie, 2020).

For assisted suicide where it is legal in the US (and where physicians do not, by law, have to be in attendance when patients ingest the deadly drugs) and to a certain extent in Canada, telemedicine has become important. Medically assisted deaths in America are increasingly taking place online, from the initial doctor's visit to the ingestion of life-ending medications. In 2019, according to the Oregon Health Authority, 57% of all assisted deaths in Oregon were attended by a physician, another health care provider, or a volunteer (Oregon Health Authority, 2019). While telemedicine is helping some people die on their own terms, it also makes the process harder on family members, who must now play a more active role in their loved one's final act.

In Canada, the usual process is an in-person assessment for the necessary second medical opinion and two independent witnesses physically present when a patient requests assisted dying. Whenever possible, patients are now being assessed remotely or online to prevent in-person contact. Provinces such as Manitoba, Saskatchewan, and British Columbia have changed the requirements by offering 'virtual assessments' by doctors as a way to reduce the risk of clinicians getting sick from Covid-19 (McCue, 2020). 'Often our work is very up close and personal. So how can we do this work in a way that's safe for everyone, but still compassionate?' said Dr. Green (Cullen, 2020). The regulations on medical opinions for assisted dying patients differ from province to province. *Dignity and Dying*, Canada, is asking medical regulating bodies to allow for more virtual assessments and some have assented. More provinces are now allowing the two independent witnesses who sign off on requests to do so virtually (Dignity in Dying, 2020).

A necessary act of compassion?

More significant than either the legislative delays or the practical changes forced by the coronavirus crisis may be its exposure of various truths about assisted dying. Most important of those is the fact that euthanasia and assisted suicide are not deemed to be necessary by all. Whereas palliative care adapted to the new and challenging situations in most areas, several euthanasia providers shut down, at least initially. In the Netherlands, the Euthanasia Expertise Centre (formerly known as End of Life Clinic), the only dedicated organization providing euthanasia and assisted suicide in the country, closed its doors for a couple of months. Its website indicated that existing procedures had been put on hold and new patients were no longer admitted. The center – which in 2019 alone ended the lives of 898 patients suffering from psychiatric problems, early-onset dementia, accumulated age-related complaints, other chronic illnesses, and terminal diseases – was willing to make an exception only for those expected to die soon and those who may have lost their capacity for decision-making. It reports that between March 17 and May 11, mobile teams consisting of a doctor and a nurse provided 91 assisted deaths, 35% less than in the same period last year (Expertisecentrum Euthanasie, 2020).[3]

Ontario, Canada, is one of the few jurisdictions where assisted dying has up-to-date statistics. These figures give us some idea of the impact of the crisis on numbers opting for assisted deaths (Health Canada, 2020).[4] Between January 1 and March 31 (a state of emergency ordering lockdown was declared in Ontario on March 17th) 669 people were euthanized; between April 1 and June 31, the number was 458, down by about a third (Office of the Chief Coroner/Ontario Forensic Pathology Service, 2020).

The Covid-crisis affected many forms of healthcare, including essential services such as cancer treatment and palliative care. Cancer treatment was scaled down due to the need to prioritize Covid-patients and to minimize the infection risks. Palliative care was also limited. At the peak of the first Covid-wave in the Netherlands, the use of palliative beds was down by about 12%.[5] Apart from the fact that the supply of palliative beds was constrained by the virus, patients, and their relatives also preferred palliative care at home where there were fewer limitations to visiting them.

In comparison, however, the consequences for assisted dying were far more radical. As indicated, the Euthanasia Expertise Centre suspended most of its services and explained its decision in early March on its website, noting that in 'the interest of public health, our patients, their loved ones and employees of the expertise center, it is no longer responsible to continue our current care provision.' It stated that 'euthanasia care cannot be identified as a top priority in healthcare'.[6] The Centre, while apologizing to prospective patients, stated: 'We would like to urge people who intend to register not to contact us at this stage and to wait for a message that we are open for new registrations' (Expertisecentrum Euthanasie, 2020). Although the Centre reopened in mid-May 2020, its capacity to receive new patients is still limited, especially psychiatric patients. Since the beginning of the Covid-crisis, half of its psychiatrists stopped providing euthanasia (Expertisecentrum Euthanasie, 2020).

Similarly, in Belgium, Jacqueline Herremans, a member of the federal commission reviewing euthanasia and president of the Belgian right to die society ADMD, has noted that there are few resources and fewer doctors available for euthanasia at the moment: 'The Corona-crisis puts euthanasia somewhat on hold.' Requests made before the confinement measures might be able to 'be honoured for patients in physical pain', she said, but they would take place without others being present (Herremans, 2020). In Canada, authorities also initially shut down services. For a process that requires two different medical assessments and witnesses, the risks involved are deemed too large. Two clinics in Ontario, where assisted dying has been legal since 2016, stopped providing this assistance because of the pandemic (one has since resumed for existing patients and those whose deaths are imminent). Health authorities there said that assisted dying is being cut back along with other 'elective services' (Grant, 2020).

All these decisions seem to undermine the most frequent justifications for assisted dying, namely the presence of intolerable pain and of unbearable physical or mental suffering.[7] Those carrying out assisted dying in the Netherlands, and those campaigning to change the law in other countries, have long insisted that assisted dying is necessary to alleviate unbearable suffering. However, the fact that some of the biggest providers of assisted dying have dramatically reduced this assistance, begs the question whether they are convinced their services are necessary; otherwise, why not brave the risk and despatch suffering patients? As recent as 2019, the director of the Euthanasia Expertise Centre stated that: 'If the situation is unbearable and there is no prospect of improvement, and euthanasia is an option, it would be almost unethical [of a doctor] not to help that person' (de Bellaigue, 2019). Yet the Centre stated a year later that euthanasia is not a top priority during the Covid-crisis.

Whereas in the Netherlands, assisted dying continues to be a 'non-normal medical intervention,' implying that a physician has no duty to provide it; it is a constitutional right in Canada. In many countries, proponents present euthanasia as the most or the only humane option for many patients. In Britain, in 2019, Nick Boles MP gave a gruesome description of suffering at the end of life, saying that the lack of provision of assisted dying forces people to 'undergo unbearable physical and psychological trauma'. Boles described this as 'a moral outrage.' Furthermore, under the title, 'The inescapable truth,' the campaign for *Dignity in Dying* claims that without assisted dying, 'seventeen people a day will suffer as they die' (Inescapable Truth, Dignity in Dying, 2019).

How then should we interpret the fact that in several countries assisted dying services were suspended? Hospice services have continued their vital service to the dying despite all of the risks involved: although the Euthanasia Expert Centre suspended its services, there are no reports of hospice closures in the Netherlands. Hospices in Ontario, where MAID services have shut, continue, rapidly organizing themselves to accommodate palliative care for terminally ill Covid-19 patients. In the UK, hospices are reported to be extraordinarily busy; in Scotland, at least one has joined forces to provide care for Covid-19 cases requiring palliative care. Most are full and senior staff are 'managing lots of clinical queries and huge fear and anxiety,' one hospice doctor reported (Taylor, 2020). They are included in Covid-19 planning groups, as a document issued by the British National Health Service (NHS) indicates. Their staff have continued working despite the crisis (Radbruch et al, 2020, Powell and Silveira, 2020, Constantini et al., 2020, Wakam et al., 2020).

What the Covid-19 crisis perhaps suggests is that the need for an assisted death is abstract rather than practical. In the Netherlands in the 1980s, assisted dying started out as the ultimate solution to impending horrible deaths. In present times, assisted dying has become something different in three respects. First, most countries that have legalized assisted dying have a high level of care for the dying, which means that intolerable pain, dyspnoea, etc., can in most cases be relieved and progress continues to be made. The reality is that most people die peaceful deaths. Where this is not the case, there seems to be a consensus that palliative care must work toward further improvements and will succeed in doing so. Thus, insofar as there is fear, this fear is often not about pain but about loneliness, meaninglessness and loss of autonomy. Many fear loss of control and find the prospect of others caring for them terrifying. Second, when it is not about fear, assisted dying is often about the preference for a controlled and manageable end. On the website of the Expertise Centre, a family member reports: 'The fact that you can consciously say goodbye makes a death by euthanasia very special' (Levenseindekliniek, 2019). Euthanasia may be 'very special,' but that does not make it an indispensable form of health care. Third, whereas initially euthanasia was a last resort to prevent a terrible death, it has increasingly become a means to prevent a terrible life. We see this in the Netherlands, where each year more than 500 people receive euthanasia who could have lived for years (Boer, 2017). It seems logical to assume that we will see a similar development in Canada, where the September 11, 2019 Quebec Superior Court ruling opens up the way for people without a foreseeable natural death to receive euthanasia.

Although some may have questions about the motives of some who provide assisted dying – there may, for example, be financial incentives – we are convinced that they are caring, dedicated people who feel that they are doing good.[8] It is possible that they feared a high profile role during the Covid-crisis in case they became seen as a 'solution'. These staff are not cowards – many are being deployed to fight the virus. But their stock in trade – the existential angst about death that seems to make euthanasia a necessary human right – seems to have at least temporarily dissipated in this time of crisis. Death, in this time of war against a disease, no longer appears a comforting friend or a useful medical treatment.

Patients who want help to die: loneliness, fear and fear of being a burden

Covid-19 brings the reality of death, the necessity of caring for others and being cared for by others, into our living rooms, making the preciousness of all lives and the tragedy of all deaths real. We see the humanity of the elderly and frail; no longer are they burdens to be despatched from this world, but victims of horrifying disease that all are invested in fighting.

But the disease also increases fear and loneliness amongst some of those most vulnerable to the disease. One of the other issues emerging as the coronavirus has forced lockdowns in various countries is that many who request an assisted death do so because they fear the isolation and loneliness forced upon them. Recent research has shown that in a considerable percentage of euthanasia cases in the Netherlands loneliness features as one of the aspects of their unbearable suffering, especially among those whose natural deaths are not reasonably foreseeable.[9] Covid-19 has only added to this predicament. In Canada, medical doctor and director of *Dying with Dignity*, Canada, Dr Chantal Perrot, noted of her patients: 'Some of them actually have said, "You know, I was planning to do this anyway and I'm cooped up. I can't go anywhere. Nobody can come and see me. So what's the point of hanging around?"' She said, 'It's sad when anybody chooses to end their life, but when they feel they have to do it under circumstances that are so isolating and challenging, it just makes it that much more sad' (Cullen, 2020).

Social workers at *Death with Dignity*, a US national advocacy organization based in Portland, Oregon, have also been answering a steady increase in calls about the coronavirus. The Executive Director of the organization, Peg Sandeen, said about 80% come from people who want medications 'just in case' the pneumonia they have proven to be the coronavirus, or so they can 'be ready' (Dembofsky, 2020). Similarly, *Dying with Dignity,* Canada has seen an uptick in calls from Canadians wanting to know if an assisted death will be available if they end up hospitalized with Covid-19. 'We're not advocating that people go out and complete a MAID process in preparation. There is no ability for an advance request at this point in time,' said its CEO Helen Long. Luc Op de Beeke, the director of the De Wending rest home in Turnhout, Belgium reports an unprecedented rise in requests for information about euthanasia, which he puts down to loneliness and isolation within his institution since the start of confinement. He explains: 'the thirst for life of these residents disappeared after two months spent without the slightest physical visit' (Van Nooten, 2020). We already know that loneliness and isolation are significant reasons why Canadians opt for an assisted death. 13.7% list it as the nature of their suffering, above 'loss of control /autonomy /independence' (Health Canada, 2020).

Others report feeling that they are burdens at a time when medical time and energy is in such short supply, particularly in the earlier phase of the lockdown when it appeared that medical services would become swamped by Covid. One question by 'Margaret' to a programme conducted by assisted dying experts asked: 'Is there a practical way that elders like myself could refuse hospitalization on the grounds that hospital beds should go to the young, health workers, first responders, and the like?' (Death with Dignity, 2020). Sandeen noted that 20% of their calls were from people who want to know what their advance directive needs to say so that if they become ill from the virus, any ventilator that would have gone to them to will instead go to someone else. 'They feel like they're older or they have a terminal illness, or for whatever reason that they feel like the ventilator should go to health care workers or to younger folks' (Death with Dignity, 2020).

Many aspects of medicine are being done in advance, whether by advance directives or by accessing an assisted death ahead of schedule to prevent Covid. The story of mental health advocate and Order of Canada recipient Pat Capponi, who recently ended her life with a medically assisted death, is perhaps typical. Her close friend Cynthia Good said Capponi moved up the date of her passing because she feared she would lose access or fall ill with Covid. 'She did not want to die that way, if she should contract it,' she said (Cullen, 2020, City News, 2020).

A rise in telemedicine

We now return to telemedicine because it, too, may impact assisted dying practice. Beginning with China, telemedicine, sometimes referred to as virtual medicine, has taken off, which inevitably has an impact on the way assisted dying happens. Ray Dorsey, director of the Center for Health and Technology at the University of Rochester Medical Center (Rochester, NY, USA) estimated that the majority of patient consultations in the United States in Covid-times are happening virtually. Dorsey suggests there has been a ten-fold increase in April 2020 after the Covid restrictions reached the United States. Sandy Buchman, president of the Canadian Medical Association, noted: 'As we confront [Covid-19], we're racing to implement virtual health-care technologies as quickly as we can. The scale and pace of change is unprecedented for Canadian health care' (Webster, 2020). It's as big a transformation as any ever before in the history of US health care. But the real question is whether these measures will stay in place after the pandemic subsides.

Because of the coronavirus, volunteers are accompanying patients and families using webcams. Physicians now complete their evaluations through telemedicine, based on recommendations released by the American Clinicians Academy on Medical Aid in Dying in March 2020. Some aid-in-dying physicians have drawn on telemedicine to reach remote patients for years. Dr Carol Parrott, a doctor who lives on an island in Washington, sees 90% of her patients online, visually examining a patient's symptoms, mobility, affect and breathing (Hanig, 2020).

The problem with virtual medicine and forward planning, as some clinicians have noted, is that personal contact is important. Covid guidance on advance care planning has largely focused on the plan itself. Success was seen as a plan recording an individual's treatment preferences. But evidence suggests that the experience of patients and their families benefit from real (physical) conversations with their health providers. Families are helped with bereavement and the reality of death and patients can be comforted by personal contact with doctors. Sarah Hopkins et al stress the importance of the process – which involves personal contact – over and above the product of such planning: 'These benefits come largely from the conversations that constitute the planning process, particularly when these occur over time and include the patient's family and loved ones' (Hopkins et al., 2020).

A family member who objects to assisted dying may more easily undercut the process when a volunteer isn't there in person to make sure a patient's final wishes are carried out. Anita Hannig, an Associate Professor of Anthropology at Brandeis University who studies assisted dying in the United States, finds that dying via telemedicine can be hard even on family members who stand behind their loved one's decision. Without a volunteer or physician present, families must assume a more active role in the dying process. That includes mixing the life-ending medications themselves, making families feel like they were facilitating – and not just morally supporting – a loved one's death. In the pre-Covid period, they were glad to outsource this delicate task. Now, they have little choice (Hanig, 2020).

A differential value on human lives

Much as the crisis has brought people together in grief and, at least initially, focused attention on its inordinate effect the high-risk groups – the elderly and those with underlying health problems – the spectre of rationing of medicine has returned. A key fear about legalized assisted dying expressed by disabled groups is that separating groups eligible for assisted dying, such as those with terminal illnesses, will inevitably target those perceived to have fewer Quality of Life Years (QALYS), which includes many disabled people. Their worries, as a recent article discussing the economic benefits of assisted dying shows, are not unfounded.[10] Turning Point, a social enterprise providing health and social care services across over 300 locations in the UK, noted that at least 22 DNR orders in April inappropriately placed on those with learning disabilities but no physical disabilities that would make them more susceptible to dying from Covid. Over the same period, Learning Disability England related that 20% of its member organizations reporting doctors placing DNR orders on the records of individuals they represent. In the US, several states including Tennessee, Washington, Kansas Pennsylvania and New York have issued protocols deprioritizing the treatment of disabled people in the event of scarce medical resources. Alabama was compelled in April by the Office for Civil Rights to abandon its crisis management policy of 'denying ventilator services to individuals based on the presence of intellectual disabilities, including 'profound mental retardation' and 'moderate to severe dementia' (Alexiou, 2020).

The medical emergency, because of its immediate (though, fortunately, in most cases unfounded) fears about a limited supply of medical care and equipment, has raised the awful question of who lives and who dies. Assisted dying, whether administered by doctor or patient, came about historically in order to make society more efficient; demand for euthanasia only included patient choice as an afterthought and there was no demand for assisted suicide until the 1930s and no focus on autonomy until the 1970s (Yuill, forthcoming). The Covid-crisis has exposed, too, elements of a ruthless medical and social utilitarianism that still values individuals differently (Boer, 2020).

As Peter Glick and Amy Cuddy said: 'Despite the patina of affection for the elderly and people with disabilities, the pandemic has revealed how we inherently devalue them.' Gunnison County in Colorado reportedly banned restaurants and bars from serving people over 60 in order not to 'spread the virus' (TRT World, 2020). Lieutenant Governor Dan Patrick of Texas went so far as suggesting that older people should voluntarily court a premature death to help save the economy (cited in Beckett, 2020). Professor Margaret MacMillan claimed that over seventies 'were not productive members of society, were not the people we need to get the economic engines going again, and we tend to be more vulnerable, so we should stay out of the way and let others get on with it.' World Health Organization (WHO) Director-General Tedros Adhanom Ghebreyesus harshly criticized this attitude: 'If anything is going to hurt the world, it is moral decay. And not taking the death of the elderly or the senior citizens as a serious issue is moral decay,' he recently observed (cited in Carbonaro, 2020).

The Temple Court Scandal in Kettering in the UK brought to light the sacrifice of elderly patients for the National Health Service. Fifteen elderly residents died, and the staff fell ill following a sudden influx of patients from NHS hospitals. None of the incoming hospital patients had been tested for the coronavirus. Before the admissions, the Northamptonshire home had been virus-free. Staff claim it became a 'dumping ground' for elderly Covid-19 patients.[11] Sending patients who test positive for Covid from hospitals into care homes with the most frail, vulnerable and at-risk elderly residents looks set to continue (Boyd, 2020).

However, positive insights may also arise from the Covid-crisis. The question is how the fact that the crisis has brought an unwanted death at the doorstep of many households relates to the narrative of an orchestrated and manageable death that is central in so many pleas for an assisted death. The Covid-crisis may remind us of the messiness of human existence, of the fact that lives cannot be lived solely according to the will of those who live them, and that death cannot be neatly set into one's diary like a work event. When the Dutch supreme court acquitted a doctor, who had euthanized an incompetent dementia patient, author and philosopher Maxim Februari wrote a critical comment in the liberal newspaper *NRC Handelsblad*. 'The decision of the Supreme Court to allow active euthanasia in deeply demented elderly had struck me as highly unfortunate and undesirable,' Februari wrote. 'But now I suddenly understand why I think it is an unwise decision: it expresses a pre-corona conception of life. An illusion of control over human behaviour' (Februari, 2020).

Conclusions

This chapter looked at changes in issues connected with assisted dying. Where it is legal (and where statistics exist for this period), the numbers of assisted deaths look to be down by 30 to 40% from April to June 2020 compared with the year 2019. There is no evidence that demand has fallen and, if anything, anecdotal evidence suggests that it has risen. Like other medical services, assisted dying, where it did happen, relied upon telemedicine and other methods employed by other medical services. More importantly, the Covid crisis has thrown into question many issues about whether the value of human lives can be compared or measured. Covid shines a spotlight on how we treat the elderly and vulnerable.

However, most significantly, the Covid-crisis has exposed assisted dying as less necessary than proponents present it, given that providers initially halted treatment altogether and resumed only limited services. Whereas other medical services continued throughout the difficulties thrown up by the crisis, the fact that assisted dying services did not suggest that those who operate the clinics may not believe as strongly in their own mission as their rhetoric suggests. Such a reorientation towards assisted dying may be one of the few beneficial effects of the ongoing crisis.

Notes

1 We use the term 'assisted suicide' because it is useful to delineate the practice where a doctor prescribes a deadly drug from the practice of the doctor administering the drug. Other terms such as medical assistance in dying (MAID, the term favoured in Canada), aid-in-dying (California), death with dignity (Oregon, Washington, Maine).
2 John Braddock argues that New Zealand's decision to legalize euthanasia 'is being advanced precisely as ruling elites are using the COVID-19 crisis to advance the conception that the elderly and vulnerable should be sacrificed' (Braddock, 2020).
3 There are anecdotic reports that even assisted dying provided by regular medical personnel happened less often, but numbers are not expected before June, 2021 (Expertisecentrum Euthanasie, 2020).
4 Although in Canada both assisted suicide and euthanasia are legal, fewer than seven deaths of the 13,946 MAID-deaths since 2016 were self-administered or assisted suicides (Health Canada, 2020).
5 Whereas the average occupancy in 2019 of the available palliative beds of 1,241 was 1,096, that number was down to about 941 during the first wave (Eijrond, 2020).
6 The wording is from March, 2020. Later, the Centre deleted these words: in a later version the reference to euthanasia not being a top priority was missing.
7 Physical pain, in fact, plays little role in requests for assisted dying. It does not feature in the top five reasons for assisted dying in Oregon (see Oregon Death With Dignity Act, 2019), or Belgium, where 12.8% reported only physical suffering, 4.8% reported only psychological suffering and the remainder reported suffering both simultaneously (Commission fédérale de Contrôle et d'Évaluation de l'Euthanasie. 2020, p. 4, Health Canada, 2020, Chart 6.1). Unbearable suffering features in most of the legislation allowing assisted dying. The Dutch legislation requires patients to be 'suffering unbearably with no prospect of improvement' (Government of the Netherlands, n.d.), the Belgian legislation uses the phrase 'unbearable physical or mental suffering' (The Belgian Act on Euthanasia, 2002). The Canadian legislation

uses the same phrase (Government of Canada, n.d.). The Oregon legislation does not mention unbearable suffering but requires that the patient must be suffering from a terminal illness (Oregon Death With Dignity Act, 2019).
8 A physician working for the Euthanasia Expert Centre receives more than 2,000 Euros for every case of assisted dying. The Centre itself receives an additional 1,200 Euros.
9 Research by Theo Boer on the basis of 4,000 euthanasia reports. Publication of this research was forbidden by the authorities on the basis that this data was confidential.
10 Euthanasia, runs the argument, prevents additional negative QALYs in the person requesting euthanasia and increases positive QALYs in one or more individuals in the population at large through the reallocation of the medical resources (Shaw and Morton, 2020, Putick, 2020).
11 John Siddle and Alan Selby, 'Coronavirus: Care home where 15 died "pressured into taking untested sick people",' *Daily Mirror*, May 16 2020, https://www.mirror.co.uk/news/uk-news/coronavirus-care-home-15-died-22039558.

References

Alexiou, G., 2020. Doctors issuing unlawful "Do Not Resuscitate" orders for disabled Covid patients "outrageous". *Forbes*, June 23. https://www.forbes.com/sites/gusalexiou/2020/06/23/unlawful-do-not-resuscitate-orders-for-disabled-Covid-patients-outrageous/#6e892a6f6cf1

Beckett, L., 2020. Older people would rather die than let Covid-19 harm US economy – Texas official. *The Guardian*, March 24. https://www.theguardian.com/world/2020/mar/24/older-people-would-rather-die-than-let-covid-19-lockdown-harm-us-economy-texas-official-dan-patrick

Boer, T., 2017. De derde evaluatie van de Wet Toetsing Levensbeëindiging en Hulp bij Zelfdoding: over de relatie van empirie, normativiteit en politiek. *Tijdschrift voor Gezondheidszorg en Ethiek TGE*, 27(4), pp. 98–104.

Boer, T., 2020. Covid-19 and the Dutch context: Some ethical comments. *Canadian Journal of Netherlandic Studies CJNS*, 21(2), pp. 1–16.

Boodman, E., 2020. A cancer patient reconsiders her end-of-life wishes, as Covid-19 brings mortality into sharper focus. https://www.statnews.com/2020/05/05/cancer-patient-reconsiders-end-of-life-wishes-as-covid-19-brings-mortality-into-focus/

Boyd, C., 2020. Second Covid-19 care home crisis fears as bosses are told they will have to accept infected hospital patients once again and place them in secure quarantine facilities. *Daily Mail*, October 14, https://www.dailymail.co.uk/news/article-8834839/Elderly-Covid-19-hospital-patients-sent-care-homes.html

Braddock, J., 2020. New Zealand to legalize euthanasia following referendum. *World Socialist Web Site* https://www.wsws.org/en/articles/2020/11/04/newz-n04.html

Bremmer, D., 2020. Pia Dijkstra (D66) over haar wet voltooid leven: "Dit is voor een selecte groep bedoeld". *Het Parool*, July 17, https://www.parool.nl/nederland/pia-dijkstra-d66-over-haar-wet-voltooid-leven-dit-is-voor-een-selecte-groep-bedoeld~b7f8accb/

Carbonaro, G., 2020. "Every life matters": WHO chief warns against COVID-19 age discrimination. *CGTN*, March 11, https://newseu.cgtn.com/news/2020-03-11/-Every-life-matters-WHO-warns-against-COVID-19-age-discrimination-OKDSHuH0gU/index.html

City News, 2020. Fears ODSP recipients may be turning to assisted dying. https://toronto.citynews.ca/video/2020/09/02/fears-odsp-recipients-may-be-turning-to-assisted-dying/

Coleman, D., 2010. Assisted suicide laws create discriminatory double standard for who gets suicide prevention and who gets suicide assistance: not dead yet responds to autonomy, Inc. *Disability and Health Journal*, 3, pp. 39–50.

Commission fédérale de Contrôle et d'Évaluation de l'Euthanasie. 2020. *Euthanasie: Chiffres d'Année 2019*. Brussels: Commission fédérale de Contrôle et d'Évaluation de l'Euthanasie.

Costantini, M., Sleeman, K.E., Peruselli, C. and Higginson, I.J. 2020. Response and role of palliative care during the COVID-19 pandemic: a national telephone survey of hospices in Italy. *Palliative Medicine*, 34(7), pp. 889–895.

Cullen, C., 2020. The pandemic is making it harder to deliver medically assisted death, doctors say. *CBC News*, April 29, https://www.cbc.ca/news/politics/pandemic-Covid-coronavirus-medically-assisted-death-maid-1.5548058

de Bellaigue, C., 2019. Death on demand: has Euthanasia gone too far? *The Guardian*, January 18, https://www.theguardian.com/news/2019/jan/18/death-on-demand-has-euthanasia-gone-too-far-netherlands-assisted-dying?

Death with Dignity, 2020. https://www.deathwithdignity.org/learn/death-with-dignity-acts/

Dembofsky, A., 2020. Isolated COVID-19 deaths have people asking about right-to-die medications. *KQED*, https://www.kqed.org/news/11814635/isolated-covid-19-deaths-have-people-asking-about-right-to-die-medications

Dignity in Dying, Canada. 2020. *Covid 19 updates*. https://www.dyingwithdignity.ca/covid19_updates

Dyer, C., 2020. Covid-19: campaigner calls for national guidance to stop DNR orders being made without discussion with patients and families. *BMJ*, 369, p. m1856. https://www.bmj.com/content/369/bmj.m1856

Eijrond, E., (tweet) (October 19, 2020) https://twitter.com/eijronderik/status/1318173847124934658/photo/1

Expertisecentrum Euthanasie, 2020. "Corona raakte het expertisecentrum in het hart". Reconstructie van een roerige periode. https://expertisecentrumeuthanasie.nl/Interviews/corona-raakte-het-expertisecentrum-in-het-hart/

Februari, M., 2020. Pas op voor de illusie van een papieren veiligheid. *NRC Handelsblad*, May 5, https://www.nrc.nl/nieuws/2020/05/05/pas-op-voor-de-illusie-van-een-papieren-veiligheid-a3998696

Finlay, I.G. and George, R. 2011. Legal physician-assisted suicide in Oregon and The Netherlands: evidence concerning the impact on patients in vulnerable groups—another perspective on Oregon's data, *Journal of Medical Ethics*, 37(3), pp. 171–174.

Government of Canada, n.d. Medical aid in dying. https://www.canada.ca/en/health-canada/services/medical-assistance-dying.html

Government of Canada, Text of Bill C-7. 2020. https://www.parl.ca/DocumentViewer/en/43-1/bill/C-7/first-reading

Government of the Netherlands, n.d., Euthanasia, assisted suicide and non-resuscitation on request. https://www.government.nl/topics/euthanasia/euthanasia-assisted-suicide-and-non-resuscitation-on-request

Grant, K., 2020. Medical assistance in dying services being cancelled in Ottawa, Hamilton areas. *Globe and Mail*, March 27. https://www.theglobeandmail.com/canada/article-medical-assistance-in-dying-services-being-cancelled-in-ottawa/

Hanig, A., 2020. Dying virtually: pandemic drives medically assisted deaths online. *The Conversation*, June 2, https://theconversation.com/dying-virtually-pandemic-drives-medically-assisted-deaths-online-139093

Harris, K., 2020. Federal government asks for another 5 months to revamp assisted dying law. *CBC*, June 11, https://www.cbc.ca/news/politics/maid-assisted-dying-lametti-1.5607681

Health Canada 2020. *First annual report on medical assistance in dying in Canada*. Ottawa: Health Canada, https://www.canada.ca/en/health-canada/services/medical-assistance-dying-annual-report-2019.html#highlights

Herremans, J., 2020. La crise du Coronavirus met quelque peu entre parenthèse l'euthanasie. *Le Journal du Médecin*, May 13, https://www.lejournaldumedecin.com/actualite/droits-du-patient-et-euthanasie-dans-la-tourmente-du-coronavirus/article-opinion-48181.html

Hopkins, S., Roberta Lovick, A., Polak, L., Bowers, B., Morgan, T., Kelly, M.P. and Barclay, S. 2020. Reassessing advance care planning in the light of Covid-19, *BMJ*, 369, p. m1927. https://www.bmj.com/content/bmj/369/bmj.m1927.full.pdf

Levenseindekliniek (End of Life Clinic), 2019. http://slk-jaarverslag-beleidsplan.nl/2018-2019

McCue, D., 2020. "I choose to be in control": some seniors weighing medically assisted death because of COVID-19. *CBC*, April 19, https://www.cbc.ca/radio/checkup/Covid-seniors-medically-assisted-dying-1.5537299

Munro, R., 2020. Locked in long term care "prison:" woman asks for assisted suicide rather than continue in COVID-19 isolation. *Kelowna Infonews*, https://infotel.ca/newsitem/locked-in-long-term-care-prison-woman-asks-for-assisted-suicide-rather-than-continue-in-Covid-19-isolation/it76041

No author, TRT World 2020. *Fighting coronavirus: Western democracies treat older people as expendable*, https://www.trtworld.com/magazine/fighting-coronavirus-western-democracies-treat-older-people-as-expendable-34707

Office of the Chief Coroner/Ontario Forensic Pathology Service, 2020. Service MAiD Data. https://drive.google.com/file/d/1_UjPvdcetGWyG9IaDZtG2gJvvI3jUeu4/view

Oregon Health Authority 2019 *Death with Dignity Act 2019 data summary*. https://www.oregon.gov/oha/PH/PROVIDERPARTNERRESOURCES/EVALUATIONRESEARCH/DEATHWITHDIGNITYACT/Documents/year22.pdf

Powell, V.D. and Silveira, M.J. 2020. What should Palliative care's response be to the COVID-19 pandemic?, *Journal of Pain and Symptom Management*, 60(1), pp. e1–e3.

Putick, H., 2020. Assisted dying will save NHS cash and provide organs, argue Scottish academics. *The Times*, 13 March, https://www.thetimes.co.uk/article/assisted-dying-will-save-nhs-cash-and-provide-organs-argue-scottish-academics-h387gdn2q

Radbruch, L., Knaul, F.M., de Lima, L., de Joncheere, C. and Bhadelia, A. 2020. Comment: the key role of palliative care in response to the COVID-19 tsunami of suffering. *The Lancet*, May 09. https://www.thelancet.com/journals/lancet/article/PIIS0140-6736(20)30964-8/fulltext

Rowe, J., 2020. The pandemic should change the way we talk about dying. *The Atlantic*, https://www.theatlantic.com/ideas/archive/2020/07/pandemic-should-change-way-we-talk-about-dying/613618/

Shaw, D. and Morton, A. 2020. Counting the costs of assisted dying. *Clinical Ethics*, 15(10), pp. 65–70.

Siddle, J. and Selby, A, 2020. Coronavirus: care home where 15 died "pressured into taking untested sick people". *Daily Mirror*, May 16, https://www.mirror.co.uk/news/uk-news/coronavirus-care-home-15-died-22039558

Taylor, Dr Ros MBE, 2020 March 28. Tweet available at https://twitter.com/hospicedoctor/status/1243888684014895112

The Belgian act on Euthanasia of May, 28th 2002. *European Journal of Health Law*, 10, pp. 329–335. https://apmonline.org/wp-content/uploads/2019/01/belgium-act-on-euthanasia.pdf

The Guardian. 2020. Dutch court approves euthanasia in cases of advanced dementia. April 21, https://www.theguardian.com/world/2020/apr/21/dutch-court-approves-euthanasia-in-cases-of-advanced-dementia

Tonnekreek, H. van der., 2020. 70-plus? Jammer dan, pech gehad. *De Telegraaf*, July 21. https://www.telegraaf.nl/watuzegt/472120398/70plus-jammer-dan-pech-gehad, (accessed February 2021).

Van Nooten, J., 2020. Stijgende vraag naar euthanasie in rusthuis: "Bewoners verliezen levenslust door gebrek aan bezoek". *HLN*, May 25, https://www.hln.be/in-de-buurt/turnhout/stijgende-vraag-naar-euthanasie-in-rusthuis-bewoners-verliezen-levenslust-door-gebrek-aan-bezoek~a892425e/

Wakam, G.K., Montgomery, J.R., Biesterveld, B.E. and Brown, C.S. 2020. Not dying alone — Modern compassionate care in the Covid-19 pandemic. *NEJM*, https://www.nejm.org/doi/pdf/10.1056/NEJMp2007781?articleTools=true

Webster, P., 2020. Virtual health care in the era of Covid-19. *The Lancet*, 295(10231), pp. 1180–1181. https://www.thelancet.com/journals/lancet/article/PIIS0140-6736(20)30818-7/fulltext

Wooton S. and Riley, L., 2020. *Last rights: The case for assisted dying*. London: Biteback Publishing.

Yuill, K., (in press). A man should be permitted to go out of this world whenever he thinks fit.' Suicide, euthanasia, and autonomy in the American press in the 1890s (forthcoming).

Part III
Impact of COVID-19 in context

12 Losing touch? Older people and COVID-19

Renske Claasje Visser

Key points

- COVID-19 has caused many governments to impose age-based restrictions without acknowledging the range of lived experience people have in similar age groups.
- Chronological age is not an adequate marker for 'oldness'.
- Psychical touch has been at the centre of many restriction measures which has caused many (older) people to experience 'touch hunger'.
- There are positives to COVID-19 and for some older people, the pandemic has offered greater opportunities to keep in touch with family and friends.

Introduction

There is an overwhelming amount of research concerned with older people and COVID-19. Much of the research on COVID-19 and older people are talking *about* older people and not engaging in conversation *with* older people. Yet, if age is as crucial in this pandemic as much research contests, then understanding how the pandemic is experienced by people assumed to be affected the most is of essence. This pandemic has laid bare the ageism that is prevalent in many societies around the globe. Analysis of newspapers, media websites and current affair magazines in Australia, the United Kingdom and the United States showed that while the three countries all had different policies with regards to nursing home visits, self-isolation and herd-immunity, the ageism depicted in the media took similar forms (Lichtenstein, 2020).

It is important to note that much research on older people and COVID-19 repeats very problematic terminology and reinforces the negative stereotypes attached to later life. Throughout this chapter, I refer to *older* people as opposed to *old* people. This is done intentionally to show the relationality of old age. Terms like 'the old' and 'the elderly' are problematic as they cannot adequately capture the range of experiences of older people within the same age 'group' (Hockey and James, 2003; Degnen, 2007). Additionally, terms like 'the elderly' and 'the old' imply a passivity and frailty that often does not reflect the lived reality of older people. People are only 'old' in relation to others, and while there are many subcategories in younger life there is an absence of categories on older age that adequately captures the range of lived experiences in later life (Hockey and James, 1993). Thus, I systematically speak of older and younger people, as opposed to old and young. While this is not perfect it implies that older people do not have a singular lived experience and that younger and older go hand in hand.

While it has been demonstrated that chronological age is not an adequate marker for 'oldness' as it cannot capture the range of lived experiences people within the same age group have (Hockey and James, 2003; Degnen, 2007; Bytheway, 2005), chronological age appears to underpin many governmental decisions on how to tackle the current pandemic. Fletcher (2020) speaks of a 'chronological quarantine' that occurred when the British government announced in March 2020 that each individual aged 70 and over should self-isolate completely for a long period of time, regardless of physical health. But this age-based response to COVID-19 is not unique to the UK.

In Finland, where the author is residing at the time of writing, the Government recommended at the end of October that indoor sports and cultural activities for people aged 18 and over would stop for the foreseeable future.[1] While this is not particularly related to older age, the Finnish Government makes a clear distinction in their policies for children and those for adults. The aim is to keep life as normal as possible for children, to hopefully avoid any negative long-term effects of COVID-19 restrictions in this group. For a while, the Finnish Government recommended older people (aged 70 and over) to refrain from physical touch, but they recently retracted this:

> The recommendation for older people to avoid physical contact is no longer in force. However, it is wise to take a cautious approach to close contacts, using individual discretion and taking into account the risk factors (Finnish Government, 2020, p. webpage).

In Denmark, the government considered all people aged 65 and over 'at risk' and advised this 'group' to self-isolate and 'cocoon' as much as possible (Clotworthy and Westendorp, 2020). Clothworthy and Westendorp (2020) conducted a telephone interview study with 32 Danish older adults between 65 and 83. They note the confusion these age-based policies caused amongst Danish older adults. As one of their participants aptly states: 'The only information you get about being in the risk group is that you're in the risk group' (Clotworthy and Westendorp, 2020, p. 171). The perceived risk of

COVID-19 to older adults in a specific chronological age group as suggested by the government did not match the feelings of older people themselves. Many older people in this study just considered COVID-19 a potential other way that they could die (Clotworthy and Westendorp, 2020). As a consequence, Clothworthy and Westendorp argue that 'regardless of their increased susceptibility to biological infection, older adults have a right to self-determination – even during a pandemic. As such, the individuals who are "at risk" should be able to claim that designation for themselves' (2020, p. 173).

Leibing notes that in Quebec, Canada a frequently repeated statement was that 'COVID-19 *only* affects older people' (2020, p. 221, emphasis in original) and that policies were based on protecting this 'group' of people who are perceived as vulnerable. She posits that:

> the all-encompassing image of 'frail older people' overshadows nuance and becomes an ideology that turns researchers and care staff into sort of Robin Hoods. Hood, who himself is a liminal figure, nevertheless fights in a clearly divided world of good and bad, in which victim and oppressor – poor and rich people – are unquestioned categories (Leibing, 2020, p. 222).

She suggests the label of 'older-person-in-need-of help' dehumanises older people and strips them of their agency. Importantly, Leibing notes, that older people living in the community were dying at a lower rate than those under 65 yet the emphasis was still on protecting frail older people (Leibing, 2020). A theme that comes to the fore in the responses from the UK (Fletcher, 2020), Denmark (Clotworthy and Westendorp, 2020) and Canada (Leibing, 2020) is that governmental responses did not take into account the experiences and opinions of older people but instead imposed restrictions to 'protect them' and supposedly for the greater good.

This chapter is concerned with the experiences of older people and looks at the literature that includes the voices of older people themselves. Offering examples from a variety of geographical locations it demonstrates the complexity and range of lived experiences older people have during COVID-19. Touch, and particularly not touching, are at the heart of preventing the spread of COVID-19. World Health Organization (WHO) guidelines for keeping safe during the pandemic state:

> Maintain at least a 1-metre distance between yourself and others to reduce your risk of infection when they cough, sneeze or speak. Maintain an even greater distance between yourself and others when indoors. The further away, the better (World Health Organization, 2020).

This advice implicitly states that not touching other people and safe distance is important to prevent the spread of the virus. They explicitly state the touch several times as well, specifically in relation to personal hygiene. 'Avoid *touching* your eyes, nose and mouth; Clean and disinfect surfaces frequently especially those which are regularly *touched*', and guidelines on wearing face masks: 'Clean your hands before you put your mask on, as well as before and after you take it off, and after you *touch* it at any time' (World Health Organization, 2020). Touch is thus framed as bad thing as touching yourself, your belongings and other people are strongly discouraged. The first section of this chapter will firstly explore the importance of touch. Secondly, it will outline how the absence of physical touch is shaping the experiences of older adults living in social isolation and lockdown conditions imposed by COVID-19. In contrast, the last section, particularly focusing on the work of Lamb (2020), looks at the positive side of living in pandemic times and shows how COVID-19 has led to innovation, resilience and new ways of being social for some older adults.

The importance of touch

Touch is an important feature of human live and the amount of physical contact can impact their general well-being.

> Our bodies have eighteen square feet of skin, which makes skin our largest sense organ. Because skin cannot shut its eyes or cover its ears, it is in a constant state of readiness to receive messages – it is always on. The first sensory input in life comes from the sense of touch while still in the womb, and touch continues to be the primary means of experiencing the world throughout infancy and well into childhood, even into aging (Field, 2014, p. 7).

While touch is still important in later life, it has been argued that the opportunities for physical touch are increasingly difficult (Field, 2014; Douglas, 2020a). It goes without saying that there are cultural variations and societal norms in what types of touch are considered important but hugs, handshakes, kisses and holding hands are all important in maintaining relationships with others. The absence of touch can negatively impact peoples' mental and physical health (Durkin, Jackson and Usher, 2020; Douglas, 2020a; Field, 2014).

Douglas (2020a) suggests that touch is essential for older people living with dementia. Touch is used as a means of communication and remaining connected with the world. Her ethnographic research in Scottish care facilities shows that while touch between family and friends and people living with dementia is currently prohibited, professional touch is deemed 'essential' (Douglas, 2020a). Douglas posits that this distinction is problematic as 'body care and its unavoidable touch do not bring only *care*. Body labour and touching bodies can also be a source of illness, infection and even death. When having fallen ill or carrying a virus, bacteria or microbe, bodies of workers can become a source of infection brought from the outside world and spread between residents' (Douglas, 2020a, p. 9, emphasis in original). So, on the one hand, touch can be comforting but on the other hand, touch can be dangerous. However, in the current climate, many older people do not have a say in what type of physical touch they would feel comfortable engaging with, and which types they would rather avoid. These decisions are not just made for older people living in care facilities but also affect older people living in the community.

Loss of touch

During the COVID-19 pandemic, a lot of older people have been isolated from their family and friends. In the Netherlands, missing intimacy and physical touch have been described as *huidhonger*, literally hunger for skin. This longing for physical touch, particularly by older people, has been a concern preceding COVID-19,[2] yet as this has been experienced by people from all parts of society the issue appeared to receive increased attention.[3] In the English language, the terms *touch hunger* and even *touch starvation* are being used (Durkin et al., 2020). In their editorial on touch hunger Durkin et al. (2020, p. 1) note:

> Touch in times of COVID-19 is restricted for our own safety and the safety of others. In these times when we must stay apart, we look for ways in which we can remain connected and acknowledge that we may also have to recognise the pain and suffering caused by the absence of touch in our own lives and the lives of our friends, family members, colleagues and patients.

Researching the impact of restrictions imposed by COVID-19 on vulnerable older adults in the Netherlands, Lemos Dekker, Vermeulen and Pols (2020) describe two case studies of older adults struggling with the measures. In their stories, loneliness and the absence of touch are telling. Catherine, a 95-year-old woman is desperate to 'reach out' to other people: 'The days take so long. I get so cold inside, cold from being lonely'. When asked what she means by this, she answers: 'I am just cold inside, I miss physical contact, touch' (Lemos Dekker et al., 2020). Catherine worries about catching the virus and, crucially, how she would have to cope with this on her own as her children would not be allowed to be with her (Lemos Dekker et al., 2020). The second case is Ben, whose wife is suspected to have Alzheimer's disease and who moved to a nursing home. Ben used to be a daily visitor until COVID came along. After being separated for 1.5 months they are able to see each other again 'through an open window, a screen of Plexiglas separating them' (Lemos Dekker et al., 2020). Ben, similarly to Cathrine, emphasises the importance of touch:

'The thing is: talking doesn't work anymore', he explains in tears. 'I'm just standing there moving up and down. I think I am somewhat erased from her aware memory at this point. So the only real form of contact we've got is touch, holding hands. But that is not allowed' (Lemos Dekker et al., 2020 online resource, no page number).

In both stories, the importance of social contact but particularly *physical* contact is emphasised. Physical touch does not need to come from humans. Animals are important companions for older people. Douglas (2020b) researches how people living with dementia in a Scottish care facility respond to therapy animals. She notes that, sadly, when the Scottish government announced social distancing measures these measures ended up extending to non-human companions, despite little evidence that they transmit the virus (Douglas, 2020b). This meant that in the care facility part of her study, the *therapet* and the volunteer accompanying this dog were no longer allowed to visit the facility. This was a great loss for many of the older residents, who had to give up their own pets before moving to this facility as animals were not allowed (Douglas, 2020b). Douglas (2020b: online resource, no page numbers) notes:

> Rusty, the gentle giant Husky therapet who visits people at River View with his human Jim, often fills this imposed loss. He never minds when Jean calls him Dingo, or when someone else squeezes his head and kisses his long, wet nose. 'For my dog', Peter, one of the therapet volunteers, told me, 'a person with dementia is just another nice human. He doesn't care if people don't remember him'. And this is exactly what many residents at River View need, yet often don't get from their fellow humans: to feel human, to be acknowledged as a person, to not be reduced to lost memory.

The therapy dogs that visit older residents contribute to older people being able to touch and pet another living being. With many care facilities and older people's homes socially isolating and visits being prohibited, older people are deprived of any opportunity for physical touch, which can attribute to the aforementioned touch hunger.

A project exploring how palliative care professionals establish relationships with dying patients and their families in times of COVID-19 describes the complexity of creating intimacy and space for touch when family members visit their dying loved one for the last time (Driessen, Borgstrom and Cohn, 2021). The authors note that personal protective equipment (PPE) which is required for staff as well as family, is a barrier in creating intimacy:

> Loved ones became hesitant about how close they could approach the dying person, while the staff were acutely aware that many patients had

often not affectionately touched anyone for days, sometimes for weeks. One consultant described how 'regulating intimacy' became one of her key tasks when dealing with visitors – not in the sense of curtailing it, but desperately trying to find ways to establish it. Modest acts of intimacy, such as the touching of somebody's arm, that normally would go unnoticed now became very obvious in their absence (Driessen et al., 2021, p. 18).

The absence of touch is creeping into every corner of society; both in people's personal environments as well as institutionalised spaces such as hospitals. For some the loss of psychical touch is a consequence of the pandemic, for others, particularly for older people living alone, this already was their everyday lived reality. Yet, while this pandemic has had very drastic and negative impacts on the lives of many people, it is also important to acknowledge the ways in which COVID-19 has brought opportunities and new ways of 'keeping in touch' particularly online.

New ways of keeping in touch

While COVID-19 has taken away many opportunities for physical touch, you can leave it to people to come up with ingenious solutions. A thing that received much media attention is a so-called 'cuddle curtain'. A plastic sheet that allows for people to safely hug without fear of contracting or spreading the virus. Media in Germany, Austria and Switzerland show a commercial that features the 'cuddle curtain' and its supposed emergence in various nursing homes (Streinzer et al., 2020). While part of everyday conversations, researchers Streinzer et al. were only able to locate one actual curtain in a private Swiss nursing home and wonder how widespread the use and appearance of these curtains actually was. A news item in England describes how a grandson made such a curtain at his grandparents' house to be able to hug his grandmother again.[4] In Toronto, this 'cuddle curtain' was termed a 'hug glove' and equally served as a means of making hugging between a family and their grandmother possible again.[5]

How popular and widespread these cuddle curtains are unclear. Interestingly in both the English and Canadian news report, they only interview the family members and not the older persons about their experience of the curtain. While these cuddle curtains are one creative example of new ways of keeping in touch, most interaction between people of all generations has moved online.

While loss of opportunities for physical touch are important to understand, it is equally important to acknowledge how new technologies offer opportunities for older people to stay in touch, or to form new connections. It has been suggested that older people face a 'double burden of exclusion' as they are deprived of both physical and digital ways of keeping in touch with their loved ones (Seifert, Cotten and Xie, 2020). While there is a digital divide and a lot of inequality having access to the internet, tablets and computers, and the programmes that facilitate virtual meetings, this is not solely based on age but points to wider inequalities in the world. Reflecting on the importance of social connections in Canadian long-term care, Ickert et al. (2020) suggest that structural issues, such as care facilities not having proper Wi-Fi access or enough tablets available, and loved ones not having these facilities at home, prevented older adults to stay in touch with their loved ones. Though knowing how to use a tablet, or having the psychical strength to use one, were noted as barriers, these larger structural issues need to be taken into account as well when considering the ways in which older people are able to keep in touch with their family and friends (Ickert et al., 2020). It is important to acknowledge the heterogeneity of older people, and while there are older people that are digitally illiterate, there is a growing group of older people perfectly capable of using various devices. Additionally, not engaging with certain devices might not be a case of lack of knowledge but a lack of means to acquire them.

Conducting ethnographic research on ageing in the United States, researchers such as anthropologist Sarah Lamb had to adapt their face-to-face research methods to phone-based or virtual ones (Lamb, 2020). Lamb conducted virtual interviews with twenty-five older adults living in the United States. A common theme amongst their pandemic stories was the notion that older people are less impacted by the pandemic than younger people. For example, Doug, aged 71 notes:

> I'd say unquestionably the quarantine is harder for the younger people. Because a lot of the older people are kind of, I won't say isolated, but they already have a home routine. ... It's almost easier for them to do the distancing. And even though everybody's social at every age, I find that the older people have it a little easier, because they don't have to worry about stopping school; they don't worry about going out on dates. You know, my son's 33 – he's still dating, and I said, 'Well, how's it going?' And he said, 'Well, I haven't been able to go out' (Lamb, 2020, p. 179).

The older adults in her study felt that their lives were less disrupted compared to those of younger people. Additionally, they felt they were probably 'more patient' and 'resilient' than younger generations. Importantly, this group of older adults adapted swiftly and were able to make use of various online communication methods such as Zoom, Facetime and Houseparty, which all proved to be fruitful platforms for social gatherings (Lamb, 2020). Lamb also received an email from one of her participants that highlights the potential for online platforms to create opportunities for new connections, and for old ones to rekindle:

> Two days ago, Jerry and I had the wonderful pleasure of Zooming with a long-lost friend of 49 years. How wonderful we all concluded that was.

The world is a mess, but Zoom has transformed our existence in it. Recommendation: Reach out and 'Zoom' someone (Lloyd, aged 71 in: Lamb, 2020, p. 181).

Another participant, Diane (aged 77), has shared many of her meals by speaker phone with a friend who is similarly widowed and living alone. Lamb's (2020) work shows the positive side of COVID-19 in that it has created space for interactions like these to be socially acceptable. Furthermore, the pandemic has caused people to 'check in' with loved ones more regularly, so people might have *more* social contacts than before (Lamb, 2020).

Burke (2020) notes that in the UK the pandemic has created various opportunities for intergenerational connections. There has been a growth in telephone befriending and various creative, mainly online, solutions were found to connect younger and older people. Despite all these positive initiatives Burke notes reaching the most isolated is difficult and that both older, as well as younger people can be digitally excluded as many initiatives demand having certain equipment and being tech-savvy (Burke, 2020). In Canada, some already existing technologies in healthcare and care facilities have been upscaled, making them accessible for more older people (Sixsmith, 2020). Yet, COVID-19 emphasises the already existing 'digital divide' (Seifert et al., 2020) and while there are some examples of positive changes and new connections the research on older people and the pandemic mainly highlights the loneliness and isolation experienced by many (Galkin, 2020; Lemos Dekker et al., 2020; Douglas, 2020a). I have heard anecdotal evidence of new connections and new ways of keeping in touch and hopefully future research will reveal additional positive examples to show that it was not all doom and gloom for older adults.

Conclusion

The COVID-19 pandemic has changed many facets of our lives. For older people, the age-based restrictions that many governments around the globe have imposed mean that many older adults have lost the opportunities to physically touch their loved ones. The restrictions solely based on chronological age deny the diversity between older people. While often lumped together as a 'group', older people can have vastly different life experiences that are shaped by, for example, health, wealth, class, religion and ethnicity. Older people live in various places including their own dwellings and nursing homes. In many places older people are not allowed to receive visitors and visits in nursing homes are either cancelled, or conducted via a see-through physical barrier (Lemos Dekker et al., 2020), or potentially through a 'cuddle curtain' (Streinzer et al., 2020). These one-size-fits-all restrictions ignore the diversity of older people and takes away their agency in deciding who will be able to visit, and who will be able to touch them.

Touch has been suggested to be an important aspect of people's wellbeing and the absence of physical touch can cause 'touch hunger' (Durkin et al., 2020). This has had a negative impact on the everyday lives of many older people across the globe. However, as Lamb (2020, p. 184) eloquently argues:

> the dominant narrative of the 'vulnerable older person' in the time of COVID-19 is misleading and even damaging in its uniformity. Older people in the pandemic are not only vulnerable, isolated, and dying. Many are also experiencing resilience, vibrant social connections, agency, and pleasure. If discourse on aging in the time of COVID-19 focuses only on vulnerability, we risk perpetuating implicit ageist assumptions.

Lamb's research in the United States has demonstrated how COVID-19 has transformed the social lives of some older adults for the better. The pandemic has moved many social interactions online and for participants in her study, this meant increased social contact and interesting new ways to connect with other people (Lamb, 2020). Thus, while we might be inclined to focus on what COVID-19 has taken from us, it is also important to reflect on what COVID-19 has given us and how some older people might have more thriving social networks compared to before the pandemic. While many of these technologies were available prior to the COVID-19 outbreak they were not used as widely as they are now. Through COVID-19, people of all ages have experienced first-hand what it is like to live in circumstances that were common among a large group of older people. Isolation and loneliness are not new and hopefully, COVID-19 will be a catalyst in continuing to bring older and younger people together and for people to think of more innovative ways to keep in touch.

Notes

1. https://thl.fi/en/web/thlfi-en/-/recommendation-to-restrict-group-hobbies-during-the-acceleration-and-spreading-stage-of-coronavirus
2. See for example: https://www.radicalevernieuwing.nl/actueel/huidhonger-een-dans-en-beweegprogramma-over-aanraking/. This project offered dance and movement workshops to older people and students. The importance of physical touch for people's general wellbeing was noted.
3. See: https://www.parool.nl/nieuws/waarom-we-massaal-huidhonger-hebben~b087e17f/
4. See: https://news.sky.com/story/coronavirus-mans-ingenious-solution-to-cuddle-his-grandma-again-goes-viral-11989880
5. See: https://www.ctvnews.ca/health/coronavirus/this-hug-glove-will-help-spread-the-love-but-not-the-coronavirus-1.4937811

References

Burke, S., 2020. Stronger together? Intergenerational connection and Covid-19. *Quality in Ageing and Older Adults*, 21(4), pp. 253–259.

Bytheway, B., 2005. Ageism and age categorization. *Journal of Social Issues*, 61(2), pp. 361–374.

Clotworthy, A. and Westendorp, R.G., 2020. Risky business: how older 'At Risk' people in Denmark evaluated their situated risk during the COVID-19 pandemic. *Anthropology & Aging*, 41(2), pp. 167–176.

Degnen, C., 2007. Minding the gap: the construction of old age and oldness amongst peers. *Journal of Aging Studies*, 21(1), pp. 69–80.

Douglas, C., 2020a. A world of touch in a no-touch pandemic. *Anthropology in Action*, Berghahn Books, 28(1), pp. 8–15.

Douglas, C., 2020b. Of dogs and their humans: late life in a more-than-human world of the COVID-19 pandemic. *Somatosphere*, [online] Available at: http://somatosphere.net/2020/of-dogs%0A-and-their-humans-late-life-in-a-more-than-human-world-of-the-covid-19-p%0Aandemic.html/.

Driessen, A., Borgstrom, E. and Cohn, S., 2021. Ways of 'being with'. Caring for dying patients at the height of the COVID-19 pandemic. *Anthropology in Action*, 28(1), pp. 16–20.

Durkin, J., Jackson, D. and Usher, K., 2020. Touch in times of COVID-19: touch hunger hurts, *Journal of Clinical Nursing*, Blackwell Publishing Ltd, 30, pp. 1–2.

Field, T., 2014. *Touch* (2nd ed.). Massachussets: MIT Press.

Finnish Government, 2020. Restrictions during the coronavirus epidemic, https://valtioneuvosto.fi/en/information-on-coronavirus/current-restrictions, [online] Available at: https://valtioneuvosto.fi/en/information-on-coronavirus/current-restrictions (Accessed: 12 January 2021).

Fletcher, J.R., 2020. Chronological quarantine and ageism: COVID-19 and gerontology's relationship with age categorisation, *Ageing and Society*, Cambridge University Press (CUP), pp. 1–14.

Galkin, K., 2020. 'The body becomes closed and squeezed up in a narrow frame': loneliness and fears of isolation in the lives of older people in rural areas in Karelia during COVID-19. *Anthropology & Aging*, 41(2), pp. 187–198.

Hockey, J. and James, A., 1993. *Growing up and growing old. Ageing and dependency in the life course.* London: Sage.

Hockey, J. and James, A., 2003. *Social Identities across the life course.* New York: Palgrave Macmillan.

Ickert, C., Rozak, H., Masek, J., Eigner, K. and Schaefer, S., 2020. Maintaining resident social connections during COVID-19: considerations for long-term care. *Gerontology and Geriatric Medicine*, SAGE Publications, 6, p. 233372142096266.

Lamb, S., 2020. On vulnerability, resilience, and age: older Americans reflect on the pandemic. *Anthropology & Aging*, 41(2), pp. 177–186.

Leibing, A., 2020. Recognizing older individuals: an essay on critical gerontology, Robin Hood, and the COVID-19 crisis. *Anthropology & Aging*, 41(2), pp. 221–229.

Lemos Dekker, N., Vermeulen, L. and Pols, J., 2020. In and outside the nursing home: On the (im)possibilities of meaningful contact while being held apart. *Somatosphere*, [online] Available at: http://somatosphere.net/2020/in-and-outside-the-nursing-home.html/ (Accessed: 18 December 2020).

Lichtenstein, B., 2020. From 'coffin dodger' to 'boomer remover': outbreaks of ageism in three countries with divergent approaches to coronavirus control. *J Gerontol B Psychol Sci Soc Sci*, XX, pp. 1–7.

Seifert, A., Cotten, S.R. and Xie, B., 2020. A double burden of exclusion? Digital and social exclusion of older adults in times of COVID-19. In Carr, D. (ed.), *The Journals of Gerontology: Series B*, Oxford University Press (OUP), XX, pp. 1–5.

Sixsmith, A., 2020. COVID-19 and AgeTech. *Quality in Ageing and Older Adults*, 21(4), pp. 247–252.

Streinzer, A., Poppinga, A., Zieringer, C., Wanka, A. and Marx, G., 2020. Familial intimacy and the 'thing' between us cuddle curtains and desires for detached relationality in Germany, Austria and Switzerland. *Anthropology in Action, Berghahn Journals*, 27(2), pp. 68–72.

World Health Organization, 2020. Coronavirus disease (COVID-19) advice for the public, [online] Available at: https://www.who.int/emergencies/diseases/novel-coronavirus-2019/advice-for-public (Accessed: 17 December 2020).

13 Between cultural necrophilia and African American activism: life and loss in the age of COVID

Kami Fletcher and Tamara Waraschinski

Key points

The following points are explored in this chapter:

- Necrophile Self
- African American deathways
- 2020 Pandemic
- 2020 Protests
- Black feminism
- African American grief/mourning
- Death Denial

Introduction: COVID-19 + white supremacy = thousands of African American deaths

On 4 April 2020, the Milwaukee Health Department announced that 87% of all persons in Wisconsin's most populous county, Milwaukee County, who had died from the coronavirus were African American. On 30 April 2020, the Virginia Department of Public Health reported that 14 of the 15 persons who died of the coronavirus in Richmond, Virginia were African American. Some Public health officials reasoned that many African Americans had pre-existing medical conditions such as diabetes, heart disease and asthma. Too often those analyses masked compounded structural inequalities present within our healthcare system. This line of reasoning even disregards the large numbers of African American essential workers who are then at risk of exposure to the disease. Other medical professionals and experts concluded that racism is a public health issue. One that extends to structural problems such as inadequate housing caused by Jim Crow redlining practices, late 20th century urban renewal policies, and 21st century gentrification (Keshavan, 2020).

Only one month into the full-scale outbreak in the U.S. and it was clear that African American communities were being disproportionately ravaged by the virus compounded by racist policies. As thousands were dying in African American communities, seven Republican governors refused to declare Stay-at-Home Orders and armed self-identified Trump supporters held Liberate-the-State protest-rallies on the courthouse steps in Pennsylvania, Michigan, Virginia, Oregon and Minnesota (Breuninger, 2020). The Stay-at-Home Orders were executed to protect the public health and safety of Americans yet, 35 of the 40 Brooklynites jailed for supposedly not following the order were African American, while police officers in Lower Manhattan passed out masks to whites in a park who openly violated the order (Southall, 2020). Following Trumpism that spouted racist and xenophobic rhetoric, self-identified white nationalists and neo-nazis protested the existence of the coronavirus (Levenson, 2017). This same sense of emboldenment led many Conservatives to not just politicize but feminize the wearing of masks and face coverings (Victor, 2020). It was evident that Conservatives, Republicans and white nationalists alike continued to play politics with Black lives. And once the 8 minute and 46 seconds video of George Floyd's murder by Minnesota police officers surfaced, African Americans responded with politicized activism and collective grief-induced agency that was not just meant to survive the pandemic but also to expose and overthrow the white supremacy weaponized by Trumpism.

Healthcare professionals, nationwide, took to social media to expose the inequalities and gross negligence associated with African American COVID-19 patients. In a 23-minute YouTube video, Nurse Nicole Sirotek blows the whistle on how African American and Hispanic coronavirus patients were murdered from hospital mismanagement and not COVID. Sirotek was part of a wave of 4,000 travel nurses who traveled from all areas of the US to go to New York City in order to help provide care to the unprecedented COVID-19 cases that had New York City hospitals over capacity. As nurses are labeled pink collar in this country, this was overwhelming women fighting to save the lives of tens of thousands of COVID patients, reminiscent of how nurses during the 1918 Spanish Flu fought on the front lines tending to 20–30 patients with 'fresh laundry, water, and fluids and food' (Clark, 2020). African American women were initially barred from the Red Cross and Nurses Corps but when welcomed were sent to Preston County, West Virginia to help save the U.S. economy since coal was the major fuel source. By October 1919, coal miners were dying in large numbers over a short period and 95% were infected with the Spanish flu, thus unable to work (Jones and Saines, 2019). Just like during the COVID-19 pandemic, African American bodies along with the poor and working class were sacrificed in order to reopen the U.S. economy.

The poor, working class, and those within communities of color were expendable. This was painfully clear with the murder of George Floyd by, then, Minnesota Police Officer, Derek Chauvin. As this chapter illustrates, this sheer amount of mourning and grief from unarmed Black women, men and children killed by the police and COVID-19, led to collective acts of resistance to white supremacy and culturally rooted ways of preserving and memorializing black life within the age of COVID. African Americans and allies in the struggle against white supremacy took to the streets in public protest, painted Black Lives Matter inspired murals, and created 'Say Their Names' cemeteries in numerous US states. Continuing, this chapter points to historical antecedents whereby African Americans used death, grief and mourning to resist – such as enslaved persons faking a funeral to cross the Canadian border for freedom or establishing autonomous Black-owned cemeteries to assert their right to be remembered in their own voice.

Using different methodologies and even different voices, ultimately as co-authors, we combined our research to address how and why the U.S. continues to go unmourning the tens of thousands of African American COVID-19 deaths that lay at the intersection of capitalism and grief illiteracy. In the first two sections, Tamara Waraschinski exposes the prevailing death denial attitude that disallowed Americans to grieve or even handle this amount of death in a healthy way – what she theorizes as the *Necrophile Self*, a cultural trait of death phobia and consumerism within the individual. In the next two sections, Kami Fletcher first historicizes the ways in which racism underlined African American deathways, the ways in which African Americans have lost their lives, arguing how death denial was never an option for African Americans. This idea dovetails into her discussion of the resiliency presence within Black grief and mourning that served as a catalyst for the 2020 international protest against structural inequality and white supremacy. Black women played a very important part in this grief-inspired activism and mourning. Therefore, the Black Feminist theories and Black women philosophies that conclude this chapter contain important lessons about Black women's activism, organizing and thinking and how it will propel a death denial culture forward.

Cultural necrophilia: revisiting death and grief illiteracy during a global pandemic

In order to investigate why COVID-19 has been especially lethal for Black (and other marginalized) communities, one has to look at the intrinsic links between capitalism, (human) life and death/ violence. In *The Necrophile Self: Contemporary Attitudes Towards Death and Its New Visibility*, Tamara Waraschinski outlined the relationship between hyper capitalism and death and grief illiteracy. More to the point, the dissertation illustrated that giving room to death has become a consumer affair and thus not approached with dignity and care. Ultimately, the point is that the dominant way of thinking about death has been channeled through the lens of capitalism that glosses over the violent means of resource and labor extraction, excess in its many forms, and unbridled consumption (Waraschinski, 2017).

Western society holds the belief that we are living in a society that mostly struggles to give death its righteous place in society. Canonical texts in *Death Studies* will lead many to assume that people in the old and new world are just bad with death and grief as thoroughly analyzed by the likes of Kübler-Ross (1976), Ariès (1974), Kellehear (2007); Becker (1973), Bauman (1992) and Elias (1985), among others. These cultural attitudes have brought forth a death positive movement that seeks to remedy our cultural failure to integrate death into the sphere of the living. Looking into the history of African American deathways, however, revealed that there is a whole different way to relate to death. Although explored later in the chapter, it is important to highlight the obliviousness of other culture's handling of death and commemorating their dead serves a purpose. It constitutes what Waraschinski calls the *Necrophile Self*.

The *Necrophile Self* is a conundrum that represents various streaks in human behavior and striving that relate to death. The *Necrophile Self* is not an identity as much as it is a theory of the psychosocial basis of pathological structures that can be found playing out in the social world as well as within the individual. It explains the struggle to give death its rightful place in society and how this impacts our sense of self. Using psychoanalytic theory as an analytical tool, it is concluded that materialism/consumerism is propped up on the shoulders of a death and grief illiterate society. What this helps to push out of view is that capitalism relies on covert and overt violence to maintain its position on the globe.

The *Necrophile Self* is an extension of Freud's death drive theory. The early Sigmund Freud (1997 [1915]) theorized that the ego is the result of the tensions between humans' innate drive to follow the lead of pleasure and navigate the world of social demands – the pleasure and reality principle. In his essay *Beyond the Pleasure Principle* (1920), Freud argues that alongside the live drive, there exists a death drive within our psyche and to expressing itself in repetitions of painful experiences and manifestations of emotional misery, as well as death, carnage, and destruction in private and inner world. After World War I and the 1918 flu pandemic, Freud's dark analysis isn't all too unsurprising. His conception of the dual drive theory is in that sense of sociological nature and the death drive should be understood as a cultural phenomenon, arising at the intersection between culture and the individual psyche.

Later psychoanalytic thinkers, Herbert Marcuse, Erich Fromm and Jacques Lacan, developed Freud's death drive theory further. Marcuse understood that the erotic drive, desire, plays a vital role in human striving, and concluded that capitalism has high-jacked desire. In his 1955 work *Eros and Civilization,* he explained how capitalism subjugates the pleasure principle and restructures people's desires for its purposes. This would lead to psychosocial pathologies expressed as the death drive, or what he labeled as Thanatos.

The term necrophilia, borrowed from Erich Fromm, claimed that the socio-economic environment dictates how an individual's character is shaped into being. Character, in turn, determines a person's consciousness towards a love of life (biophilia) or a disdain, maybe even hatred for, life (necrophilia). He sees destructiveness not as parallel, but alternative to biophilia that each individual faces in one's lifetime. If the conditions are such that the love of life is suppressed, then the psychological predisposition for destruction offers itself as an alternative. He writes:

> If man cannot create anything or move anybody, he cannot break out of the prison of his total narcissism, he can escape the unbearable sense of vital impotence and nothingness only by affirming himself in the act of destruction of the life that he is unable to create ... for destruction all that is necessary is strong arms, or a knife or a gun (Fromm, 1973, p. 366).

In ordinary terms, necrophilia denotes the sexual attraction to a dead body or body parts. In Fromm's usage of the term (as well in Marcuse's usage of the term Thanatos) he hinted at the underlying drive that had lost its life affirming touch, but tapped into something excessive, destructive and repulsive that is located beyond the biological (i.e. killing for survival).

Another aspect of the *Necrophile Self* is that of the pursuit of symbolic immortality. Zygmunt Bauman (2007) argues that we live in a time when the pleasure principle is fused with the reality principle, and, not unlike Marcuse, suggests that human desires are now aligned with capitalistic demands and practices, which aim at the control of the environment and extraction of resources by economic and institutional forces, as well as control over the individual and the body on a personal level. People are influenced by chimerical consumer fantasies that help shape an identity that is preoccupied with creating an idealistic sense of self or individualism through chasing material desires that seem only two days of prime shipping away. In Bauman's book, *Mortality, Immortality, and Other Life Strategies* (1992), he labels these mechanisms 'immortality strategies', which are methods of emotional survival that extend the meaning of an individual's life beyond the individual self. In other words, it is a desperate attempt to give life meaning, while simultaneously keeping mortality awareness at a distance (Waraschinski, 2017, p. 6).

This concurs with Ernest Becker's understanding of the pursuit of a heroic ideal or symbolic standard that acts as buttress to one's death anxiety, 'cultural values condensed into an ideal form of humanity' (Darell and Pyszczynski, 2016, p. 3).

> In man a working level of narcissism is inseparable from self-esteem, from a basic sense of self-worth. [...] his sense of self-worth is

constituted symbolically, his cherished narcissism feeds on symbols, on an abstract idea of his own worth, an idea composed of sounds, words, and images, in the air, in the mind, on paper (Becker, 1973, p. 3).

Becker's theory that preserving and building self-worth through aligning oneself through the dominant cultural ideals holds the key to fending off the terror death evokes in the individual. From Becker's work Terror Management Theory (TMT) has evolved and successfully shown through gathering empirical data, that indeed, reminders of one's mortality increase defensive view of one's worldview (Darell and Pyszczynski, 2016, p. 6). By strengthening these psychological structures through pursuing social standards and ideals, death anxiety is held at bay (Darell and Pyszczynski, 2016, p. 10).

The link between death denial and White supremacy

Terror Management Theory explains the functioning of striving towards a cultural ideal to boost and protect one's self-esteem. Self-esteem functions like a psychic lubricant for social settings and thus promotes better social outcomes. What needs more attention in this line of assessment, however, is that these cultural heroic ideals are shaped by white supremacist patriarchal capitalist ideologies. Waraschinski wrote of the *Necrophile Self* as:

> the illusion of an independent self, which at its core has fused the reality and pleasure principles, leading to excess and overconsumption. This fusion corresponds to the modern (perverted) immortality strategy (the obsessive meaning-making attempt) of the necrophile self that is located within the death drive, the spectral undeadness that demands an enjoyment of life in excess – jouissance (Waraschinski, 2017, p. 105).

A core Lacanian concept important to this line of thought is jouissance. In Lacanian thought, jouissance is understood as the death drive pushing to reach beyond the pleasure and reality principle, a sort of pull towards the enjoyment of life in excess, but in total disregard of its potentially deadly and inhumane consequences. 'Culture is embedded in the excess of its denial' (Waraschinski, 2017, p. 105). To be more exact, there is a refusal to acknowledge the failure and cruelty of the modern, consumerist and capitalist mindset that demands to control the environment and attempts to extract not only life, but also death out of it. At the same time, it provides little space to address end-of-life matters appropriately.

However, being ill-equipped to deal with death and dying on an emotional level has certain functions that benefit capitalism as well as White Supremacy. For one, it helps to occlude the lethal material realities that capitalisms' success relies on. The frantic behavior of entitlement, extraction, excess, unbridled consumption that we can observe around death is also that of White Supremacy, because long before medical advancements bettered health, prolonged life and pushed death out of the consciousness of modern (white) people, capitalism succeeded through racist and violent methods. Historically, Black people have had a complicated relationship to the U.S. economy because as enslaved persons, they *were* the wealth, resources and means of production. The institution of plantation slavery dehumanized African Americans, exploited their labor in life and still capitalized off their bodies in death. Marc Lamont Hill reminds us that America was built on this 'racial capitalism', where the construct of race served to exploit their labor to build and fortify the nation-state. Black bodies are seen as mere 'sites of wealth extraction rather than humanity' (Hill, 2020, pp. 17–18).

Given this history of exploitation and oppression, that used to solely operate through the mechanism of complete dehumanization, death and grief illiteracy now, too, serve the ever churning machinery of hyper capitalism. We can further see this in the argument we've heard so often during the 2020 crisis in the U.S., that the COVID death toll of the vulnerable would be miniscule compared to the 'sacrifice' of closing the economy. Hill refers to this as 'Corona capitalism, in which healing is an industry and survival a luxury' (Hill, 2020, p. 19). Corona capitalism isn't something new, but rather an extension of pre-existing predatory capitalist practices that have led to the surplus loss of lives during the COVID-19 pandemic (i.e. healthcare is not a human right but just another commodity). It also highlights the fact that crises are exploited by the powerful and rich in collaboration with governments to further their financial superiority. The term also explains the dangers of living in a white supremacist capitalist empire, that exposes the disposability of Black, Native and Brown communities, the elderly, poor, disabled and generally, marginalized people. The proximity to death makes one disposable and though that one becomes more exploitable (Hill, 2020, p. 21).

In 2020, we have witnessed African Americans, as well as Latin and Native Americans die at much higher rates while they still have to summon their strength to protest for basic human rights. But these groups are not the only segments of society that staged protests during the pandemic. Conservative and far-right groups protested the public health mandates like wearing masks, or Stay-At-Home Orders that were implemented to curtail the spread of the virus by the Democratic Governor Gretchen Whitmer in April 2020. In May 2020, heavily armed and unmasked protesters stormed the Michigan State House and angrily demanded the reversal of these mandates they'd labeled as 'tyranny' (Solener, 2020). While the Democratic Gov. Gretchen Whitmer had to regularly deal with death threats for her COVID position, the maliciousness of these anti-lockdown sentiments culminated in October when the FBI forfeited a kidnapping plot, schemed by far right white supremacist terror militias. In an essay published by the *Atlantic* in October 2020 Whitmer made it clear that the President himself is to be held accountable for emboldening white supremacists and their violent strategies since he had actively encouraged people to express hostility towards Whitmer (2020).

It is not a coincidence that the calls to open the economy were uttered after it became clear that marginalized communities are the one's suffering most during this crisis. We live in a society conditioned to think in market terms and that encourages us to be a consumer rather than a participant in democracy. Hill warns us that this leads to a 'politics of disposability' (Hill, 2020, p. 41) in which individuals are only as valuable as their ability to consume or produce. The most vulnerable to the pandemic belong to a social segment that has long been denied protection, care and investment. In market terms, which is structured by the logic of white supremacy, patriarchy and capitalism, their economic value is low, and 'the moment you become no longer exploitable, you become death-eligible' (Hill, 2020, p. 43).

Making the suffering and deaths from underrepresented communities invisible has consistently been a strategy to suppress uncomfortable conversations about social justice, accountability and social change. I have yet to see a greater public acknowledgment of the emotional toll this pandemic has taken on pretty much everyone, especially those who have lost someone. *The New York Times* had a special edition once the death toll reached 100,000. Its front cover was only the name of the first 1,000 who succumbed to the disease. The fact that there seems to be no room (besides small local grassroots events) to acknowledge the staggering number of lives lost isn't just because we are still counting bodies in this on-going pandemic. Racism also includes the white entitlement to remain oblivious of the suffering of others.

Another function of death and grief illiteracy is that it protects white innocence. Being surprised by the depths of suffering and struggle of marginalized people or being ill-equipped to respond appropriately to death and grief are hallmarks of protecting the innocence of whiteness. James Baldwin's words still hold true to this day:

> [...] this is the crime of which I accuse my country and my countrymen, and for which neither I nor time nor history will ever forgive them, that they have destroyed and are destroying hundreds of thousands of lives and do not know it and do not want to know it. [...] But it is not permissible that the authors of devastation should also be innocent. It is the innocence which constitutes the crime (Baldwin, 1963, p. 17).

The question we must ask is, 'what has to be excised from the white mind that renders a society death and grief illiterate, while simultaneously coexisting with other Latin, Indigenous and Black cultures, that have very different approaches to death and grief?' What is at play is the *Necrophile Self* that has its status in the world taken for granted and assumes this position through open and subtle violence and thus needs to maintain a narrow understanding and outlook on vulnerability, mourning and death. Death itself vanishes as an existential possibility in a white modern understanding of life because awareness of it has to be kept at the lowest level possible for capitalism to thrive. Hill observes that:

> American culture is committed to nostalgia, erasure, and outright dishonesty as its response to trauma. Instead of reckoning with our violent history of conquest and plunder, we tell romantic stories of brave and principled European explorers. Rather than viewing slavery as a foundational component of this country, with ongoing impacts in every sector of our lives, we dismiss it as a brief and morally troublesome interruption to an otherwise principle and longstanding journey toward democracy. We ignore painful truths as a strategy for maintaining national pride and justifying acts of evil (Hill, 2020, p. 53).

This mechanism allows white Americans to remain oblivious of racism and their unearned power in the culture, further, it makes them complacent and indifferent towards the systems they are benefiting from, even though these very systems kill those on the margins. As a broader cultural consequence, this has led to a society that doesn't offer space for end-of-life and grief matters for anyone, let alone fathom those segments of society that have historically been denied their humanity. The result is surplus suffering, rooted in a death denialist, violence addicted, consumerist, necrophile culture of which the entire collective, no matter what social status, class and race, has been affected.

Death denial runs counter to African American deathways. If death was so-called denied because more Americans sent their sick kin to die in hospitals, so out of sight, and strides in American medicine were designed to extend life instead of accept death, then what of the Jim Crow segregation that denied African Americans hospital care? What of the thousands of African Americans who were unnaturally killed by white supremacy and therefore denied a deathbed? What of the Black men, women and children experimented on in life and death to advance American medicine? Are their lives extended? In *The Price for Their Pound of Flesh: The Value of the Enslaved, from Womb to Grave, in the Building of a Nation*, Daina Ramey Berry (2017) says that it was not their life that was extended from advancements in medicine but the ways they could be exploited in death. Through tedious archival work, Berry illustrates how America's most reputable medical schools participated in what she calls the cadaver trade of enslaved bodies – medical schools were in need of cadavers and looked to exploit the unprotected enslaved dead body.

African American deathways amidst COVID-19, the 2020 pandemic and White supremacy

The sheer number of COVID-19 deaths in African American communities has to make a death-denying culture reckon with itself because racism underscored these deaths. At the writing of this chapter, *The COVID Tracking Project* put American fatalities at 309,449 with 51,385 of those deaths African American. The question of why African Americans were dying at nearly 2.5 times the rate of White Americans had to be asked. Some medical professionals pushed the narrative that pre-existing conditions (diabetes, heart disease, asthma) were the reasons for the disparity and our Nation's doctor implied that African Americans' alcohol and tobacco consumption was a leading cause in these COVID-19 related deaths. But as an April 2020 Aljazeera headline so bluntly put it 'Racism: The most dangerous "pre-existing condition"' (Bonhomme, 2020). Racism is the underlying culprit when African American children are twice as likely to be asthmatic which has everything to do with historically racist redlining practices that date back to FDR's New Deal, namely the 1934 National Housing Act (NHA) that systemically pushed government financial institutions to underinvest in largely Black populated neighborhoods and city-centers while simultaneously pushing developers to build segregated white suburbs (Greer, 2014). Research conducted in New York City, Los Angeles, San Francisco and Oakland from 2006 until 2017, top public policy and health professionals found that 80 years later, the vast majority of premature babies born to African American and Latinx women or with low birth rates were living within these same redlined neighborhoods (Krieger et. al., 2020; Nardone et. al., 2020). Low birth rate is directly correlated with childhood asthma showing the direct correlation between African American deaths and structural racism.

COVID-19 deaths revealed historic racist policies that have directly contributed to African American deaths. In the 1920s through the 1960s as African Americans migrated out of the south to northern and western cities by the hundreds of thousands, racist housing policies locked them into slums. Slum lords took advantage of this influx and subdivided already cramped apartments without increasing property maintenance. As lead-based paint chipped and dust spread, generations of African Americans, still today, suffer from lead poisoning (Wheeler and Broadwater, 2015). Racist housing policies locked African Americans into geographical areas that continually bordered the more air polluted areas, shut off access to healthy food and even clean drinking water as is the cases of Flint Michigan and Eudora, Arkansas ('Eudora Residents Not Happy with Water Quality, City Says Work is Being Done to Resolve It', 2019).

Reports revealed that when African Americans did contract the coronavirus, they were either woefully under cared for by doctors and healthcare professionals or just not believed and therefore turned away from hospitals, which led to loss of life. A story surfaced of Rana Zoe Mangin, a Brooklyn Social Studies teacher, who died of the coronavirus after she was not believed when EMTs answered her 911 call and even after she made her way to the hospital and was examined by doctors (Brown, 2020). This racial empathy gap speaks to the larger issue of institutionalized and even government sanctioned experimentation on perceived 'immuned' Black bodies, especially so when one examines the 2 April 2020 comments by two French doctors who seriously suggested Africans as the so-called logical test subjects for new COVID-19 trials happening in Europe and Australia (Rosman, 2020).

There is history to the racist idea that somehow Black people are immune to disease. Based on the idea that African Americans are not real people but Jezebel-Mammy-Brute-Coon-Pickaninny caricatures, public sentiment developed that contagions and diseases just work differently on Black people. Operating on the racist belief that Black women did not feel pain in the ways that white women did, Black women who fell ill from issues due to abnormalities with their reproductive systems were vulnerable to experimentation. In *Medical Bondage: Race, Gender, and the Origins of American Gynecology,* Deirdre Cooper Owens (2018) unequivocally shows how American gynecology was advanced from the forceful experimentation of enslaved women. The subtext is that slaveholders were invested in treating/curing slave women's bodies so as to restore and fortify their labor force. There is a shift that happens once these enslaved women and their labor are freed and believed to not have value if their labor is not perpetually controlled by white society. Therefore, unlike during the antebellum era where Black bodies were enslaved to white slaveholders, now post emancipation, there is no vested interest in Black life because whites do not universally control Black labor.

A strong shift to devaluing Black life in the post emancipation period, African Americans were viewed as dispensable, which made them vulnerable to experimentation. An antebellum 'immuned' Black body becomes a Black 'diseased' body post emancipation and all one had to do was to look at the disease-infested shanty towns across the south where most Black folk were relegated to justify their assumptions. So for 40 years (1932–1972) when doctors – operating under the auspices of the U.S. government – researched how syphilis affected the so-called Negro, and therefore left hundreds of Black men untreated, even after the invention of penicillin, one understands that the experiment was more about learning from the dying/dead African American body. As Dr. Oliver Wenger of the United States Public Health Service admitted in a July 1933 letter 'We have no further interest in these patients *until they die*' (Van West, n.d., emphasis in original).

By all accounts, the American government and the general public have left and continually leave African Americans to die. As the numbers of African Americans who have died from COVID-19 reach astronomical proportions in only a few months, once again, African Americans have been left to die.

Addressing the question of why African Americans (who make up 13% of the American population) make up 19% of the COVID-19 deaths is essential in understanding racism as a direct cause of African American death. In addition to inadequate housing and run-down neighborhoods, racism minimizes, marginalizes, devalues African American life and ultimately kills African Americans. This became especially true when George Floyd was murdered amidst the coronavirus outbreak. Cell phone video footage (recorded by bystanders) went viral of Floyd, an African American father and hometown football hero, being murdered by Minneapolis police. On 25 May 2020, Minneapolis Police were called to Cup Foods Convenient Store over George Floyd's alleged use of a counterfeit twenty-dollar bill. As police used excessive force to apprehend Floyd who was completely subdued in handcuffs behind his back and forced to lay face-down on the street, near the curb, senior officer Derek Chauvin kneeled on Floyd's neck for 8 minutes and 46 seconds. Floyd pleaded that he could not breathe and when he quieted, one bystander pleaded for the officers to check for a pulse while one shouted that Floyd was unresponsive. But with his hand in his pants pocket, Chauvin callously kneeled on Floyd's neck and proceeded to murder Floyd amidst the crowd that had gathered, and police officers called to the scene for backup.

When it comes to the pandemic of 2020, death was not the great equalizer. The virus had exposed a truth that had been hidden in Death Studies for far too long about death and equality – that there is institutionalized and even government sanctioned devaluation of Black life that is accepted and repeated in public norms and behavior. The racist systems fueled by racist ideology that is further normalized by public belief in racist stereotypes all underline African American death ways, or ways in which African Americans die. As Karla Holloway and Maurice Jackson remind us, Black people do not just die but they die differently, unnatural and in 'mournful collectives and disconcerting ways' (Jackson, 1977; Holloway, 2003). African American deathways illustrate the white supremacy that lynched them from trees, the law-and-order racism that beat and subdued them to death, the color-blind racism that weaponized the neighborhood watch and white nationalist to their demise. In this Black Lives Matter era, fighting COVID-19 and racism is synonymous. The murder of George Floyd amidst a pandemic made this painstakingly clear.

African American deathways as a response to dehumanized Black Life and dishonored Black Death

In this Black Lives Matter era, African Americans made the American death denial culture bear witness to the resiliency of African American grief and mourning. Meeting in the streets the day after George Floyd was murdered under common shared grief, protestors created a space for public mourning. This is significant because as scholar Candi Cann argues, in the 21st century there is no literal space for mourning, particularly for those deemed marginal; therefore, Black and Brown peoples appropriating public space, place and time, democratizes their grief (Cann, 2014). Holding high, Black Lives Matter inspired signage and wearing R.I.P. T-Shirts, these marginalized mourners literally carved out space on public property through culturally ascribed mourning wear and collective voices to not just mourn and grieve but also to perhaps be recognized as the bereaved. Among other things, the protests were an expression of grief – grieving the loss of George Floyd and the many, many African Americans who have lost their lives to the white supremacy disguised as law-and-order criminal justice.

Establishing the protestors as mourners and marginalized mourners, at that, is important because then the protest gets repositioned as one way in which African Americans are purposefully and openly, in a very strategic way, illustrating the impact of loss and grief and the dismissal of African Americans as bereaved in American society. The 'Say Their Names' Cemetery created in Minnesota was perhaps the best example of claiming bereavement displayed during the 2020 protests. Artists Anna Barber and Connor Wright printed the name, as well as date, age and place where African Americans were killed by police, along with the phrase 'Rest In Power' onto white poster boards; and with metal stakes positioned them as headstones in a city-owned public park. Twenty-two-year-olds Barber and Wright said they wanted to humanize the listing of African Americans killed by the police. The memorial garnered attention from around the country but most importantly the immediate community in which it was created. Community members cared for the 'Say Their Name' Cemetery by re-erecting all postboard gravestones that toppled over and protected it by placing plastic bags over the ephemeral headstones to shield it from rain. They even held vigils to show a unified remembrance that was also encouraged to act and incite macro-level change.

Public memorialization then is key to moving Black grief and mourning from margin to center, especially because Black grief is overlooked, dismissed and frankly misunderstood. The 'Say Their Name' Cemetery became a sacred space of remembering and validating the very idea that George Floyd and all other African Americans murdered by the police needed and must be remembered – that they each were part of families and communities that are incomplete in their absence. Cemeteries, also labeled cities of the dead, are historical treasure troves and genealogical gold mines. Researchers like Foster and Eckert (2003) have used cemeteries to uncover and literally map entire towns thought lost to history, understanding the demographics and even ethnic and migratory patterns over time. Genealogists and others in search of family history have used the space to fill in their family trees. This is especially important to African Americans who were dehumanized within the U.S. Census records, i.e. listed as slaves and counted as a number, and purposefully omitted from pre-emancipation burial, death and marriage records.

The 'Say Their Name' Cemetery also lays bare the deeply rooted racism in American death culture because as rhetoric scholar Elizabethada Wright (2005) clearly states, 'not only do cemeteries remind us of what and how we overlook memories, they make evident what is so difficult to see, the unseeable, what is not there'. Therefore the 'Say Their Name' Cemetery makes Americans confront the very racism and white supremacy that are the root cause of so many African American deaths. The memorial is made up of a little under 100 symbolic headstones – only some deaths, not meant to be comprehensive. Grouping together African American deaths from police brutality powerfully pushes back against a narrative of American death culture that not only marginalizes African American gravesites but also one that blatantly disrespects Black cemeteries. African Americans are not allowed to rest in peace because their gravesites are vandalized, shot up even, as is the case with Emmett Till whose historical grave marker is now bulletproof. Headline after headline reveal how gravestones are defaced at African Americans cemeteries – cemeteries that only inter African Americans due to Jim Crow regulations or due to purposeful ownership and operation. Historically, African American cemeteries have been purposely neglected, segregated and underfunded because society does not view them as sacred spaces part of America's national memory. Instead, these sacred spaces have been sacrificed in the name of urban planning that is supposed to enrich the American way of life. As a result, thriving Black communities and towns, where African American cemeteries were established, were gutted by highways and interstates and suburban neighborhoods. Cemeteries play a very important role in not just individual memory but also serve as important sites of national memory. Having our society recognize the importance of slave cemeteries and African American cemeteries – historic and Jim Crowed – helps America remember its African American death stories and therefore tell the pain of the truth.

Arguably what makes death so impactful on life is the cemetery because it plays a very important role in making sure the memory of that person, community and/or event lives on. In a society where Black life is devalued, nationally protected, respected and valued Black cemeteries are activism. The truth of this point comes in February 2019 when Representative Alma S. Adams introduced the African American Burial Grounds Network bill in order for these spaces to have federal dollars and federal protection to ensure their preservation and restoration. By making slave cemeteries part of the historical plantation tours instead of segregated knowledge, Americans can start to deal with and heal from the trauma of slavery. By recognizing historic Black cemeteries and Jim Crowed Black sections, Americans can start to understand how our society operates within the legacy of slavery and that racism did not end with the abolishment of slavery but was fortified in its aftermath.

Therefore, creating the cemetery memorial for all the African Americans who lost their lives to police shootings, the memorial doubled as a site of grief and mourning but moreover as a catalyst for how protestors could encourage social justice activism. Remembering those African Americans who died senselessly at the hands of white racist violence is radically powerful. The memory forces American whites to confront the racism, the whiteness and the culture of complicitness within and surrounding American death norms when it comes to the death of African Americans. It is in the memory that we fight for justice and it is in the memorial that protestors do the work to fight against systemic racism and oppression.

Along with allies, African Americans channeled their grief into activism becoming politicized change agents fighting for justice. African American deathways positioned death as resistance. And COVID-19 publicized and mobilized Black grief in unprecedented ways. White society bore witness to George Floyd's Homegoing. The gold casket, seen as ostentation according to white death norms, was his family memorializing him with the highest of honor and respect because African Americans have historically used death material culture to resist and use last rites as a tool to subvert the racist, stereotypes caricature of thug and brute. White society watched as Black people celebrated his life and used grief and mourning to continuously fight for justice.

Conclusion: Black feminist and womanist frameworks as ways through the crisis

Malcolm X once said that the most disrespected person in this society is the Black woman. Being a Black woman in what bell hooks calls the 'white supremacist capitalist patriarchy' (2004) is being in a position of constantly having to assess one's safety and the safety of one's community. The Combahee River Collective observed that a person living at the intersection of womanhood, Blackness and queerness experiences an even more complex layer of social oppression (Taylor, 2017). Intersectionality is about structural exposure and vulnerability to violence and Black women are more often put in a position in which they cannot afford to be death illiterate; plus, historically they have been those tending to the life-death-life cycle. Therefore, the current predicament cannot be undone without the perspective of the very population segment that is highly vulnerable to these structural violences.

During the height of the coronavirus outbreak, a news headline declared 'Black Women -The most vulnerable in the wake of the COVID-19 Global Pandemic' (Harris, 2020). As the article argued, Black women and women of color are most vulnerable to the systems of oppression amplified by the coronavirus, i.e. racial empathy gap and maternal health. Black women are then ground zero for addressing the devastation left in the wake of COVID-19 but not as passive subjects to be studied. Womanism and Black feminist theory provide frameworks that, taken together, are primed to push back on cultural necrophilia and address centuries-old racial inequality underlining American death culture.

Womanist Layli Phillips reminds that Black women's historical position and inclusive activism speaks for all members of humanity. Phillips writes that Black women:

> have developed the ability to think and reason using multiple perspectives simultaneously, moving in and out of different cognitive, ideological, cultural, emotional, social, or spiritual frames with relative ease – and the ability to harmonize and coordinate a variety of forms and methods of social movement to respond synthetically and with specificity to an ever changing variety of social problems and conditions (Phillips, 2006, p. xxxix).

Womanism allows Black women to address their problems while simultaneously addressing society's ills. Said another way, if the White Supremacy that undergirds American death culture is addressed by and for Black women, it ends up addressing it for the whole of society. More still, Black women's activism is inclusive. When sociologist Patricia Hill Collins (2002) coined the phrase 'Black Feminist Thought', she put forth a theory that cantered Black women, i.e. experiences, knowledge and heritage, and used this standpoint as the basis for Black women's empowerment and activism in all spaces we inhabit. As a standpoint theory, Black feminist theory is inclusive – at its core is a clear connection between Black women's consciousness and power that leads to an epistemology of truth for all oppressed groups. Black womaness that sits at the axis of intersectionality – class, race, sexuality, gender, nationality, religion, age is important to examining how oppressed. Black women – experiences, knowledge and heritage – is instrumental in post pandemic America.

A Black feminist/womanist analysis of big data regarding the pandemic is needed, because this approach centers the need of vulnerable communities right from the start. Considering the framework through which data was collected and assessed, and further who then gets to shape decisions and policies based on the interpretations, is incredibly important. Adopting a Black feminist/womanist lens for data evaluation is invaluable because it centers on the importance of care. That means the material realities of oppressed communities are not being overlooked and devalued anymore, instead their stories would be highlighted. Kim Gallon, founder and director of COVID Black, a Black Digital Humanities Collective located at Purdue University, argues that a 'Black feminist ethics of care' should be applied in looking at data. The Black feminist perspective of care isn't reduced and devalued to labor as within a white patriarchal capitalist context but rooted in the Black community and thus holds transformational power to better the lives of those struggling. This is accomplished by sharing power and engaging community partners. But this isn't all, she reminds us:

> Instead, data analysis derives its power and meaning from the community through call-and-response. Effective data analysis is not only cut

off when the community is unable to demonstrate its capacity to generate knowledge, it also loses its transformative potential (Gallon, 2020).

With this lens, the pitfalls of big data would be avoided because spreadsheets and graphs by design fail to reveal the gravity of the situation and lived experience. Gallon warns us:

> Thus, in as much as big data is valuable in identifying health disparities, it compresses Black humanity, a contested premise in the United States, into quantitative containers that offer a final dehumanizing insult in its inability to represent the Black lived experience (Gallon, 2020).

Badly interpreted data cannot lead to good policy change. Doing 'business as usual' won't help the U.S. recover from the devastating loss of lives in the year 2020 and beyond. A way towards a more equal and hopefully less lethal future is by telling these stories behind the data, telling the stories of those who have passed on and their survivors.

This is just a first step on a long road towards healing and the complexity of the situation demands to address many things simultaneously. We need to find ways to structurally make the invisible suffering seen and then find ways to offer support. Systematic changes in many areas of life, society and culture are needed to pull away from the influence of this death cult, this reckless, necrophile culture.

References

Ariès, P., 1974. *Western attitudes towards death: from the middle ages to the present.* Middlesex: Penguin Books.
Baldwin, J., 1985 [1963]. The fire next time. In Baldwin, J. (ed.), *The price of the ticket: collected nonfiction 1948-1985.* New York, NY: St. Martin's, pp. 333–379.
Bauman, Z., 1992. *Mortality, immortality and other life strategies.* Cambridge: Polity.
Bauman, Z., 2007. The reality principle and the pleasure principle strike a deal. In Elliott, A. (ed.), *The contemporary Bauman reader.* Milton Park and New York: Routledge, pp. 187–197.
Becker, E., 1973. *The denial of death.* New York, NY: The Free Press.
Berry, D.R., 2017. *The price for their pound of flesh: The value of the enslaved, from womb to grave, in the building of a nation.* New York, NY: Beacon Press.
Bonhomme, E., 2020. Racism: The most dangerous 'pre-existing condition'. *Aljazeera.* Available at: https://www.aljazeera.com/opinions/2020/4/16/racism-the-most-dangerous-pre-existing-condition/ (Accessed: 24 January 2021).
Branigin, A., 2020. Surgeon General Jerome Adams tells Black people to lay off alcohol, tobacco, and drugs to prevent COVID-19 deaths: 'Do it for your big mama'. *The Root.* Available at: https://www.theroot.com/surgeon-general-jerome-adams-tells-black-people-to-lay-1842797456 (Accessed: 24 January 2021).

Breuninger, K., 2020. Trump demands states 'LIBERATE' after he issues new coronavirus guidelines and protests pop up. *CNBC*. Available at: https://www.cnbc.com/2020/04/17/coronavirus-trump-demands-states-liberate-amid-protests.html (Accessed: 24 January 2021).

Brown, E., 2020. Black women have long faced racism in healthcare. COVID-19 is only amplifying it. *The Appeal*. Available at: https://theappeal.org/black-women-coronavirus-healthcare/ (Accessed: 24 January 2021).

Cann, C., 2014. *Virtual afterlives: grieving the dead in the twenty-first century.* Lexington, KY: Kentucky University Press.

Clark, J., 2020. Calm, cool, courageous: nursing and the 1918 influenza pandemic. *Barbara Bates Center for the Study of The History of Nursing Collection.* University of Pennsylvania School of Nursing. Available at: https://www.nursing.upenn.edu/history/publications/calm-cool-courageous/ (Accessed: 24 January 2021).

Collins, P.H., 2002. *Black feminist thought: knowledge, consciousness, and the politics of empowerment.* New York, NY: Routledge.

Darell, A. and Pyszczynski, T., 2016. Terror management theory: exploring the role of death in life. In Harvell A. and Nisbett G.S. (eds.), *Denying death: An interdisciplinary approach to Terror Management Theory.* New York, NY: Routledge, pp. 1–15.

Elias, N., 1985. *The loneliness of the dying.* Oxford: Blackwell.

Foster, G. and C. Eckert, 2003. Up from the grave: a sociohistorical reconstruction of an African American community from cemetery data in the rural midwest. *Journal of Black Studies*, 33(4), pp. 468–489.

Freud, S., 1961 [1920]. *Beyond the pleasure principle.* New York, NY: WW Norton & Company.

Freud, S., 1997 [1915]. *General psychological theory: theories of paranoia, masochism, repression, melancholia, the unconscious, the libido, and other aspects of the human psyche.* New York, NY: Touchstone.

Fromm, E., 1973. *The anatomy of human destructiveness.* New York, NY: Holt, Rinehart and Winston.

Gallon, K., 2020. 'Care' and COVID-19: a call for Black feminist data analytics, part II. *Medium – COVID Black*. Available at: https://medium.com/@ktgallon/care-and-covid-19-a-call-for-black-feminist-data-analytics-part-ii-77d903f0d9e2 (Accessed: 24 January 2021).

Greer, J.L., 2014. Historic home mortgage redlining in Chicago. *Journal of the Illinois State Historical Society*, 107(2), pp. 204–233.

Harris, I., 2020. Black women – the most vulnerable in the wake of the COVID-19 global pandemic. Women's Way. Available at: https://womensway.org/black-women-the-most-vulnerable-in-the-wake-of-the-covid-19-global-pandemic/ (Accessed: 24 January 2021).

Hill, M.L., 2020. Black women – the most vulnerable in the wake of the COVID-19 global pandemic. Women's Way. Available at: https://womensway.org/black-women-the-most-vulnerable-in-the-wake-of-the-covid-19-global-pandemic/ (Accessed: 24 January 2021).

Hooks, B., 2004. *The will to change: men, masculinity, and love.* New York, NY: Simon & Schuster.

Holloway, K., 2003. *Passed on: African American mourning stories: a memorial.* Durham, NC: Duke University Press.

Jackson, M., 1977. The Black experience with death: a brief analysis through Black writings. In Kalish, R. (ed.), *Death and dying: Views from many cultures*. New York and Amityville: Baywood Publishing Company.

Jones, M.M. and Saines, M., 2019. The eighteen of 1918-1919: black nurses and the great flu pandemic in the United States. *American Journal of Public Health*, 109(6), pp. 877–884.

Kellehear, A., 2007. *A social history of dying*. Cambridge: Cambridge University Press.

Keshavan, M., 2020. 'The direct result of racism': Covid-19 lays bare how discrimination drives health disparities among Black people. *STAT*. Available at: https://www.statnews.com/2020/06/09/systemic-racism-black-health-disparities/ (Accessed: 24 January 2021).

Krieger, N., Van Wye, G, Huynh, M., Waterman, P.D., Maduro, G., Li, W., Gwynn, R.C., Barbot O and Bassett, M.T., 2020. Structural racism, historical redlining, and risk of preterm birth in New York City, 2013-2017. *American Journal of Public Health*, 110(7), pp. 1046–1053.

Kübler-Ross, E., 1976. *On death and dying*. New York, NY: Macmillan Publishing.

Levenson, Z., 2017. Articulating Trumpism. *Berkeley Journal of Sociology*, 61, pp. 8–15.

Mrian Moser, J. and Saines, M., 2019. The eighteen of 1918-1919: Black nurses and the great flu pandemic in the United States. *American Journal of Public Health*, 109(6), pp. 877–884.

myarklamiss.com, 2019. Eudora residents not happy with water quality, city says work is being done to resolve it. *Nexstar, Inc*. Available at: https://www.myarklamiss.com/news/local-news/residents-not-happy-with-water-quality-city-says-work-is-being-done-to-resolve-it/ (Accessed: 24 January 2021).

Nardone, A.L., Casey, J.A., Rudolph, K.E., Karasek, D., Mujahid, M. and Morello-Frosch, R., 2020. Associations between historical redlining and birth outcomes from 2006 through 2015 in California. *PloS One*, 15(8), p. e0237241.

Owens, D.C., 2018. *Medical bondage: race, gender, and the origins of American gynecology*. Athens, GA: University of Georgia Press.

Phillips, L., 2006. *The womanist reader*. London, UK: Taylor & Francis.

Rosman, R., 2020. Racism row as French doctors suggest virus vaccine test in Africa. *Aljazeera*. Available at: https://www.aljazeera.com/news/2020/4/4/racism-row-as-french-doctors-suggest-virus-vaccine-test-in-africa (Accessed: 24 January 2021).

Solener, A., 2020. Armed protesters storm Michigan State House over COVID-19 Lockdown. *Forbes*. Available at: https://www.forbes.com/sites/andrewsolender/2020/04/30/armed-protesters-storm-michigan-state-house-over-covid-19-lockdown/?sh=4ab4a75d69b5 (Accessed: 24 January 2021).

Southall, A., 2020. Scrutiny of social-distancing policing as 35 of 40 arrested are Black. *The New York Times*. Available at: https://www.nytimes.com/2020/05/07/nyregion/nypd-social-distancing-race-coronavirus.html (Accessed: 24 January 2021).

Taylor, K., 2017. *How we get free: Black feminism and the Combahee River Collective*. Chicago, IL: Haymarket Books.

Victor, D., 2020. Coronavirus safety runs into a stubborn barrier: Masculinity. *The New York Times*. Available at: https://www.nytimes.com/2020/10/10/us/politics/trump-biden-masks-masculinity.html (Accessed: 24 January 2021).

Waraschinski, T., 2017. *The necrophile self: Contemporary attitudes towards death and its new visibility*. Dissertation. South Australia, SA: University of Adelaide. https://digital.library.adelaide.edu.au/dspace/bitstream/2440/113580/2/Waraschinski2018_PhD.pdf (Accessed: 24 January 2021).

Wheeler, T.B. and Broadwater, L., 2015. Lead paint: Despite progress, hundreds of Maryland children still poisoned. *Baltimore Sun*. Available at: https://www.baltimoresun.com/news/investigations/bs-md-lead-poisoning-gaps-20151213-story.html (Accessed: 24 January 2021).

Whitmer, G., 2020. The plot to kidnap me. *The Atlantic*. Available at: https://www.theatlantic.com/ideas/archive/2020/10/plot-kidnap-me/616866/ (Accessed: 24 January 2021).

Wright, E.A., 2005. Rhetorical spaces in memorial places: the cemetery as a rhetorical memory place/space. *Rhetoric Society Quarterly*, 34(4) pp. 51–81.

14 The biopolitics and stigma of the HIV and Covid-19 pandemics

Jason Schaub

Key points

- Different health scares create varying societal responses; when a small number of groups are at greater risk, increased stigma is applied to them.
- Governments and policymakers are interested in controlling and managing how individual citizens use their bodies through their lives, as these are mechanisms of creating resources.
- HIV-related stigma has significant effects on the grief experience, and contributes to disenfranchised grief, where loss is identified as illegitimate.
- There are some actions that can help individuals and communities respond to health scares, such as community action and engaging deliberately with healthcare initiatives.

Humans have experienced a series of widespread disease transmissions across the entirety of their existence; it is assumed that pandemics existed before there were written records. The more (in)famous of these pandemics killed millions and resulted in significant societal change. Each version of this trope is transmitted and affects populations differently. Bubonic plague was a bacterial disease that swept through Europe and Asia in 14th century, transmitted by being bitten by infected fleas. The Cholera pandemics travelled between Europe and Asia in the early 19th century and is a bacterial disease that often infects people through contaminated drinking water. The 1918 Flu pandemic (often erroneously called 'Spanish Flu') was a viral disease prominent between 1918 and 1920 and killed between 20 and 50 million people. Because of the lack of knowledge of how these were transmitted before modern scientific techniques, uncertain transmission mechanisms often caused re-affirmation of religion's centrality in society and an increased societal pressure to follow religious doctrine. Another effect of the spread of a deadly disease was an increased distrust of outsiders, as unfamiliar people could bring infection into a community from elsewhere (LaSala, 2020). As a result, when these diseases were spreading 'outsiders' were deemed more threatening than they were perceived to be during healthier times. These pandemics brought significant fear and reprisals of anyone that might increase the risk for a community.

More recently, the HIV pandemic's first cases were identified in early 1980s in gay men in the USA. Because of a long and inconsistent gestation period, it was difficult in this early phase to identify how HIV was transmitted. It affected people already marginalised by society: gay men and IV drug users, although had been present in other communities before it became known to Western public health officials (Greene, 2007). HIV was so strongly associated with gay men that one of the earliest names was gay-related immune deficiency (or GRID). Significant variation in infection rates for different populations resulted in considerable public shaming of 'lifestyle choices' that appeared to increase the likelihood of contracting the virus; earlier concerns centred around the use of amyl nitrate ('poppers') and a possible reaction to semen (Greene, 2007). HIV is now known to be transmitted through contact with bodily fluids, predominantly semen and blood, and does not infect people through surfaces (such as door handles) or aerosol (such as coughing). The public health responses, as a result of the high death rate and connection to specific populations, were grim and frightening, seeking to scare people into behavioural changes (such as using condoms or not sharing needles). Because of advances in treatment, it is now considered a chronic condition, and people living with managed HIV are expected to have a full life span, and when the virus is managed by medication, are unable to transmit the virus to others, even during unprotected sex (this is the basis of the U=U campaign) (Carter, 2020).

The HIV pandemic had significant physical effects on communities and individuals. Many thousands of people experienced a slow, torturous death from opportunistic infections with confusing presentations (such as infections previously unknown in humans). The lack of understanding about transmission routes resulted in significant discrimination and fear of those that were deemed 'high-risk'. Some partners were not allowed to visit sick patients, and there were challenges finding healthcare and funeral service providers (Loue and Lamb, 2020). The devastating impact on some populations gave rise to strong community action (Gessen, 2020), producing such organisations as ACT-UP (Gould, 2009). This community action responded to individuals' needs as well as more systemic political activism (Omoto and Crain, 1999). Activism often sought to improve the policy and healthcare responses, which were often ineffective, and can be interpreted as an indication of the lack of respect for the marginalised groups most affected by HIV.

Moving to the most recent pandemic in human history, Covid-19 was first identified in late 2019, following the rapid rise of respiratory illnesses and fatalities associated with the novel SARS-CoV-2 coronavirus (Jacob et al.,

2020). Given the outline of other chapters in this book, this chapter contains less detail about the general context of Covid-19. The disease was declared a global pandemic in March 2020 by the World Health Organisation (WHO). The novel coronavirus (Covid-19) has spread rapidly across the globe and is now known to be transmitted through contact with surfaces and from aerosol droplets. It was quickly identified as having greater impact on older people, but was much more easily transmitted than HIV, and the wider population felt more at risk from Covid-19 than from HIV (Loue and Lamb, 2020). Much of the safety felt by society during the HIV pandemic was because it was predominantly identified as a 'gay disease' and the bulk of society felt safe from this risk, feeling that they had no sexual contact with men who have sex with other men.

There are striking similarities in these last two examples. Both pandemics have been characterised by widespread uncertainty, challenges with identifying and treating the disease, sweeping health reforms, and pervasive illness and death which disproportionately affect people of Black and minority ethnicity (Millett, 2020; Quinn et al., 2020). Individual responsibility towards other people has been prominent across both pandemics (Loue and Lamb, 2020). Younger people have also received less attention and focus (both of prevention and treatment) (DeLong et al., 2020). Conspiracy theories have spread widely with deadly impacts. Behaviours that are deemed to increase transmission have been criminalised (Seiler et al., 2020). Families have not been allowed to visit sick loved ones in hospital (LaSala, 2020). Anxieties about asymptomatic people resulted in demands for mandatory (i.e. forced) quarantine for anyone infected (Loue and Lamb, 2020; National Research Council US, 1993) and of the healthcare workers working with them (Edelman et al., 2020).

When attempting to understand what can be learned from the HIV and Covid-19 pandemics and how they differ, conceptual frameworks are useful mechanisms to analyse the experience and societal responses. The following sections explore the concepts of biopolitics and stigma, and how they can help inform an analysis of the differing experiences and responses to these two pandemics. In addition, there are some lessons from the difficult experience of the HIV pandemic that can provide some suggestions for our current and future responses to Covid-19.

Biopolitics

Biopolitics (and its active form, *biopower*) is a concept explaining that political activities are organised around the propagation of life and, as a result, are significantly interested in controlling the body (Lemke et al., 2011). It is most famously associated with Michel Foucault; he outlined these concepts in *History of Sexuality* (1976a), although the term has been used by a range of scholars. Governments are interested in controlling the population's bodies because of the importance of physical action to producing resources

(Foucault, 1976b). Given the concept's focus on governmental organisation and control of the physicality of citizens, it is useful to apply to the pandemics under consideration here, HIV and Covid-19.

Before the current political structures of nation-states, society was organised around monarchies. Foucault suggested that during this time period, governments (as personified by the monarch) were simplistically engaged in the physical lives of their subjects and their primary options were to take one's life or allow one to live. He argued that this control has mutated in the current time period and that modern political structures have the 'power to "make" live and "let" die' (Foucault, 1976b, p. 241). Whilst the language is slightly stilted, as with all things Foucauldian, it is selected deliberately. The 'make' is important, as it relates to the deliberate engagement of political actors into the life actions of its citizens. The change required that governments examine (and seek to control) the ways that citizens' bodies act and interact, activity that is conceptualised as *biopower*. These forces are most prominently observed in health and healthcare (although not exclusively). In addition, modern political actors exert control on individual bodies as well as the population as a whole. For example, considering individual effects, HIV criminalisation around 'unsafe' sex; for Covid-19 this includes policies about mask-wearing; when considering societal-wide effects, in HIV this included slow policy responses encouraging medical treatments, for Covid-19 this includes nation-states controlling entry of those from outside. Foucault would describe this as the 'explosion of numerous and diverse techniques for achieving the subjugations of bodies and the control of populations' (1976, p. 140). It is important to point out that the mobilisation of this concept does not examine whether the control is beneficial to the citizens – that is not the determining factor, so whilst some of these controls reduce transmission and save lives, they can still be conceptualised as a place where the state engages in control over individual or societal bodies.

Biopolitics can be applied to an analysis of both pandemics when, during the HIV pandemic, political actors presented gay men as problematic (because of perceived promiscuity) and, therefore, deserving of the horrible death wrought by AIDS. More recently, these same actors consider whether protecting older people from Covid-19 is worth affecting children's schooling, given children's relatively safer experience of contraction and transmission (HM Government, 2020). A central component of biopolitics is that bodies are something to be managed and controlled and can be seen as 'a border that should be simultaneously respected and overcome, one that seems to be both natural and given but also artificial and transformable' (Lemke et al., 2011, pp. 4–5). Government actors are, therefore, concerned with how to manipulate and alter the ways that citizens' bodies move through their lives. It is helpful to reflect at this point that *biopower* here is typified by quarantines and government measures seeking to restrict the movement of bodies ('lockdown') which is affected by how individuals exert free will, such as by breaking these rules and seeking to make individual choices contrary to policy.

What is striking about these pandemics is that countries responded to them in ways that support the conceptualisations. For example, during the HIV pandemic, 'conservative ideas about the nation, race, and sexual behaviour stepped to the front' (Ailio, 2013, p. 261), and during Covid-19, the space expectations that were rapidly introduced to address transmission implications of close contact.

When political actors become focussed on individual bodies' activities, such as the use of condoms or mask-wearing, this creates anxiety in the individual, as policies are, by their creation, porous and imperfect, and individual activities are not perfectly represented (Hodson, 2020). For HIV policies considering condom use were only strictly applied to gay men, and if there were mistakes, then the responsibility for transmission resided with the men involved, not, for example, in the manufacturer of a faulty condom. There was not a corresponding blanket expectation that heterosexual couples would use condoms in every sexual encounter. Condoms can be equated with another body-covering measure, face masks, which have become significantly identified as part of the public health response to Covid-19). During the early phase of the Covid-19 pandemic, there was uncertainty about the benefits of mask-wearing (Martin et al., 2020). In addition, it can be difficult for people to accurately assess how close two bodies can be without a ubiquitous measuring tool, and individuals needed significant time to adjust to these new social norms. These changes increased anxiety in citizens, many of whom appeared to be trying to carefully follow the guidance but were uncertain as to whether they were doing so correctly. This anxiety encourages individuals to seek certainty, which can be translated into stigmatising societal scapegoats, either individuals or communities that are deemed to be 'dangerous' to the political body (Cohen, 1972). The differing presentations and experiences of this stigma are examined in the following section.

Stigma

HIV and Covid-19 laid bare some structural inequalities present in modern life, with marginalised populations bearing the brunt of both diseases. During both pandemics, society sought those to blame, and stigmatised those perceived as 'different', either nationally or socially. HIV had a devastating impact on Haitian communities (Malow et al., 2010), and people from Haiti were early identified as potentially at greater risk, causing significant retribution (Santana and Dancy, 2000). Covid-19, being first identified in China, has infamously been called the 'Chinese virus' by many including the-then American President Trump, with attacks and discrimination of Chinese-appearing individuals in Western countries as a result of this conflation (Human Rights Watch, 2020).

Table 14.1 Experiential and policy differences

HIV/AIDS	Covid-19
Slow and hyper specialised drug response that took over six years to develop.	Enormous and relatively speedy reaction (e.g. several vaccines in little more than a year).
Being HIV+ resulted in shame, even in the gay community – with responsibility for not practising safe sex.	Given the ubiquity of the virus and ease of transmission, everyone feels sympathy for coronavirus victims.
AIDS has a very high mortality rate, killing a majority of those that contracted HIV without treatment.	Covid-19 has a much lower mortality rate, and many people that contract it have no, or very mild, symptoms.
Healthcare workers were unlikely to contract HIV from working with patients (except for a few unfortunate workers who accidentally were contaminated with infected blood).	Health workers are highly vulnerable to coronavirus, and shortages of protective equipment only increase this vulnerability.
Anthony Fauci (Director of US National Institute of Allergy and Infectious Diseases) was seen as blocking the release of life-saving viral treatment drugs.	Anthony Fauci is seen as important to maintaining order and trust in scientific process.

*adapted from Greene, 2007; LaSala, 2020; White, 2020.

Whilst the two pandemics present with significant similarities, as seen above, there are notable divergences. These differences can be conceptualised as a result of differing levels of stigma, primarily because 'HIV reflects the health, moral and racial dimensions of stigma theorized by Goffman' (Logie, 2020, p. 1) (see Table 14.1).

The above table suggests people infected with Covid-19 experience less stigma likely because of widespread and easy transmission – how can a society apply stigma to every member? An example of the impact of stigma on the reaction to the disease was the disastrously slow development of effective treatment for HIV which caused thousands of infections and deaths. Vociferous activism sought to reach policymakers with little response for years. Some of the more famous actions were invading the Food and Drug Administration (FDA) building in an attempt to get the FDA to meet with people with HIV about allowing very unwell patients access to an experimental medication; another example was when hundreds of people converged on Wall Street and blocked traffic by lying in the street, with over 100 people being arrested – this last example was a frequently used tactic of 'street theatre' (Haldi, 1999) that can be analysed as an act of political activism using bodies (DeLuca, 1999) in a population's employment of biopolitics. Ronald Reagan, then president of the United States of America, did not mention HIV or AIDS until September 1985 (over four years after the initial concerns were raised), even though there had been years of multiple requests for engagement by public health officials. The shame experienced for contracting HIV or developing AIDS was presented as a result of poor lifestyle choices, and contrasting this to Covid-19, where the coronavirus is often described as impossible to avoid. The stigma applied during the HIV pandemic is only able to be created by society because of the perceived restricted nature of who is at risk, as identified above, this was originally identified as gay men and IV drug users. When a more widespread infection occurs and everyone is at risk, stigma is not able to be applied with as much focus and is diffused to a more generalised anxiety. This anxiety is therefore directed to outsiders, who are perceived to be bringing the infection into a location from elsewhere (as with Covid-19), rather than contracting (or spreading) the disease as a result of deviance (as with HIV).

The stigma experienced by those that contracted or died of HIV/AIDS meant that their grief was dismissed or invalidated by the surrounding society. Disenfranchised grief is a concept that originated in the work following the AIDS crisis and is useful to consider in relation to the differential presentation and experience of these pandemics. This theory and its applications are discussed by Doka in detail earlier in this volume (see Chapter 2). The term relates to grief that is perceived to be inappropriate, and the griever is encouraged to reduce their grief symptoms (Doka, 1989). Stigma has an effect on societal perceptions of the validity of grief, for example, during the HIV pandemic, grieving someone who died from AIDS could be invalidated by others because of the perceived 'responsibility' of the dead person for their actions, which society could perceive as deviant. During the HIV pandemic, there was also significant proximity stigma, as partners of those that died from AIDS were often perceived to have HIV without symptoms, and experienced stigma from wider society. The mourning process is identified as 'illegitimate and unnecessary' in disenfranchised grief (Green and Grant, 2008; McNutt and Yakushko, 2013). It is important to note that because 'AIDS-related deaths are untimely, not developmentally expected' there is less preparation for them than other, more expected types of death (Doka and Martin, 2010). In contrast, grievers of those that have sadly died from Covid-19 are not identified as having engaged in significant risk or deviance and are more likely to receive public support and validation of their grief. Without the stigma created as a result of the narrower population at risk as in HIV, grief related to Covid-19 is perceived as appropriate.

The disenfranchised grief of AIDS-related loss also includes a more personal poignancy, since grieving partners were often concerned that they may have contracted HIV from a deceased partner (Patlamazoglou et al., 2018). This additional burden creates a 'more intense and long lasting' connection to the deceased (Walter, 2003, p. 35). These situations can have complicated effects on the grief experience and can increase survivor guilt or AIDS-related death anxiety (Neimeyer and Anderson, 2002) as well as negative feelings towards the partner. In addition, there is evidence that the HIV-related stigma can affect non-AIDS-related partner bereavements (O'Brien, Forrest and Austin, 2002). This last means that even those deaths not related to HIV can be blighted by HIV stigma.

Lessons from HIV for the Covid-19 pandemic

Whilst these pandemics have not been experienced similarly because of the differing rates of infection and transmissibility, there are, nonetheless, areas of knowledge that can be applied from the HIV pandemic to the societal experience of Covid-19. It is important to acknowledge that healthcare knowledge has improved in the 40 years since HIV became a global concern, and the rapid deployment of resources to combat the worldwide threat of Covid-19 is an indication of this progression. The public health campaigns that have generally worked to address the effects of HIV inform and empower people, rather than shaming those that are identified as at risk because of deviance (Hodson, 2020). Another ineffective mechanism for combatting the spread is criminalising those infected or transmitting the disease (Molldrem, Hussain and McClelland, 2020). Improving the knowledge of the public will help them avoid infection and transmission. Public health campaigns that aim to provide clear, understandable guidance are effective. Communicating public health guidance has been a significant challenge in the UK's response to Covid-19, as the policy guidance has moved repeatedly and often with little notice.

Another important lesson that can be drawn from the HIV pandemic is the power and benefit of the fierce community response. This response had several arms: individual support to help those suffering from the disease and associated grief; community activities to address the effects of rapid human loss and societal change; and political activism to gain policymaker's attention and demand changes that improve (and save) lives. The community engagement and volunteering are often identified as 'a positive and empowering response to the HIV epidemic that developed within the gay community and has grown in scope to be critically important in society's response to HIV' (Omoto and Crain, 1999, p. 205). The engagement generated a worldwide community that developed internal support mechanisms, often because the community did not think that their needs would be met by policymakers. Whilst there have been some community responses to Covid-19, a more activated community response to support individuals may work to combat the more pernicious effects of the pandemic, namely isolation and anxiety (Miller, 2020). Returning to biopolitics for a moment, the lesson of community engagement can be conceptualised 'about the power of communities coming together to take care of one another, to touch one another, to act, using bodies – often frail bodies, always endangered bodies, sometimes even dead bodies – to fight' (Gessen, 2020, n.p.). The physical ramifications of these diseases are central to our responses, and society should engage as a community to address the bodily effect of the illness and associated grief, which can take varied forms depending on the duration of trauma and differing experiences of loss.

Interestingly, there is some evidence that gay men that lived through the HIV pandemic have some skills that can be usefully applied to the current pandemic (Quinn et al., 2020). This includes understanding the benefits of engaging in collective action, and experience of following new and complex public health protocols. This knowledge, while painfully gained, can be applied to the current pandemic and provided some men sense that they had the skills to manage the Covid-19 pandemic that their cis/heterosexual peers did not likely have. It would be helpful to consider how we could draw on this knowledge and apply it to current and future pandemics. People that lived through the HIV pandemic could provide examples of how to engage with community action as a way to combat increased anxiety from a lack of agency. It is also likely that if we drew on their experiences, this may go some way to reduce HIV-related stigma, by identifying how their knowledge can improve society.

Conclusion

It is helpful to examine how government actors engage deliberately into individual lives through controlling the body and are concerned with how the population is affected by health issue. Using *biopolitics*, this chapter has examined how both governments and individual citizens mobilise and interact in ways that are affected by changes to public health challenges. Whilst the two pandemics under examination in this chapter share some similarities (viral, global) there are marked differences, particularly in the stigma experienced by those at risk. When a narrower range of groups are identified as at risk, these groups are stigmatised by the wider society and behaviour that increases risk is ascribed with increased 'deviance'. It is important during health crises to balance public health priorities with individual responsibility, and there is a great deal that future pandemics can learn from previous experiences, such as these axioms drawn from the HIV crisis: to act as if you are infected, that everyone is at risk and that government and organisations cannot save you.

References

Ailio, J., 2013. Liberal thanatopolitics and the HIV/AIDS pandemic. *Alternatives*, 38(3), pp. 256–267.

Carter, M., 2020. U=U improves gay men's sense of self and many believe it will reduce HIV-related stigma. *NAM: aidsmap*. 11 November. Available at: https://www.aidsmap.com/news/nov-2020/uu-improves-gay-mens-sense-self-and-many-believe-it-will-reduce-hiv-related-stigma (Accessed: 4 October 2020)

Cohen, S., 1972. *Folk devils and moral panics: The creation of the mods and rockers*. Hove: Psychology Press.

DeLong, S.M., Denison, J.A., Yang, C., Agwu, A., Alexander, K.A., Kaufman, M.R. and Arrington-Sanders, R., 2020. From HIV to COVID-19: focusing on and engaging adolescents and young adults during the pandemic. *American Journal of Public Health,* 110(11), pp. 1650–1652. Doi: 10.2105/AJPH.2020.305915

DeLuca, K.M., 1999. Unruly arguments: the body rhetoric of earth first!, ACT UP, and Queer Nation. *Argumentation and Advocacy,* 36(1), pp. 9–21.

Doka, K.J., 1989. *Disenfranchised grief: Recognizing hidden sorrow.* Lexington: Lexington Books.

Doka, K.J. and Martin, T.L., 2010. *Grieving beyond gender: understanding the ways men and women mourn* (2nd ed.). Hoboken: Taylor & Francis Group.

Edelman, E.J., Aoun-Barakat, L., Villanueva, M. and Friedland, G., 2020. Confronting another pandemic: lessons from HIV can inform our COVID-19 response. *AIDS and Behavior,* 24, pp. 1977–1979. Doi: 10.1007/s10461-020-02908-z

Foucault, M., 1976a. *The history of sexuality* (Vol. 1). Paris: Éditions Gallimard.

Foucault, M., 1976b. *'Society Must Be Defended' Lectures at the College de France.* London: Picador Press.

Gessen, M., 2020. What lessons does the AIDS crisis offer for the coronavirus pandemic? *The New Yorker.* Available at: https://www.newyorker.com/news/our-columnists/what-lessons-does-the-aids-crisis-offer-for-the-coronavirus-pandemic. (Accessed: 4 November 2020).

Gould, D.B., 2009. *Moving politics: emotion and ACT UP's fight against AIDS.* Chicago: University of Chicago Press.

Green, L. and Grant, V., 2008. Gagged grief and beleaguered bereavements: an analysis of multidisciplinary theory and research relating to same sex partnership bereavement. *Sexualities,* 11(3), pp. 275–300. doi:10.1177/1363460708089421.

Greene, W.C., 2007. A history of AIDS: looking back to see ahead. *European Journal of Immunology,* 37(S1), pp. S94–S102.

Haldi, A., 1999. AIDS, anger and activism: ACT UP as a social movement organization. In Jo Freeman and Victoria Johnson (eds.), *Waves of protest: Social movements since the sixties*: Chapter 7. London, UK: Rowman & Littlefield, pp. 135–150.

Hodson, M., 2020. Safer breathing: how safe is 'safe'?. *Gay Men's Health Project* [blog]. 28 October. Available at: https://www.gmfa.org.uk/fs180-how-safe-is-safe.

HM Government, 2020. *Children's Task and Finish Group: Update to 4th Nov 2020 paper on children, schools and transmission.* London, England, UK: Scientific Advisory Group for Emergencies (SAGE).

Human Rights Watch, 2020. Covid-19 fueling anti-Asian racism and xenophobia worldwide: national action plans needed to counter intolerance. Available at: https://www.hrw.org/news/2020/05/12/Covid-19-fueling-anti-asian-racism-and-xenophobia-worldwide (Accessed: 20 October 2020).

Jacob, L., Smith, L., Butler, L., Barnett, Y., Grabovac, I., McDermott, D., Armstrong, N., Yakkundi, A., and Tully, M.A., 2020. Challenges in the practice of sexual medicine in the time of COVID-19 in the United Kingdom. *Journal of Sexual Medicine,* 17(7). Doi: 10.1016/j.jsxm.2020.05.001

National Research Council (US), 1993. 'Panel on Monitoring the Social Impact of the AIDS Epidemic'. In A.R. Jonsen and I. Stryker (eds.), *The social impact of AIDS in the United States.* Washington, DC: National Academies Press, pp. 117–157.

LaSala, M.C., 2020. Comparing COVID-19 and AIDS from a gay male perspective the not-so-hidden lessons of a pandemic. *Psychology Today.* Available at: https://www.psychologytoday.com/us/blog/gay-and-lesbian-well-being/202003/comparing-Covid-19-and-aids-gay-male-perspective. (Accessed 23 September 2020).

Lemke, T., Casper, M.J. and Moore, L.J., 2011. *Biopolitics: an advanced introduction*. New York City: NYU Press.

Logie, C.H., 2020. Lessons learned from HIV can inform our approach to COVID-19 stigma. *Journal of the International AIDS Society*, 23(5), p. e25504. Doi: 10.1002/jia2.25504

Loue, S. and Lamb, E., 2020. Retraumatized: COVID-19, the specter of HIV/AIDS, and reorienting responsibility. *Logos Universality Mentality Education Novelty: Philosophy & Humanistic Sciences*, 8(1), pp. 01–07. Doi: 10.18662/lumenphs/8.1/31

Malow, R., Rosenberg, R., Lichtenstein, B. and Dévieux, J.G., 2010. The impact of disaster on HIV in Haiti and priority areas related to the Haitian crisis. *The Journal of the Association of Nurses in AIDS Care: JANAC*, 21(3), pp. 283–288.

Martin, G.P., Hanna, E., McCartney, M. and Dingwall, R., 2020. Science, society, and policy in the face of uncertainty: reflections on the debate around face coverings for the public during COVID-19. *Critical Public Health*, 30(5), pp: 501–508.

McNutt, B. and Yakushko, O., 2013. Disenfranchised grief among lesbian and gay bereaved individuals. *Journal of LGBT Issues in Counseling*, 7(1), pp. 87–116. Doi: 10.1080/15538605.2013.758345.

Miller, E.A., 2020. Protecting and improving the lives of older adults in the COVID-19 Era. *Journal of Aging & Social Policy*, 32(4-5), pp. 297–309.

Millett, G.A., 2020. New Pathogen, Same Disparities: Why COVID-19 and HIV Remain Prevalent in US Communities of Color and Implications for Ending the HIV Epidemic. *Journal of the International AIDS Society*, e25639. Doi: 10.1002/jia2.25639

Molldrem, S., Hussain, M.I. and McClelland, A., 2020. Alternatives to sharing COVID-19 data with law enforcement: recommendations for stakeholders. *Health Policy*. [e-pub]. Doi: 10.1016/j.healthpol.2020.10.015.

Neimeyer, R. A., and Anderson, A., 2002. Meaning reconstruction theory. In N. Thompson (ed.), *Loss and grief*. New York, NY: Palgrave, pp. 45–64.

O'Brien, J. M., Forrest, L. M., and Austin, A. E. (2002) Death of a partner: Perspectives of heterosexual and gay men. *Journal of Health Psychology*, 7(3), pp. 317–328. Doi:10.1177/1359105302007003222

Omoto, A. and Crain, A.L., 1999. AIDS volunteerism: lesbian and gay community-based responses to HIV'. In T. G. Heckman (ed.), *AIDS, identity, and community: the HIV epidemic and lesbians and gay men. Archives of sexual behavior*. Thousand Oaks: Sage, pp. 187–209.

Patlamazoglou, L., Simmonds, J.G. and Snell, T.L., 2018. Same-sex partner bereavement: non-HIV-related loss and new research directions. *OMEGA-Journal of Death and Dying*, 78(2), pp. 178–196.

Quinn, K.G., Walsh, J.L., John, S.A. and Nyitray, A.G., 2020. 'I Feel Almost as Though I've Lived This Before': insights from sexual and gender minority men on coping with COVID-19. *AIDS and Behavior*, pp. 1–8. Doi: 10.1007/s10461-020-03036-4.

Santana, M.A. and Dancy, B.L., 2000. The stigma of being named 'AIDS carriers' on Haitian-American women. *Health Care for Women International*, 21(3), pp. 161–171.

Seiler, N.K., Vanecek, A., Heyison, C. and Horton, K., 2020. The risks of criminalizing COVID-19 exposure: lessons from HIV. *Human Rights Brief*, 24(1), Art. 3. pp. 5–17. Available at: https://digitalcommons.wcl.american.edu/hrbrief/vol24/iss1/3

Walter, T. (2003). Historical and cultural variants on the good death. *bmj*, 327(7408), pp. 218–220.

White, E., 2020. Fear, bigotry and misinformation – this reminds me of the 1980s Aids pandemic. *The Guardian*. 6 April. Available at: https://www.theguardian.com/commentisfree/2020/apr/06/1980s-aids-pandemic-coronavirus-gay-community-survive. (Accessed: 15 October 2020).

15 Suicide in the context of the COVID-19 pandemic

*Mohammed A. Mamun and
Jannatul Mawa Misti*

Key points

- COVID-19 pandemic has increased psychological suffering leading to more suicide incidences
- Unusual suicidal case (e.g. suicide pact) are also reported during the ongoing COVID-19 pandemic
- Fear of COVID-19, economic crisis, issues related to lockdown etc. are the prominent suicide casualties
- Implementing appropriate theories for a better understanding of suicide risk factors is needed

The COVID-19 pandemic and mental health

The ongoing pandemic, the Coronavirus Disease 2019 (COVID-19) has drastically altered the structure of people's way of living across the world. The COVID-19 is a physical condition that is caused by a newly emergent coronavirus called SARS-CoV-2. The virus was newly introduced on 31 December 2019, in Wuhan province, China (World Health Organization [WHO], 2020a). Following a report of a cluster of cases of 'viral pneumonia' in Wuhan, the WHO came to learn about the new virus. The most common symptoms of the COVID-19 infection include (i) fever, (ii) dry cough and (iii) fatigue; however, other symptoms that are less common and may affect some patients are: (i) loss of taste or smell, (ii) nasal congestion, (iii) conjunctivitis (i.e. red eyes), (iv) sore throat, (v) headache, (vi) muscle or joint pain, (vii) different types of skin rash, (viii) nausea or vomiting, (ix) diarrhea, (x) chills or dizziness etc. (WHO, 2020a). In the severe form of its infection, people experience (i) shortness of breath, (ii) loss of appetite, (iii) confusion, (iv) persistent pain or pressure in the chest and (v) high temperature (above 38 °C) (WHO, 2020a). Additionally, irritability, confusion, reduced consciousness (sometimes associated with seizures), depression, anxiety, sleep problems, more severe and rare neurological complications such as strokes, brain inflammation, delirium and nerve damage etc.; which are the frequently occurring symptoms related to psychological illness are also included as the COVID-19 symptoms by the WHO (2020a). Thus, it's evident that people infected with the virus have to suffer from psychological conditions.

Under the unexpected circumstances (e.g. surge in virus infection rate without availability of proper treatment or vaccine to control), the governments are advocating adopting some of the implementing programs to suppress the virus rapid transmission. The most common and effective preventive measures including restriction on social interaction and movement, alleviation on travelling, school closure, office closure, isolation for the virus infected cases, quarantine for the suspected cases etc. along with mandatorily maintaining personal hygiene practices, are being followed during the current pandemic like the previous outbreaks e.g. SARS in 2003, Ebola in 2014 etc. (Gualano et al., 2020; Leaune et al., 2020; Mamun and Griffiths, 2020a). There is no doubt for the effectiveness of the aforementioned strategies for suppressing the virus transmission. More evidently, 44% to 96% and 31% to 76%, COVID-19 incident and death rates, respectively, are estimated for these people having taken no quarantine measures (Nussbaumer-Streit et al., 2020). But, studies suggest people do not feel the necessity of being quarantined. A study in Toronto, Canada, conducted during the SARS outbreak in 2003 reported that 15% of the quarantined people do not think they should be placed into quarantine (Hawryluck et al., 2004). The same study also found elevated mental health problems among the quarantined people. Like this, all forms of separation like quarantine, isolation etc., imposes an emotional toll to people including depression, anxiety, stress, sleep problems, exhaustion, detachment, irritability, poor concentration, deterioration of work performance and so on (Hossain, Sultana and Purohit, 2020). And posttraumatic stress-related symptoms are most common after the quarantine period, even these problems persist after a long period; for example, three years after the quarantine period (Brooks et al., 2020; Hossain et al., 2020).

The rapidly changing situation related to the pandemic has drastically also altered the global economy. Besides, the uncertainties and fears related to the virus, along with mass lockdowns and economic recession, are alleged for elevated mental health sufferings (Krishnamoorthy et al., 2020; Pedrosa et al., 2020). In summary, the ongoing pandemic triggers the common mental health stressors including longer duration of quarantine, fear of being infected with the virus, frustration and boredom feeling, inadequate basic supplies, inadequate information and misinformation, stigma and financial constriction, making people psychologically more vulnerable (Brooks et al., 2020). Thus, people are experiencing more psychological comorbidities than 'normal' periods. For instance, a systematic review reports 40% as the pooled prevalence of poor sleep quality, 34%

stress and psychological distress, 30% insomnia, 27% post-traumatic stress symptoms, 26% anxiety and 26% depression (Krishnamoorthy et al., 2020). These sufferings diversely affect people belonging to the different groups. Group specific (including general population, students, schoolchildren, hospitality, sport and entertainment industry employees, elderly individuals, healthcare professionals, economically disadvantaged groups, homeless, prisoners, rural population and psychiatric patients etc.) mental health problems are discussed in more details by Khan et al. (2020) and Pedrosa et al. (2020).

What is suicide?

Suicide is ultimate direction of taking one's life, whereas the victims end their lives intentionally. In oppose, suicidal behaviour refers to the acts related to taking one's life. The stages of suicidal behaviour include (i) suicidal ideation or thoughts, (ii) suicide plan and (iii) suicide attempt (Klonsky, May and Saffer, 2016; Mamun et al., 2020b). A death by suicide has to cross these stages in a forward direction. As reported by the WHO (2020b), any typical suicide death is completed after more than 20 attempts. However, every 40 seconds there is at least one suicide occurred, which accounts nearly 800,000 deaths every year (WHO, 2020b). Suicide is regarded as the 18th leading cause of death, accounting 1.4% of all deaths globally (WHO, 2020b). However, suicide can be prevented by effective and evidence-based interventions focusing on different cohorts.

Prior pandemics and suicide

There is enough evidence on suicide rate increment during and following a pandemic (Leaune et al., 2020). For instance, significant suicide mortality increment is observed in the 1889–1894 Russian Influenza outbreak in Europe (United Kingdom, Ireland and France) (Smith, 1995), the 1918 influenza outbreak (Wasserman, 1992), and the 2003 SARS epidemic in Hong Kong (Cheung, Chau and Yip, 2008) However, in respect to the type of viral outbreak (like the ongoing COVID-19 outbreak) related suicide studies, available studies can be categorised into three types, that is, (i) Coronaviruses, (ii) Influenza viruses and (iii) Ebola virus (Leaune et al., 2020).

Coronaviruses related pandemic and suicide

Chan et al. (2006) and Cheung et al. (2008) found that suicide rate increased significantly; but the coronavirus seropositivity and suicide attempts relationship was not significantly found in the USA (Okusaga et al., 2011). In addition, drug overdose-related suicide attempters' visits to the emergency department has been reported by a non-significant increase trend during the peak of the 2003 SARS epidemic in Taiwan (Huang et al., 2005).

Influenza viruses related pandemic and suicide

In respect to influenza virus related outbreaks, Wasserman (1992) and Smith (1995) observed significant suicide increment during the pandemics, while influenza seropositivity B and suicide attempt was significantly associated, but not for seropositivity A in depressed individuals (Okusaga et al., 2011). But, non-adult individuals' suicide attempts in respect to being infected with influenza virus was found non-significant in the United States over five influenza seasons (2009–2013) (Harrington et al., 2018).

Ebola virus related pandemic and suicide

A study was conducted by Keita et al. (2017) observing the PostEboGui cohort in Guinea, where the cohort is under the observation of clinical, immuno-virological, psychological, and socio-anthropological effects of the Ebola virus infection for a 24-month period following discharge from the Ebola Treatment Center. The study found, one of the people having suicidal ideation, whereas three attempted suicide out of 256 subjects within 12 months of being discharged from the Ebola Treatment Centers (Keita et al., 2017).

Factors affecting the suicidality

There is dearth of epidemiological studies addressing the risk factor related to suicide mortalities. However, the available information suggests that suicide of females was found significantly higher during the 2003 SARS epidemic in Hong Kong (Chan et al., 2006), but the gender-based disparities in suicide mortality was diminished in the years to come in the same context (Cheung et al., 2008). There was no significant role of age, marital status, socio-economic status (e.g. unemployed and vice versa) in respect to suicide as reported by Yip et al. (2010). However, four risk factors are suggested based on prior studies, that is (i) fear of being infected (the first and most affecting factor), (ii) being socially isolated, (iii) empiercing normal life disruption and (iv) experiencing long-term illness burden (Cheung et al., 2008; Yip et al., 2010).

Suicide in the context of the COVID-19 pandemic

Adequate evidence suggests that there are profound psychological and social effects turned by the COVID-19 pandemic (John et al., 2020). The disruptions of social normal life, economic stability, including mental instabilities undoubtedly link with the common mediators leading suicidality and actual suicide occurrences.

Modelling approaches estimating suicide rate

There are a few studies forecasting the impact of the ongoing COVID-19 pandemic on suicide rates (John et al., 2020). These modelling approaches are based on district assumptions, whereas the impact of unemployment on suicide is mostly focused (Chang et al., 2013; Stuckler et al., 2009). Besides, the role of physical distancing measures is also considered in a study (Moser et al., 2020). For instance, a US study considered the three possible scenarios of unemployment rate changes, that is (i) no significant change (i.e. 3.6% for 2020, 3.7% for 2021); (ii) moderate increase reflecting the unemployment rates in 2008–2009 (i.e. 5.8% for 2020, 9.3% for 2021); and (iii) extreme increase (i.e. 24% for 2020, 18% for 2021). It is worthy of note that the suicide rate in the US was 14.8 per 100,000 in 2018; which is predicted (i) 15.7 for 2020 and 16.2 for 2021; (ii) 16.9 for 2020 and 17.5 for 2021; and (iii) 17.0 for 2020 and 17.4 for 2021, for respective scenarios (McIntyre and Lee, 2020). Similarly, 1% increment of global suicide is predicated by Kawohl and Nordt (2020); whereas the suicide rate risen is predicted 145% for Switzerland (Moser et al., 2020).

Suicidal behaviours: prevalence rate

There are limited epidemiological studies addressing the suicidal behaviours (i.e. suicidal ideation, suicide plan and suicide attempt) compared to other aspects of psychiatric epidemiology. Ammerman et al. (2020) conducting an online study via Amazon Mechanical Turk within 3–4 April 2020 among a total of 970 US general population, found 17.5% and 4.9% past-month active suicidal ideation and suicide attempt, respectively. Contradictorily, another two US studies conducted through Qualtrics Panels using quota sampling methods reported (i) 4.6% and 1.2% past-month suicidal ideation and suicide attempts, respectively, among 10,625 subjects (survey time: 18 March to 4 April) (Bryan, Bryan and Baker, 2020), (ii) 10.7% seriously considered suicide in past 30 days, among 5,412 subjects (survey time: 2 to 8 April) (Czeisler et al., 2020). In the end, these studies reporting different prevalence rate figures may be as of lack of representativeness of the sample and sampling strategies used.

Similarly, 18% and 5% of the UK participants reported experiencing suicide or self-harm thoughts and attempts, respectively, within the first month of lockdown (Iob, Steptoe and Fancourt, 2020). Another Colombian study observed 7.6% of the participants at a high suicide risk assessing by the four items CES-D-IS, where within a total score of 12, 9 was considered for the cutoff score (Caballero-Domínguez et al., 2020). There are two studies assessing COVID-19 related suicidal behaviours in Bangladesh, reported 5% to 6.1% suicidal behaviour aftermath the pandemic (Mamun et al., 2021, 2020a). While, 15.7% of the participants with mental suffering (vs. 0.9% control group; $p = 0.003$) reported having suicidality in China

(Hao et al., 2020); whereas 1.1% general people reported experiencing suicidal thoughts over several days by another study (Wu et al., 2020). Similarly, a 20.2% increment in suicidal behaviours is reported in a sample in Greece (Kaparounaki et al., 2020). A very non-representative sample, claimed 5.1% of global participants having suicidal ideation, although the study didn't specify how much time was considered for the suicidal ideation assessment (Sharif et al., 2020).

Risk factors related to suicidal behaviours

Although suicide is a complex phenomenon, where identifying its causality is yet considered as a gray zone. Some of the studies carried out investigating the risk factors related to suicidal behaviours during the COVID-19 pandemic. Off the studies, the risk factors leading suicidality can be categorised into three groups; (i) mental health, (ii) socio-economic and (iii) COVID-19 related issues. The common mental health issues included as anxiety (Lee, 2020), insomnia (Killgore et al., 2020b; Mamun et al., 2021), fear and worry relating to COVID-19 (Killgore et al., 2020b); loneliness (Killgore et al., 2020a); pre-existing mental illness history (Hao et al., 2020; Plomecka et al., 2020). However, in the sense of socio-demographics, young, female, not married, alcohol users, higher illness comorbidity, more social media users etc. were observed for higher suicidal ideation (Mamun et al., 2021). In addition, having less knowledge about COVID-19, engaging in less preventive COVID-19 behaviours, fear related to COVID-19 were identified for suicidality risk factors related to COVID-19 (Mamun et al., 2021). In contrast, no evidence of an increased risk of suicidality amongst those living in states with either stay-at-home orders or restrictions on large gatherings in place compared with states without these measures, but participants reporting ongoing arguments with a partner and serious legal problems and concerns about a life-threatening illness or injury were responsible for higher suicidal behaviours (Bryan et al., 2020).

Reasons of actual suicide occurrences

A number of case (or case series) studies published based on the press media reporting suicide news related to the COVID-19 pandemic. In the very early, Mamun and Griffiths (2020a) reported a Bangladeshi adult's suicide as of fear of contamination with the virus, and social negligence imposed by the victim native villagers. Later on, economic crises was reported for suicide causality by another Bangladeshi case-series study (Bhuiyan et al., 2020), which was also alluded in Pakistan (Mamun and Ullah, 2020). Additionally, fear of COVID-19 infection was reported the second most suicide reasons in Pakistan (Mamun and Ullah, 2020). But, Dsouza et al. (2020) investigated in India, a total of 69 suicide cases, which is the highest case-series study in COVID-19 context; the study observed that fear of COVID-19 infection as the prominent suicide causality accounting in a total of 21 cases and following this, economic crisis was reported in a total of 19-case. Other suicide reasons were reported to be (i) infected with the virus, (ii) xenophobia and social boycott, (iii) pressure to be quarantined, (iv) loneliness and missing family, (v) COVID-19 work-related stress, (vi) lack of alcohol access and (vii) feeling distressed because of exam postponement (Dsouza et al., 2020). These studies failed to identify any profession specific suicide reasons, which turned Mamun et al. (2020c) investigating a cohort-wise suicide analysis. Considering the situation, Indian celebrity suicides were analyzed, where depression was found as the main suicide reason, which is far different than the findings reported by other studies not considering the profession-wise suicidality risk factors.

In addition, there is a few studies that reported more than one suicide at a time, which can be generally referred to suicide pact. More specifically, six-suicidality pact cases were reported from Bangladesh, India, Malaysia, and the USA by Griffiths and Mamun (2020), whereas (i) fear of contamination, (ii) economic issue and (iii) missing family were found as the suicide reasons. Besides, a mother-son suicide pact was reported from Bangladesh, blaming online schooling related family conflicts (Mamun, Chandrima and Griffiths, 2020). In addition, infanticide-suicide pact from Saudi Arabia was reported, whereas retrenched from job and fear of being infected with COVID-19 was suspected for the suicide reasons (Mamun et al., 2020). Lastly, Mamun (2020) reported a very unusual suicide pact, that is triadic suicide pact, whereas an Indian whole family consisting with a total of three members, committed suicide. However, the suicide reasons were suggested to be (i) economic distress, (ii) feeling burden of disability and sick people and (iii) being stubborn as of not getting hospital treatment (Mamun, 2020).

Theories of suicide in the COVID-19 context

Suicide is a multiple, complex phenomenon and often misunderstood behaviour, which is usually linked with the interaction between the factors related to socio-demographic, family and personal history, stressful life events, and neurobiological (Klonsky et al., 2016; Mamun et al., 2020c; Mamun and Griffiths, 2020b). For understanding the suicidal behaviours to actual suicide occurrence, numerous theories explaining the direction of suicidality were proposed and explained from time to time. However, these theories can be separated into two categories (i. traditional approach and ii. ideation-to-action framework) based on the role of suicide risk factors (Klonsky et al., 2016). In the traditional approach, suicide risk factors are treated as a unitary construct; but differentiation between the factors of suicidal ideation and suicide attempt can be retrieved from the ideation-to-action framework (Klonsky et al., 2016; Klonsky and May, 2014). However, some of the suicide theories under the two-category are briefly discussed below.

Traditional approach

Suicide risk factors are treated in a manner of unitary construct in the traditional approach. That means, the theories belonging to this category failed to explain the differentiated role of suicide risk factor between the suicidal ideators and suicide attempters (Klonsky et al., 2016). Despite the limitations, these theories enormously help in conducting suicide research and adopting preventive approaches (Klonsky et al., 2016). Some of the major theories of suicide can be noted as (i) biological theory, (ii) psychodynamic theory, (iii) sociological theory, (iv) hopelessness theory, (v) psychache theory, (vi) escape theory and (vii) emotion dysregulation theory, to name a few (Selby, Joiner and Ribeiro, 2014). Biological theories tried to explain suicide resulting from genetic biological predispositions and life stressors; whereas the role of social isolation in suicide was emphasised in sociological theory; similarly, suicide is thought as the response of overwhelming pain in the psychache theory (Selby et al., 2014).

Ideation-to-action framework

For understanding of the suicide risk factors in respect to the development of suicidal ideation and the progression from ideation to suicide attempts, ideation-to-action framework is proposed (Klonsky et al., 2016). The theories belonging to this category are able to distinct the suicide predictors' role in suicidality, which helps tremendously for adopting suicide preventive approaches across different stages. To date, three theories (i. interpersonal theory of suicide, ii. integrated motivational-volitional theory and iii. three-step theory) are available explaining the ideation-to-action framework (Klonsky et al., 2016). According to the interpersonal theory of suicide, perceived burdensomeness and thwarted belongingness lead to suicidal ideation, and later on, suicide attempt happens if the ideators acquired capability for suicide (Selby et al., 2014). Defeat and entrapment, which are facilitated by threat-to-self and motivational moderators is the main factor causing suicidal ideation, and capability, impulsivity, planning, access to means, imitation and other volitional moderators are regarded as the factors causing progression from ideation to suicide attempts – based on the integrated motivational-volitional theory (Klonsky et al., 2016). Lastly, the most recent theory of suicide, that is three-step theory, explain combination of pain and hopelessness as the factors of occurring suicidal ideation, whereas dispositional, acquired, and practical contributors to increased capacity for suicide are regarded for further progression (Klonsky and May, 2015).

Concluding remarks

The present chapter highlights an overview on suicide related to the current COVID-19 pandemic. Although huge studies have been conducted assessing suicidal behaviours, there were no prior studies linking with any of suicide theories to the best of knowledge. But, suicide being a multiple complex phenomenon, which is usually misunderstood. Thus, implementing appropriate theories for better understanding of suicide risk factors in the context of COVID-19 outbreak is highly recommended. Such studies can be helpful in developing preventive measures for suicide. In this case, risk and protective factors for suicidal behaviours are supposed to be adequately understood. During and after the COVID-19 pandemic, the urgent implementation of suicide preventive approaches is of public health importance. In this regard, the present writing can be helpful in providing a better insight of suicide during the ongoing COVID-19 pandemic.

Acknowledgements

The authors would like to acknowledge that their affiliation, that is the Centre for Health Innovation, Networking, Training, Action and Research – Bangladesh (CHINTA Research Bangladesh) was formerly known as the Undergraduate Research Organization.

References

Ammerman, B.A., Burke, T.A., Jacobucci, R. and McClure, K., 2020. Preliminary investigation of the association between COVID-19 and suicidal thoughts and behaviors in the US. *Journal of Psychiatric Research*, 134, pp. 32–38. https://doi.org/10.1016/j.jpsychires.2020.12.037

Bhuiyan, A.K.M.I., Sakib, N., Pakpour, A.H., Griffiths, M.D. and Mamun, M.A., 2020. COVID-19-related suicides in Bangladesh due to lockdown and economic factors: Case study evidence from media reports. *International Journal of Mental Health and Addiction*, Epub ahead of print. https://doi.org/10.1007/s11469-020-00307-y

Brooks, S.K., Webster, R.K., Smith, L.E., Woodland, L., Wessely, S., Greenberg, N. and Rubin, G.J., 2020. The psychological impact of quarantine and how to reduce it: Rapid review of the evidence. *The Lancet*, 395, pp. 912–920. https://doi.org/10.1016/S0140-6736(20)30460-8

Bryan, C.J., Bryan, A.O. and Baker, J.C., 2020. Associations among state-level physical distancing measures and suicidal thoughts and behaviors among U.S. adults during the early COVID-19 pandemic. *Suicide and Life Threatening Behaviour*, 50, pp. 1223–1229. https://doi.org/10.1111/sltb.12653

Caballero-Domínguez, C.C., Jiménez-Villamizar, M.P. and Campo-Arias, A., 2020. Suicide risk during the lockdown due to coronavirus disease (COVID-19) in Colombia. *Death Studies*, pp. 1–6. https://doi.org/10.1080/07481187.2020.1784312

Chan, S.M.S., Chiu, F.K.H., Lam, C.W.L., Leung, P.Y.V. and Conwell, Y., 2006. Elderly suicide and the 2003 SARS epidemic in Hong Kong. *International Journal of Geriatric Psychiatry: A Journal of the Psychiatry of Late Life and Allied Sciences*, 21(2), pp. 113–118. https://doi.org/10.1002/gps.1432

Chang, S.-S., Stuckler, D., Yip, P. and Gunnell, D., 2013. Impact of 2008 global economic crisis on suicide: time trend study in 54 countries. *BMJ*, 347, p. f5239. https://doi.org/10.1136/bmj.f5239

Cheung, Y.T., Chau, P.H. and Yip, P.S.F., 2008. A revisit on older adults suicides and Severe Acute Respiratory Syndrome (SARS) epidemic in Hong Kong. *International Journal of Geriatric Psychiatry: A Journal of the Psychiatry of Late Life and Allied Sciences*, 23(12), pp. 1231–1238. https://doi.org/10.1002/gps.2056

Czeisler, M.É., Lane, R.I., Petrosky, E., Wiley, J.F., Christensen, A., Njai, R., Weaver, M.D., Robbins, R., Facer-Childs, E.R. and Barger, L.K., 2020. Mental health, substance use, and suicidal ideation during the COVID-19 pandemic—United States, June 24–30, 2020. *Morbidity and Mortality Weekly Report*, 69(32), p. 1049. https://doi.org/10.15585/mmwr.mm6932a1

Dsouza, D.D., Quadros, S., Hyderabadwala, Z.J. and Mamun, M.A., 2020. Aggregated COVID-19 suicide incidences in India: Fear of COVID-19 infection is the prominent causative factor. *Psychiatry Research*, 290, p. e113145. https://doi.org/10.1016/j.psychres.2020.113145

Griffiths, M.D. and Mamun, M.A., 2020. COVID-19 suicidal behavior among couples and suicide pacts: Case study evidence from press reports. *Psychiatry Research*, 289, p. e113105. https://doi.org/10.1016/j.psychres.2020.113105

Gualano, M.R., Lo Moro, G., Voglino, G., Bert, F. and Siliquini, R., 2020. Effects of Covid-19 lockdown on mental health and sleep disturbances in Italy. *International Journal of Environmental Research and Public Health*, 17(13), p. 4779. https://doi.org/10.3390/ijerph17134779

Hao, F., Tan, W., Jiang, L., Zhang, L., Zhao, X., Zou, Y., Hu, Y., Luo, X., Jiang, X. and McIntyre, R.S., 2020. Do psychiatric patients experience more psychiatric symptoms during COVID-19 pandemic and lockdown? A case-control study with service and research implications for immunopsychiatry. *Brain, Behavior, and Immunity*, 87, pp. 100–106. https://doi.org/10.1016/j.bbi.2020.04.069

Harrington, R., Adimadhyam, S., Lee, T.A., Schumock, G.T. and Antoon, J.W., 2018. The relationship between oseltamivir and suicide in pediatric patients. *The Annals of Family Medicine*, 16(2), pp. 145–148. https://doi.org/10.1370/afm.2183

Hawryluck, L., Gold, W.L., Robinson, S., Pogorski, S., Galea, S. and Styra, R., 2004. SARS control and psychological effects of quarantine, Toronto, Canada. *Emerging Infectious Diseases*, 10(7), pp. 1206–1212. https://doi.org/10.3201/eid1007.030703

Hossain, M.M., Sultana, A., and Purohit, N., 2020. Mental health outcomes of quarantine and isolation for infection prevention: a systematic umbrella review of the global evidence. *SSRN Electron*, pp. 1–27. https://doi.org/10.2139/ssrn.3561265

Huang, C.-C., Yen, D.H.-T., Huang, H.-H., Kao, W.-F., Wang, L.-M., Huang, C.-I. and Lee, C.-H., 2005. Impact of severe acute respiratory syndrome (SARS) outbreaks on the use of emergency department medical resources. *Journal of Chinese Medical Association*, 68(6), pp. 254–259. https://doi.org/10.1016/S1726-4901(09)70146-7

Iob, E., Steptoe, A. and Fancourt, D., 2020. Abuse, self-harm and suicidal ideation in the UK during the COVID-19 pandemic. *British Journal of Psychiatry*, 217, pp. 543–546. https://doi.org/10.1192/bjp.2020.130

John, A., Okolie, C., Eyles, E., Webb, R.T., Schmidt, L., McGuiness, L.A., Olorisade, B.K., Arensman, E., Hawton, K., and Kapur, N., 2020. The impact of the COVID-19 pandemic on self-harm and suicidal behaviour: a living systematic review. *F1000Research*, 9, p. 1097. https://doi.org/10.12688/f1000research.25522.1

Kaparounaki, C.K., Patsali, M.E., Mousa, D.P.V., Papadopoulou, E.V.K., Papadopoulou, K.K.K. and Fountoulakis, K.N., 2020. University students' mental health amidst the COVID-19 quarantine in Greece. *Psychiatry Research*, 290, p. 113111. https://doi.org/10.1016/j.psychres.2020.11311

Kawohl, W. and Nordt, C., 2020. COVID-19, unemployment, and suicide. *The Lancet Psychiatry*, 7, pp. 389–390. https://doi.org/10.1016/S2215-0366(20)30141-3

Keita, M.M., Taverne, B., Savané, S.S., March, L., Doukoure, M., Sow, M.S., Touré, A., Etard, J.F., Barry, M. and Delaporte, E., 2017. Depressive symptoms among survivors of Ebola virus disease in Conakry (Guinea): preliminary results of the PostEboGui cohort. *BMC Psychiatry*, 17, p. 127. https://doi.org/10.1186/s12888-017-1280-8

Khan, K.S., Mamun, M.A., Griffiths, M.D. and Ullah, I., 2020. The mental health impact of the COVID-19 pandemic across different cohorts. *International Journal of Mental Health and Addiction*, Epub ahead of print. https://doi.org/10.1007/s11469-020-00367-0

Killgore, W.D.S., Cloonen, S.A., Taylor, E.C. and Dailey, N.S., 2020a. Loneliness: A signature mental health concern in the era of COVID-19. *Psychiatry Research*, 290, p. 113117. https://doi.org/10.1016/j.psychres.2020.113117

Killgore, W.D.S., Cloonen, S.A., Taylor, E.C., Fernandez, F., Grandner, M.A. and Dailey, N.S., 2020b. Suicidal ideation during the COVID-19 pandemic: the role of insomnia. *Psychiatry Research*, 290, p. 113134. https://doi.org/10.1016/j.psychres.2020.113134

Klonsky, E.D. and May, A.M., 2014. Differentiating suicide attempters from suicide ideators: A critical frontier for suicidology research. *Suicide and Life-Threatening Behavior*, 44(1), pp. 1–5. https://doi.org/10.1111/sltb.12068

Klonsky, E.D. and May, A.M., 2015. The three-step theory (3ST): A new theory of suicide rooted in the 'ideation-to-action' framework. *International Journal of Cognitive Therapy*, 8(2), pp. 114–129. https://doi.org/10.1521/ijct.2015.8.2.114

Klonsky, E.D., May, A.M. and Saffer, B.Y., 2016. Suicide, suicide attempts, and suicidal ideation. *Annual Review of Clinical Psychology*, 12, pp. 307–330. https://doi.org/10.1146/annurev-clinpsy-021815-093204

Krishnamoorthy, Y., Nagarajan, R., Saya, G.K. and Menon, V., 2020. Prevalence of psychological morbidities among general population, healthcare workers and COVID-19 patients amidst the COVID-19 pandemic: A systematic review and meta-analysis. *Psychiatry Research*, 293, p. 113382. https://doi.org/10.1016/j.psychres.2020.113382

Leaune, E., Samuel, M., Oh, H., Poulet, E. and Brunelin, J., 2020. Suicidal behaviors and ideation during emerging viral disease outbreaks before the COVID-19 pandemic: A systematic rapid review. *Preventive Medicine*, 141, p. 106264. https://doi.org/10.1016/j.ypmed.2020.106264

Lee, S.A., 2020. Coronavirus anxiety scale: a brief mental health screener for COVID-19 related anxiety. *Death Studies*, 44, pp. 393–401. https://doi.org/10.1080/07481187.2020.1748481

Mamun, M.A., 2020. The first COVID-19 triadic (homicide!)-suicide pact: do economic distress, disability, sickness, and treatment negligence matter? *Perspective in Psychiatric Care*, Epub ahead of print. https://doi.org/10.1111/ppc.12686

Mamun, M.A. and Griffiths, M.D., 2020a. First COVID-19 suicide case in Bangladesh due to fear of COVID-19 and xenophobia: possible suicide prevention strategies. *Asian Journal of Psychiatry*, 51, p. 102073. https://doi.org/10.1016/j.ajp.2020.102073

Mamun, M.A. and Griffiths, M.D., 2020b. Mandatory Junior School Certificate exams and young teenage suicides in Bangladesh: a response to Arafat (2020). *International Journal of Mental Health and Addiction*, Epub ahead of print. https://doi.org/10.1007/s11469-020-00324-x

Mamun, M.A. and Ullah, I., 2020. COVID-19 suicides in Pakistan, dying off not COVID-19 fear but poverty?–The forthcoming economic challenges for a developing country. *Brain, Behavior and Immunity*, 87, pp. 163–166. https://doi.org/10.1016/j.bbi.2020.05.028

Mamun, M.A., Chandrima, R.M. and Griffiths, M.D., 2020. Mother and son suicide pact due to COVID-19-related online learning issues in Bangladesh: an unusual case report. *International Journal of Mental Health and Addiction*, Epub ahead of print. https://doi.org/10.1007/s11469-020-00362-5

Mamun, M.A., Bhuiyan, A.K.M.I. and Manzar, M.D., 2020. The first COVID-19 infanticide-suicide case: financial crisis and fear of COVID-19 infection are the causative factors. *Asian Journal of Psychiatry*, 54, p. 102365. https://doi.org/10.1016/j.ajp.2020.102365

Mamun, M.A., Akter, T., Zohra, F., Sakib, N., Bhuiyan, A.K.M.I., Banik, P.C. and Muhit, M., 2020a. Prevalence and risk factors of COVID-19 suicidal behavior in Bangladeshi population: are healthcare professionals at greater risk? *Heliyon*, 6, p. 05259. https://doi.org/10.1016/j.heliyon.2020.e05259

Mamun, M.A., Rayhan, I., Akter, K. and Griffiths, M., 2020b. Prevalence and predisposing factors of suicidal ideation among the university students in Bangladesh: a single-site survey. *International Journal of Mental Health and Addiction*, Epub ahead of print. https://doi.org/10.1007/s11469-020-00403-z

Mamun, M.A., Siddique, A.B., Sikder, M.T. and Griffiths, M.D., 2020c. Student suicide risk and gender: a retrospective study from Bangladeshi press reports. *International Journal of Mental Health and Addiction*, Epub ahead of print. https://doi.org/10.1007/s11469-020-00267-3

Mamun, M.A., Sakib, N., Gozal, D., Bhuiyan, A.K.M.I., Hossain, S., Bodrud-Doza, M., Al Mamun, F., Hosen, I., Safiq, M.B. and Abdullah, A.H., 2021. The COVID-19 pandemic and serious psychological consequences in Bangladesh: a population-based nationwide study. *Journal of Affective Disorders*, 279, pp. 462–472. https://doi.org/10.1016/j.jad.2020.10.036

McIntyre, R.S. and Lee, Y., 2020. Preventing suicide in the context of the COVID-19 pandemic. *World Psychiatry*, 19, pp. 250–251. https://doi.org/10.1002/wps.20767

Moser, D.A., Glaus, J., Frangou, S. and Schechter, D.S., 2020. Years of life lost due to the psychosocial consequences of COVID-19 mitigation strategies based on Swiss data. *European Psychiatry*, 63(1), e58. https://doi.org/10.1192/j.eurpsy.2020.56

Nussbaumer-Streit, B., Mayr, V., Dobrescu, A.I., Chapman, A., Persad, E., Klerings, I., Wagner, G., Siebert, U., Ledinger, D. and Zachariah, C., 2020. Quarantine alone or in combination with other public health measures to control COVID-19: a rapid review. *Cochrane Database of Systematic Reviews*, Epub ahead of print. https://doi.org/10.1002/14651858.CD013574.pub2

Okusaga, O., Yolken, R.H., Langenberg, P., Lapidus, M., Arling, T.A., Dickerson, F.B., Scrandis, D.A., Severance, E., Cabassa, J.A. and Balis, T., 2011. Association of seropositivity for influenza and coronaviruses with history of mood disorders and suicide attempts. *Journal of Affective Disorders*, 130, pp. 220–225. https://doi.org/10.1016/j.jad.2010.09.029

Pedrosa, A.L., Bitencourt, L., Fróes, A.C.F., Cazumbá, M.L.B., Campos, R.G.B., de Brito, S.B.C.S. and e Silva, A.C., 2020. Emotional, behavioral, and psychological impact of the COVID-19 pandemic. *Frontiers in Psychology*, 11, p. 2635. https://doi.org/10.3389/fpsyg.2020.566212

Plomecka, M.B., Gobbi, S., Neckels, R., Radziński, P., Skórko, B., Lazerri, S., Almazidou, K., Dedić, A., Bakalović, A. and Hrustić, L., 2020. Mental health impact of COVID-19: a global study of risk and resilience factors. *Frontiers in Psychiatry*, 11, p. 581426. https://doi.org/10.3389/fpsyt.2020.581426

Selby, E.A., Joiner Jr., T.E. and Ribeiro, J.D., 2014. Comprehensive theories of suicidal behaviors. In *The Oxford Handbook of Suicide and Self-Injury*. Oxford Library of Psychology. Oxford University Press, New York, NY, US, pp. 286–307. https://doi.org/10.1093/oxfordhb/9780195388565.013.0016

Sharif, S., Amin, F., Hafiz, M., Benzel, E., Peev, N.A., Dahlan, R.H., Enchev, Y., Pereira, P. and Vaishya, S., 2020. COVID 19-depression and neurosurgeons. *World Neurosurgery*, 140, pp. e401–e410. https://doi.org/10.1016/j.wneu.2020.06.007

Smith, F.B., 1995. The Russian Influenza in the United Kingdom, 1889–1894. *Social History of Medicine*, 8(1), pp. 55–73. https://doi.org/10.1093/shm/8.1.55

Stuckler, D., Basu, S., Suhrcke, M., Coutts, A. and McKee, M., 2009. The public health effect of economic crises and alternative policy responses in Europe: an empirical analysis. *The Lancet*, 374, pp. 315–323. https://doi.org/10.1016/S0140-6736(09)61124-7

Wasserman, I.M., 1992. The impact of epidemic, war, prohibition and media on suicide: United States, 1910–1920. *Suicide and Life-Threatening Behavior*, 22(2), pp. 240–254.

World Health Organization, 2020a. Coronavirus Disease (COVID-19). Available at: https://www.who.int/emergencies/diseases/novel-coronavirus-2019/question-and-answers-hub/q-a-detail/coronavirus-disease-covid-19 (Accessed: 18 December 2020).

World Health Organization, 2020b. Mental health and substance use: suicide data. Available at: https://www.who.int/teams/mental-health-and-substance-use/suicide-data (Accessed: 12 February 2021).

Wu, C., Hu, X., Song, J., Yang, D., Xu, J., Cheng, K., Chen, D., Zhong, M., Jiang, J. and Xiong, W., 2020. Mental health status and related influencing factors of COVID-19 survivors in Wuhan, China. *Clinical and Translational Medicine*, Epub ahead of print. https://doi.org/10.1002/ctm2.52

Yip, P.S.F., Cheung, Y.T., Chau, P.H. and Law, Y.W., 2010. The impact of epidemic outbreak: the case of severe acute respiratory syndrome (SARS) and suicide among older adults in Hong Kong. *Crisis: The Journal of Crisis Intervention and Suicide Prevention*, 31(2), pp. 86–92. https://doi.org/10.1027/0227-5910/a000015

16 Death and dying during the COVID-19 pandemic: the Indian context

Apurva Kumar Pandya and Khyati Tripathi

Key points

- The COVID-19 pandemic has resulted in large number of deaths and disrupted essential death rituals.
- Deaths from COVID-19 have provoked collective and prolonged grief which has become a public health concern.
- The grief associated with COVID-19 death has significant psychological repercussions for the bereaved. This chapter brings out issues around death and grief in the COVID-19 pandemic especially with respect to the religion-specific death rituals and the stigma attached with the COVID dead bodies.
- It builds discussion on the handling of COVID-19 dead bodies and questions the concept of 'dignity in death' in the Indian context.
- From a public health perspective, the concept of death, dying and grief should be acclimatised within clinical and institutional contexts. Health care providers need to be sensitised to respond to grief in the current pandemic climate.
- The need to normalise conversations about death and dying by promoting death literacy and dialogue in public spaces to enhance the potential of creating the compassionate communities is emphasised, too. Lastly, implications for therapeutic practice and research are discussed.

Introduction

The COVID-19 pandemic has questioned the concept of 'dignity in death'. Losing a loved one to the pandemic is tragic indeed but not being able to give the dead a dignified farewell is even more heart wrenching for the family and relatives. The death rituals form an inevitable part of the process. It would be apt to say that rituals have a psychological significance for the bereaved. Rituals and practices surrounding death and dying help the bereaved to overcome grief (Jahangir and Hamid, 2020). These rituals and ceremonies aid the bereaved to express their feelings, offer a significant, culturally normative map for the expressions of emotions while helping them adjust without the deceased person to some extent (Adams, 2020; Pietkiewicz, 2012; Mohanty, 2003). However, the pandemic has altered these rituals and religious customs around death and dying throughout the world. The funeral services have been carried out with restrictions in place, particularly with respect to the body-specific death rituals performed for the deceased (for example, cleansing of the body) and the number of people allowed to attend the funeral. Given the communicable nature of the virus, 'distance' is being maintained with the 'infectious' body. Thus, also restricting the 'normal' bereavement and grief process that entails saying goodbye to the dead via physical touch (of his/her cold lifeless body), being in close proximity with the deceased or by simply attending the deceased's funeral in person.

In this chapter, the authors examined the changing nature of death, dying and mourning due to the COVID-19 pandemic in India especially with respect to the religion-specific death rituals, 'dignity in death' and the stigma attached with the COVID dead bodies. For the same, the authors rapidly reviewed existing literature on the topic and mapped newspaper articles on the theme. Also, two cases have been used as the primary source of data in the study. Lastly, the chapter discusses the implications of this knowledge on therapeutic practice and research.

Changing the nature of death, dying and mourning in COVID-19

In order to mitigate the effects of the pandemic, safety measures such as social distancing, restrictions on social movements and visits to the healthcare institutions have been commonly put into practice (Wallace et al., 2020). In various health care institutions, the infected patients have been kept in isolation with an aim to reduce the spread of the virus. Though quarantining is an important part of the process, but less attention has been paid to the potential repercussions of the same on the mental health of the patients, as well as their families (Hamid and Jahangir, 2020). Patients with severe infection are dying in isolation in absence of their loved ones. In cases where the infected individuals are taken care of at home, visits from the extended family members and relatives are rare because of the social distancing regulation in place (Ingravallo, 2020). In both the situations, the dying person and the bereaved feel helpless, unable to provide comfort to each other.

Throughout the world, new guidelines and policies for the management of the dead bodies, funerals and burials have been implemented to contain the spread of the infection (Wallace et al., 2020). The Indian Government also released guidelines with respect to funerals (burials and cremations) amid the COVID-19 pandemic on 15 March 2020 (Government of India, Ministry of Health and Family Welfare, 2020). These guidelines indicate that only immediate family members are allowed to participate in these ceremonies provided the social distancing rules are followed (maintaining a distance of at least 2 meters). The number of people attending the funeral have also been restricted to a maximum of 20. Those with COVID-19 symptoms or in quarantine are not allowed to attend funerals. No rituals involving any physical contact with the deceased like touching, hugging or cleansing can be performed. In rare cases, few of the bereaved can take part in the last rites, provided they wear Proper Protective Equipment (PPE). While on the one hand, this regulation might have contributed to controlling the spread of COVID-19, on the other, it has definitely complicated the experiences of grief (Wallace et al., 2020).

In India, reports began surfacing within a week of mandatory social distancing painting a distressing scenario of people dying alone in hospital beds, away from their loved ones; of families being unable to unite to bid a loved one goodbye because they live in different parts of the city, or country, of undignified treatment to dead bodies; of the suspicion and stigma that follows those who survive the deceased, because neighbours and outsiders speculate and whisper the possible cause of death. The findings of the study conducted in Kashmir, India revealed that the deceased mostly died in isolation and mourning the loss was highly challenging in the absence of in-person support (Hamid and Jahangir, 2020). The inability to perform the last rites added yet another layer of grief which resulted in prolonged grief among the bereaved and impacted their overall wellbeing (Hamid and Jahangir, 2020).

Death rituals, stigma and coping in the era of COVID-19

Death rituals can vary greatly from culture to culture, often depending on religion, traditions, and beliefs. Each society has its own customs and rituals for death and mourning (Mohanty, 2003). Although, there are differences in death rituals across cultures, the common thread that runs through these culture-specific rituals is cohesion and social connection (Weir, 2020). Rituals and practices surrounding death and dying help the bereaved to overcome grief (Jahangir and Hamid, 2020). These rituals and ceremonies apart from playing other roles like honouring the deceased, as per the religious beliefs and preparing the deceased for their journey to the 'other' world, also help the bereaved cope with the emotion of loss (Hamid and Jahangir, 2020; Pietkiewicz, 2012).

Stigma attached to the COVID dead bodies

Death is considered to be a taboo topic, conversations about which are considered to be unsavory in many cultures. But contradictorily, the rapid spread of the COVID-19 pandemic and deaths across the globe resulted in the fear of death and it became an important topic of discussion, as Pentaris (2020) mentioned in one of the seminars on COVID-19 death and dying, 'the pandemic has brought death to our doorstep'. The pandemic did not just forcefully assimilate 'death' in our lives but also provoked social stigma and discriminatory behaviours against the infected patients and dead bodies. The disposal of the COVID dead bodies has also been met with a lot of resistance and caused heated debates across the country. Their funerals have been protested against by the people living around the cemeteries and crematoria fueled by the fear of contracting the infection from the 'burning' (among Hindu) or the 'buried' (among Muslim and Christian) dead body (Johari, 2020). Instances of stigma associated with dead bodies have been documented such as a driver denying transporting the 'infected' dead bodies to burial sites or crematoria and mishandling of dead bodies by hospital staff while burying or cremating (Biswas, 2020; Mehta, 2020). Though WHO (2020) released the guidelines for preventing and addressing stigma associated with COVID-19, however, it does not talk about the stigma related with COVID-19 dead bodies. In many instances, mishandling of dead bodies were commonly reported. During the initial months, due to space constraints in the hospitals and long waiting hours to cremate the bodies in the designated crematoria, corpses started piling-up in hospitals in different cities (Joshi, 2020). Often relatives were not informed about the death or misinformed. These are in contrast with the constitutional provision. In the Indian Constitution, the Article 21 considers mishandling of dead bodies as a violation. The Indian Supreme Court had to intervene eventually and directed the Government to ensure dignity in death by disposing off the bodies respectfully.

Religion-specific death rituals

Most funerals in India are faith-based and guided by the community guidelines unlike the funerals in the UK or the US where people of different faiths can 'choose' to cremate the dead. In India, the mourning rituals take place in an elaborate fashion and aim at short-term needs of the bereaved. However, loss and grief can have long-term effects. The feeling of grief continues to impact the bereaved person long after the religiously and socially observed period of mourning has ended. The social support for the bereaved is limited; religious rituals often spread from 13 to 40 days and few rituals are performed once in a year. Following two cases illustrate the scenario of death rituals during the pandemic and the associated coping (or the lack of it).

Death rituals in Islam (Shia Muslim, Central Gujarat): case 1

This case is about a young Indian man, 46-year-old, Asif (pseudonym) whose father succumbed to COVID-19 unexpectedly during the lockdown (phase 3.0). Being a doctor, Asif volunteered as part of a medical team with Municipal Corporation during the lockdown and post-lockdown in containment zones near his residential area. During his volunteering tenure, he and his father, both contracted the infection and were under isolation at home. However, his father (86 years old) had severe symptoms requiring hospitalisation. His father was initially denied hospitalisation at a Government Hospital. With a lot of effort, admission was secured in a hospital and he was put on a ventilator. As per the protocol, COVID-19 dead bodies were either buried or cremated based on the deceased's religion by the hospital staff. The bodies were cremated/buried without involving the families of deceased to help keep them safe from the infection.

After three days of hospitalisation, Asif's father died. Collective bathing of the dead body, enshrouding the dead body in white cotton cloth, funeral prayer and burial are important rituals in Islam after death. However, these rituals were not followed, and Asif's father's dead body was buried in a special graveyard dedicated for COVID-19 burials.

Asif was burdened with guilt; he considered himself responsible for his father contracting the infection. He carried anger and self-hatred for not being around his father to take care of him during his last moments and could not attend the last rites as he was in quarantine.

Rituals that consist of *ghusl* or washing of dead bodies, *kafan* or shrouding the body with pieces of cloth and finally *salat al-janazah*, i.e. a funeral prayer are obligatory in the Islam. To cope with the guilt and intrapsychic conflicts imposed by not performing rituals, Asif paid more attention to the performing rituals for the peace of his father's soul. He read the Quran and watched YouTube lectures of Shia *Imam* (Islamic priest). According to him, in Islam, three days of mourning is observed by increased devotion, receiving visitors and condolences. However, lockdown due to COVID-19 did not allow relatives to visit his place, he received condolences over voice calls and video calls. He poured his emotions out to one of his colleagues who encouraged him to express. He started praying five times a day, offered food to those in need, and started fasting. He visited his father's graveyard each day with flowers for 40 days and apologised for his inability to have provided a dignified farewell to his father.

After a month of his father's death, Asif discovered that Imam declared COVID-19 pandemic as a war and hence those dying in this pandemic/war are to be considered as martyrs. This gave great relief to Asif that his late father will be identified as a martyr which instilled some dignity for his father in death which Asif had assumed was lost completely.

Death rituals in Hinduism (Brahmin, South Gujarat): case 2

Seema (pseudonym), 45 years old, lost her husband to COVID-19. He was suffering from a rare cancer and during his treatment was diagnosed with COVID-19. She urged the doctor, as well as the hospital administrator to allow her to meet her husband as she wanted to spend some time with him. But as per the protocol, unfortunately, she was not permitted. After her husband died, she was allowed to see his body but from a distance. She longed to sit beside him and caress him but felt completely helpless.

She was shook by her husband's death and felt disoriented given the daunting responsibilities of managing a business, supporting the education of her younger son and impending marriage of a daughter. She was inundated with sorrow and the guilt of not having been able to take enough care of her husband in his last days. She stopped eating and the absence of rituals took away the opportunity for her to express her warmth and care for her husband vicariously by engaging in the ritualistic actions which could have given her the feeling of 'having done something' for him.

In Hinduism, the dead body is cleansed by the family members or others very close to the deceased. The body is covered in shrouds and dressed in flower garlands (Davies, 2017). According to the Hindu death rituals, the body should remain at the home until cremated within 24 hours of death which is referred to as *Antyesti*. It is customary for family and friends to visit the home of the bereaved to offer their condolences. This also enables the bereaved, as well as the visitors to share their grief and stories about the deceased. Seema felt that rituals were not followed, and her husband's dead body was cremated hastily by the authorities in her absence. She could not give him a befitting farewell. In Hindu Brahmins belonging to Gujarat, on the third day, *Beshnu* is organised at home. On this day relatives visit and *bhajans* or hymns are sung. The bereaved are allowed to mourn and express their sorrows with each visitor. But during the extended lockdown (when a gathering of more than 20 people was not allowed), Beshnu was organised virtually using Google Meet. This online experience of Beshnu, however, was not as impactful as Seema felt bereft of the personal 'physical' space to express her emotions and connect with the fellow mourners.

Traditionally, the Hindu mourning period ranges from 13 to 40 days and the family performed the yearly *shraddh* to remember the deceased. Throughout this time, families display a picture of their loved one as a symbol of his vicarious presence, adorned with a garland of flowers. Visitors are welcomed during this period. On the 13th day of mourning, it's common for the grieving family to hold a ceremony *(termu)* where they perform rituals to help release the soul of the deceased in the presence of relatives. Given the pandemic, all the rituals were performed in the presence of close family members only. Relatives interacted with the bereaved over telephone or via video calls, the unusualness of which suck out the comfort to express one's pain of losing a loved one.

Reflections on case scenarios: theoretical perspective

Grief and bereavement are unavoidable, multidimensional and complex experiences (Gesi et al., 2020; Zhai and Du, 2020). The grief in the COVID-19 pandemic occur against the backdrop of multiple losses such as loss of everyday routine, financial stability, and social life. All of these have added to the complexity to grief and bereavement. While unexpected illness is linked to anticipatory grief, the fear of what the future may hold after a loved one's demise can lead to complicated grief (Shore et al., 2016). Researches have acknowledged the fact that the grief associated with COVID-19 death has significant psychological repercussions on the bereaved (Goveas and Shear, 2020; Menzies, Neimeyer and Menzies, 2020; Simon, Saxe and Marmar, 2020) and can also trigger the onset or relapse of psychiatric and physical disorders (Fried et al., 2015)

Indeed, COVID-19 has restricted the expression of grief. Although in Islam and Hinduism, death is accepted and viewed as a natural part of life, stigma associated with COVID-19 death and unique treatment of COVID dead bodies as different from the non-COVID dead bodies has propelled guilt and anger. Both case scenarios have represented multiple emotional, cognitive, and behavioural reactions after a loss (Worden, 2018). Anticipatory grief occurred in the second case scenario more explicitly. Anticipatory grief occurs prior to a loss, as distinguished from grief occurring at or after a loss (Aldrich, 1974). Complicated grief was a central theme and emerged in both case scenarios. Complicated grief entails (1) a sense of disbelief regarding the death; (2) anger and bitterness over the death; (3) intense yearning and longing for the deceased; and (4) preoccupation with thoughts of the deceased that often include distressing and intrusive thoughts related to the death (Shear et al., 2005). However, Shear et al. have not explained adjustment with grief and normalisation process. Kübler-Ross's (1969) five-stage theory of grief explains the different stages of grief. The five-stages that the theory discusses are denial, anger, bargain, depression and acceptance. Asif and Seema, both (as presented in case scenarios) experienced feelings of disbelief for what had happened for some time and were angry for not being allowed to participate in the funeral. Both of them expressed resentment and guilt for not taking enough care of the deceased. Finally, with time, both of them adapted coping strategies such as daily activities and rituals and navigated their grief journey. The construction of meaning was key for dealing with grief, in both the cases (Neimeyer and Sands, 2011).

Both tried to bargain with the health system to gain more time with the loved one. Asif convinced the hospital administrator to allow him to meet his father once and being a health professional, he was allowed to meet him wearing PPE whereas, in the case of Seema, she yearned to be with her husband but was allowed to see him from a distance. Hall (2011) claimed that loss provides the possibility of life-enhancing 'post-traumatic' growth as the individual integrates the lessons of loss and resilience. This process was echoed in the case scenarios as both individuals adapted religious activities to cope with the situation. These coping responses were aligned with the 'dual-process model' proposed by Stroebe and Schut (1999). This model conceptualises grief process as an oscillation between two modes, a 'loss orientation' mode when the griever engages in emotion-focused coping, and a 'restoration orientation' mode when the griever engages in problem-focused coping. For example, five times *namaaz,* reading Quran etc., and chanting and praying incessantly were religious coping strategies adopted by both of them. Furthermore, the use of technology (e.g. phone/video calls) and conversations with colleagues played an important role for Asif in helping him express his grief. In case scenario two, close family members and relatives facilitated the expression of grief for the bereaved Seema.

Historically, grief is theorised as an individual, intrapsychic phenomenon (Granek, 2010; Hamilton, 2016; Hall, 2011), paying less attention to the impacts of wider social and public health contexts and processes that shape the experience of grief (Breen et al., 2020; Neimeyer, Klass and Dennis, 2014). Lately, Macdonald (2020) proclaimed that society in general is grief-denying. The experience of grief can be compounded by the common, socially awkward, and maladapted responses to grief (Breen et al., 2019). Further, the COVID-19 pandemic is acknowledged as the scariest public health emergency where millions of bereaved people worldwide have been left behind (Gesi et al., 2020). It has impacted the social and community functioning. Therefore, the approach to address grief and bereavement need to focus on the larger society from public health perspective, rather than just individual.

With the fear of transmission of the coronavirus and as per the COVID-19 protocols, mourning is no longer the collective experience as it used to be. A son could not perform last funeral rites personally, wife could not hug the body of her husband and a bereaved son was unable to attend the last rites of a parent. Death rituals (for example, ghusl, kafan and salat al-janazah in Islam; antyesti and beshnu in Hinduism; or cleansing and dressing-up the body in both Islam and Hinduism) were either omitted or witnessed virtually. There were instances where families were denied opportunities to say goodbye before a death or had the choice to only say goodbye over the phone or via a video call. These are instances of roadblocks to bereavement and grief and how people navigate through grief. Being consoled is an important aspect of grief but in the COVID-19 era, it is often skipped that makes grief and bereavement more challenging (Ramadas and Vijayakumar, 2020).

Dying with dignity in the times of COVID-19

Dying with dignity has been a challenge during the COVID-19 pandemic. This pandemic has in many cases robbed people off the opportunity to say a final goodbye to their loved ones. It has deprived the deceased of their dignity and has heightened the grief of those left behind. The pandemic has left patients isolated in hospitals to die alone, without the presence of close family members. A recent systematic review reported that hospitalised patients placed in isolation for medical reasons were more likely to experience loneliness, depression, anxiety, anger, and loss of self-esteem (Chochinov, Bolton and Sareen, 2020). Furthermore, less time spent with them by health care providers adversely impact patient recovery (Chochinov et al., 2020). Studies have shown that loneliness is a risk factor not only for mental disorders (Abad, Fearday and Safdar, 2010) but may also generate fear of death. Lack of social support, distress, and not feeling valued or respected, especial in hospital settings, can undermine a dying patient's sense of dignity (Chochinov, 2007).

Implications for practice and research

The complex and rapid changes from COVID-19 impact the experience of grief. With increasing transmission of COVID-19 across the world, it is expected to experience fear of death while more deaths toll at unprecedented rates. The number of people experiencing anticipatory grief and complicated grief increases continuously. In order to preserve dignity, care-safeguard the connectedness between relatives and COVID-19 inpatients and to improve the communication between medical staff and relatives, it is important to keep family members updated about the patient's health developments, and eventually allowing visitations (with proper precautions) as the condition gets worse. This can lower the psychological impact on the bereaved during the current pandemic. It can protect the dignity of patients who are dying, as well. Differential treatment and isolation may cause a sense of disrespect and distress not only among COVID-19 patients (Cazeau, 2020) but also among their loved ones and family members. Therefore, ensuring respectful management and disposal of dead bodies is imperative. Existing mental health services and psychosocial support helplines need to be responsive to the fear of death and facilitate the overcoming of anticipatory and complicated grief. Chochinov (2007) studied the ABCD (Attitude, Behaviour, Compassion and Dialogue) of dignity conserving care which ensured dignified death and facilitated grief among the bereaved. This approach enabled health care providers with compassionate dialogues with patients that facilitated expression of anticipatory grief of patients and eased grief of the bereaved. Recognising, responding, and validating emotional responses is effective in addressing anticipatory grief of patients, family members and friends (Shore et al., 2016). Approaching difficult conversations directly (e.g. discussing emotions, grief, overall patient and family distress, desired ritual or spiritual practices) and discussions of funeral plans are recommended as 'advanced care planning conversations' (Hui and Bruera, 2014; Rogne, 2013). Research by Wallace and colleagues (2020) has shown that the way dying patients perceive themselves is reflective of health care provider attitudes toward them. This is the most ardent predictor of maintaining dignity. Further, connecting families to resources to help them consider post-death planning needs and referral to additional grief support through telehealth services is an important consideration to mitigate grief (Wallace et al., 2020).

Health care providers play an important role in dignity-conserving care of patients, as well as support patients' family members navigate bereavement amidst this and any future pandemic. In this context, healthcare providers need to be oriented on dignity-conserving care, quality communication by incorporating this topic in the routine training and COVID-19 related training programmes. Considering the long-lasting nature of the pandemic and the possibility of future pandemic, dignity-conserving care should be planned in advance and the curriculum of medical, nursing and psychiatry education should be provisioned accordingly. Importantly, healthcare providers' self-care should not be undermined as healthcare providers also face grief (Nelson and Kaminsky, 2020). Healthcare providers' self-care should be part of dignity-conserving care programme to enable healthcare provider to manage their grief. Self-awareness was endorsed as a key strategy for health care providers to overcome stress and grief (Kearney et al., 2009). In 2017, Gibson shared some self-care strategies for disaster responders to help them cope with stress and grief. These include being able to take breaks, feeling prepared and informed in facilitating your response role, being aware of local resources and services to refer patients for additional recovery assistance, and having adequate supervision and peer support. More interventions around dignity-conserving care are needed to generate evidence around the same. The longitudinal study of COVID-19 impact on bereaved can be insightful in understanding a resilient trajectory.

The death rituals form an inevitable part of culture. The non-performance of certain essential death rituals like the cleansing of the body or getting together with the extended family to mourn has psychological impact on the bereaved. As suggested by Ramadas and Vijayakumar (2020), bereaved should be allowed sufficient time to say goodbye, adhering to the COVID-19 safety protocols; religious rituals as per the needs of the family should be facilitated incorporating safety protocols. Restricted visits and virtual family meetings should be encouraged. Culturally sensitive and religiously appropriate alternative rituals should be documented and promoted.

Specialised mental health services (online or onsite) which are appreciative of religious and spiritual rituals could foster healthy coping. Future studies need to assess effectiveness of spiritual and religious practices in alleviating psychological distress and facilitate grief process. Promoting research on death and developing protocols or standards for counselling and psychotherapeutic practice, as well as healthcare practice for end-of-life care of patients and their loved ones is warranted.

It is important to re-iterate what Breen and colleagues (2020) have anticipated – a grief literate society. Generating grief literacy can augment the concept of death and grief process, thereby further enhancing the potential of the compassionate society. Hopefully, this chapter provides useful information and helpful insights into a major life event affecting everyone at some stage in their lives especially in the context of COVID-19 pandemic in India.

References

Abad, C., Fearday, A. and Safdar, N., 2010. Adverse effects of isolation in hospitalized patients: a systematic review. *The Journal of Hospital Infection*, 76(2), pp. 97–102. https://doi.org/10.1016/j.jhin.2010.04.027

Adams, K.M., 2020. Part 1: Ritual and grief in the time of COVID-19. The conversation project. Available at: https://theconversationproject.org/tcp-blog/ritual-and-grief-in-the-time-of-covid-19 (Accessed: 2 January 2021).

Aldrich, C.K., 1974. Some dynamics of anticipatory grief. In Schoenberg, B., Carr, A.C., Kutscher, A. H., Peretz, D. and Goldberg, I. (eds.), *Anticipatory grief*. New York, NY: Columbia University Press, pp. 3–9.

Biswas, S., 2020. Our neighbors made us COVID-19 pariahs. BCC News. Available at: https://www.bbc.com/news/world-asia-india-53418762 (Accessed: 2 January 2021).

Breen, L.J., Szylit, R., Gilbert, K.R., Macpherson, C., Murphy, I., Nadeau, J.W., Reis, E., Silva, D., Wiegand, D.L. and International Work Group on Death, Dying, and Bereavement, 2019. Invitation to grief in the family context. *Death Studies*, 43(3), pp. 173–182. Doi: 10.1111/j.1467-6427.2010.00495.x

Breen, L.J., Kawashima, D., Joy, K., Cadell, S., Roth, D., Chow, A. and Macdonald, M.E., 2020. Grief literacy: A call to action for compassionate communities. *Death Studies*, pp. 1–9. Doi: 10.1080/07481187.2020.1739780

Cazeau, N., 2020. Social Isolation: Managing psychological distress in hospitalized patients during the COVID-19 pandemic. *Clinical Journal of Oncology Nursing*, 24(5), pp. 472–474.

Chochinov, H.M., 2007. Dignity and the essence of medicine: the A, B, C, and D of dignity conserving care. *BMJ*, 335(7612), pp. 184–187.

Chochinov, H.M., Bolton, J. and Sareen, J., 2020. Death, dying, and dignity in the time of the COVID-19 pandemic. *Journal of Palliative Medicine*, 23(10), pp. 1294–1295. https://doi.org/10.1089/jpm.2020.0406

Davies, D., 2017. *Death, ritual and belief: The rhetoric of funerary rites*. London, UK: Bloomsbury Publishing.

Fried, E. I., Bockting, C., Arjadi, R., Borsboom, D., Amshoff, M., Cramer, A.O., Epskamp, S., Tuerlinckx, F., Carr, D. and Stroebe, M., 2015. From loss to loneliness: The relationship between bereavement and depressive symptoms. *Journal of Abnormal Psychology*, 124(2), pp. 256–265. https://doi.org/10.1037/abn0000028

Gesi, C., Carmassi, C., Cerveri, G., Carpita, B., Cremone, I., Dell'Osso, L., 2020. Complicated grief: What to expect after the coronavirus pandemic. *Frontiers in Psychiatry*, online. 11, 489. https://doi.org/10.3389/fpsyt.2020.00489

Gibson A., 2017. An inquiry into older disaster responders' secondary traumatic stress. *Innovation in Aging*, 1(Suppl 1), pp. 1016–1017. https://doi.org/10.1093/geroni/igx004.3691

Government of India, Ministry of Health and Family Welfare, 2020. COVID-19: Guidelines on dead body management. Available at: https://www.mohfw.gov.in/pdf/

1584423700568_COVID19GuidlinesonDeadbodymanagement.pdf&ved=2ahUKEwj UqO6ZupqAhXLSH0KHcliCZEQFjAAegQIAhAB&usg=AOvVaw1NFmG1Wo_ s5c6LPccHUM6t&cshid=1595510789171 (Accessed: 28 November 2020).

Goveas, J.S. and Shear, M.K., 2020. Grief and the COVID-19 pandemic in older adults. *The American Journal of Geriatric Psychiatry*, 28(10), pp. 1119–1125. https://doi.org/10.1016/j.jagp.2020.06.021

Granek, L., 2010. Grief as pathology: the evolution of grief theory in psychology from Freud to the present. *History of Psychology*, 13(1), pp. 46–73. https://doi.org/10.1037/a0016991

Hall, C., 2011. Beyond Kübler-Ross: recent developments in our understanding of grief and bereavement. *InPsych*, 33(6). Available at: https://www.psychology.org.au/publications/inpsych/2011/december/hall/ (Accessed: 8 January 2021).

Hamid, W. and Jahangir, M.S., 2020. Dying, death and mourning amid COVID-19 pandemic in Kashmir: a qualitative study. *OMEGA—Journal of Death and Dying*, online. https://doi.org/10.1177/0030222820953708

Hamilton I.J., 2016. Understanding grief and bereavement. *The British Journal of General Practice*, 66(651), p. 523. https://doi.org/10.3399/bjgp16X687325

Hui, D. and Bruera, E. (eds.), (2014). *Internal medicine issues in palliative cancer care*. England, Oxford: Oxford University Press.

Ingravallo, F., 2020. Death in the era of the COVID-19 pandemic. *Lancet Public Health*, 5(5), p. e258. https://doi.org/10.1016/S2468-2667(20)30079-7

Jahangir, M.S. and Hamid, W., 2020. Mapping mourning among Muslims of Kashmir: analysis of religious principles and current practices. *OMEGA—Journal of Death and Dying*, online. https://doi.org/10.1177/0030222820911544

Johari, A., 2020. No dignity in death: How ignorance, irrational fears are obstructing coronavirus funerals. www.scroll.in. Available at: https://scroll.in/article/960101/no-dignity-in-death-how-ignorance-irrational-fears-are-obstructing-coronavirus-funerals. (Accessed: 8 January 2021).

Joshi, S., 2020. Mishandling of dead bodies. Available at: https://www.vice.com/en/article/5dz373/covid-19-%20%20has-overwhelmed-indias-ability-to-dispose-of-its-dead (Accessed: 7 January 2021).

Kearney, M. K., Weininger, R. B., Vachon, M. L., Harrison, R. L., and Mount, B. M., 2009. Self-care of physicians caring for patients at the end of life: Being connected... a key to my survival. *JAMA*, 301(11), pp. 1155–E1. https://doi.org/10.1001/jama.2009.352

Kübler-Ross, E., 1969. *On death and dying*. New York, NY: Macmillan.

Macdonald, M.E., 2020. The denial of grief: Reflections from a decade of anthropological research on parental bereavement and child death. In M.H. Jacobsen and A. Petersen (eds.), *Exploring grief: towards a sociology of sorrow*. London, UK: Routledge, pp. 125–149.

Mehta, S., 2020. Stigma shrouds bodies of COVID patients. Times of India. Available at: https://timesofindia.indiatimes.com/city/visakhapatnam/ashes-cant-contain-virus-can-be-given-to-relatives-after-cremation-say-docs/articleshow/76986945.cms. (Accessed: 8 January 2021).

Menzies, R., Neimeyer, R. and Menzies, R., 2020. Death anxiety, loss, and grief in the time of COVID-19. *Behaviour Change*, 37(3), pp. 111–115. doi:10.1017/bec.2020.10

Mohanty, S.B., 2003. Death rituals and practices of the Hill Saora of Orissa [Doctoral dissertation, Utkal University].

Neimeyer, R. and Sands, D., 2011. Meaning reconstruction in bereavement: from principles to practice. In Neimeyer R, Winokuer H., Harris D. and Thornton, G., (eds.), *Grief and bereavement in contemporary society: bridging research and practice*. New York, NY: Routledge, pp. 9–22.

Neimeyer, R.A., Klass, D. and Dennis, M.R., 2014. A social constructionist account of grief: loss and the narration of meaning. *Death Studies*, 38(6–10), pp. 485–498. https://doi.org/10.1080/07481187.2014.913454

Nelson, B. and Kaminsky, D.B., 2020. COVID-19's crushing mental health toll on health care workers. *Cancer Cytopathology*, 128(9), pp. 597–598.

Pentaris, P., 2020. *COVID-19 death and dying- Let's talk now to take firm actions*. Organised by Gored Action Services, University of Greenwich and The Collective for Radical Death Studies. 29th May 2020 (Online).

Pietkiewicz, I., 2012. Burial rituals and cultural changes in the polish community—A qualitative study. *Polish Psychological Bulletin*, 43(4), pp. 288–309.

Ramadas, S. and Vijayakumar, S., 2020. Disenfranchised grief and Covid-19: How do we make it less painful? *Indian Journal of Medical Ethics*, Online. https://doi.org/10.20529/IJME.2020.128

Rogne, L. (ed.), 2013. *Advance care planning: communicating about matters of life and death*. New York, NY: Springer Publishing Company.

Shear, K., Frank E, Houck, P.R. and Reynolds, C.F., 2005. Treatment of complicated grief: a randomised controlled trial. *JAMA*, 293(21), pp. 2601–2608.

Shore, J.C., Gelber, M.W., Koch, L.M. and Sower, E., 2016. Anticipatory grief: an evidence-based approach. *Journal of Hospice & Palliative Nursing*, 18(1), pp. 15–19.

Simon, N.M., Saxe, G.N., Marmar, C.R., 2020. Mental health disorders related to COVID-19–related deaths. *JAMA*, 324(15):1493–1494. doi:10.1001/jama.2020.19632

Stroebe, M. and Schut, H., 1999. The dual process model of coping with bereavement: rationale and description. *Death Study*, 23(3), pp. 197–224.

Wallace, C.L., Wladkowski, S.P., Gibson, A. and White, P., 2020. Grief during the COVID-19 pandemic: Considerations for palliative care providers. *Journal of Pain and Symptom Management*, 60(1), pp. e70–e76. https://doi.org/10.1016/j.jpainsymman.2020.04.012

Weir, K., 2020. Grief and COVID-19: Saying goodbye in the age of physical distancing. *American Psychological Association*. Available at: https://www.apa.org/topics/covid-19/grief-distance (Accessed: 28 November 2020).

Worden, J.W., 2018. *Grief counseling and grief therapy: a handbook for the mental health practitioner*. New York, NY: Springer Publishing Company.

WHO, 2020. A guide to preventing and addressing social stigma associated with COVID. Available at: https://www.who.int/publications/m/item/a-guide-to-preventing-and-addressing-social-stigma-associated-with-covid-19?gclid=CjwKCAjwrKr8BRB_EiwA7eFapr1uAotDtqyOwihwsjUUtK0bP4V672A6ezQduTl3SyGUVKSRJJgVkBoCg_oQAvD_BwE (Accessed: 8 January 2021).

Zhai, Y. and Du, X., 2020. Loss and grief amidst Covid-19: a path to adaptation and resilience. *Brain, Behaviour and Immunity*, 87, pp. 80–81. https://doi.org/10.1016/j.bbi.2020

Index

Note: *Italicized* page numbers refer to figures, **bold** page numbers refer to tables

Abdulwahab, I.M. 21
ACT-UP 230
Adams, A.S. 222
advanced care planning (ACP) 111–113
African American Burial Grounds Network bill 222
African Americans 1–2, 10, 209–211; and antebellum immuned Black body 219; Black feminist/womanist frameworks 223–225; Black grief 221–223; COVID-19 deaths 218–220; and death denial 217; deathways 218–223; Jim Crow laws 222; and White supremacy 214–217
age: and coronavirus anxiety 42, 43, 46, 50; and COVID-19 vulnerability 1–2, 17, 148; and governments' response to COVID-19 198–199; inequalities based on 22; and social death 84, 90; *see also* older people
agency 48, 49, 84; loss of/ reduced 84, 91; political 63; self-agency 49; and social death 61, 82, 84–86, 89
Agency of Integrated Care 143
AIDS *see* HIV/AIDS
alcohol use 30, 166
Alzheimer's disease 201
amendable mortality 78
anticipatory grief 260; *see also* grief in COVID-19 pandemic
Antyesti 259
anxiety 2, 9, 30, 169; in context of COVID-19 41–42
APM Research Lab 1
Araya, R. 162
Ariès, P. 18, 212

Asians 1
assembly, limitations on 32, 35
assisted dying 9–10, 178–190; as act of compassion 182–185; in Canada 180–181, 183–184; legal developments 179–181; in Netherlands 179, 185; overview 178–179; patients 185–187; practical application of 181–182; and telemedicine 187–188; in the UK 180; and value of human lives 188–189
assisted suicide 9–10, 178; in United States 182; *see also* suicide
AstraZeneca 4
asymptomatic cases 30
Atlas Obscura 69
The Atrocity Paradigm (Card) 83
avoidable mortality 77, 78–80, 87–88, 89–90
awareness context 81

Baldwin, J. 216
Bangladesh 171; suicide reasons in 246
Barber, A. 221
Bauman, Z. 86, 211, 213
Becker, E. 211, 213–214
Beechside Home 152
Belgium, assisted dying in 180
bereavement 168–170, 260–261
Berry, D.R. 217
Beshnu 259
Beveridge Report (1942) 123
Beyond the Pleasure Principle (Freud) 212
bhajans 259
Biehl, J. 85
biological death 81

Index

biological theory of suicide 248
biophilia 213
biopolitics 10–11, 229–237; definition of 231
biopower 231–232
bipolar 162
Black 1–2; bodies 215, 219; feminist theories 10, 223–225; maladaptive mourning 47–48
Black, Asian and Minority Ethnic (BAME) groups 88–90
Black Lives Matter 211, 220–221
Black women 223–225
Boer, T. 9, 178–190
Boles, Nick 184
Breen, L.J. 263
bubonic plague 229
Buchman, S. 187
Burke, S. 205
Burrell 66–67
Butler, Judith 87

Canada 165, 166; assisted dying in 180–181, 183–184; older people in 199
cancer trials 9
Cann, C. 220
Captain Tom Foundation 125
Card, Claudia 83, 85
care homes 9, 146–159; COVID-19 in 147–150; deaths in 90–92, 147–150, *148*; definition of 147; demographics 147; end of life care 151; population of residents 147; preventable mortality in 90–92; risk reduction 150–151; in the UK 146–147
Care Quality Commission (CQC) 110, 150, 152
caregivers 9, 37, 111, 134, 172
case fatality rate, probability of 1
cemeteries 221–222, 257
Center for Disease Control and Prevention 35
Center for Health and Technology 187
Centre for Global Mental Health 162
Chan, S.M.S. 243
changes 168–170
Chauvin, Derek 210, 220
Chee, W.Y. 8, 134–144
Cheng, H.W.B. 20
children 2; death of 20
Children in Need 131
Chile 165

China 29, 62, 63, 102, 165, 169, 187, 233, 241
Chinese virus 233
Chochinov, H.M. 262
cholera 229
Church of England 128
clinical death 81
Clinical frailty score (CFS) 105
Clothworthy, A. 199
The Collaborative 165
collectivism 108
Collins, P.H. 224
Combahee River Collective 223
Compassion in Care 152
Compassionate Funerals 64, 65–66, 67
Completed Life Act (Netherlands) 179
complicated grief 260
condoms 233
Corona capitalism 215
coronavirus anxiety 41–42
Coronavirus Anxiety Scale (CAS) 7, 42–44, **45**
COVID Tracking Project 218
Covid wards 21
COVID-19: in context 30–31; deaths 1, 29; number of cases worldwide 29; overview 1; preventive measures 242; stigma 233–235; symptoms of 241–242
Covid-19 Bereaved Families for Justice 21
COVID-19 pandemic: biopolitics of 229–237; and HIV pandemic 231–237; identification of 230; lessons from HIV pandemic 236–237; third wave of 102; transmission of 231
COVID-19 patients: African American 210; Hispanic 210; mental health of 165–166
cremation 66, 70, 135, 255, 257–258, 259
Cremation Vessels 70
crematoria 66, 257
Crimean War (1853-1856) 129
Cuddy, A. 189
cultural necrophilia 211–214
cyberbullying 131

D66 (political party) 179
Davies, Douglas 8, 121–132
de Beeke, L. 186
De Wending rest home 186
dead bodies, stigma attached to 257
death: biological 81; changing nature of

255–256; clinical 81; concealment in modern socities 19; during the COVID-19 pandemic 255–264; familiarity with 17–24; institutionalisation of 19, 21; non-COVID-19 32; politicisation of 23–24; pre-COVID-19 visibility of death 18–20; premature 17, 19; pre-modernity 18; probability of 1; visibility of 20–22
death cafes 20
death causation guilt 31
death denial 217
death doulas 20
death rates 6, 23, 31, 34, 41, 150, 230, 242
death rituals 256–259; in Hinduism 259; in Islam 258; omission of 261; religion-specific 257–259; stigma attached to COVID-19 dead bodies 256–257
death signs 81
death studies 7
death talks 20, 22
Death with Dignity 186
deaths, non-COVID-19 134–144; acceptance of early death 142–143; care factor unique to COVID-19 pandemic 136; cases 135, 139–140; and communication barriers 136–137; disenfranchised grief in 137; dying in isolation 141–142; ethical concerns in 141; funerary restrictions and constraints 142; grief entrapped by pandemics 143; grief of 136; impact on the bereaved 137–138; making meaning of 138; maladaptive grief in 138–139; moral distress in 141; non-COVID-19 134–144; overview 134; pandemic as shield for acute grief reactions 143; and public health priority 143–144; resource allocation 140–141; and social isolation 137–138
deaths from COVID-19: African Americans 218–220; dying alone 35; ethical issues in 32; and process of dying 32; and racism 218; spiritual issues in 32, 36; stigma attached to dead bodies 256–257; in United States 29, 218; unpredictability 31
dehumanising practices 89
dementia 84, 162, 200
Denmark 198

Department of Health and Social Care (DHSC) 149
depression 9, 30, 162, 169
Deprivation of Liberty Safeguards (DoLS) 151–152
dialogue, developing 52
digital divide 167–168
Dignity and Dying 182
Dijkstra, P. 179
disabled people 188
disenfranchised grief 234
disruption of routine 30
do not attempt cardio-pulmonary resuscitation (DNACPR) policies in 109–110
do not attempt resuscitation order (DNAR) 150
Doka, K.J. 6, 29–38, 235
domestic abuse 30, 167
do-not-resuscitate (DNR) notices 178, 188
Dorsey, R. 187
Douglas, C. 200–201, 202
Dsouza, D.D. 246
dual sovereignty 130–131
dual-process model of grief 34–35, 261
Durkheim, E. 85, 128–129
Durkin, J. 201
dying: changing nature of 255–256; during the COVID-19 pandemic 255–264; with dignity 261–262
Dying with Dignity 186

eating disorders 162
Ebola virus 244
Eckert, C. 221
Elias, N. 212
emotion dysregulation theory of suicide 248
emotions, regulation of 52–53
End of Life Clinic 182
end-of-life decisions 101–114; advanced care planning 111–113; best interest decisions in 108; best practice principles 113–114; in care home situations 109; in COVID-19 107–110; decision aids 110–111; emotive nature of 105; factors in 105–107; legal challenges in 109; overview 101–102; and rationing resources 101–105; shared-decision making in 109, 110–111
Ernst, J. 84

Eros and Civilization (Marcuse) 212
escape theory of suicide 248
ethnic minorities 2, 22–23, 88, 89
ethnicity 1–2, 22, 50, 231
euthanasia 86, 178–179; legality of 180; in Netherlands 179, 185; *see also* assisted dying
Euthanasia Expertise Centre 182–183
evil, secular theory of 83
extrusive social death 83, 90; *see also* social death

Facebook Live 66, 67
FaceTime 167, 204
Fauci, A. **234**
Februari, M. 189
Federal Bureau of Investigation (FBI) 215
Fenestra 70
Finland 198
Finnerty, G. 9, 160–173
Fletcher, K. 10, 198, 209–225
Floyd, George 10, 209, 220, 221, 223
Fong, M. 8, 134–144
Food and Drug Administration (FDA) 234
Foster, G. 221
Foster, J. 9, 160–173
Foucault, M. 231–232
Frankl, V. 49
Freud, S. 33, 212
Fromm, E. 212, 213
funeral directors 19, 64–67
funerals 7, 32, 255–256; guidelines and policies 255; online 21, 64–67; restrictions 135, 139, 140, 142; rituals 36, 37–38; and stigma attached to COVID dead bodies 257; streaming 64–67

G20 Leader's Summit 4
Gallon, K. 224–225
Gaudi, A. 78
gay men 10, 230
gay-related immune deficiency (GRID) *see* HIV/AIDS
gender 2
genocide 7, 83, 91–92
Germany 171
ghusl 258
Gibson, A. 263
Gilhooly, M.L. 82, 86
Giroux, H. 86

GitHub Diaries 64
Glaser, B.G. 81, 84
Glick, P. 189
Global Burden of Disease 161
Goffman, E. 81, 84
Google Meet 66
Gorer, G. 19
The Great North Run 131
grief in COVID-19 pandemic 7, 29–38, 44–45, 260–261; anticipatory grief 260; complicated grief 260; coping with 34–36; course of 35; disenfranchised grief 235; dual-process model of grief 34–35, 261; ethical issues in 32; interventive approaches to 36–38; medical/health personnel 33; models 34–35; non-death losses 33–34; overview 29–30; persons dying from other causes 32; persons mourning COVID-19 deaths 31–32; and process of dying 32; validation 36–37
Griffiths, M.D. 246–247
Guenther, L. 86–87, 91
guilt: death causation 31; moral 32; survivor 31, 37
Guinea 244

H1N1 102, 105
H5N1 (avian influenza) 102, 105
Hage, G. 85
Haiti 233
Hall, C. 260
Hancock, Matt (UK Health Secretary) 21
handwashing 49
Hannig, A. 188
health workers, mental health of 165
Healthcare Quality Improvement Partnership (HQIP) 172
Herremans, Jacqueline 183
Hill, M. 215, 217
Hinduism, death rituals in 259
Hispanic patients 210
History of Sexuality (Foucault) 231–232
HIV/AIDS 10, 229–237; biopolitics 232–233; and COVID-19 pandemic 231–237; criminalisation 232; disenfranchised grief 235; first cases 230; stigma 233–235; transmission of 230
Holloway, K. 220
Holocaust 49, 86
home palliative care 139–140

Hopkins, S. 188
hospices 184
Houseparty 204
housing 167
huidhonger 201
Hurricane Katrina 85

Ickert, C. 204
ideation-to-action framework of suicide 248
immortality strategies 213
India 171; death and dying in 255–264; suicide reasons in 246–247
Indigenous Americans 1
inequalities 22–23
infant, mortality rates 18
influenza virus 244
Instagram 67
intensive care units (ITUs) 123
intensive therapy unit 129
International Cemetery, Cremation and Funeral Association 64
International Classification of Diseases (ICD) 45, 78–79, 90
International Monetary Fund (IMF) 4
International Severe Acute Respiratory and Emerging Infection (ISARIC) 110
Internet 167–168
interpersonal theory of suicide 248
intervening in meaning 53–54
intrusive social death 83, 90; *see also* social death
Islam, death rituals in 258
Italy 102, 165

Jackson, M. 220
Jameton, A. 33
Jarvis 70
Jeffrey, D.I. 105
Jim Crow laws 222
job loss 31, 34, 169
Johnson, Boris 127

kafan 258
Kalish, R.A. 81
Kardashian, Kim 62
Keita, M.M. 244
Kellehear, A. 212
Králová, J. 7
Kübler-Ross, E. 212, 260

Lacan, J. 212
Lamb. Sarah 204–205

language, surmounting the limits of 53
lead poisoning 218
Learning Disability England 188
Lee, A. 8, 134–144
Lee, R.L. 20
Lee, S.A. 7, 40–54
Leibing, A. 199
Lemmos Dekker, N. 201
Li, Jiabao 62–63
liminality 124
live streaming 66
loneliness 2, 185–187
Long, Helen 186
losses 168–170; complications 36; employment 31, 34, 50; income 31, 34; multiple 31; non-death 33–34; opportunities 34
loss-orientation mode 261
Lovell, A.M. 85
Luxembourg, assisted dying in 180
Lynn, Vera 126

Macdonald, M.E. 261
MAID services 184
Malcom X. 223
Mamun, M.A. 11, 246–247
Mangin, R.Z. 219
Marcuse, H. 212
mask-wearing 49, 215, 232, 233
mass media 3
Mauss, M. 85
media coverage 23–24
Medical Bondage: Race, Gender, and the Origins of American Gynecology (Owens) 219
medical/health personnel, grief experienced by 33
medicine, rationing 102–105
memorials, online 60–71; communications technologies in 64–67; in countries with land scarcity for burials 62; funeral directors' use of 64–67; overview 60–71; and social media 60, 67–68; technologies used in 61; virtual memorial gardens 61
mental, neurological and substance use disorders (MNS) 162
Mental Capacity Assessments 165
mental health 9; and bereavement 168–170; and change 168–170; and COVID-19 163–167, 241–243; of COVID-19 patients and their families 165–166; development assistance for

163; disorders 162; of elderly 166; of health workers 165; and housing 167; and internet connection 167–168; and losses 168–170; overview 160–161; people with existing mental illness 164–165; pre-COVID-19 161–163; and social connections 167; suicidal intention *170*, 170–172
Mental Health Act 169–170
Mental Health Foundation 169
mental health hospitals 81
mental health in COVID-19 pandemic 160–173
MERS-CoV (Middle East Respiratory Syndrome – coronavirus) 5, 105
Microsoft Teams 167
Milman, E. 7, 40–54
Milne, A.J. 9, 146–159
minority ethnic groups 2
Misti, J.M. 11
MIT Media Lab 62
Mols, H. 128–129
monarch 124–126
Moore, T. 125
moral distress 33, 141
moral guilt 32
Mors Britannica study 123
Mortality, Immortality, and Other Life Strategies (Bauman) 213
mortality rates, infant 18
Moug, S. 106
mourning 255–256
Mourning and Melancholia (Freud) 33
Mulkay, M. 84
multiple losses, experience of 31
Muslim burials 64–65

namaaz 261
National Council for Palliative Care 131
National Health Service (NHS) 8, 101–102; applause for 124; cultural destiny 127; dual sovereignty 130–131; medical-political messages 123–124; and monarch 124–126; and religion 127–128; ritual-symbolism 123–124; and sacrality 128–129; and spirituality paradox 131; worldview model 121–123
National Health Services (NHS) 61–62
National Housing Act (NHA) 218
National Institute for Health and Clinical Excellence (NICE) 101–102
Native Americans 215

necrophile self 10, 211–214
The Necrophile Self: Contemporary Attitudes Towards Death and Its New Visibility (Waraschinski) 211–213, 214, 217
necrophilia 213
Neimeyer, R. 7, 35, 40–54
Netherlands, assisted dying in 179, 185
New Deal 218
New Orleans Charity Hospital 85
New York Times 216
Nightingale, Florence 129
non-Covid-19 related deaths 8–9
North Korean defectors 85
Norwood, F. 86
NRC Handelsblad (newspaper) 189

older people 2, 10, 197–206; in Canada 199; with dementia 200; in Denmark 198–199; in Finland 198; mental health of 165–166; overview 197–198; risks for death 31; social distancing 199; touch and touching 199–205
Oliver, David 155
online learning 30
online memorials 60–71; communications technologies in 64–67; in countries with land scarcity for burials 62; funeral directors' use of 64–67; overview 60–71; and social media 60, 67–68; technologies used in 61; virtual memorial gardens 61
online scams 131
Ontario, assisted dying in 183–184
Oregon Health Authority 182
Organisation for Economic Co-operation and Development (OECD) 78
Otsuchi, Japan 69
Owens, D.C. 219

Pakistan 165; suicide reasons in 246
Palestinian suicide bombing 85–86
palliative care 139–140
pandemic distress 48–51
Pandemic Grief Scale (PGS) 7, 46–48, **47**
pandemics, and suicides 243–244
Pandya, A.K. 11
Parrott, C. 187
Patrick, D. 189
Patterson, 90
Patterson, H.O. 80, 83, 84, 88
Pattison, N. 8, 101–114

Paul, S. 20
Pentaris, P. 9, 17–24, 160–173, 257
Perrot, Chantal 186
personal protective equipment (PPE) 129, 149–150, 152, 202–203, 256
personhood 82
Pfizer 4
Philippines 165
Phillips, L. 110, 224
physical distancing 38
Pikachu 69
Pitsillides, S. 7
Player Two (short film) 68
Poetic Endings 64–65
Pokémon 69
Pokémon Go 69
politics of disposability 216
Pols, J. 201
The Pornography of Death (Gorer) 19
post-traumatic stress syndrome (PTSD) 9, 169
premature death 17, 19
preventable mortality 78, 87; in BAME communities 89; of care home residents 90–92; and socioeconomic inequalities 79; theoretical exceptions 89, 91
The Price for Their Pound of Flesh: The Value of the Enslaved, from Womb to Grave, in the Building of a Nation (Berry) 217
prolonged grief disorder 47
psycho-dynamic theory of suicide 248
psychological death 81–82
psychological effects 2
psychoses 162
Public Accounts Committee 152
Public Health England (PHE) 149
public protective equipment (PPE) 22

Qingming Festival 62
quality of life years (QALYS) 188
quarantines 8–9, 32, 35, 38
Quebec, older people in 199

race 1–2
racism, in United States 218
Ramadas, S. 263
Rando, Therese A. 34
Rappaport, R. 128–129
rationing 102–105
Reagan, Ronald 234
restoration orientation mode 261

Riley, S. 180
ritual-symbolism 123–124
Rockwood Clinical Frailty Scale 102
Roosevelt, Franklin 218
Rushford, Marcus 127
Russian influenza outbreak (1889-1894) 243
Ryan, L. 8, 101–114
sacrality 128–129

Sagrada Família 78
salat al-janazah 258
Samaritans UK 171
Sandeen, P. 186–187
SARS epidemic 243
SARS-CoV (Severe Acute Respiratory Syndrome – coronavirus) 5, 243
SARS-Cov-2 (Severe Acute Respiratory Syndrome – coronavirus – 2) *see* COVID-19
Sasaki, Itaru 69
Saudi Arabia 171
'Say Their Names' Cemetery 221–223
Schaub, J. 229–237
schizophrenia 162
Schut, H. 34–35, 261
Scientific Advisory Group for Emergencies (SAGE) 154
screening, for suffering and symptomalogy 51–52
secure base, for client reflection and action 53
Selman, L.E. 66–67
seropositivity 244
severe acute respiratory syndrome (SARS) 102, 105
severe cases 30
shadow pandemic 44
Shahul-Hameed, M. 9, 160–173
Shears, Joanna 64–65
Shipman, Harold 121–132
shraddh 259
Sina Weibo 62–63
Sirotek, Nicole 210
Skype 167
slavery 7
slaves 84
Smith, F.B. 244
social contact 202
social death 7, 77–93; archaeology of 80–84; axceptions 91–92; in BAME communities 88–90; exceptions 84–87; extrusive 83, 90; and genocide 83,

91–92; and interdisciplinary death studies 81–83; intrusive 83, 90; overview 78–80; schools of thought on 80–84; of social state 86; and social viabIlity 91–92
social distancing 127, 199; and dying 256
social isolation 30, 37, 137–138, 169
social media 3; and online memorials 60, 67–68
social vitality 91–92
sociological theory of suicide 248
Spain 165
Spanish flu 210, 229, 243
spillover event 5
spiritual issues 32, 36
spirituality paradox 131
stay-at-home orders 209, 215
stigma 233–235
Strauss, A.L. 81, 84
stress 169
stressors 50
Stroebe, M. 34–35, 261
structural invisibility 84, 89
Sudnow, D. 81, 84
suicidal behaviour 11; definition of 243; prevalence rate 245–246; stages of 243
suicidal intention 170–172
suicide 11, 241–249; annual deaths from 243; and coronaviruses related pandemic 243–244; and COVID-19 pandemic 245–247; definition of 243; and Ebola virus related pandemic 244; factors affecTing suicidality 244; ideation-to-action framework 248; and influenza viruses related epidemic 244; and prior pandemics 243–244; rate 245; reasons of actual occUrrences 246–247; risk factors 248; theories of 247–248
Suicide Act 1961 (UK) 180
suicide bombing 85
survivor guilt 31, 37
Sweeting, H.N. 82, 86
symptoms: multiple 31; non-specificity of 30
symptoms of Covid-19 241–242
syphilis 219

Talkspace 165
telemedicine 182, 187–188
telepresence 7
Temple Court Scandal 189
Teo, W. 8, 134–144

termu 259
terror management theory (TMT) 214
Thanatos 212, 213
theoretical exceptions 89, 91
therapy dogs 202
Thomas, J.C. 105
Till, E. 222
Tomorrow will be a Good Day (Moore) 125
Tonnekreek, Hummie van der 179
touch and touching 199–200; importance of 200–201; loss of 200–213; news ways of 203–205; touch hunger 201; touch starvation 201; WHO guidelines on 199–200
travel restrictions 32, 35, 38
treatable mortality 78
Tripathi, K. 11
Trump, Donald 127, 233
Trumpism 209
Turner, Victor 84, 124
Turning Point 188
Twitter 62, 67, 104

undocumented immigrants 84
UNESCO 167
Unfinished Farewell (memorial project) 62–63, *63*
United Nations 4
United States: assisted dying in 180; cases in 29, 35; COVID-19 deaths 218–220; deaths in 29, 35
United States Public Health Service 219

vaccines 4, 38, **234**, 242
validation 36–37
Van Gennep, Arnold 84, 124
Vermeulen, L. 201
Vijayakumar, S. 263
virtual memorial gardens 61
Visser, R. 10, 197–206

Wallace, C.L. 262
Wallace, J. 7
Walter, T. 19
Wang, S. 8, 134–144
Waraschinski, T. 10
00WARTHERAPY00 (username) 68
Wasserman, I.M. 244
Wenger, O. 219
Wenliang, Li 62–64
Wesley Media 66
Westerndorp, R.A. 199

WhatsApp 64–65, 67, 167
White supremacy 209–211, 214–217, 224
Whitner, G. 215–216
Wi-Fi access 204
Wind Telephone 69
Winter, Louise 64–65
Woodthorpe, K. 6, 17–24
Wootton, S. 180
Worden, J. William 34
World Bank Group 4
World Health Organization (WHO) 4, 199
worldview model 121–123, 121–132
worthwhile life 86, 92
Wright, C. 221
Wright, E. 222
Wu, Laobai 62–63

XBox 68

Yong, W.C. 8, 134–144
youth 2
YouTube 68
Yuill, K. 9, 178–190

Zaman, H. 64–66, 66, 67
Zero Suicide Alliance 171
Zoom 64–65, 66, 167, 204

Milton Keynes UK
Ingram Content Group UK Ltd.
UKHW030709231124
451456UK00020B/276